CIVIL WAR JOURNAL™

The Battles

CIVIL WAR

JOURNAL™

The Battles

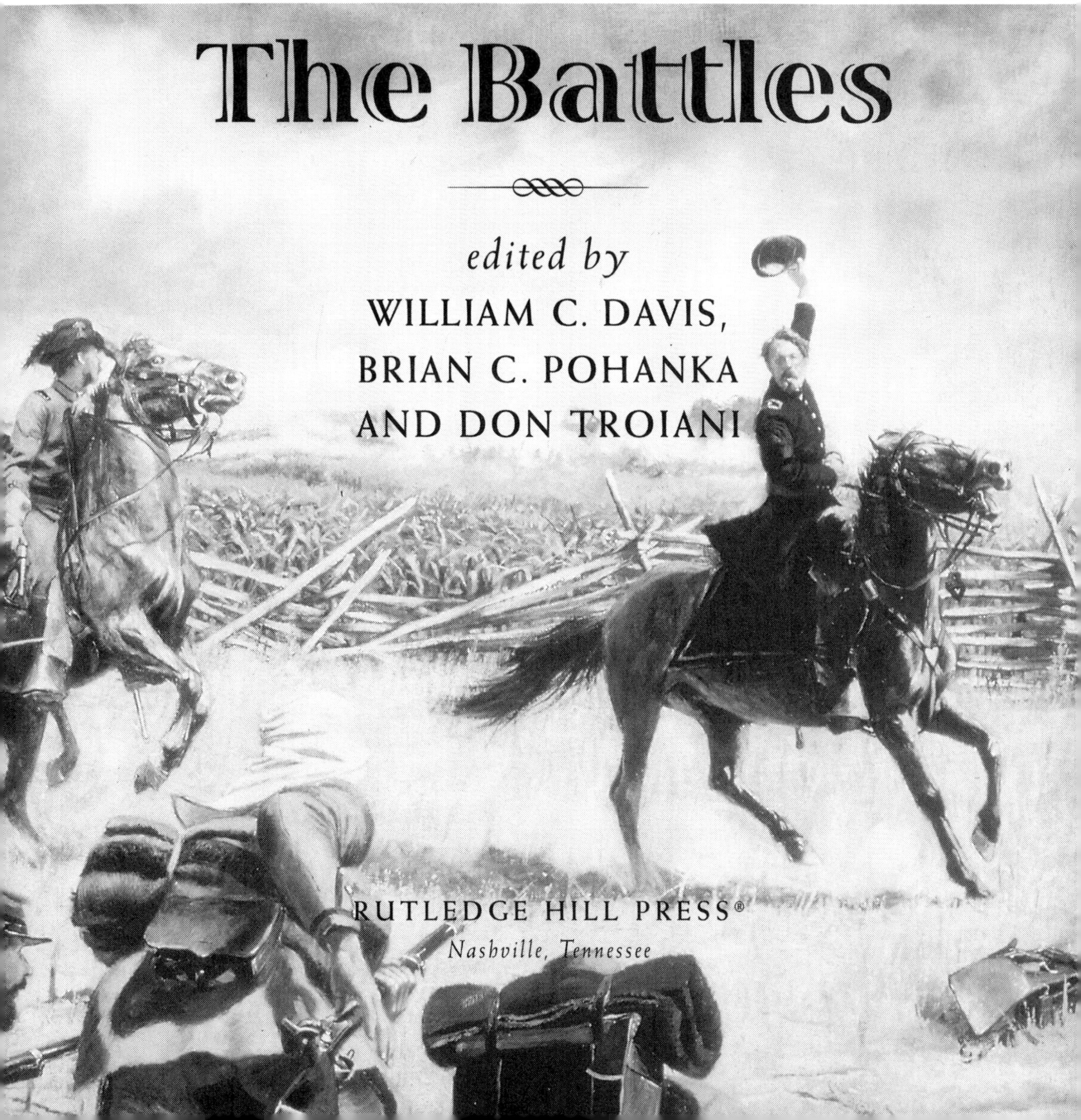

edited by

WILLIAM C. DAVIS,
BRIAN C. POHANKA
AND DON TROIANI

RUTLEDGE HILL PRESS®

Nashville, Tennessee

Published in Nashville, Tennessee, by Rutledge Hill Press®, 211 Seventh Avenue North, Nashville, Tennessee 37219. Distributed in Canada by H. B. Fenn and Co., Ltd., 34 Nixon Road, Bolton, Ontario L7E 1W2. Distributed in Australia by The Five Mile Press, 22 Summit Road, Noble Park, Victoria 3174. Distributed in New Zealand by Tandem Press, 2 Rugby Road, Birkenhead, Auckland 10. Distributed in the United Kingdom by Verulam Press, Ltd., 152a Park Street Lane, Park Street, St. Albans, Hertfordshire AL2 2AU.

Typography by Compass Communications, Inc., Nashville, Tennessee.

The maps on pages 19, 66, 67, 102, 124, 147, 172, 252, 256, 262, 353, 403, 412, 431, 436, and 448 copyright © 1998 by Arcadia Editions, Ltd., Shirley, Derbyshire, England.

Pages 456–59 constitute an extension of this copyright page.

Library of Congress Cataloging-in-Publication Data

Civil War journal / edited by William C. Davis, Brian C. Pohanka, and Don Troiani.
    p. cm.
    Fifty-two edited scripts from the television program Civil War journal.
    Includes bibliographical references and index.
    Contents: [2] The Battles
    ISBN 1-55853-438-5
    1. United States—History—Civil War, 1861–1865. I. Davis, William C., 1946– . II. Pohanka, Brian C., 1955– . III. Troiani, Don. IV. Civil War journal (Television program)
E468.C6247 1997
973.7′8—dc21   97-6861
                                            CIP

Printed in the United States of America.
1 2 3 4 5 6 7 8 9 — 01 00 99 98

Contents

Preface

WHAT FOLLOWS IS not a comprehensive history of the battles that raged across the United States between April 1861 and April 1865; the three million men who bore arms during that time clashed in more than a thousand encounters. Here we were limited by the scope of the television series of which we were all a part, the History Channel's *Civil War Journal*. As episodes created for television and video, potential topics had to be evaluated on the basis of availability of representational art and photographs. At the same time, several engagements were discussed in other episodes, particularly those dealing with biographies. The short list of battles that eventually arose in those production meetings emerged with two dramatic emphases: the eastern theater and Gettysburg.

There was little question that we would begin with Fort Sumter. It was here that the shots that arced across Charleston Harbor, illuminating the night and to some extent entertaining the townspeople, would echo terribly across the country for four years. There was also the irony that after hours of shelling one another, no lives were lost in the exchange of fire that launched the country's costliest war in terms of human lives.

While we could not be comprehensive regarding the combat that colored the war, we could touch on most aspects of the fighting in which Americans engaged during the Civil War. This included the loss of innocence at Manassas, the resourcefulness of naval architects in building the first iron fleets, the way of life in occupied New Orleans, the bloodiest one day of the war (Antietam), the bloodiest two days of the war (Chickamauga), the bloodiest three days of the war (Gettysburg), the most one-sided battle (Fredericksburg), the longest sieges (Vicksburg and Charleston), and the most decisive battle (Nashville). All were pivotal battles.

Of more than a thousand engagements fought during the war, these few have risen to lasting fascination and prominence, some even regarded as "turning points." The battles included here are some that caused the greatest casualties, produced the greatest feats of heroism, and won or lost major campaigns. They decided the course of the war in the East and the West, set the standard for valor and sacrifice, defined who the American soldier was to be in this war and in the future, and established the American military tradition.

As we reviewed the other episodes, we chose three topical studies to complement the stories of these battles: a description of the life of foot soldiers during the war, the Iron Brigade, and the Fifty-fourth Massachusetts. Hardly enough can be said for the men who left families and homes for the hardships of army life. Too easily they lose their individuality as numbers and statistics. Similarly, units like the Iron Brigade and the Fifty-fourth Massachusetts earned reputations on the battlefield that have dimmed with the passage of time. We have tried to polish those for a new generation of Civil War enthusiasts. We also wanted to clarify some misperceptions generated by other media regarding the Fifty-fourth.

Union or Confederate, Civil War volunteers were trained in the complex choreography of nineteenth-century tactics—repetitive drills intended, as one veteran put it, "to sink the individual in the soldier." Elbow to elbow, rank on rank, these compact blocks of humanity marched time and again into the jaws of death. It was not uncommon for a regiment to lose 40 or 60 percent of its men in a single engagement; and some units lost even more. That those young Americans could endure the horrific carnage and fight on says a great deal about discipline and regimental pride; but above all it reveals the idealism, belief, and devotion to cause and country that motivated the combatants on both sides.

The text for each chapter was taken from the script for the corresponding show and only slightly embellished to enhance readability. An effort was made throughout to maintain the voice, nuance, and inflection conveyed by the many experts who made this a distinctive body of work. Their words are set off in the text with superscript bullets; open bullets (°) mark the beginning of a speaker's words and solid bullets (•) indicate the conclusion. Attribution is indicated by initials in the left margin, and these initials are identified on the first page of each chapter.

WILLIAM C. DAVIS
BRIAN C. POHANKA
DON TROIANI

Acknowledgments

We would be remiss in acknowledging the many people involved in this project if we did not express appreciation to the following writers whose scripts undergird this book. They are Don Cambou (Gettysburg: The Civilians), Arthur Drooker (Gettysburg: The President), Kellie Flanagan (Fredericksburg), Martin Gillam (Charleston, Chickamauga-Chattanooga), Martin Kent (The Iron Brigade), Rob Kirk (The *Monitor* vs. the *Virginia*), Rob Lihani (Gettysburg: The Battle), Pam Moore (Fifty-fourth Massachusetts), Noah Morowitz (First Manassas), Rhys Thomas (Antietam, Vicksburg, Franklin-Nashville), Laura Verklan (Fort Sumter, New Orleans), Noah Morowitz (Foot Soldiers), and Kellie Flanagan (Gettysburg: The Unsung Heroes). Dana B. Shoaf and JoAnna McDonald assisted in the writing of the captions.

A book such as this is dependent on the willingness of archives, museums, historical societies, universities, and private collectors to allow us access to their collections for photographs. We cannot be profuse enough in our thanks to Marty Baldessari; JoAnna McDonald, Tom Freeman; John and Troy Leib; Alan T. Nolan; Lloyd Ostendorf; Herb Peck; Charles V. Perry, M.D.; Harry Roach; Joe Umble; Elwood Christ, Adams County Historical Society; Sam Jorgensen, American Heritage Engravings; Gail Quezada and Noel Blackwell, AmSouth Bank N.A., Mobile, Alabama; Larry Schwartz, Archive Photos; Mary Bell, Buffalo and Erie County Historical Society; Lance Herdegen, Carroll College Institute for Civil War Studies; Thomas Y. Cartwright, Carter House; Leith Rohr and Matthew Cook, Chicago Historical Society; Pat Ricci and Christine Harvey, Confederate Memorial Hall; Carolyn Picciano, Connecticut State Archives; Jennifer Pelland, Farnsworth House Military (Gettysburg); John Tucker and Richard W. Hatcher III, Fort Sumter National Monument; David L. Preston, Fredericksburg National Park; Joseph M. Judge, Hampton Roads Naval Museum; Jo-Val Codling, Historical Art Prints; John Magill and Sally Stassi, Historic New Orleans Collection; Jennie Rathbun, Houghton Library, Harvard University; Kim Bauer, Illinois State Historical Library; Joan Caron, Kunhardt Productions, Inc.; Marie C. Boltz, Special Collections, Lehigh University; Petie Bogen-Garrett and Audrey C. Johnson, The Library of Virginia; James F. Sefcik, Claudia Kheel, and Shannon Glasheen, Louisiana State Museum; John Pemberton and Dina Hill, Mariners' Museum; Chris Steele, Massachusetts Historical Society; Judy Simonsen, Milwaukee County Historical Society; Bonnie Wilson, Minnesota Historical Society; Cory Hudgins and Terry Hudgins, Museum of the Confederacy; Dale L. Neighbors and John Kuss, New-York Historical Society; Earl Iames, North Carolina State Archives; Gordon A. Cotton, Old Court House Museum; Kathy Flynn, Peabody Essex Museum; Mike Sherbon, Pennsylvania State Archives; Frank Wood, The Picture Bank; Lea Kemp, Rochester Museum and Science Center; Pat Hatch, South Carolina Historical Society; Beth Bilderbeck, South Caroliniana Library; Andy Kranshaar, State Historical Society of Wisconsin; Stephen Cox, Tennessee State Museum; Lee Miller and Courtney Page, Special Collections, Tulane University; John E. White, Southern Historical Collection, University of North Carolina; Mike Winey and Randy Hackenburg, U.S. Army Military History Institute; Alan Aimone and Sheila Biles, Special Collections, U.S. Military Academy Library; Pat Dursi and Dave Meschutt, U.S. Military Academy Museum; AnnMarie Price, Virginia Historical Society; Amber Woods, Wadsworth Atheneum; and Ann Sindelir and Barbara Billings, Western Reserve Historical Society.

We have enjoyed working with the editors of Rutledge Hill Press in the production of this volume and look forward to completing the series with the next book.

The Contributors

ONE OF the distinctive elements of *Civil War Journal* is the authority conveyed by the fifty scholars, historians, curators, and descendants who infused each topic with something of themselves, bringing the leaders alive for a television audience. Their comments have been marked throughout the text, with an open superscript bullet (°) indicating the beginning and a solid superscript bullet (•) marking the conclusion of direct quotations from the television script. Initials appear in the left margin designating attribution. Each chapter's opening page includes a list in the lower right hand corner of the experts whose voices can be heard on the pages that follow. Their names are reproduced here in two lists, one arranged by last name and another by initials.

ECB	*Edwin C. Bearss*, chief historian and special assistant to the director for military sites, National Park Service	GAC	*Gregory A. Cocco*, historian and author
AWB	*Arthur W. Bergeron Jr.*, historian	GC	*Gordon A. Cotton*, curator, Old Court House Museum
GSB	*Gabor S. Boritt*, author	CC	*Carl Cruz*, descendant of William Carney
TLB	*Timothy L. Burgess*, Civil War historian		
GCC	*Glen C. Cangelosi*, Confederate Museum, New Orleans	WCD	*William C. Davis*, historian and author
TC	*Tina Cappetta*, historical researcher	PE	*Pat Eymard*, curator, Confederate Museum, New Orleans
TYC	*Thomas Y. Cartwright*, military curator and historian, Carter House, Franklin, Tennessee	EFG	*Elizabeth Fox-Genovese*, historian and author, Emory University
RC	*Raphael Cassimere Jr.*, professor, University of New Orleans	REF	*Roy E. Frampton*, guide, Gettysburg Battlefield
CC	*Catherine Clinton*, professor, Harvard University	WAF	*William A. Frassanito*, historian and author
GC	*George Coblyn*, descendant of Eli George Biddle	GWG	*Gary W. Gallagher*, professor of history, Pennsylvania State University

CG   *Charles Glatfelter,* Adams County Historical Society

AWG   *A. Wilson Greene,* president, Association for the Preservation of Civil War Sites

WWG   *William W. Gwaltney,* historian and author

KGH   *Kathy George Harrison,* historian, Gettysburg National Military Park

SH   *Scott Hartwig,* historian, Gettysburg National Military Park

CGH   *Chester G. Hearn,* author

JJH   *John J. Hennessy,* historian and author

LH   *Lance Herdegen,* author

DH   *Dina Hill, Monitor* National Marine Sanctuary

BH   *Bobby Horton,* musician

JH   *James Horton,* professor, George Washington University

RKK   *Robert K. Krick,* National Park Service, Civil War author and historian/Army of Northern Virginia

JL   *Joe Logsdon,* professor of history, University of New Orleans

TL   *Thomas Lowry,* author

HM   *Howard Madaus,* curator, Firearms Buffalo Bill Historical Center

RM   *Ross Massey,* historian, Battle of Nashville Preservation Society

JMM   *James M. McPherson,* professor of history, Princeton University

CN   *Chris Nelson,* historian

AN   *Alan Nolan,* historian and author

JO   *James Ogden,* historian, Chickamauga and Chattanooga National Military Park

FO   *Frank O'Reilly,* historian, Fredericksburg National Military Park

JSP   *John S. Patterson,* American studies, Pennsylvania State University, Harrisburg

EWP   *Ernest W. Peterkin,* captain, U.S. Naval Reserve, retired; historian

DP   *Donald Pfanz,* staff historian, Fredericksburg National Military Park

BP   *Brian Pohanka,* historian and film consultant

CDR   *Colan D. Ratliff,* naval architectural historian

JIR   *James I. Robertson Jr.,* Alumni Distinguished Professor of History, Virginia Tech, Blacksburg, Virginia

ALR   *Armstead L. Robinson,* historian

DR   *David Roth,* Civil War historian

JAS   *Jacob A. Sheads,* historian and Gettysburg native

WS   *Wiley Sword,* historian and author

DT   *Don Troiani,* artist and historian

GU   *Gregory Urwin,* professor, University of Arkansas

WGW   *William G. Williams,* author

TJW   *Terrence J. Winschel,* historian, Vicksburg National Military Park

SRW   *Stephen R. Wise,* author

PMZ   *Paul M. Zall,* research scholar, Huntington Library

ALR	Armstead L. Robinson	FO	Frank O'Reilly	PE	Pat Eymard
AN	Alan Nolan	GAC	Gregory A. Cocco	PMZ	Paul M. Zall
AWB	Arthur W. Bergeron Jr.	GC	George Coblyn	RC	Raphael Cassimere Jr.
AWG	A. Wilson Greene	GC	Gordon A. Cotton	REF	Roy E. Frampton
BH	Bobby Horton	GCC	Glen C. Cangelosi	RKK	Robert K. Krick
BP	Brian Pohanka	GSB	Gabor S. Boritt	RM	Ross Massey
CC	Carl Cruz	GU	Gregory Urwin	SH	Scott Hartwig
CC	Catherine Clinton	GWG	Gary W. Gallagher	SRW	Stephen R. Wise
CDR	Colan D. Ratliff	HM	Howard Madaus	TC	Tina Cappetta
CG	Charles Glatfelter	JAS	Jacob A. Sheads	TJW	Terrence J. Winschel
CGH	Chester G. Hearn	JH	James Horton	TL	Thomas Lowry
CN	Chris Nelson	JIR	James I. Robertson Jr.	TLB	Timothy L. Burgess
DH	Dina Hill	JJH	John J. Hennessy	TYC	Thomas Y. Cartwright
DP	Donald Pfanz	JL	Joe Logsdon	WAF	William A. Frassanito
DR	David Roth	JMM	James M. McPherson	WCD	William C. Davis
DT	Don Troiani	JO	James Ogden	WGW	William G. Williams
ECB	Edwin C. Bearss	JSP	John S. Patterson	WS	Wiley Sword
EFG	Elizabeth Fox-Genovese	KGH	Kathy George Harrison	WWG	William W. Gwaltney
EWP	Ernest W. Peterkin	LH	Lance Herdegen		

Key to Maps

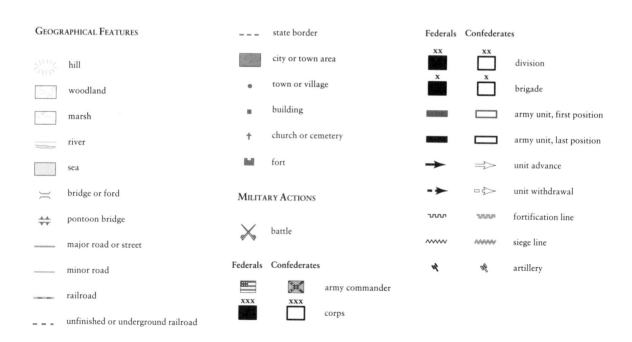

GEOGRAPHICAL FEATURES

- hill
- woodland
- marsh
- river
- sea
- bridge or ford
- pontoon bridge
- major road or street
- minor road
- railroad
- unfinished or underground railroad

- – – state border
- city or town area
- town or village
- building
- † church or cemetery
- fort

MILITARY ACTIONS

- battle

Federals Confederates
- army commander
- xxx / xxx corps

Federals Confederates
- xx / xx division
- x / x brigade
- army unit, first position
- army unit, last position
- unit advance
- unit withdrawal
- fortification line
- siege line
- artillery

CIVIL WAR JOURNAL™

The Battles

FORT SUMTER

The BOMBARDMENT OF FORT SUMTER ignited the bloodiest conflict in American history, a war in which 620,000 Americans lost their lives. It was a war with many facets: a war of power between two rival presidents of one nation, a war of honor for one officer who would carry the weight of the war for the rest of his life, and ultimately a war of hope for millions of black Americans who dreamed of freedom.

ALR °The roots of the Civil War lay in the American Revolution and the founding of the republic. Between the Revolution and the Civil War there was a growing series of political conflicts between slave states and free states over what the national policy should be on issues affecting slavery.•

These sectional tensions came to a climax in the mid-nineteenth century; a war between the states seemed inevitable. Two years before his election to the White House, Abraham Lincoln predicted that war would come. During an unsuccessful bid for the Senate, in a speech that focused on the issue of slavery, he said to his listeners: "I believe this government cannot endure permanently half-slave and half-free."

BP °Slavery was certainly the most important cause of the Civil War, although some have argued that slavery did not cause the war because the typical southerner did not own slaves and the typical northerner did not particularly care whether black Americans were freed or not. While that observation is true, the institution of slavery precipitated the war because slavery was the most crucial right that the South saw as being threatened.• The Civil War

CC	Catherine Clinton
WCD	William C. Davis
EFG	Elizabeth Fox-Genovese
WWG	William W. Gwaltney
BP	Brian Pohanka
ALR	Armstead L. Robinson
DR	David Roth

The South enjoyed a monopoly on the world's cotton for most of the first half of the nineteenth century and saw no reason to expect anything different for the 1860s. In fact, when war came in 1861, the Confederacy anticipated the European nations would pressure the North by every means to keep the cotton corridors open. This cotton economy required a large labor force and perpetuated slavery as the most efficient WWG *means for cultivating this cash crop. In the photograph above (left), despite its being an image from a region occupied by the Northern army, contrabands (as slaves in Union-held areas were called) sort through ginned cotton. The severity of this way of life is apparent in the demeanor of the slave family above (right) and the condition of their living quarters as they were photographed in 1863 near Fredericksburg.*

was fought over the right of individual states to determine how their voters wanted to live, and slavery was the most visible example of a challenge to this right.

In the 1860s slavery was virtually abolished in the North, but in the South, which had a population of nine million people, four million were slaves. Roughly one in every seven Americans was a slave.

°The practice of slavery in the United States was something of an aberration. It had run its course in almost every Western nation by the beginning of the nineteenth century and probably would have ceased to exist in the American South had it not been rejuvenated by the invention of the mechanical cotton gin, which made slavery profitable again. Most towns in the South had slave markets, where slaves were treated very much like cattle and prices were based on a slave's skills. The agrarian nature of the southern economy—which prospered on cotton, sugar, and tobacco—called for a large work force whose primary virtue was endurance. In that environment, slaves worked "from can to can't"; that is, from when one "can see" in the morning, when the sun came up, until "can't see" at night, when the sun went down.

To maintain the institution of slavery, the southern slave owners had to maintain a balance of terror and

humanity.• In return for obedience and productivity, slaves received food and shelter. Punishment was administered for disobedience, but not in such ways as to hamper future productivity. Of course, consistent disobe-
EFG dience was dealt with severely, and °some slaves did everything they could to resist.• They knew their white masters had power over them because the law of the land protected slavery, but many slaves were determined to find freedom in the North.

In the late 1850s a small but highly vocal abolitionist movement spread across the North proclaiming that slavery was inhumane and immoral. The well-known orator Frederick Douglass, a self-freed slave who had been born to a slave mother and a white slaveholding father, became a voice for all slaves who yearned to be free. During one of his speeches, Douglass argued, "The vital question at stake is not whether slavery shall be extended or limited, but whether the four million now held in bondage are men, entitled to the rights and liberties of men."

Disagreement over slavery led to conflicts between the two cultures in the United States: the industrialized, free-labor North and the agricultural, slave-labor South. The
EFG issue, however, was not really one of racism, because °in the 1850s northerners were every bit as racist as southerners. Instead it was a question of the nature of society• and economics, but ultimately it became an issue of political power.

At the 1860 Democratic convention in Charleston the issues of states' rights and slavery split the party. The northern Democrats were determined to reject the proslavery plank of the southern Democrats and chose Stephen Douglas as their standard-bearer. Douglas, however, was abhorred by the southerners. William L. Yancey of Alabama bluntly demanded, "We are in a position to ask you to yield." The northerners refused, and so Yancey and fifty other delegates walked out, held their own convention, and nominated Vice President John C. Breckinridge as their candidate.

James L. Petigru (above), a respected Charleston jurist, was a Unionist. After the state declared its independence on December 20, 1860, he allegedly told a friend, "South Carolina is too small for a republic and too large for an insane asylum."

Opposite page: Taken prior to his election as president, this is the only known full-length photograph of Abraham Lincoln. Although he had repeatedly stated that he would not act against slavery in those states in which it already existed, he was viewed as an abolitionist in the South, and his election polarized the secessionist movement. Lincoln's most direct statement about the fragmenting Union was made in his inaugural address, March 4, 1861: "In your hands, my dissatisfied fellow-countrymen, and not in mine, is the momentous issue of civil war. . . . You have no oath registered in Heaven to destroy the government, while I shall have the most solemn one to 'preserve, protect, and defend' it."

WCD

As the country expanded and territories sought statehood, the U.S. Congress and the White House debated whether slavery would be allowed to expand into the western frontier, which at that time was everything west of Kansas. °As long as there were an equal number of free states and slave states, there would be an equal number of senators in Congress from the North and from the South. Thus that branch of Congress would not be dominated by either side.●

During the decades before the war, a series of compromises were devised in Congress that allowed new states to be admitted while maintaining the balance between slave and free states. The first compromise occurred in 1818 when Missouri petitioned Congress for admission as a slave state, which would have given the slave states a majority in the Senate. The situation was resolved when Maine separated from Massachusetts in 1819 and petitioned for statehood as a free state. Congress, however, still had to address the question of slavery in the area acquired by the 1803 Louisiana Purchase. In legislation known as the Missouri Compromise, Missouri was admitted to the Union with the stipulation that slavery would be limited in the Louisiana Purchase to those territories below latitude 36°30′.

When the question of slavery in the new territories aroused sectional tensions again thirty years later, Congress honored the 36°30′ boundary line in legislation dubbed the Compromise of 1850. Four years later, however, the Kansas-Nebraska Act voided the Missouri Compromise by dissolving the geographical boundary of slavery and allowing the settlers of Kansas and Nebraska to determine by popular vote whether their territories would be open or closed to slavery. Nebraska was admitted as a free state, but Kansas became a battleground. Ultimately Kansas was admitted as a free state, but only after five constitutions had been drafted and two hundred lives had been lost in "Bleeding Kansas."

Regional animosity escalated between North and South when the compromises of the past failed and no further agreements could be reached. As tensions climaxed following the presidential election of 1860, the outgoing president, James Buchanan, did nothing to address the problem.

Steadfast opposition to the expansion of slavery and the increasing influence of abo-
ALR litionists forced °southerners to face the reality that they would no longer have an opportunity to expand the areas that would reflect their way of life. They had to decide if they needed to organize their own national government that would view the expansion of slavery favorably.•

By the late 1850s southern states were actively discussing the concept of seceding from the Union, a right they believed the Constitution allowed. Building on the political legacy of John C. Calhoun, South Carolina became the cradle of the secessionist movement.

WCD °South Carolina had always been the seedbed of secessionist sentiment. Further-
more, the state, and particularly Charleston, was very much in the hands of prominent pro-secessionist politicians and newspaper editors who came to be called "fire-eaters," a name give to them because they were so rabid about secession they were said to spit fire when they spoke of it.•

One of the South's leading secessionists was a sixty-one-year-old Virginian named Edmund Ruffin. He was an agricultural sci-
WCD entist and a writer who °had a vision of northerners as "the vile Yankee race." There was no room for compromise with him. When members of his own family remained loyal to the Union, he had nothing further to do with them.•

It was not only southern men who dis-
cussed secession from the Union. Women like Mary Chesnut, a descendant of Charleston's elite and wife of Sen. James Chesnut, also joined in the debate. She maintained a diary that became famous

In an 1860 Louis Maurer cartoon entitled "Three 'Outs' and One 'Run,'" the presidential race was compared to a baseball game. Lincoln's opponents (from left to right: Union Party nominee John Bell, Northern Democrat Stephen A. Douglas, and Southern Democrat John C. Breckinridge) have fouled out, or in the jargon of the game at the time, they have been "skunk'd," which is reenforced by the skunk on the field. The bats are labeled with the primary positions of the respective parties in regard to slavery. Douglas credits the Republican's success to the bat he uses, a fence rail that is inscribed "equal rights and free territory."

THE NATIONAL GAME. THREE "OUTS" AND ONE "RUN".
ABRAHAM WINNING THE BALL.

after the war for its behind-the-scenes look at the Confederacy. Regarding separation from the United States, she wrote, "We are divorced, North and South, because we have hated each other so."

By 1860 some southerners wanted to leave the Union immediately while others wanted to compromise with the North and avert bloodshed. In the presidential election of 1860, a northern politician emerged who finally ended the debate and solidified the South against the North. That man was a lanky former congressman from Illinois who had campaigned against slavery as a senatorial candidate and who was then campaigning even stronger against its spread as a presidential candidate. His name was Abraham Lincoln.

LINCOLN DID NOT start the debate on slavery, but he crystallized it when he said, "A house divided against itself cannot stand." His growing popularity in the North and the likelihood that the South would split its votes among the other candidates worried southern politicians who still hoped to keep the country together. They wanted to believe Lincoln when he said he would not interfere with slavery in states where it already existed, but they did not trust him.

WCD °Because of the myth that has grown up around the benevolent "Father Abraham," the intensely political side of Lincoln tends to be forgotten.• While Lincoln the candidate could be ambiguous, other men who were close to him, like his law partner, William Herndon, announced, "Liberty and slavery, civilization and barbarism, one or the other must perish on this continent," implying that Lincoln would pursue an aggressive abolitionist agenda.

Lincoln seemed destined to be a politician. He was born in a Kentucky log cabin to poor farmers. Self-taught, he developed an interest in politics, first becoming a lawyer, then an Illinois state legislator, and later a U.S. congressman. His wife, Mary Todd, was a Kentucky belle. Although he was born a southerner and married a southerner, Lincoln rose through the political ranks of Illinois as a campaigner against slavery.

By 1860 he had become the North's most important spokesman on the issue, and abolition was an issue that everyone, northerners and southerners, associated with Lincoln's campaign for the presidency. Running against him were Stephen Douglas, a northern Democrat who had once beaten Lincoln for a seat in the U.S. Senate; John C. Breckinridge of Kentucky, a southern Democrat who had been vice president under President James Buchanan; and John Bell, a Tennessean who wanted to

Mary Boykin Chesnut was the wife of South Carolina Sen. James Chesnut Jr. Her descriptive diary, which she maintained throughout the war, provides tremendous insight into civilian life during the war. Her writing is more than a chronicle of events, but a commentary filled with her opinions and experiences. On hearing the first shots in Charleston Harbor, she noted, "I sprang out of bed, and on my knees— prostrate—I prayed as I never prayed before." In addition, she wrote of her conversations with other significant Southern wives, such as First Lady Varina Davis, and maintained a record of their perceptions as well as her own.

On November 8, 1860, the citizens of Savannah, Georgia, celebrated the unveiling of their first flag. The secessionist banner had a picture of a rattlesnake, the same emblem as in the American Revolution, and the words, "Don't tread on me." Two months later, Georgia seceded from the Union, January 19, 1861. Scenes like this spread throughout the South. On April 30, the Confederacy's vice president, Alexander Stephens of Georgia, stated, "We have ten millions of people with us, heart and hand, to defend us to the death. . . . God is on our side, and who shall be against us?"

In late November 1860, Secretary of War John B. Floyd—a Virginian— appointed Maj. Robert Anderson commander of the three federal forts in Charleston Harbor: Moultrie, Sumter, and Castle Pinckney. Floyd hoped that Anderson's Kentucky heritage, his Georgian wife, and the fact that he had been a slave owner would not aggravate matters in this hotbed of secessionism. Shortly after arriving at Fort Moultrie, Anderson assessed his vulnerability and decided to move his command to the harbor fort—Sumter.

William Waud, an Englishman, sketched these slaves mounting a cannon at Cummings Point on Morris Island as the South Carolina military constructed its circle of fire around Fort Sumter. By April 11, six thousand southerners surrounded the small garrison in the harbor fort. More than thirty cannon and eighteen mortars were aimed at the federals from batteries on James Island (including Fort Johnson), Cummings Point, Mount Pleasant, and Sullivan's Island (including Fort Moultrie). When the firing began, Anderson restricted his men to the lower casemates, limiting his response to twenty-one guns.

preserve the Union. Each of Lincoln's opponents hoped the nation would turn to him as the alternative to Lincoln. Yet the South recognized that the four-man presidential race—with two of the candidates being southerners and the third a northerner who preached compromise with the South—probably assured Lincoln of the White House.

BP °Southerners viewed Lincoln as a man who assailed their institutions and denied them their rights. His election pushed the inevitable confrontation at Sumter even closer because South Carolina wanted nothing to do with him. Carolinians knew that Lincoln was not going to vacillate the way Buchanan had.•

DR °With the election of Lincoln impending, South Carolina threatened to secede. If that secession occurred, northern leaders wanted someone in charge of the Charleston forts and arsenal who would not alarm the Carolinians further.• When it became virtu-
ALR ally certain that Lincoln would win, °President Buchanan and Secretary of War John B. Floyd, a Virginian, sent one of their most reliable officers, Maj. Robert Anderson, to Charleston.•

The choice of Anderson was meant to soothe south-
BP ern fears because °he was a southerner, a Kentuckian whose family owned slaves. Furthermore, his wife was from Georgia, and he had served in the Mexican War

with many other southern-born officers then in the army. Anderson was a graduate of and a former instructor at West Point. Politically, his sympathies were probably southern, but his loyalty and his devotion were to the federal government.° At the same time °he was a tragic man. His life had been full of ironies. Thus the worst place for him to have been sent in November 1860 was to command the federal troops in Charleston. The tug-of-war inside him between his southern sympathies, on the one hand, and his duty to his uniform and his flag, on the other, tore him apart emotionally.°

Anderson himself had no doubts about his loyalties. In a letter he wrote before leaving New York for Charleston's Fort Moultrie, he said, "In this controversy between the North and South, my sympathies are entirely with the South." That did not mean, however, that Anderson would ignore his duty to his government. He took command of °the garrison at Fort Moultrie, which also included the harbor fort known as Sumter. His was a very small garrison, a mere eighty-four soldiers, many of whom had their wives and children with them. Moultrie was also virtually indefensible against the people Anderson feared he might have to fight.°

In 1780 the residents of Charleston built a rampart to protect the town from British invasion. By the 1800s a section of the rampart in downtown Charleston was used as a state arsenal and guardhouse. The arsenal was called "the Citadel" because of the building's design. In December 1842 the South Carolina legislature established a college at the arsenal, and three months later the state militia guards were replaced by twenty young men—the first South Carolina Corps of Cadets—and the college became known as the Citadel Academy. As tensions rose in the aftermath of South Carolina's secession, cadets from the Citadel were assigned to a battery on Morris Island. On January 9, 1861, that battery opened fire on a federal supply ship, Star of the West, turning the vessel back to sea and away from Anderson's command at Sumter.

11

Named after Revolutionary war hero Thomas Sumter, this brick-and-masonry fort dominated Charleston Harbor and was 3.3 miles from the heart of the city. Its isolated position made it a stronger defensive position than Moultrie. The original plans called for three tiers of 146 guns manned by 650 men. Work on the fort, however, was not complete. The barracks were unfinished and only 15 guns had been mounted. The parade ground was cluttered with building materials: 5,600 shot and shell and 66 unmounted guns. These details were unknown to the southerners. As soon as Anderson and his men occupied the fort they began mounting more cannon and preparing for the inevitable battle.

Built on the tip of Sullivan's Island on the site of a fort first defended against the British during the American Revolution, Fort Moultrie was surrounded by houses whose DR °rooftops dwarfed the fort's twelve-foot-high walls. Quickly, Anderson saw that Moultrie was a death trap.• Moreover, Charleston's secessionist citizens knew everything about the fort. The fort's gate had always been open to them.

Some officers, such as Capt. Abner Doubleday, a staunch abolitionist and Anderson's second in command, were skeptical of the new commander's loyalty to the Union. Doubleday wrote, "Major Anderson was neither timid nor irresolute. . . . Unfortunately, he desired not only to save the Union, but to save slavery with it." Lincoln's supposed upcoming election meant that it would not be long before Anderson would have to prove his loyalty.

The issue of the legality of leaving the Union was crystal clear to the secessionists. They could go when they EFG pleased. °Secession was grounded in the notion that ultimate sovereignty resided in the states, not in the federal government. Southern theorists argued that the Constitution had been ratified by the states, not the country's citizens.• With that distinction being made, the secessionists argued that any state's elected representatives could take their state out of the Union at any time.

Just one month after Lincoln's election, a secessionist convention met in Charleston, and on December 20, 1860, South Carolina became the first state to secede from the Union. The new republic of South Carolina and the United States now had a common problem, although each viewed it differently. The United States had two major forts, Fort Moultrie and Fort Sumter, within South Carolina's borders and wanted to retain ownership of those forts. South Carolina preferred that everything formerly owned by the United States should be deeded over to it.

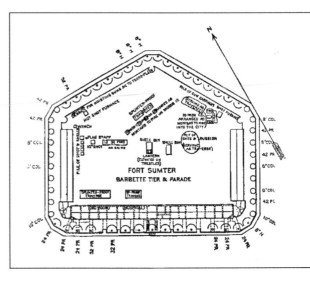

It was obvious to everyone that a fight for the forts was imminent. Because Moultrie was the more difficult to defend, °Anderson decided to abandon it. He had tangible evidence that the Carolinians were about to begin hostilities. He could move to any of the forts in Charleston where he felt he could protect his garrison, and so he made the fateful decision to leave Fort Moultrie and occupy Fort Sumter.•

A three-story brick fort constructed after the War of 1812 for protection against foreign invasions and named after the Revolutionary War hero Thomas Sumter, Fort Sumter was the safest bastion in the harbor for Anderson and his tiny garrison. Its walls were tall and thick, and any attack would have to come from more than a mile away over open water. °Sumter was virtually impregnable. Round shot could not break through its heavy brick walls. The fort had been designed to mount 135 guns, and even though it stood unfinished in the middle of Charleston Harbor, it was Anderson's safest point.•

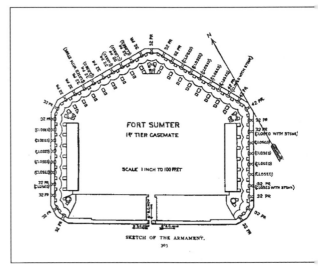

On December 26, under a moonlit sky and while the civilians of Charleston slept, Anderson evacuated his eighty-four soldiers and their forty-five wives and children from Fort Moultrie to Fort Sumter. He °did not inform any of his officers of his decision, even Doubleday, his second in command, until moments before the movement to Sumter was to take place.•

Sumter was a part of the system of coastal defenses developed after the War of 1812. It was the largest of the Charleston defenses, hunkering on a shoal a mile across the harbor from Moultrie. Work had begun on the installation in 1829, but it took ten years to create the man-made island of granite "leavings" on which the fort rested.

13

In December 1860, Francis W. Pickens (near right) was elected governor of South Carolina. At the height of the Sumter controversy the state was spending twenty thousand dollars a day for the defense of Charleston, and many shipping companies began avoiding South Carolina's largest harbor. In addition to the lost revenues, Pickens and others saw the Sumter situation as a symbol of control. The fort belonged to the republic of South Carolina, not to the United States. In response to Anderson's move to Sumter, Pickens ordered all federal installations seized, including Forts Moultrie and Johnson and Castle Pinckney, which became components in the circle of iron around Anderson and his men.

A career soldier, P. G. T. Beauregard (far right) had been an engineer on Winfield Scott's staff during the Mexican War, earned two brevet promotions, and was wounded twice. Between the wars he was assigned to coastal construction projects. Beauregard has the dubious distinction of serving the shortest period as superintendent at the military academy at West Point—five days, January 23–28, 1861. Transferred when he counseled a cadet to see which way he would go if Louisiana seceded, Beauregard resigned from the army to accept a brigadier's commission in the South and command of the troops around Charleston. He had been Anderson's pupil when the latter had taught gunnery at West Point.

With the evacuation, Anderson proved that his first loyalty was to the U.S. government. His officers and men no longer doubted him. Proving his sentiments further, he had Moultrie's guns spiked and also burned their carriages so these could not be of immediate use to the Carolinians. As a final act, he had Fort Moultrie's flagpole chopped down so no secessionist flag could be immediately unfurled over U.S. property.

DR °The next day, December 27, Charlestonians awoke to see smoke rising over Moultrie and the U.S. flag flying over Fort Sumter.• The South declared Anderson a traitor as volunteers occupied Moultrie and the remaining federal installations around Charleston. South Carolina Gov. Francis Pickens wasted no time demanding

EFG the surrender of Fort Sumter. °The ordinance of secession, in the view of the secessionists, justified their taking possession of Fort Sumter because it was part of their territory and they had declared themselves a sovereign state.•

WCD °South Carolina secessionists expected these Yankee soldiers would evacuate the federal forts without a fight because they were no longer Yankee property. They even sent commissioners to Washington to negotiate the purchase of the property.• Fort Sumter, however, was not for sale, and the newly elected president would risk war to keep it.

DURING THE FIRST few months of 1861, Fort Sumter became a symbol of the battle for territory between North and South, but for the soldiers and civilians stranded within the fort's walls, it became a battle for survival against the cold, constant winds, hunger, isolation from the rest of the nation, and the realization that one day they might come under fire. According to Doubleday, "We wondered how long those boys would keep up their enthusiasm amidst the real war, which was now fast approaching."

DR   °January 1861 was a bitter month. It was extremely cold, and the women and the children suffered tremendously inside the fort. They had very little fuel, very little wood for fires. When Doubleday's wife came out to the fort, he had to chop up a mahogany table for kindling to keep her warm.•

Both sides knew that Sumter's small garrison could not hold out for long. When first occupied, the fort had supplies for only four months, and the secessionists blocked all attempts to purchase groceries from civilian

In February 1861, Charleston photographer George Cook journeyed to Sumter and persuaded Anderson and his officers to sit for him. Those standing are (from left to right): Capt. Truman Seymour, Lt. George W. Snyder, Lt. Jefferson C. Davis, 2d Lt. Richard K. Meade, and Capt. Theodore Talbot. Those seated are (from left to right) Capt. Abner Doubleday, Maj. Robert Anderson, Assistant Surgeon Samuel W. Crawford, and Capt. John G. Foster. All but Meade, Snyder, and Talbot would be generals by the end of the war. Only one, Meade, resigned his commission to fight for the South.

Sixty-seven-year-old Edmund Ruffin of Virginia was an ardent secessionist and writer. Ruffin moved to Charleston to celebrate South Carolina's withdrawal from the Union and was made an honorary member of the Palmetto Guard, a local militia. On April 12, Ruffin fired the first shot of the Iron Battery on Morris Island at Fort Sumter. He was elated that war had come at last. Four years later, following the surrender of the Confederacy, Ruffin shot himself. A portion of his suicide note read, "I here repeat my unmitigated hatred to . . . the vile Yankee race."

When Anderson realized how vulnerable his men were at Fort Moultrie, he evacuated the fort. Prior to their departure (right), the federal troops burned gun carriages and wrecked the cannon by hammering steel rods into the vent pipe of the guns, rendering them useless.

sources. President Buchanan sent a supply ship, the *Star of the West*, to Fort Sumter in mid-January 1861, but Carolina troops immediately fired on the vessel when it neared the harbor. Defenseless against attack, the *Star* withdrew. Anderson watched the episode without taking action himself.

BP °The U.S. government was providing Anderson with lackluster direction. Had he been more aggressive by firing on the South Carolinians when the *Star of the West* attempted to resupply Sumter, he could have touched off the war four months earlier. He could have ignited the spark, but he chose to do everything possible to avoid that.•

Weeks passed and the garrison's food supplies dwindled. With no end to the conflict in sight, Anderson evacuated the women and children to New York. After the families had bid a tearful farewell, °he ordered his men to prepare the fort for combat, which included lifting some heavy artillery into place.• Despite this preparation, by early April 1861 Anderson told his men—and the Confederates—that the fort had only a few days' rations left. Rather than be shelled out of the fort, the soldiers might be starved out.

DR

Either way, the South Carolinians were finally ready to take the fort. That had not always been the case. For the first few months all they could do was bluster and boast. The threat to bombard Fort Sumter had been a hollow one because the secessionists did not have sufficient trained men or the gunpowder to fire on it. Four months, however, had given them time to train troops and surround Sumter with what they called "a ring of fire." While the soldiers in the fort were preparing for a deadly struggle, the Carolinians were confidently preparing for their place in history. Diarist Mary Chesnut observed, "This Southern Confederacy must be supported now by calm determination and cool brains, for the stake is life or death."

By February 1861 seven states had seceded from the Union—Alabama, Florida, Georgia, Louisiana, Mississippi, South Carolina, and Texas. All of these sent representatives to a meeting in Montgomery, Alabama, to form the Confederate States of America. While there, the representatives selected a conservative former U.S. senator from Mississippi, Jefferson Davis, as president. Davis, a Mexican War hero who had also previously served the United States as secretary of war, recognized that the South was undertaking a deadly course. Summoned to Montgomery from his Mississippi plantation, Davis wrote of his inauguration to his wife, Varina: "The audience was large and brilliant. Upon my weary heart was

On the evening of December 26, 1860, Anderson and his men set out for Fort Sumter. The major had kept the move confidential and had only told his officers the night before. Ironically, Anderson's father, Capt. Richard Anderson, had defended Fort Moultrie during the American Revolution and had been forced to surrender to the British. The federal soldiers quietly moved across the water to Sumter with little incident. In the morning, crowds in Charleston saw smoke rising from Moultrie. When they saw the Stars and Stripes flying over Sumter, they realized the federals had moved to the stronger position. Governor Pickens demanded that Anderson return to Moultrie, otherwise the occupation of Sumter would be viewed as a belligerent act, and he so informed the government in Washington.

Anderson's responsibilities as garrison commander included ensuring the safety of the families who lived on post. As the tension over Sumter increased and food supplies dwindled, he evacuated the women and children from the harbor fort on February 3, 1861. They were allowed to depart for New York on the steamship Marion.

On January 5, 1861, the Star of the West *left New York Harbor and headed toward South Carolina. Its mission was to resupply Anderson's troops. News of this expedition did not reach the federal commander until January 8, and he had no instructions from Washington on what his role should be if the ship drew fire as it approached. The next day the federals saw the ship approach Charleston waters. Confederate gunners opened up while Anderson and his men looked on in frustration. Without orders, the major would not commit the Union to war. Within minutes the ship turned about and withdrew. In the sketch at right, Fort Moultrie is to the left, and Morris Island is to the right.*

showered smiles . . . but beyond them, I saw trouble and thorns innumerable."

Davis was a perceptive man who knew the dangers of attacking Fort Sumter. Like Lincoln, he was the son of a Kentucky farmer, but he had moved to Mississippi to make his fortune in cotton. Davis had been educated at West Point, where he was three years behind Robert Anderson, now the enemy at Fort Sumter. After a short military career fighting Indians and Mexicans, Davis had been a U.S. congressman, senator, and cabinet member. He had been the South's spokesman throughout the 1850s. Until drafted by the Confederacy, Davis had been

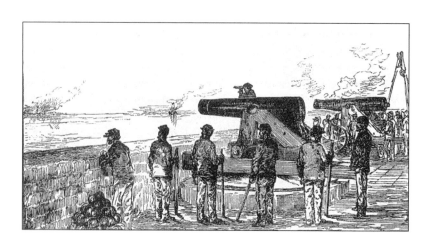

WCD ready to retire to his Mississippi plantation. He °did not want the presidency of the Confederacy. His preference would have been to stay on his plantation and not get involved in what was going to happen. At the same time he did not believe the North would let the South go without a fight.•

Lincoln had made the federal government's position quite clear in his March 4 inaugural address: "The power confided in me will be used to hold, occupy, and possess the property and places belonging to the government. In your hands, my dissatisfied fellow countrymen, and not in mine, is the momentous issue of civil war."

Fort Sumter, very visible in the harbor of one of the South's largest cities, had become much more than just a fort to the North. It had become a symbol of federal

ALR power. °In the states that had seceded, southerners had successfully seized control of all federal property. Court-houses, customs houses, post offices, arsenals, and forts had all come under the control of the southerners. Only

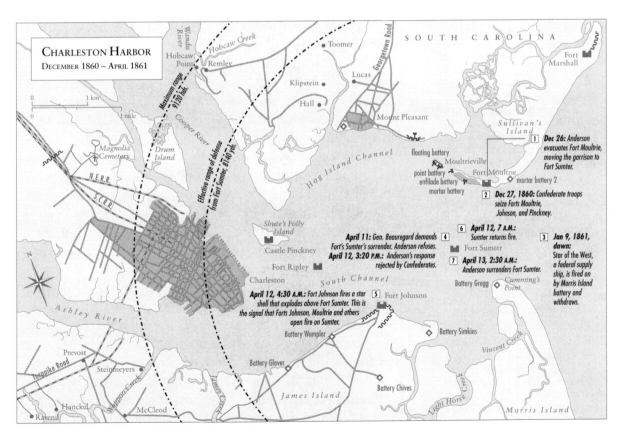

CHARLESTON HARBOR
DECEMBER 1860 – APRIL 1861

SOUTH CAROLINA

1 Dec 26: Anderson evacuates Fort Moultrie, moving the garrison to Fort Sumter.

2 Dec 27, 1860: Confederate troops seize Forts Moultrie, Johnson, and Pinckney.

6 April 12, 7 A.M.: Sumter returns fire.

3 Jan 9, 1861, dawn: Star of the West, a federal supply ship, is fired on by Morris Island battery and withdraws.

April 11: Gen. Beauregard demands 4 Fort's Sumter's surrender. Anderson refuses.
April 12, 3:20 P.M.: Anderson's response rejected by Confederates.

7 April 13, 2:30 A.M.: Anderson surrenders Fort Sumter.

April 12, 4:30 A.M.: Fort Johnson fires a star 5 shell that explodes above Fort Sumter. This is the signal that Forts Johnson, Moultrie and others open fire on Sumter.

In the engraving of the attack on Fort Sumer above, the fort's apex points toward Fort Moultrie on Sullivan's Island. Fourteen Confederate cannon and ten mortars fired from Moultrie. A floating battery near the island concentrated four guns on Sumter, and from James Island, west of Sumter, Fort Johnson was made up of five cannon. At the tip of Morris Island, south of the fort, eleven guns had been erected. To man the guns on Morris Island and to storm the fort, if necessary, Beauregard mustered 6,000 soldiers. Anderson and approximately 127 men were surrounded. In all, forty-six cannon threw shot and shell into the fort. Anderson countered with twenty-one guns.

At 4:30 A.M. on April 12, 1861, the first shot of the Civil War was fired (right). Sumter's outer layer had been faced with brick to make the barracks fireproof. To counter this the Confederates placed cannonballs in a huge oven and heated them until they were red-hot. These "hot shot" lodged inside the walls and set the wood afire.

The body to the right of the center cannon was added by the artist to make the engraving more dramatic. No one on either side was killed during the first engagement of the war.

a few places, like Fort Sumter, remained in federal hands. The North would not allow the South to annex these installations. Lincoln could not let them go.•

Anderson watched all this political maneuvering on both sides with a grim sense of reality. On March 5, the day after Lincoln's inauguration, he sent the president a letter urgently requesting relief: "I confess that I would not be willing to risk my reputation on an attempt to throw reinforcements into this harbor . . . for our relief rendered necessary by the limited supply of our provisions."

During the next six weeks the U.S. president agonized over what he should do about Fort Sumter. °Lincoln the politician knew that Sumter was a possible opening wedge to war. His primary commitment to the people, however, was the preservation of the Union. Thus abandoning Sumter to the Confederates would have been a concession he could not make.• After weeks of sleepless nights and chronic headaches, Lincoln came up with a plan that could lure the South into war by forcing it to fire the first shot.

THE SIEGE OF Fort Sumter has been called one of the most brilliant and bloodless clashes of the Civil War. It was a battle fought before the cruelty of warfare touched the hearts and minds of all Americans. While it was fought, families sat perched on their rooftops to watch the blazing spectacle of bombs bursting in air. The action at Fort Sumter began as a gentlemen's war between the North and South, but its gentlemen's good-

will was lost in the smoke over Charleston Harbor and led to the bloodiest four years in American history.

On April 12, 1861, hours before dawn, the first shots of the Civil War echoed across the harbor of Charleston. Charlestonians, the most vocal of all secessionists, were excited to finally hear the cannons roar. One of them, William Merritt Bristol, said, "All the pent-up hatred of the past months and years is voiced in the thunder of these cannon, and the people seem almost beside themselves in the exultation of a freedom they deem already won." A reporter for the *Charleston Courier* wrote: "The clustering shells illuminated the sky above us. Hail upon Sumter's side—this first great scene in the opening drama of this momentous history."

BP By April 1861 °Fort Sumter had become a symbol. In the weeks leading up to this bombardment there was no piece of real estate in the country more symbolic and more important to both sides than this little island and CC its battered fort.• °The engagement at Sumter occurred before there was even a hint of the losses to come, when the great dreams of glory were untouched by any reality.•

Anderson, like Lincoln and the Confederates, knew that the opening shot was drawing near. On April 7, 1861, he wrote, "My heart is not in the war, which I see is thus to be commenced." On April 8 Lincoln sent a letter

On the morning of April 13 the Union soldiers within Sumter casually ate their breakfast and then went back to their guns to answer the Confederate bombardment. More hot shot was falling inside the barracks. The fort frequently caught fire. By 10:00 A.M. the blaze was virtually out of control, and the Confederate mortar shells exploding on the parade ground made any attempts to extinguish the fire impossible. At noon the entire barracks was aflame, and the blaze crept close to three hundred barrels of gunpowder. Anderson quickly ordered every available man to move the powder kegs.

Anderson decided it was too dangerous to use the barbette guns on the upper level. Instead, he ordered his men to the twenty-one guns sheltered in the vaulted masonry casemates on the lower level. These cannon were huge 32- and 42-pounders; they were quite deadly against ships but less effective against masonry forts or earthworks. To compound the problem, there were no fuses for the explosive shells, thus the federals used solid shot. Moreover, the garrison ran low on cartridge bags. On the second day Anderson ordered his gunners to slow their rate of fire to one shot every ten minutes.

to the Confederates warning them that a fleet of warships with provisions was sailing to Sumter.

The waiting game was over. Lincoln's announcement was a crafty one that, on the surface, seemed to fly in the face of conventional military secrecy regarding the movements of one's navy. °The decision to do it reflected the masterfulness of the Lincoln administration. If Confederate gunners would open up on the fleet, or open up on the fort in the process of receiving the supplies, the Confederate government would be maneuvered into firing the first shot.•

Lincoln's letter was passed to Gen. Pierre Gustave Toutant Beauregard, commander of the Confederate forces at Charleston. °Beauregard was a Creole from Louisiana who could speak better French than English. Some critics said that he was barely tall enough for his own name, but he was a capable officer with a magnetic personality.•

With a deadline set in the form of a federal relief mission soon to be on its way, communication increased between Anderson and the Confederates surrounding him. °A review of the correspondence between Anderson and Beauregard reveals a sense of the respect the two men felt for each other. This respect probably had its beginning at West Point, where Beauregard had been tutored by Anderson. It was very much a gentlemen's war at that point.•

°Anderson finally received word, on April 10, that a relief fleet was en route with provisions. He realized that there was probably no way war could be averted. As he walked alone among the guns of the fort's lower deck, his head bowed, undoubtedly in prayer, he realized that all he had done over the past four months had been for naught.•

DR On April 11 Jefferson Davis ordered Beauregard to send a group of commissioners to Fort Sumter. °They gave Anderson an ultimatum: Either evacuate the fort or he would be fired upon. Anderson, however, had not received orders from Washington authorizing him to evacuate the fort. His duty as an American officer would not allow him to surrender the fort without battle.• As the commissioners departed, Anderson shook their hands and confided to them: "Gentlemen, if you do not batter us to pieces, we shall be starved out in a few days."

DR That bit of information added a new wrinkle to the negotiations. °Beauregard was instructed to find out when Anderson would agree to leave, and so the commissioners returned to Fort Sumter. Anderson told them he would leave the fort on April 15 unless the fort was going to be resupplied or unless the Confederates would open fire.•

His response disappointed Beauregard. Lincoln's supply fleet was approaching. If the fort were resupplied, there would be no pressing need for Anderson to

Local news reports lauded the role of Fort Moultrie, shown below, in the artillery duel with Fort Sumter: "The advantage was unquestionably upon the side of Fort Moultrie. In that fort not a gun was dismounted, not a wound received, not the slightest permanent injury sustained by any of its defenses, while every ball from Fort Moultrie left its mark on Fort Sumter. . . . The last two or three hours before dark, Major Anderson devoted himself exclusively to Fort Moultrie, and the two fortresses had a grand duello. Game to the last, though much more exposed, Fort Moultrie held her own, and it is believed, a little more than her own."

surrender, and the standoff might drag on for many more months. In the early morning hours Beauregard sent word to Anderson through the commissioners that the Confederates would open fire in one hour.

°They looked at their watches. Anderson realized that around 4:40 A.M. the war would start. The Confederate representatives left Fort Sumter for James Island, where they met with the battery commander. The stage was set for the firing of the first shot.•

It would not be a fair fight. Inside Fort Sumter were 127 men (84 federal soldiers and officers and 43 non-combatant laborers). More than 6,000 Confederates stationed at ten batteries and two forts surrounded the harbor fort. Confederate Lt. George S. James, a former U.S. Army officer at Fort Johnson, was ordered to prepare his guns to fire the first shot. °It was a momentous event: the first shot of the war. James looked at Roger Pryor, a former U.S. representative turned leading fire-eater and secessionist, and gave him the option of firing the first shot.• Pryor, however, declined, professing that he could not fire the first gun of the war.

°So James instructed his second in command, Lt. Henry S. Farley, to prepare one of his mortars for action. When James next looked at his watch, it was 4:30. Farley yanked the lanyard and fired the first round. It was a splendid shot that burned for nearly thirteen seconds but struck nothing. Moments later, Virginian Edmund Ruffin pulled the lanyard that fired the first shot from Morris

Island that struck Fort Sumter. Thus commenced the debate of who fired the first shot.

In only a matter of moments all the guns that were aimed at Fort Sumter opened up, and within twenty minutes, Anderson and his garrison were surrounded by a deadly ring of fire.• The townspeople who had been waiting now knew that war had finally come. Only a handful suspected what the firing would bring the South. Mary Chesnut wrote that when she heard the heavy booming of a cannon, "I sprang out of bed, and on my knees—prostrate—I prayed as I never prayed before."

WCD   °The rooftops were soon crowded with people. Mary Chesnut managed to sit down on a chimney, not realizing a fire was burning beneath her, and her dress caught fire. Hundreds if not thousands of people looked on the bombardment as a kind of show. They took it for granted the Yankees would not fight back and there would be a glorious victory.•

For the first several hours forty-seven Confederate guns fired upon Sumter, but Anderson did not return the fire because

DR   in the predawn darkness °his gunners would be firing blindly into the night. Rather than deploy his men prematurely, he assembled them at reveille. Around seven o'clock, they moved to the guns.•

The photograph below was taken April 15, 1861, one day after Anderson's surrender, by either George Cook or F. K. Houston of Charleston. The damaged original flagpole occupies the foreground, and the ruins of the officers quarters and the main sally port fill the background. This part of the fort drew fire from Fort Moultrie's guns.

Former U.S. senator Louis T. Wigfall (left) from Texas was serving as a volunteer on Beauregard's staff. When he saw Sumter's flagpole fall, Wigfall—without any authority—commandeered a boat and was rowed to the fort, where he met with Anderson and suggested the major might wish to surrender. Since the fort had exhausted all but four kegs of powder, Anderson agreed. Around 1:30 P.M., April 14, the federal commander hoisted a white flag on a makeshift pole. The garrison agreed to evacuate the next day and were allowed to give a gun salute to their flag.

Sixteen-year-old John Styles Bird (right) had joined the Palmetto Guard in 1858. Flag-bearer of his unit, he had acquired the flag from Charles E. Mills, captain of the brig John H. Jones, who had added a red star to a Palmetto flag as symbolic of the southern republic's independence. From December 1860 through March 1861 the flag flew over the arsenal, the old Charleston lighthouse on Morris Island, and Stevens's Iron Battery. When Sumter surrendered, Bird's flag was used to meet U.S. barges approaching Morris Island. The Palmetto Guard was then designated as one of the units to occupy Fort Sumter. As the last federal was leaving the facility, Bird secured a pole and planted his flag on the parapet of the fort. Later Bird and the flag went into combat at First Manassas. In 1862 he was discharged with a disability and returned home with the flag, which stayed in his family until 1979.

Captain Doubleday fired Fort Sumter's first return shot at Edmund Ruffin's battery on Morris Island. That pleased the old secessionist. He later said, "I was fearful that Major Anderson did not intend to fire at all. It would have cheapened our conquest of the fort."

Anderson resisted any urges to strike out at anyone WCD other than those who were shooting at him. He °could have fired on civilian targets in downtown Charleston had he chosen, but he did not. He did not want to make things worse than they already were, and he also had very limited resources with which to fire back.•

Fort Sumter's return fire had little effect on the DR opposing forces. °That was disheartening to all the Union soldiers during that first day's action. Anderson had determined that he would not allow his men to leave the security of the lower casemates to go to the top tier of the fort, where the heaviest artillery was emplaced.•

On the second day of battle, Anderson's men took the DR war into their own hands. °Sgt. John Carmody climbed the spiral stairways to the top tier. Knowing that all of the guns in the top deck were loaded and aimed, he yanked the lanyards and fired the guns against Anderson's orders. Two other sergeants saw what had happened and climbed the staircase to fire the rest of the guns.• While the gesture was brave, it was futile. Fort Sumter was outmanned and outgunned.

DR The Confederates increased the pressure. °The gunners inside Fort Moultrie heated their cannonballs until they were red hot and then fired them into Sumter's supposedly fireproof barracks.• That turned the tide of the battle. By midmorning the fort was an inferno. The smoke and fires were so intense that Anderson's men were suffocating. Amidst the pandemonium, Anderson noticed that the garrison flag had been shot down.

WCD °Viewed from the shore, it looked as if the federals had taken the flag down themselves—a sign of surrender. Yet before Beauregard could do anything, former U.S. Sen. Louis T. Wigfall of Texas, a man who viewed himself as a sort of Confederate knight errant but was more of a pest to the Confederate leadership, took it upon himself to go out to the fort and present terms for its surrender.• Wigfall acknowledged the bravery of the Sumter defenders and said to Anderson, "You have defended your flag nobly, sir. It is madness to preserve this useless resistance."

Anderson looked around him at the fires raging in the barracks. He knew he had food for only one more day and that Lincoln's supply ships were nowhere near. He and his men had honored their commitment to their country as long as they could. Anderson declared defeat and told Wigfall, "I have already stated my terms for evacuation to General Beauregard. Instead of noon on the fifteenth, I will go now."

This image was among the first to be taken of the interior of Sumter after the departure of Anderson and his men. F. K. Houston of Charleston brought his camera to the fort the day after the Confederates took possession. The hot-shot furnace can be seen to the left of the makeshift flagpole, and a gun crew stands with one of the converted Columbiads posing for the photographer's benefit in addition to the small work crew in the center foreground. The flag is one of the earliest versions of the Stars and Bars, and seven stars can be seen clearly. The fort's beacon lantern has been removed from its place on the parapet, resting elsewhere on the parade ground. The damage sustained by the fire ignited during the bombardment can be seen in the officers quarters in the left background. Work has begun in the far right, along the second rank of casemates, enclosing the area, possibly for soldiers quarters.

IT WAS WITH a heavy but proud heart that Anderson filed his final report on April 15, 1861: "Having defended Fort Sumter for thirty-four hours until the quarters were entirely burned . . . I accepted the terms of evacuation offered."

The siege of Fort Sumter was remarkable in at least one aspect. After thirty-five hundred rounds of fire, neither side had suffered any deaths. Anderson told one Confederate that he was proud to serve his country without taking the life of a fellow human being.

The surrender terms were simple and generous. °Anderson would be allowed to leave the fort with his flag flying and with his men carrying their arms with them. He would also be allowed to fire a one-hundred-gun salute in honor of his flag. Furthermore, the men would leave, not as prisoners, but would simply board a ship and go to the North. They were the most lenient terms anybody received during the war.•

°On April 14, the day that Anderson was planning to leave Fort Sumter, his men prepared to fire the one-hundred-gun salute. After the twenty-seventh round, one of the guns prematurely exploded, tearing off the arm of Pvt. Daniel Hough, an immigrant from Ireland. He was killed instantly, making him the first casualty of

Notable Southerners visited the fort after its surrender (left). The tall figure in the center of the crowd is believed to be Wade Hampton. Governor Pickens may also be within the group. The men stand near a Columbiad mounted as a mortar but not used during the action. This Columbiad is either an 8- or 10-inch Model 1844. These huge guns weighed between 15,000 and 22,000 pounds and fired 65- or 100-pound solid shot. They were deployed primarily as seacoast artillery pieces. Most of Sumter's Columbiads had been placed at the upper level.

The workmen brought to Sumter after the fort's surrender have completed the enclosing of the second tier (right), which was probably the occasion for taking this group picture. The loss of the barracks to fire during the bombardment led to a need for supplemental housing for troops stationed at the fort.

the war. Another man standing next to Hough was mortally wounded, so the "bloodless" battle was ultimately not bloodless at all.•

Anderson, shaken by the death, reduced the ceremony to a fifty-gun salute. The following morning he and his men whistled "Yankee Doodle" as they boarded a ship for New York, where they received a hero's welcome. °No one in the North did not know Robert Anderson's name.•

Instant fame, however, bothered Anderson. °His experience at Fort Sumter essentially broke his heart. He was made a brigadier general immediately and called a hero in the North, but he became an ill man almost overnight. Emotionally and mentally, the battle pushed him to a point from which he could not recover.•

°After the surrender of Fort Sumter, because he was a Kentuckian, Anderson was sent to the Bluegrass State to do what he could to keep that state in the Union, and he succeeded. Midway through the war, however, his health failed, and he was retired from the service. He went to New York City, where he retained possession of the Fort Sumter flags.•

While Anderson himself was forced to withdraw from the war after his experience at Fort Sumter, his staff parlayed their experience into larger military

On April 15 President Lincoln called for seventy-five thousand volunteers to put down the southern rebellion. In short order the Northern states responded with overwhelming support for the government. On April 19 (above left) the Seventh Regiment of the New York National Guard paraded through the streets of Manhattan, down Broadway to the docks, and were cheered along the route by thousands of flag-waving New Yorkers.

In Michigan (above right), Detroit civic leaders held a rally in Campus Martius to recruit volunteers. Some in the crowd mistook the call for the imposition of a draft and began to protest, turning the rally into a riot. The riot was seen as a black mark upon the patriotism of Detroit, Wayne County, and Michigan. To remedy this, the governor called for a special regiment of volunteers in addition to the six requested by Lincoln to "rescue the honor of Detroit."

Anderson and his men were hailed as the "heroes of Fort Sumter." A commemorative medal was struck with the Major's likeness on one side (below) and Liberty heroically supporting the banner of the Union on the other (above). It was awarded to all the men of the Sumter garrison. The episode, however, had disheartened Anderson, and he became ill, feeling partially responsible for the war.

careers. Many of them went on to become Union generals, although one lieutenant resigned and joined the Confederate army. °Most of Anderson's troops, certainly most of his officers, stood by him in this crisis and admired him.•

Fort Sumter itself became a rallying cry for the North. Lincoln immediately called for seventy-five thousand volunteers to join the Union cause, but that call drove four more southern states out of the Union. Arkansas, North Carolina, Tennessee, and Virginia aligned with the other seven, bringing the Confederacy to a total of eleven states.

As the war raged on for four bloody years, Fort Sumter never left the spotlight. °Precisely because it was a symbol of Confederate victory, the North wanted it back. Nevertheless, Federal forces would spend a great deal of effort and suffer a great many casualties before Sumter was back in Union hands.•

Between 1863 and 1865, the Union navy bombarded Fort Sumter eleven times, including an all-out attack by ironclads that resulted in an embarrassing Northern defeat. A Union landing party that tried to sneak ashore was repulsed with heavy losses. Fired upon from Union-held Morris Island just three-quarters of a mile away by °some of the heaviest artillery then known, Fort Sumter was turned into a pile of rubble.• Over the course of the war, its three walls were reduced to one wall by the shelling.

Yet the rubble that was left of Fort Sumter was still defensible rubble. In fact, the broken bricks from Union shell fire were just pushed in front of sand walls to make the fort even stronger. In the end, Confederate Fort Sumter was never taken by Union gunfire.

On February 18, 1865, Federal soldiers stationed at Morris Island were puzzled to see no banner displayed above Fort Sumter. The morning before a brand-new Confederate flag had flown from the flagpole. Some men rowed over to investigate and discovered that the Confederate garrison had abandoned the fort in the middle of the night. They then rowed into Charleston, discovered it was no longer defended, and captured the city. Their first task was to extinguish the raging fires that threatened to consume the houses and buildings that had not already been destroyed by four years of war and two years of constant bombardment.

The city was fortunate to surrender to whom it did. Union Gen. William T. Sherman, whose army had bypassed Charleston in favor of marching on Columbia, wrote: "In our march through South Carolina, every man seemed to burn any kind of property he could put the torch to. South Carolina paid the dearest penalty of any state in the Confederacy, for if South Carolina had not been so persistent in going to war, there would have been no war for years to come."

Robert E. Lee's surrender at Appomattox on April 9, 1865, precipitated a victory celebration at Fort Sumter on April 14. Four years to the day of his surrender, Gen. Robert Anderson was invited to raise the U.S. flag over the fort. It was a moving moment for the old soldier who said: "I thank God that I have lived to see this day

In the euphoria of victory and with a sense of urgency to follow up the capture of Fort Sumter, South Carolina Governor Pickens wrote General Beauregard urging him to attack Washington while the Federal government was in chaos. His handwriting betrays his anxiousness to solidify the second American revolution with a quick strike against the government before the North could assemble an army and invade the South.

After the surrender of Sumter, Robert Anderson was promoted to brigadier general (left) and given charge of the Department of Kentucky, where his primary task was to prevent that state's seceding and joining the Confederacy. With him in that capacity was William T. Sherman, who had served previously with Anderson from 1842 to 1846 in Charleston. Both Lieutenant Sherman and Captain Anderson had occasionally viewed the ships dumping their loads of ore to create the pile upon which Fort Sumter would be built later. Ill health led Anderson to retire from the military in 1863. He returned to Sumter as a brevet major general (right) in 1865.

. . . to perform, perhaps, the last act of my life, of duty to my country."

°That night in the Charleston Hotel, Anderson raised a glass to toast the health of President Lincoln, who had been invited to the ceremonies but had chosen not to attend. Instead, that night the president attended a play in Washington, D.C., where one of the final shots of the Civil War rang out.•

Lincoln was assassinated on April 14 by John Wilkes Booth, an actor and Confederate sympathizer. The Union victory the president so desperately wanted had cost him his life. Yet his was not the last death.

The war that started at Charleston claimed one of its last victims on June 17, 1865, when Edmund Ruffin, the old fire-eater who had loosed one of the first shots on Fort Sumter and who vowed never to live under Yankee rule, committed suicide. Before he died, he had a few last words for the people he had fired upon on April 12, 1861: "In my latest writing and utterance, I here repeat my unmitigated hatred to . . . the vile Yankee race."

Although a bloodless battle, Fort Sumter will forever symbolize the opening drama to a war where freedom was won and more than 620,000 lives were lost. Union Maj. Robert Anderson ultimately became a casualty of Fort Sumter, for he carried the burden of the battle to his grave. In 1871, at age sixty-five, he died in Nice, France.

Four years to the day of the surrender, Maj. Gen. Robert Anderson returned to the rubble that remained of the fort. In ceremonies that day he raised the same flag that had flown over the garrison in 1861. Addressing the crowd and dignitaries, he said, "I restore to its proper place this flag which floated here during peace, before the first act of this cruel Rebellion. I thank God that I have lived to see this day, and to be here to perform this, perhaps the last act of my life, of duty to my country." The guests included Harriet Beecher Stowe, whose father delivered the keynote speech. Most of the dignitaries in attendance that day were leading abolitionists, and the crowd included three thousand recently emancipated African Americans. Most of the townspeople, however, stayed away. President Lincoln had been invited, but he had declined in favor of attending a play. The next day the Sumter flag was lowered to half-mast, following news of the president's assassination.

His body was returned to the United States and buried at West Point, his coffin covered by the flag of the country he had so honorably served.

THE FOOT SOLDIER'S LIFE

At THE START OF THE CIVIL WAR, hundreds of thousands of men—and the occasional woman who hid her sex—left their cities, fishing villages, farms, and factories to fight for the future of America. These foot soldiers wore their nicknames proudly. Johnny Reb saw himself as fighting the second American Revolution, finishing the noble work of the Founding Fathers. Billy Yank battled in defense of the new and precious form of government called democracy. Most Americans, both Northerners and Southerners, were idealists ready to fight and die to preserve their vision of freedom. The country was caught up in the heroic image of glorious battles fought by brave men. It seemed that everyone wanted to be a soldier.

CN °They signed up because their brothers and their best friends were signing up, and they would be thought a coward if they did not follow one another. They signed up because the uniforms were heroic-looking and girls liked boys in uniforms. They signed up because brass bands came into town and played patriotic songs. It sounded like a lot of fun, and they did not want to be left behind. They signed up because the war was going to be a great adventure.°

Thomas O'Pierce, who would one day be a Union sergeant, described his experience: "It was a fine sight to see them in bright arms and polished accoutrements, marching to the music of four splendid brass bands. Oh, who would not be a soldier?"

Both North and South were gripped by a euphoria that was not dampened by the reality of war because few

WCD	William C. Davis
BH	Bobby Horton
TL	Thomas Lowry
CN	Chris Nelson
BP	Brian Pohanka
JIR	James I. Robertson Jr.
DT	Don Troiani

35

Crowds of civilians (above left) watch the Seventy-third Ohio Infantry as the regiment stands rigidly for a photographer in the streets of Chillicothe. Leading the column is the regimental band, while behind the musicians can be seen a detachment of spade- and ax-wielding "pioneers," specialized soldiers who cleared the regiment's route of march through heavily timbered country. The unit's nine companies, one short of the customary ten, follow in succession, each headed by its company officer.

An American flag (above right) snaps crisply in the wind as men of the First Connecticut Heavy Artillery march smartly past orderly rows of tents pitched on the grounds of Fort Richardson, Virginia, one of the many bastions that ringed Washington, D.C. Although outfitted and trained as infantry and artillerists, heavy artillerymen primarily functioned as garrison troops until 1864, when Lt. Gen. Ulysses S. Grant began using them as foot soldiers during his overland campaign. The "heavies" were derided as "paper collar soldiers" by the Army of the Potomac's hard-bitten veterans until they proved their courage in numerous battles.

citizens had ever seen combat firsthand. The veterans of the American Revolution, more than eighty years earlier, were nearly all dead. There were a few generals around from the War of 1812, but they were old and their warnings about the gore of fighting fell on deaf ears. The most recent armed conflict, the war with Mexico in 1846, had been conducted so far away that most people knew of it only from books and newspaper articles. Few people were acquainted with the armless or legless Mexican War veterans to ask what combat had been like.

°Most of the young men enlisting in 1861 went to war with great enthusiasm. They believed war was going to be grand and painless, wonderful and clean. They believed that if death came, it would surely come to someone else.•

The politicians on both sides did little to warn the citizens of war's horrors. Before any battles were fought, one congressman in a speech offered to mop up all the blood that would be shed in the coming war with his handkerchief.

°Each saw the other side as cowardly, undedicated, and unmotivated. Each had the notion that his side, with God behind it, had a monopoly on courage. As a result, the soldiers on both sides thought that there would be little danger in this war. They believed it was a matter of standing up, showing the flag, giving a rousing shout for home and glory, making one great charge, and putting

the enemy to flight.• In fact, some worried that there would not be enough war to go around. James Cooper, a soldier from Tennessee, wrote, "I was tormented by feverish anxiety before I joined my regiment, for fear the fighting would be over before I got a chance to get into it." Cooper need not have worried. There would be thousands of battles and hundreds of thousands of deaths over four years.

The soldiers on both sides who joined up did so with their friends. Fathers and sons and brothers enlisted in the same companies. Whole classes of college students served in the same regiment. Some regiments had reputations before they even put on a
JIR uniform. °The Sixth New York Infantry came from the

Soldiers had a daily routine of assigned chores, which included preparing their own meals (above right). Despite such activities, the men inevitably had time on their hands (above left), and the use and abuse of liquor was prevalent throughout the ranks (below left), from the highest general to the lowliest private. A group of enlisted men (below right), many with their sleeves rolled up for the tasks at hand, illustrates some of the work they performed daily: chopping firewood, hauling water for cooking and cleaning, and food preparation. The rest just sit and wait. Such moments could be filled with idle talk, card playing, smoking, drinking, singing, or wondering what the army would do next.

Army life allowed many soldiers to take to gambling (above left) as a way of passing time and flaunting the rigid confines of Victorian civilian society. In addition to cards, other games of chance appeared at camp as well. These included boxing matches (above right), baseball games (below left), and cockfights (below right). Boxing champions were the pride of their regiments and were granted special privileges—until they lost. Baseball was played roughly, allowing a man to be thrown out if he were struck by the ball. Defeated roosters, regardless of how many victories they had beneath their belt, were eaten.

tough Lower East Side of Manhattan. The rumor was it took a jail record to enlist. On the other hand, the Thirty-third Illinois Infantry was called the Teachers Regiment because most of its officers had been college professors prior to the Civil War. It was alleged they would not obey an order unless the syntax and the grammar were correct.•

Physically, the soldiers looked much alike at the start of the war. They were young, most between eighteen and thirty years old. They were only of medium height, averaging five feet six inches to five feet eight inches. Anyone taller than six feet was looked on as unusual. Thin by today's standards, they weighed an average of 140 pounds. Farming was the most common occupation on both sides.

Only their ethnic origins set the two sides broadly apart. The Southerners came from Scottish, Irish, Welsh, English, and some French stock, with their roots in America going back one hundred years to colonial times. The Union army may have been all "Yankees" to the average Southerner, but tens of thousands were literally right off the boat, immigrants from Ireland and the German states, who were sometimes coerced to sign enlistment papers with the lure of future citizenship and quick bounty money.

Walt Whitman, a struggling poet before the war and a nurse during it, described the fighting men: "The actual soldier, North and South, with all his ways, his incredible dauntlessness, habits, practices, tastes, language, his fierce friendship, his appetite, rankness, his superb strength and animality, lawless gait, and a hundred unnamed lights and shades of the same, will never be written."

To the younger recruits, going to war coincided with their physical maturation as adults. °For the first time they were away from the control of mother and small-town politicians and church authorities, all of the controlling influences they had ever known. When they came to a big city and encountered "sophisticated" women with somewhat different moral backgrounds, they became drunk and disorderly. They cut all restraint loose since they were a long way from home.•

For many Federal soldiers their first experience with life in the big city came in the camps around the nation's

"Tilly," Pvt. C. D. Sides of the Fifth North Carolina Infantry wrote his wife in February 1863, "I must go on Drill right now. I will finish as soon as I come in." He later returned and picked up his pen. "It is Just Drill Drill . . . This embraces the whol[e] day." Sides's annoyance stands as a universal statement for the thousands of Northern and Southern troops irritated and exasperated by the countless sun-baked, snow-swept, or rain-soaked hours they spent on drill fields throughout the four years of the conflict. Drill, though, was a necessary evil in turning clumsy green troops into tough veterans capable of maneuvering on a chaotic battlefield. Above, the Twenty-second New York State Militia goes through its paces at Harpers Ferry.

capital, Washington City—and the nation's capital was ready to receive them. Downtown Washington was one huge red-light district with hundreds of bordellos and thousands of women ready to make the acquaintance of the young soldiers. °The provost marshal, the equivalent of the military police today, compiled a consumers guide to the whorehouses in Washington. Eighty-seven bordellos were listed and ranked on a scale of one to four. The list included the bordellos' addresses, the madams' names, and the number of women working there.• The list, however, was no guarantee of safety. °The lower down on the social scale of whoredom that a soldier went, the greater his chance of contracting venereal diseases for which there were no cures. Soldiers who were infected with gonorrhea—what they called "the clap" or "the pox"—had it for life.• By war's end, one quarter of the Union army was infected with venereal disease, but the average soldier seemed not to care. Massachusetts Pvt. Eli Veezy boasted: "I had a gay old time, I'll tell you. Lager beer, and in the evening, horizontal refreshments, or in plainer words, riding a Dutch gal."

Giving in to weaknesses of the flesh was not purely a Union foible. °Richmond, Atlanta, and Charleston all had problems with prostitutes,• but it would take an exasperated Federal general in Union-occupied Nashville,

WCD Tennessee, to come up with a truly creative solution. °He ordered all the prostitutes in the city rounded up, put on a steamboat, and sent down the Cumberland River in 1863. He did not care where they went, as long as they were out of Nashville.•

The steamboat carrying the prostitutes tried to put into port several times, but it was refused at every stop. The ship of whores made it all the way to Cincinnati before the Union secretary of war ordered the vessel

TL back to Nashville. When the ladies returned, °the army instituted the first program of legalized prostitution and issued licenses to the prostitutes. To maintain the license, a woman had to get a certificate of health every seven days. With this sort of control, there was a great decrease in venereal disease and an increase in the soldiers' health.•

Soon the training near the big cities was over, and the armies moved into the field, drawing nearer to an inevitable clash. As they got closer to the reality that someone on the other side would soon be shooting at them, the men contemplated how they would react.

JIR Many struggled with the demon of fear. °While they feared death, what they feared even more was "to show the white feather," to display cowardice in battle. This was the one unpardonable sin a soldier could commit. If he ran, he was never again accepted by his messmates.•

Arrayed here are the typical contents of a volunteer's knapsack. Clockwise from the top are wool mittens and a rubberized rain hat cover, most likely sent from home; issue shoes or "brogans"; cotton socks purchased by the soldier to replace the wool ones issued by the government; gaiters, universally despised by the troops and soon discarded; a shelter half; comb, shaving mirror; razor; candle holder; pocket diary; a treasured photo; writing kit and materials; and a colorful neckerchief. In the center, a U.S. Army issue blanket lies topped by a comfortable cotton shirt, also probably sent to the soldier by a caring relative.

Despite the presence of weaponry, this 1862 camp of the Third Kentucky Confederate Infantry near Corinth, Mississippi, comfortably situated beneath moss-laden shade trees, has a tranquil, languid air about it. One can almost smell the tangy wood smoke and hear the pleasant cacophony of clucking chickens, hissing cook pots, the murmur and laughter of men playing cards, conversations under tents and leafy arbors, or the preparation of the evening meal. This scene was preserved by Conrad Wise Chapman, an artist who served in the Third and later in the Forty-sixth Virginia Infantry.

No systematic training existed during the Civil War that would acclimate a volunteer soldier to the shock and gore of battle. While hours of drill could make a soldier adept at handling his weapon and marching in a straight line, nothing prepared him for the moment when the bullets began to fly and his comrade collapsed in a bloody heap; when he could not hear the screamed commands of his officers over what an Indiana infantryman called the "rush and roar of battle," although they stood but a few feet away. Little wonder that the survivors of such carnage considered themselves lucky members of a special brotherhood born out of blood.

Combat also caused many men to flee from the army. Below, two ragged and forlorn Confederate deserters pose for a Northern photographer. In a sense they were lucky. If they had been caught by their own troops, they might have been hanged or shot—common punishments for this serious offense. Although desertion was a common problem on both sides, the Confederacy was particularly plagued by the problem during the last year of the war. Many Southerners slipped away at the behest of their wives to return to their struggling households.

It did not take long for romantic visions of glory to vanish in the savage chaos of actual battle. It would take only one skirmish for a soldier to realize that real war meant real horror. °Seeing friends with legs blown off, a neighbor disemboweled, or a regiment cut to pieces impressed these citizen soldiers with the reality that war was deadly serious. Many untested soldiers fled and felt ashamed for running.•

"I have heard and seen pictures of battles. They would all be in a line, all standing in a nice level field fighting, a number of ladies taking care of the wounded. But it isn't so," wrote Pvt. William Grarely.

°Some men were able to cope with the excitement and exhilaration of battle. They found that after the first few minutes of combat, they lost their fear and were caught up in the fight. The thrill made them feel almost oblivious to enemy bullets—until one finally struck them.•

Others recognized the absurdity of standing in a line shooting at other men standing in another line just a few hundred yards away. Daniel Ashby of the Eighth Georgia Regiment wrote: "My first thought was, 'This is unfair. Somebody's to blame for getting us all killed.' I didn't come out here to fight this way. I wish the earth would crack open and let me drop in."

Attended by female nurses and hospital stewards, wounded bluecoats, many cradling the bandaged stumps of their amputated limbs, sit before the camera's lens in Washington's Carver Hospital. Before the Civil War, it was unthinkable for a lady to work in such an ungenteel, dirty place as a hospital. The strains of war, however, broke down this societal restriction, and Northern and Southern women rushed to the aid of the wounded. Their attentiveness helped save countless injured soldiers, and the improved conditions of hospitals late in the war are generally attributed to the reforms women inspired concerning cleanliness and hygiene.

Below, a yard near Savage's Station, Virginia, seethes with the Federal human wreckage of the battle of Gaines's Mill, one of the engagements that comprised the Seven Days' battles of 1862. Compounding the troubles of these men, the Union army retreated from this area, leaving them to become prisoners. In the foreground an overworked doctor tries to treat a soldier's mauled leg. The troops wearing the straw hats are from the Sixteenth New York Infantry, known to have worn the distinctive headgear during this campaign.

FOR MOST MEN, combat would be the defining moment of their lives, and the experience of battle changed them forever. Awakened as if from a dream, they began the transformation from citizens into warriors. Oliver Wendell Holmes Jr., a Harvard student turned Federal officer who would survive the war to become a justice of the U.S. Supreme Court, wrote: "We have shared the incommunicable experience of war. We have felt, we still feel, the passion of life to its top. In our youths, our hearts were touched with fire."

Although war changed men's thoughts of life and death, it did not necessarily WCD make them obedient soldiers. °Discipline was something foreign to their nature. They were volunteers. They had not made—and did not intend to make—a career of the military. Because of this, some have said that the troops of the Civil War were the best fighters and the BP worst soldiers in American history.• °The New York Fire Zouaves, for instance, were brawny athletic firemen who failed as a regiment because they would not obey their officers. The firemen expected war to be fought in the same way in

Soldiers endeavored to make their huts as homey as possible, building fireplaces and using scrap lumber to construct bunk beds and shelves to hold treasured photographs of loved ones. Pegs would be placed in the walls to hold clothing, muskets, and equipment, while one corner could be reserved for a roughly fashioned table and chairs. The men would share the duties and chores of cooking and cleaning, and many long-lasting friendships were forged in such rustic domiciles. One bluecoated veteran's memories of camp life prompted him to construct this model of the hut he shared with his mates on Folly Island, South Carolina.

which they had operated the engine house. There they fought with other fire companies for the privilege of putting out a fire. The New York firemen thought that all war took was brawn and a sense of adventure. They failed to realize it also required discipline.•

The best volunteers knew that discipline was instilled through the mind–numbing repetition of drill maneuvers and learning to march, to quickly form a line of battle, to deploy in a skirmish line, BP and to do battle with bayonets. °They would groan at the command "Fall in for company drill," because it was sheer exertion for hours on end. They could perform these maneuvers backward and in their sleep, but still they drilled. That was the point of drilling, however. Drilling kept the soldiers busy and occupied their time. Officers could not afford to give the men time to brood, to get melancholy, or to think too hard.• If the men were busy, they were becoming better soldiers.

Much of the time was spent on the march. For men ignorant of their commanders' plans, the seemingly endless marching was almost unbearable. "Here we are marching from one end of Virginia to the other, wearing ourselves out, and yet nothing is accomplished by it. My God, hasten the end of this accursed war, then we can once more enjoy the comforts of home and never, never march again," wrote one member of the Nineteenth Massachusetts.

While Federal soldiers complained of marching, JIR Southerners complained of chronic shortages. °At any given time, one-third of any Confederate army would be barefoot. The men would often be without blankets or changes of clothes. They simply wore what they had until the clothing deteriorated and literally rotted off.•

The Southerners had to make do with what was available, and that frequently forced them to do things that would normally be distasteful. °When the Confederates were on a battlefield, one of the first things they did was to remove the shoes of the Union dead and sometimes

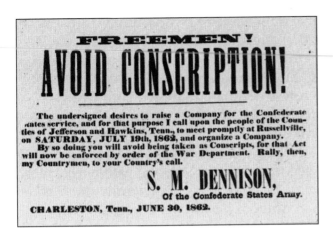

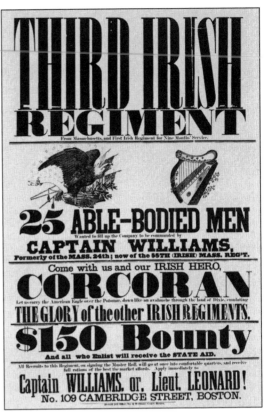

the wounded. On occasion, Rebel soldiers, still in the act of a charge or an advance, would stop to find shoes.•

Soldiers on both sides could be hot, cold, poorly equipped, lonely, and frightened, but perhaps no hardship elicited more complaints than the quantity and quality of their food. Neither side mastered the almost impossible task of feeding its huge army in a time before refrigeration and any preservatives other than salt and vinegar. Delivery of fresh vegetables and fruit to the front was impossible as that sort of food would rot long before reaching the men. The process of canning food had been refined, but the quantities necessary to feed hundreds of thousands overwhelmed the factories. Herds of live cattle were sometimes driven to the armies, which resulted in the occasional rustling raid by both sides. More often, both sides ate—or tried to eat—beef or pork that had been so heavily salted at the processing plant it was almost unpalatable, even to those who were starving.

°Human stomachs were subjected to some of the vilest concoctions ever devised by man and labeled as food. Federal troops were issued a three-inch-square cracker made of flour and water, known as hardtack, that was normally shipped south in wooden crates marked on the sides with the large letters "B.C.," signifying that the hardtack was consigned to the brigade commissary. The soldiers, however, said that the letters really meant

JIR

The casualties incurred by the Confederacy in the first year of the war prompted Richmond to pass America's first draft law on April 16, 1862. This law stated that all men between the ages of eighteen and thirty-five could be required to serve in the military for up to three years. Although extremely unpopular with the Southern people, the draft did increase the number of men in the Rebel army. Many men, in fact, volunteered rather than risk the stigma of being drafted, a fact reinforced by the Tennessee recruiting poster above (left).

Many Northern recruiting posters often played on ethnic pride. The juxtaposition of the Irish Harp with the American Eagle on the broadside above (right) hints at another reason many immigrants joined the ranks. By serving in the army or navy they hoped to gain acceptance in American society and enhance their families' chances for financial success in the New World.

Walt Whitman, best known to Americans for his powerful, cadenced poetry and writing, did not fight in the Civil War, but he witnessed its horrors while working as a volunteer aide in hospitals in Washington, D.C. The teeming masses of the sick and mangled victims of war had a profound effect on him. In February 1863, he described for readers of the New York Times *the conditions he witnessed: "every form of wound, . . . every kind of malady, . . . are here in steady motion. The soldier's hospital! How many sleepless nights, how many woman's tears, how many long and aching hours and days of suspense, from every one of the Middle, Eastern and Western States, have concentrated here!"*

WCD the stuff had been made before Christ and was just now getting to the battlefield.• °Hardtack was always stale by the time it got to the soldiers, leading to nicknames like "tooth collars" or "sheet iron crackers." If the hardtack was not stale, it was frequently infested with weevils. That led to the unappetizing but perhaps descriptive name of "worm castles" because of the vermin infestations. The soldiers ate the crackers anyway.•

The Confederates would capture and eat the Federal hardtack when they could get it. Even wormy crackers were better than nothing. As the war dragged on, the Southern armies faced the constant threat of starvation. At times Confederate soldiers were forced to steal cracked corn from the rations given to their horses and mules.

The officers of both armies, sharing the same fate as their men, knew that the key to a successful fighting force was through its stomach. "Despondency, like a black and poisonous mist, began to invade hearts before so tough and buoyant. Feed a soldier well and he will fight gaily. Starve him, and break him down with fatigue, and he will despond," wrote Confederate Capt. John Esten Cooke.

TL Sometimes the outcome of battles turned on the soldiers' hunger. °At the battle of Shiloh, Tennessee, in April 1862, the Confederates made a surprise attack on the Yankee camp early in the morning. The Yankees fell back,

Confederate cavalrymen of Jeb Stuart's famous command gather around a blazing fire to ward of the chill air of a fall evening and to watch a camp servant dancing to the banjo playing of "Sweeny," a favorite musician of Stuart's troopers. William Blackford, one of Stuart's officers, found that the "tinkle" of Sweeny's instrument often rejuvenated the horse soldiers after long marches. Indeed, the relaxing plucking of a banjo was a welcome sound in the bivouacs of the tired, war weary, and homesick combatants of both sides.

leaving their just-cooked breakfast behind, and the Confederates stopped their successful charge to eat the abandoned steaming meals. Although their officers yelled to continue the attack, the Southerners ignored them. They were hungry, and they relinquished a great advantage and lost valuable minutes, which the Federals used to mount a defense from which they would come back the next day to defeat the Confederates.•

Because neither army could regularly supply its men with adequate food, both °armies became like a plague of locusts. They would descend on the population, and every pig, chicken, sheep, and sweet potato would be taken and eaten.• Farmers, or more often the farmers' wives left behind while the men were off fighting, resorted to hiding provisions.

While starvation demoralized the armies, disease was the deadliest enemy of all soldiers. Before the war, many of these men were accustomed to living in wide-open spaces with few neighbors in sight. They drank fresh water from wells. They placed their outhouses well away from their water supply. When it was hot, they rested in the shade. When it was cold or rainy, they stayed inside by the fire. When they were sick, they sent for a doctor.

That civilized lifestyle went by the wayside during the war. Thousands of men were thrown together in tent cities. Water drawn from streams or lakes was often contaminated by human and animal waste. Food, spoiled or not, was eaten because there was nothing else to eat. Standards for digging latrines were often ignored, as doctors had little understanding of the concepts connecting germs and viruses with human health. °Many Civil War recruits had no resistance to many diseases because they came from isolated rural areas where they had not been exposed to childhood diseases that helped to build up resistance to infection. When measles or smallpox cropped up in camp, it quickly spread and became an epidemic.•

The battlefield toll was nothing compared to what could happen to the men in camp. °Two men died in camp for every man who was killed on the battlefield. Sickness wiped out these men by the tens of thousands.•

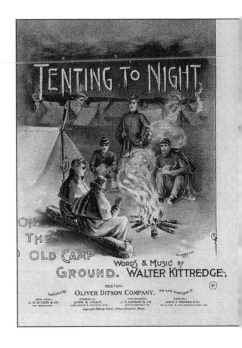

A surge in the production of sheet music occurred in the early 1860s, driven by the thirst of soldiers and civilians for songs related to the military experience. This cover advertises the piece "Tenting Tonight on the Old Camp Ground," a song with sentimental verses that touched the heartstrings of Northerners and Southerners alike: "We are tired of war on the old camp ground, many are the dead and gone, of the brave and true who left their homes, others have been wounded long. Many are the hearts that are weary tonight, wishing for the war to cease."

The static nature of the war's winter months, when armies settled into large, city-sized camps, allowed mothers, sisters, and wives to visit their respective male companions (above left). Officers' wives could even stay with their husbands if they wished, as those of rank were entitled to larger and more private quarters. Sometimes, spouses of enlisted men would stay in nearby hotels if they were available. The presence of a pretty, fashionably dressed woman in camp would inspire gawks and stares from warriors starved for the sight and company of the "fairer sex."

For those not fortunate enough to have a female friend in camp—there was always the camaraderie of the mess table. In this photograph (above right), men of the Third New Hampshire Infantry settle down to dinner outside of their tents on Hilton Head, South Carolina, in 1862. The drummer sitting on his instrument, although he most likely played the mess call that alerted the men that the food was ready, apparently had to wait his turn for a seat at the table.

Hospitalization was no solution. In fact, it could result in a quicker death. °Men with relatively slight wounds would write joyful letters from the hospital saying that they would soon be on their way home. Often the next letter the family would receive would be from a hospital nurse saying that the soldier had died. Sepsis or gangrene had set in, and the spreading bacteria had killed him, not his minor wound.•

John William DeForest described a hospital near his camp: "Two–thirds of the regiment are buried or in hospital. We can distinctly hear the screams and the howls of the patients in their crazy fits. They cannot be kept in their wretched beds, but stagger about, jabbering and muttering insanities until they lie down and die in their ragged, dirty uniforms."

Field hospitals, set up on the battlefield after the fighting was over, were horrific, both medically and psychologically. °One aspect that made it so nauseating was the widespread practice of taking hundreds of wounded men to a barnyard or an open field and simply laying them on the ground around the operating table. While they waited their turn, these men had to listen to the screams and yells of the patients being operated on by a doctor. They lay there watching the growing mound of amputated arms and legs pile up. These waiting men knew that at some point they would be placed on the table and undergo the same kind of operation.•

Walt Whitman, the poet who learned about hospitals while nursing his wounded brother following the battle of Fredericksburg, wrote: "Future years will never know

48

Northern troops, tanned faces contrasting with their white bodies, take a refreshing swim in Virginia's North Anna River during Grant's overland campaign in May 1864. In the background, the fire-scorched remains of a ruined bridge bear testament to the destructive nature of war.

the seething hell and infernal background of this war. Oh, the sad scenes I witness, scenes of death, anguish, amputations, friendlessness, hungering, and thirsting young hearts."

Horrible as it was, the battlefield experience actually brought soldiers closer. The shared suffering bound soldiers together as nothing else could. It made their comrades dearer than brothers. It molded them into an army.

"The strongest ties between human beings are not cemented in safety, luxury, and comfort. It is the dividing by a hungry soldier, with a hungrier comrade, the last morsel of meat, the binding up of each others' wounds, the lending of courage from one heart to another. These are what create the strongest bonds between human beings," wrote Capt. Horace H. Shaw of the First Maine Infantry Regiment.

Although the majority of those who fought in the war ranged in age from eighteen to thirty, some men were in their fourth—with a rare few in their fifth—decade of life. Gustave A. Schurman, pictured below, represents younger warriors who had yet to see their eighteenth birthday, those between twelve and seventeen years of age. Schurman served as a bugler on Union Gen. Philip Kearny's staff until Kearny was killed by Rebel fire at the battle of Chantilly, Virginia, in September 1862.

SURVIVING BULLETS, CANNON fire, starvation, and camp diseases were only part of being a soldier. For the men who survived the ravages of army life, the war became the ultimate test of willpower. The soldiers had to learn to

JIR summon the inner strength to continue. °Maintaining morale as the war went along was an overpowering issue. The casualties piled up far beyond anyone's expectations. As the suffering increased, maintaining high spirits was difficult for Johnny Rebs and Billy Yanks alike.

The loneliness of being away from home became over-

WCD powering.• °Homesickness actually killed some men. They simply gave up, losing all spirit. They became

The music of military bands like the one above (left) could inspire troops during combat and even affect the outcome of a fight. At the 1862 engagement of Williamsburg, Virginia, Yankee Brig. Gen. Samuel Heintzelman, in an effort to stabilize a hard-pressed battle line, exhorted an idle band to "Play! Play! It's all you're good for. Play, damn it! Play some marching tune! Play 'Yankee Doodle,' or any doodle you can think of!" The chastised musicians summarily struck up a tune, the Northerners' resolve stiffened, and the retreat was ended. Bandsmen also served the armies as stretcher bearers, clearing the field of dead and wounded men after the conclusion of a battle.

The tensions of the battlefield were sometimes relieved by combative sports. Above (right) Rebel soldiers engage in a vigorous "snow-balling" match, a common wintertime activity in camps on both sides of the Mason-Dixon Line. One of the more noteworthy snowball fights took place during the Southern Army of Tennessee's 1864 winter bivouac near Dalton, Georgia. This "engagement" pitted Georgia troops against those from Tennessee, and one Volunteer State colonel reported that the "heavens" rang with the yells of "thousands" of combatants and the "air was striped with tracks of flying snow-balls" for "two hours or longer." After a momentary lull in the action, the Tennesseans mounted a final massed charge that gained victory and possession of the contested field.

lethargic, sitting around, not eating, not taking care of themselves. They waited to die.• "Oh, would that I was at home! I have often dreamt that I was at home and how nice it was. But lo and behold, when I wake up, I am in this blame old tent," wrote Illinois Pvt. Alfred C. Huff.

For many, the quickest way to boost morale was from a bottle. °Nineteenth-century American soldiers were hard drinkers. If they found a supply of liquor in a farmhouse they would often drink themselves into a stupor until the liquor was gone.• °As soon as they were liquored up, they would start fighting. The records contain accounts of murders, stabbings, and all kinds of accidents with muskets that can be tied to drunkenness.•

The generals, who were not above taking a bottle themselves, recognized the problem but could do little about it other than complain. Union Maj. Gen. George B. McClellan wrote: "No one evil so much obstructed an army as the degrading vice of drunkenness. Total abstinence from intoxicating liquor would be worth 50,000 men to the Armies of the United States."

Drinking offered only a temporary sanctuary from army life, so other diversions were needed. °The soldiers found that camp life consisted of about 7 days of fighting a year and 358 days of boredom, sitting around trying to find something to do. Gambling was a natural diversion. Wherever two or more soldiers got together, a blanket went down on the ground, the cards and the dice came out, and money began to change hands.•

Although common, gambling was considered a sin by most men, who believed it posed a threat to their

The foot soldiers in the foreground (left) on the parade ground of Fort Pulaski, Georgia, surely must have envied their baseball-playing comrades cavorting behind them. This is perhaps the earliest photographic depiction of the national pastime in existence. If time and circumstances did not permit an organized game, well-worn baseballs were always pulled from knapsacks for a quick game of catch.

CN immortal souls. °When the armies would draw close to do battle, the path of the troops could be charted by the cards, dice, and liquor bottles scattered on the ground. The soldiers would throw away everything sinful before they would fight, not wanting to die with these "devices of the devil" on their bodies.• °Of course, at the end of the battle, most of these soldiers would go back looking for the cards and the dice that they had discarded, and the gambling would resume.•

There was more to camp-life amusements than getting drunk and playing card games, however. The soldiers loved their fun and excelled at creating amusements, including sports. °Many kinds of recreational sports were popular in the Civil War, including high jumps, long-distance running, wrestling matches, snowball fights, theatricals, and poetry readings. If it helped them to forget about the war for a few minutes, the soldiers did it.•

Sometimes the sports took on the same violence as the battlefield. °Football was well established, although it was more like rugby than today's game, particularly since some games had as many as a hundred men on each side. Everybody more or less piled up in a huge melee in the middle of the field.•

°One wintertime diversion was snowball fights, often spontaneous, unplanned events that involved dozens, hundreds, or even thousands of men, as brigades would challenge and fight other brigades. The fights would resemble real combat, with officers planning tactics such as diversions and flank attacks. Just as in real battles, the attacks would have dire consequences with serious

Shortly after the soldiers had set up camp, sutlers—civilians who peddled a variety of goods—would establish places of business, like the one pictured above (left). Although sutlers dealt in a variety of dry goods, their chief "stock of goods . . . answered the demands of the stomach," according to a Massachusetts artilleryman. Sutlers were notorious for inflated prices, causing one soldier from Illinois to grouse that a sutler would gladly "skin a louse for its hide and tallow." This frustration sometimes built among the men until a swarm of them would raid the offending peddler's tent and simply take what they wished.

Opposing teams composed of volunteers of the First Maryland Infantry (U.S.) enthusiastically swarm pell-mell toward an unfortunate ball carrier during a football game (above right). Far behind baseball in popularity during the Civil War, football remained close to its rugby origins and little resembled the game today. Occasionally, an overly aggressive player would take a swing at an opponent, and the game would break down into a wild melee of fisticuffs.

injuries, bloody noses, and broken bones. Occasionally an officer would try to intervene and stop the fight, which usually had bad consequences for him because everyone would turn on him. The men would pelt him with snowballs and drive him off the field.•

The most popular game was baseball, a sport that had been played for years, long before the modern-day myth alleged that Union Gen. Abner Doubleday had invented the game. °By the time the Civil War started in early 1861, baseball had already been called America's game by Walt Whitman, and the sportswriters in the New York papers were referring to it as the national pastime. Regimental commanders encouraged their men to play baseball because it was obviously good exercise, and if the men were playing baseball, they were not getting drunk or chasing women.•

°The rules of the game were different from the modern-day version. When the batter hit the ball and the fielder picked it up, the fielder then had to hit the batter with the ball to put the runner out. This sometimes caused some injuries and fistfights between teams.• It could get even more dangerous than that. °There was an incident where a Union regiment was playing ball, and somebody hit a long drive to center field. The center fielder went for it, got a little too close to the nearby Confederate lines, and was shot. What really angered his comrades, however, was that the Confederates captured the ball, the only baseball in Alexandria, Texas.•

Sports in camp were a healthy diversion, but that did not stop the men from thinking about sex. While the bordellos around the big cities were off-limits and women in the flesh were usually not available, pictures of and stories about women were easy to buy. Soldiers devoured reading material of all types, including packages that arrived discreetly in plain paper covers. °The soldiers received many catalogs through the mail from pornographers in New York City. Some of the merchandise depicted were pictures such as *The Temptation of Saint Anthony*, showing the naked charms of the evil ones. Other items included pornographic novels and various kinds of sexual devices and novelties, such as dildos, condoms, and pictures of people in various sexual poses, some so small they could be concealed in stick pins.•

Meanwhile, the vast majority of mail the soldiers received was personal. No letters were more treasured than those from loved ones back home. One soldier, Pvt. Robert Goodyear of the Twenty-seventh Connecticut, said it best when he wrote: "The soldier looks upon a letter from home as a perfect godsend, sent as it were by some kind ministering angel to cheer his dark and weary hours."

°Those soldiers who could write, wrote letters incessantly. Those who could not, dictated letters to their friends. Letters were their everyday link to parents, sweethearts, relatives, and friends back home. The important thing was not what they wrote, but the fact that they were maintaining contact with the people with whom they had grown up and the home to which they hoped to return after the war was over.•

Sometimes, sadly, the last time parents might hear from a soldier would be by his own writing. °In some instances a soldier would be mortally wounded but still have time to think of home. He would spend his last earthly efforts dictating a letter or passing word along to someone to convey the message to a loved one that he would not be coming back.• One North Carolina officer, mortally wounded at Gettysburg, had just enough energy

Head shorn and wearing a placard indicating his crime of theft, a doleful Yankee volunteer is drummed out of camp in disgrace. While this punishment was publicly degrading, and soldiers could add to the humiliation by showering the guilty party with insults and rotten food, it was not as physically brutal as some other forms of army discipline. Troops could be "bucked and gagged" or bound in an uncomfortable squatting position with their hands tied around their knees and held with a stick, keeping the arms in place by locking the elbows and knees together, and another stick tightly secured in their mouth. Those convicted of offenses in the artillery could find themselves tied to the spare wheel of a caisson and subjected to a painful pounding and jolting as the battery advanced over rock-strewn and uneven dirt roads.

53

The trappings of civility in this mess scene (above left)—glass condiment bottles, bone china, white tablecloth, and the table and chairs—would indicate the presence of officers even if their shoulder straps were not visible. The rank-and-file soldiers made do with much plainer dining accessories, frequently cooking their food on tin plates or ersatz frying pans made out of the unsoldered halves of discarded canteens. Many an enlisted man also affixed a wire bail to a tin can that had originally contained peaches, or some other foodstuff, to have a serviceable "boiler" for his coffee.

A crowd of infantrymen (above right), joined by a convalescing comrade, celebrate the end of drill by lustily singing at the top of their lungs. The singing of songs, both bawdy and sentimental, was a favorite pastime around the campfires and bivouacs of the blue and the gray. Rebels sang songs like "Stonewall Jackson's Way," Yanks crooned to the verses of "John Brown's Body," while songs like "Home, Sweet Home" brought tears to the eyes of the men of both armies. In many cases, soldiers sang whether they could carry a tune or not. One soldier compared another's voice to "a cross between the bray of a jackass and the note of a turkey buzzard."

left to scrawl a note to his father, "I died with my face toward the enemy," on a blood-stained piece of paper. The short note made it to North Carolina and became a treasured family heirloom.

John Mosely, another Southerner writing from Gettysburg, tried to break the news gently to his family: "Dear mother, I am here, a prisoner of war, and mortally wounded. I hope I may live long enough to hear the shouts of victory yet. But do not mourn my loss. I had hoped to have been spared, but a righteous God has ordered it otherwise. Farewell to you all. Your son, John." Mosely was buried on the Gettysburg battlefield. Fortunately his was one of the few Confederate graves marked by a headboard. The Mosely family from Alabama was able to come to the Pennsylvania town after the war and take him home.•

LETTERS TO AND from home helped the men connect with the families they left behind. Music filled the gap when those letters did not arrive. Oliver Wendell Holmes Jr., a prolific writer and observer of camp life, noted: "Every old infantryman will remember how the tears flowed down his tanned and roughened cheeks as the tender melody of 'Home, Sweet Home' floated through the evening air and came to him like a blessed benediction."

Throughout the Civil War, music was the glue that held armies together. For men in the ranks, music was the best means of expression and the greatest source of inspiration. °A recruiting officer would often take great pains to make his first recruit the local bandleader. Once the bandleader was signed up, the officer would then march the band into the town square where they would strike up "Yankee Doodle Dandy" or "Hail Columbia" or one of the patriotic tunes of the day. The boys would come flocking to the sound of the music, and the officer would be waiting with his enlistment papers. The brass band with the big bass drum was one of the principal inducements for men to sign up to go off to war.•

Music at the start of the war reflected the feelings of both sides: War was glorious and heroic. °Early war tunes were happy and upbeat, reflecting the ignorance of the population to the destructiveness of war. The songs reflected the joy, excitement, happiness, and bravado of the soldiers who believed they were going to thrash the other side quickly and return home safely.•

Once in the army, volunteers were quick to find fault with their new officers, but the only way they could do anything about that was to sing about it. °Throughout these tunes, even when they were complaining about something in a humorous way, both sides kept a sense of optimism, such as in the song "The Brass Mounted Army" that made fun of the officers.•

Soldiers who could play instruments were very popular. °Banjo players were in demand because the banjo was a new instrument. Fiddlers were important because the fiddle was the most popular dance instrument of the period. Nighttime would find everyone around the campfire learning a new tune. When everybody learned the songs, they would carry that same spirit into the drill and on the march.•

Music was important to the armies, not only to keep up the men's spirits in camp, but to help them keep time on long marches. Many regiments went to war with their

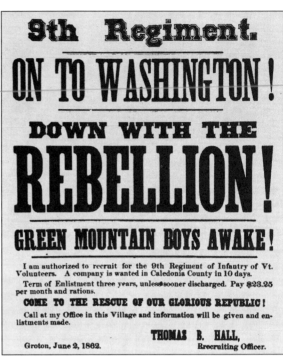

This enthusiastic and enticing poster offers, perhaps fraudulently, a much higher rate of pay than the thirteen dollars Federal privates usually made and was used to entice young men of the Green Mountain State to serve their country by joining the Ninth Vermont. The regiment was fully recruited and mustered into service by July 9, 1862, and then spent much of its service on less than glamorous guard and fatigue duties until the fall of 1864, when it was engaged in several battles near Richmond. By the end of the organization's three-year term of service in December 1865, 44 members of the Ninth had fallen in combat while 281 of its men died of various diseases. Losing more men to disease than bullets was common among many regiments.

A staged fracas imitates a real fight, a common enough occurrence among bored and weary troops. Although liquor was often the culprit behind such disputes, some tussles broke out over the most trivial of circumstances. New Yorker Charles Belknap got into a row when a camp mate tossed some "chewed . . . bits of apple" into his face. Belknap retaliated by throwing a "little piece of soap" at his assailant, and soon both men were thrashing about, trying to rub soap in each other's face. Through the "help . . . [of] God," Belknap regained his temper and calmed the situation. He admitted, though, that some of the onlookers, no doubt feeling cheated out of a good show, called him a coward for not continuing the scrape.

Although the armies did not issue such items, this wood-encased shaving mirror is an example of the type of dry goods troops could purchase from sutlers. Such extraneous items were often left behind or pitched from overloaded knapsacks when the volunteers went on the march; the majority of soldiers tried their best to stay as clean as possible when in the field.

town's brass band leading the way. The music on the march also °bound the men that much closer to each other. When they went into the ultimate test of battle, the men could depend more and more upon each other. Once the battle was underway, the musicians would usually trade their instruments for stretchers to carry the wounded from the battlefield to the field hospitals. Music contributed greatly to that sense of increased unity.•

The bands played °not only marching tunes and anthems but jaunty dance music, waltzes, and popular tunes that would be performed to bolster the troops' spirits as they deployed.• Sometimes this playing was not a good idea. On one of the nights at Gettysburg, the Union artillery used the playing of a Confederate brass band to aim their cannon. The band stopped once it realized it was a target.

Arthur Fremantle, a British colonel and an observer of the war from the Confederate perspective, noted: "When the cannonade was at its height, the Confederate band began to play polkas and waltzes. It sounded very curious accompanied by the hissing and bursting of the shells."

Just as men rushed to grab their regimental flag when the color-bearer was shot, musicians filled the gap left by fallen comrades. It almost did not matter what type of music was played on the field as long as it was played. At Antietam, one man substituted for an entire regimental band. °A fiddler went up to his colonel and asked to "fiddle us in." The man played "Granny, Does Your Dog Bite? Hellfire, No" as the soldiers counterattacked.•

As the war wound on and the enthusiasm for fighting faded, the music changed. It began to reflect an increasing sense of despair. The soldiers started thinking more about home and death than battlefield glories. °Camp favorites became songs of loneliness and homesickness, the heart-wrenching songs that reflected what was deep in the men's souls. Popular songs later in the war were "When This Cruel War Is Over," "Just Before the Battle, Mother," and "Tenting Tonight on the Old Camp Ground."• °The songs could be so sad and moving that the commanders would try to ban the singing of certain songs to keep the soldiers' morale from flagging.•

On occasion, the soldiers on opposite sides would be brought together by the common bonds they shared through music. °It was at the battle of Stones River, Tennessee, fought on New Year's Eve 1862, that soldiers on both sides realized, through music, just how alike they were. On the night before the battle the men on both sides were huddled in the darkness. Early in the evening, a Union band began to play some of the great Union songs, and as it finished each song, the Union soldiers would applaud. Their applause was joined by the thousands of Confederates who were in position just across the field. Toward the end of the evening, the band began to pack up its instruments. From across the way the Confederates shouted, "Play some of our songs!" The Union musicians unpacked and played some of the songs that were dear to the Southern soldiers. For the last song that night the band struck up the opening chords to "Home, Sweet Home." It is estimated that eighty-one thousand men, the total of the two armies, sang that song together. It was the greatest chorus in the history of the Western Hemisphere. Three days later, twenty-three thousand of those voices would sing no more.•

WHEN EACH SIDE'S music seemed to prove that the enemy was not so devilish, some soldiers took it upon

A "soldier . . . [is] never to be satisfied without he has a . . . pipe in his mouth," stated one volunteer in the 116th Pennsylvania. Indeed, many soldiers reserved a pocket in their coats for a pipe and a bag of tobacco, welcome "friends" at the end of a long day of marching or fatigue duty. Several of the pipes below were carved from briarwood or mountain laurel roots by troops in their spare time, and they range in size from the large, long-stemmed variety used in camp, to the smaller-bowled style often carried on campaign. In the center is a brass match-safe. Secured by a hinged lid, the "lucifers" could be withdrawn from the safe as needed and struck across the container's serrated bottom.

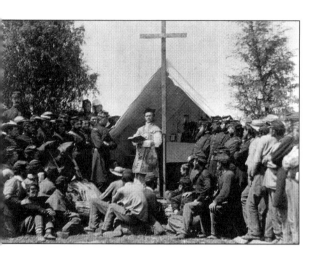

Beneath a cross made of surplus lumber, Catholic infantrymen gather above (left) for mass. With the presence of death from disease and combat so close, soldiers often found comfort in religion, despite a predilection for gambling and womanizing. Organizations such as the Christian Commission and the South Carolina Tract Society tried to reinforce the warriors' adherence to the Lord's Word by distributing pocket Bibles and religious booklets. One such pamphlet was dramatically entitled Sufferings of the Lost, *while another warned of eternal misery for those who did not forego the evils of vice.*

Of course, all camps had to feed their men. While soldiers in stationary camps could sometimes get a steady diet of fresh beef and bread prepared by camp cooks, such as the gentleman standing at the ready outside of his log "kitchen" (top right), their fare while on campaign was much more monotonous. To supplement their diet, soldiers of both armies took to "foraging," or taking food from the homesteads along their marching routes.

themselves to make an occasional unofficial peace. Officially, the blue and the gray were mortal enemies, sworn to destroy each other. Unofficially, they were high-spirited young men, united by blood and history. In the calm between the battles, truces were sometimes arranged and opposing armies gathered together to sing or enjoy a swimming hole, sharing moments of brotherhood.

Gilbert A. Hayes, a private with the Sixty-third Pennsylvania, wrote: "It was a singular sight to see. The soldiers of two great, hostile armies, bantering and joking together. It was not uncommon to see an equal number of 'graybacks' and 'bluebellies,' as they facetiously termed each other, enjoying a game of draw poker."

Although their political leaders no doubt frowned upon the fraternization, the common soldier saw little wrong with visiting with his enemy. °The men in blue and gray were from the same country, they spoke the same language, they worshiped the same God, and their past was a common tradition. They would often exchange newspapers and swap tobacco for coffee. Frequently when they would part, they would kneel and pray together, asking for the others' safety. Moments later, they were enemy soldiers again.•

This concern for the enemy was often displayed on the battlefield. °These were young men who recognized a common bond of suffering. There were many instances of soldiers climbing over the lines during a battle to bring water to wounded enemy soldiers who were crying for help.• To the soldiers, the political questions of the war were for politicians. The men fighting the war cared about the human cost of it.

"We believed that those who stood against us held convictions just as sacred as ours. And we respected them as every man with a heart must respect those who give all for their beliefs," wrote Union officer Oliver Wendell Holmes Jr.

Sometimes the fraternization between sides was purely practical. °After a battle, it was necessary to try to remove the bodies between the lines and to bury them as quickly as possible before they were attacked by animals and before decomposition started. A man might proudly serve as a Johnny Reb, or equally proudly as a Billy Yank, but in death he lost his identity. The gravediggers of both sides just saw young boys, fallen on the field. Often the dead of both sides were simply dumped into a mass grave.•

It was just before the battle, when they knew that they would face death, that the soldiers expressed appreciation for the life they had lived. °Many soldiers commented on the day of battle how clean the air was and how bright

In the photo at the bottom left soldiers of the First Rhode Island await their turn in the barber's chair. Union veteran John Billings recollected that not all camp barbers were proficient in their craft, however. Some used razors "of the most barbarous sort" that mangled their victims nearly as badly as if they had been in battle. Hence, some troops shaved themselves, but they too, Billings asserted, "frequently shed . . . innocent blood in the service of their country while undergoing the operation."

While his "pards," or friends, scribble letters home, a Northern soldier diligently repairs a worn item of his clothing (bottom right). In a society characterized by a strong division of labor, most men, with the exception of tailors, had not handled a needle and thread before they enlisted. The shoddy nature of army clothing, sparse uniform issues, and wear and tear soon forced soldiers to reach for their "housewife," or sewing kit. Some men became surprisingly adept at repairing and altering clothing and hired out their services to those less skillful.

Holidays created uncommon sights among the ranks. In the picture to the right some infantrymen, one whimsically dressed in a festooned woman's hoop, parade through camp celebrating Christmas and New Year's. If possible, troops would celebrate Christmas with an elaborate dinner. Capt. Edgar Richards of the Ninety-sixth Pennsylvania wrote that the "subject of stuffing" had divided his mess into "two violent cliques . . . , the oyster and onion factions." Although he left no record as to which prevailed, he did explain that the "onion faction" argued that its preferred seasoning should be adopted on "national grounds" as it dubiously claimed the correct pronunciation of "onion" was actually "union."

the sun was. They heard birds sing; they smelled honeysuckle. A number of soldiers took these peaceful signs as omens. They wondered if they were experiencing their last feelings on earth.• °Just before the fighting began, soldiers would pray, cry, or maybe even laugh hysterically. Some would be very quiet, thinking about what was about to happen. Most would read their pocket Bibles, write a last-minute letter home, or look at pictures of loved ones. They prepared themselves for death.•

Some prepared more than others. Many seemed to sense that they were about to die. °Those soldiers would write their names and hometowns on a slip of paper and put it somewhere in their clothing, just in case they were killed. They did not want to be one of those thousands of men who would spend eternity under headstones that read "Unknown."•

It was the waiting to be under fire, wounded, or killed that seemed to bother soldiers the most. All they could do was wait in the woods and behind the rocks, listening to the din of battle that was just out of sight but not out of hearing. °These men realized it was in that moment that their lives took on some meaning more than just the everyday routine of being a farmer or being a clerk or being a teacher.•

"We lay there about eight minutes, and yet it seemed an age to me. My heart seemed to thump the ground as hard as the enemy's bullets. Twice I exclaimed aloud, 'My God! Why don't they order us to charge?'" wrote one Union sergeant.

CN °When the shooting started, these men would walk elbow to elbow into volleys of musketry and canister fire that tore swaths through their line. Few would fail to pick up their regiment's flag even though eight or nine or more had fallen carrying it. These men served with their comrades. Their brothers in arms were dearer than blood brothers to them. They could not let them down; they could not let the regiment down. That was the code by which these men lived and the code by which these men died.•

JIR °The Johnny Rebs and Billy Yanks who survived the war were quite aware that they had been a part of something that was too big to comprehend, and they took a great deal of pride in that. They celebrated each other's courage at reunions, such as that held at Gettysburg after the turn of the century. They sat side by side reminiscing, talking of what they had done, the sights they had seen, and the experiences they had felt. These aged men, who grew old with dignity, died as compatriots.•

One of the most poignant descriptions of the timeless bond born on the battlefield comes from William Shakespeare's *Henry V:* "We few, we happy few, we band of brothers; for he today that sheds his blood with me shall be my brother. . . . And gentlemen . . . now abed shall think themselves accursed they were not here. . . . Old men forget; yet all shall be forgot, but he'll remember with advantages what feats he did that day."

The soldiers of the Civil War were fiercely independent, passionately loyal, sometimes crude, and often noble. Above all, the fighting men of the war were uniquely American. Three million strong, these citizen soldiers shared an adventure of unspeakable suffering and enduring pride. They began their epic journey as Rebs and Yanks, but they concluded it as Americans.

Oliver Wendell Holmes Jr. graduated from Harvard and became an officer in the Twentieth Massachusetts. Pictured as a lieutenant above, Holmes went on to a distinguished law career after the war, most notably as an associate justice of the U.S. Supreme Court. His greatest contribution to the Union cause may have occurred on July 12, 1864, at Fort Stevens, one of the sixty enclosed bastions that ringed the national capital. During Jubal Early's 1864 raid on Maryland, which encroached on the capital defenses, Abraham Lincoln twice ventured to the front to witness the action. On his second visit he came under fire. Fascinated with the sight, he continued peering over the earthworks until Holmes, then a captain, shouted, "Get down, you fool!"

61

FIRST MANASSAS

The CIVIL WAR WAS THE CLIMAX OF fifty years of growing tension between the North and the South. For most of the nineteenth century the two major regions of the country had been looking for some final resolution to the disputes over states' rights and slavery. Compromises had been offered, sometimes tried, and always rejected as failed policies. By 1861 the only alternative left was war.

War, however, was an abstract concept to almost everyone in the United States. Wars were fought between Americans and foreigners, not between men of common heritage and beliefs. A few political leaders worried what war between brothers would bring.

"All the armies of Europe, Asia, and Africa combined with all the treasures of the Earth could not by force take a drink from the Ohio or make a track on the Blue Ridge in a trial of a thousand years. If destruction be our lot, we must ourselves be its author and finisher," wrote Illinois state legislator Abraham Lincoln in 1838. "As a nation of free men, we must live through all time or die by suicide."

Twenty-three years later the United States was about to do exactly what worried Lincoln. The difference in 1861 was that while the questions and political arguments were the same as they had always been, the technology of war had greatly advanced. The potential for death and destruction on a grand scale had arrived, but even the generals who had fought America's past wars did not know it.

After Fort Sumter there had been a few skirmishes between Northern and Southern soldiers at Big Bethel,

WCD	William C. Davis
GWG	Gary W. Gallagher
JJH	John J. Hennessy
RKK	Robert K. Krick
BP	Brian Pohanka
JIR	James I. Robertson Jr.

The two youths on these pages enlisted during the patriotic surge that swept over the nation following the bombardment of Fort Sumter. In general, these recruits and thousands like them had no prior military experience, which meant that both North and South faced a tremendous task in turning these men and boys into soldiers. Companies were quickly formed and ceremoniously sent off to army camps where discipline was strict and the training stringent. Both armies used the same manual—Hardee's Tactics—to master the fundamentals of shooting and maneuvering. They learned to act and react to bugle and drum calls. They slept on the ground or in tents and arranged their quarters to meet their tastes and preferences. Both sides paid infantry and artillery privates eleven dollars a month and cavalry twelve dollars. The Yankees increased the pay to thirteen dollars at one point, and by the end of the war the rate had been increased to sixteen dollars a month. The Rebels increased their pay once, to twenty dollars a month, but by then Confederate currency was

(continued on next page)

Rich Mountain, and Corrick's Ford in Virginia, with both sides suffering only a handful of casualties. The big battle that both sides sincerely believed would decide the war came in July 1861, barely twenty miles from Washington, D.C., on the plains around Manassas Junction, Virginia. It was in this battle that North and South first experienced the horror of modern combat.

GWG °Before Bull Run, or Manassas, no Americans really understood what the war would mean. They could not, because there was nothing in the American experience that had prepared them for what they were going to have to endure.•

JIR °Both sides were living in a dream world where war was viewed romantically. Men dashed to the recruiting offices, absolutely petrified the war might end before they could fight. They wanted a chance to seek their red badge of courage, as a battle wound was called in those days.•

°Neither side expected the other to be able to fight WCD well, so both went forward filled with the confidence that not only would they have victory but they would have an easy victory. It would be a short war—a summer's war—and by fall they would all be home.• Instead, for four long years no one except the dead and mangled returned home. The reality of what war was really like hit home after the battle in July 1861, a battle with two names.

JIR °Each side chose to name the battles differently. The North named battles after the closest stream or geographic feature, while the South named the same battle after the closest town. Thus this first major action was called the battle of Bull Run in the North, after the shallow stream cutting across the battlefield. In the South, it would be known as the battle of Manassas, after Manassas Junction, a nearby railroad town.•

It was almost inevitable that the first major battle would be fought where it was. The Confederates had been massing at the junction for days to protect the vital railroad, which ran west into the Shenandoah Valley, where a Southern army was stationed. °The attention of the world was focused on the Manassas-Washington front• because everyone knew that America, long divided by economic and cultural differences, had finally reached the breaking point. °While there were many issues that divided North and South, the issue that polarized the conflict was slavery. That was an issue people could easily understand as a moral issue, and it was one that inflamed people's passions.•

Slavery was a simple enough concept in the minds of Southern leaders like Confederate Vice President Alexander Stephens, who wrote, "Our new government is founded upon the great truth that the Negro is not equal to the white man." In the 1860s °almost half of the Southern population were slaves. The average Southerner wondered what would happen if all of those slaves were suddenly free. Who would take care of them? Moreover, there was a mostly unvoiced fear of "racial amalgamation," the belief that if the slaves became free, sooner or later whites and blacks would intermingle. This thought terrified Southern society and culture.•

When Lincoln was elected in 1860, the South believed he would push for the abolition of all slavery, even though Lincoln promised explicitly that he would protect slavery in states where it already existed. The South, nevertheless, did not believe him. By the time of his inauguration in March 1861, seven states from the Deep South had left the Union of thirty-four states to form their own new nation, the Confederacy, named after a political notion that the South should form a confederation of slaveholding states that would be separate from the United States.

°The Southerners viewed themselves as fighting a second American Revolution. They were seeking liberty and independence, just as the American colonies had

(continued from previous page)

worthless. Pay was usually four to six months late for the Federals and twelve months or more for Southerners. The scourge of enlistment, however, was measles, which spread through the ranks of both sides mercilessly. Yet all this paled in contrast to each man's baptism by fire in his first combat.

done in 1776. When they were called "rebels" and Southern soldiers were nicknamed "Johnny Rebs," they took no offense. Their grandparents had been called rebels by the British government.•

Just weeks after Lincoln took office, Southern forces fired on and captured Fort Sumter in Charleston Harbor, South Carolina. °The firing on Fort Sumter on April 12, 1861, was like a lightning bolt hitting a powder keg. It released all the pent-up emotions of decades.• War was a reality, and both sides were thrilled.

"The military excitement in Washington is intense. Civil war is actually upon us, and, strange to say, brings a feeling of relief. The suspense is over," wrote Ohio Congressman John Sherman, foster brother of William Tecumseh Sherman.

Almost before the smoke had cleared from Fort Sumter, Lincoln called for seventy-five thousand troops to crush the rebellion staged by the Deep South states. Outraged that Lincoln would order them to raise troops

1 Federal forces concentrate on Virginia's northern border.

2 **July 21:** McDowell's Federal forces some 37,000-strong meet the combined forces of Beauregard and Johnston at Manassas Junction. The battle of Bull Run ensues. The Federals withdraw in confusion toward the Washington defenses.

3 **Oct. 21:** Reconnaissance by the Union into northern Virginia result in clash at Ball's Bluff in which Federals are surprised and defeated by a Confederate brigade.

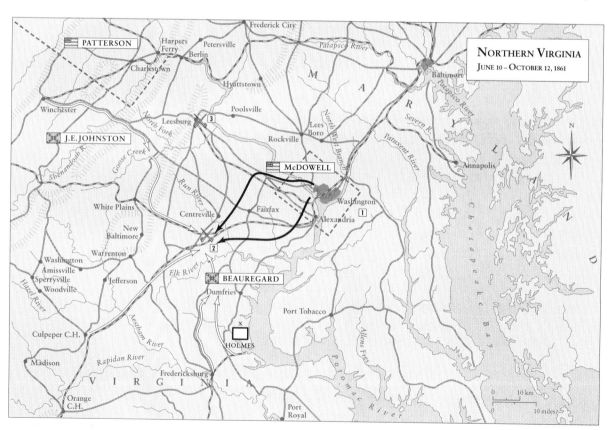

to attack their neighbors, the four remaining Upper South states—Arkansas, North Carolina, Tennessee, and Virginia—joined the Confederacy. °In their eyes, Lincoln was not raising an army to defend the flag, which was his constitutional obligation. Rather, he was invading the South, an act that threatened the sovereignty of the border states.• Southerners would not allow that to happen without a fight.

"If we are conquered, we will be driven penniless and dishonored from the land of our birth. I had rather fall in its cause than to see my country dismantled of its glory and independence," wrote William A. Smith, a volunteer with the Fourteenth North Carolina Regiment.

The reason behind the Southerner's will to fight was simple in his mind. °He was fighting in defense of his hearth and his home. The Union army was an invader. It was coming into his country to overrun his land, to take away what he had been able to scrape together through a lifetime.• Southerners were fighting in self-defense, but

1 · *July 21, night:* Intending to outflank the Confederate left, McDowell moves 10,000 men from Centreville heading west and south.

2 · *8:30 A.M.:* The Confederate defenders of Stone Bridge learn the Federals are at Sudley Ford. Brig. Gen. N. G. Evans moves portion of his command to meet the Federal retreat.

3 · *A.M.:* Evans opposes Federal moves.

4 · Outnumbered, Evans's force withdraws to Henry House Hill, where it makes a stand.

5 · *Afternoon:* For several hours, the front line pushes up and down on Henry House Hill.

6 · Confederates withdraw from Henry House Hill. Gen. Thomas Jackson leads in fresh Confederate troops.

7 · *4 P.M.:* Confederate attack forces Federals to retreat toward Centreville.

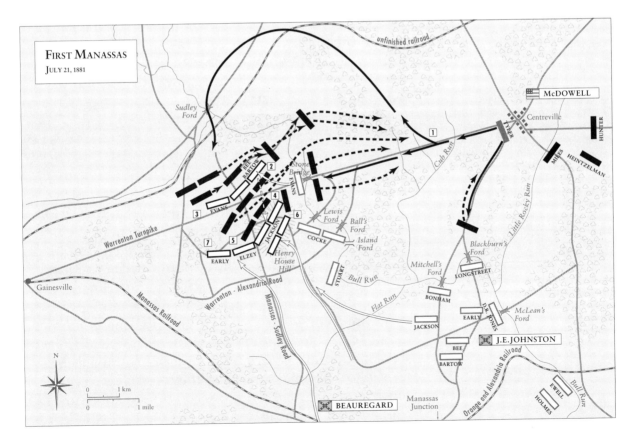

At the outbreak of the war, Irvin McDowell was a staff officer in the adjutant general's office in Washington. As one of the youngest and most fit for field command of the army staff in 1861, he was given his star and command of the army assembling in the capital. Pressured to act prematurely, McDowell devised a workable plan of attack; unfortunately it required an army, and all McDowell had was a mob. Against him stood his former West Point classmate P. G. T. Beauregard, who was already being lauded as the hero of Fort Sumter.

JIR they could not understand what motivated Northern boys to get involved in a war that was none of their business °and die for something as vague and flimsy as "the Union."•

GWG °To nineteenth-century Northerners, however, the Union represented a democratic beacon to the rest of JIR the world.• °One out of every five Billy Yanks was an GWG immigrant,• °and the rest were not far removed. These immigrants were willing to put their lives on the line for the United States, especially if it meant they would be accepted as citizens more quickly. This deep-seated immigrant mentality influenced many Yankees to believe that were this beacon of democracy to be snuffed out by the dismemberment of the Union, the world would lose something it could never again regain. There might never again be another spark that would lead to another democratic society such as the United States. To the people of the North that was something worth fighting and dying for.•

JIR °THE BATTLE OF Bull Run was much more than a battle. It was an omen of what was to come and what would be the bloodiest era in all of American history.• The men who fought here were common men, mostly farmers who had lived all their lives within a few miles of their birthplaces. Most had no direct knowledge of war. Their experience of combat was limited to the heroic tales of George Washington and the Revolution. The citizen soldiers who flocked to the battlefields from Maine to Texas expected to share in some glorious adventure.

WCD °The sense of enthusiasm, excitement, and desire to take part in this war touched every segment of the population. Women could not legally be soldiers, but in several cities, especially in the South, special shooting galleries were set up to teach women to use firearms, so they could be some last line of defense and to give them the feeling that they were contributing to the war effort. Many blacks, both free and slave, were anxious to serve. Thousands of Confederate slaves wanted to fight for the Confederate army, and they were accepted as musicians, teamsters, cooks, servants, and sometimes as soldiers. The blacks fought because the Yankees were invading their homeland just as much as they were invading the homeland of white settlers. The coming war was an all-encompassing experience that swallowed everyone involved.•

"Standing before a long mirror, I put in many hours of weary work and soon thought myself quite a soldier," bragged Union soldier Elisha Hunt Rhodes, an articulate man who kept a diary of his war experiences.

The expectations and experiences were no different for the young Confederates. "Every young fellow who went to war got a kiss from his best girl, and, as it was the first that many of us had ever enjoyed, it is not surprising that a last farewell is repeated over and over again before we actually took our departure," wrote J. P. Cannon, of the Twenty-seventh Alabama Regiment.

The soldiers on both sides had been influenced to fight by their politicians, their newspapers, their RKK churches, their friends, and everyone they knew. °The entire society was at war. There was almost no opportunity *not* to go to war. The drums were beating, the bands were playing, and the girls were at the county courthouse watching while almost every able-bodied male of the appropriate age signed up with all of his friends, neighbors, brothers, cousins, and other relatives. The community was going to war, and they went with them.• For many soldiers, it would be the most stirring moment in their lives.

"At last the regiment was formed in companies, and we marched. Was there ever such an ovation? Handkerchiefs fluttered in the air like myriads of white butterflies. An avenue of brave, honest faces smiled upon us as we passed, and sent sunshine into our hearts that lives there still," wrote Fitz James O'Brien of the Seventy-ninth New York, a flashy unit made up mostly of Scottish descendants who intended to fight their battles wearing kilts BP and ribboned caps. °Before the first battles there was no accepted standard that one side would wear gray and the other would wear blue. Instead, there was a colorful hodgepodge of uniforms, a bewildering variety of weaponry, and a great deal of enthusiasm.•

In the weeks before Bull Run as the Confederates gathered around Manassas Junction, Washington became the

A native of Louisiana, Pierre Gustave Toutant Beauregard graduated in 1838 ranked second in a class of forty-five at West Point (McDowell was ranked twenty-third). He stood five feet seven inches, weighed about 150 pounds, and had an olive complexion and graying hair. At the age of forty-three Beauregard was the first Confederate given the rank of brigadier general. Like most officers of the period, he was a great admirer of Napoleonic tactics and even imitated the language and expressions used by the French emperor. In preparation for the Federal assault at Manassas, Beauregard issued grandiloquent orders that echoed the Little Corporal. The language of the orders, however, was almost impossible for his commanders to comprehend, and one canard contends that the Southern commander ordered one of his regiments to attack another Southern regiment.

On May 24, 1861, Union troops marched into Alexandria, Virginia. Twenty-four-year-old Col. Elmer E. Ellsworth of the New York Fire Zovaves along with seven comrades determined to remove a Confederate flag from the Marshall House Hotel. He cut down the banner and started down the stairs. The innkeeper, James Jackson, encountered Ellsworth at the third-floor landing and leveled a double-barreled shotgun at the colonel. Cpl. Francis Brownell attempted to divert the shot, but the blast killed Ellsworth. Brownell fired his musket at Jackson and then bayoneted him. Ellsworth became a martyr for the North; Jackson was mourned in the South.

focal point for Union activity. Elisha Hunt Rhodes arrived with his regiment and wrote: "Hurrah! We are in Washington, and what a city! Mud, pigs, geese, Negroes, palaces, shanties everywhere! I was not well pleased with the appearance of the city, but was struck by the magnitude of the public buildings."

JIR °These militia units gathered in the national capital to defend the Union. Washington was alive, not with the reality of war, but with the excitement for it.• One of the most colorful regiments in town was the Eleventh New York, better known as the New York Fire Zouaves, comprised entirely of New York City firemen and dressed in colorful uniforms in imitation of French Algerian soldiers.

BP °The Fire Zouaves, commanded by Col. Elmer E. Ellsworth, a close friend of President Abraham Lincoln, were one of the most reckless, undisciplined, rowdy, hard-to-control bunch of scoundrels that ever camped in Washington. At one time they cavorted across the unfinished dome of the Capitol, but they had their good side, too, and once ran past the camp sentries to help battle a fire that broke out at Willard's Hotel.• They were one of the first Union units to experience death when on May 24, 1861, Ellsworth was shot and killed by an Alexandria, Virginia, innkeeper after Ellsworth tore down a Confederate flag from the hotel flagstaff. The innkeeper was also killed.

BP °"Remember Ellsworth!" became a Union battle cry. To the North this was an outrageous murder of a great national celebrity, a dashing young hero who had made a name for himself in prewar America by creating and leading one of the nation's best-known and best-drilled militia units.• Ellsworth was the first Federal officer to die in the war, although ironically, he was shot by a civilian, not a Confederate soldier.

WCD °Lincoln, who had met Ellsworth when he had clerked in Lincoln's law office in Illinois, went into mourning upon hearing of the incident. Ellsworth, twenty-four, was almost like a son to the fifty-two-year-old president. This was only the first of many times that Lincoln would personally feel the pain of loss in the war.•

Perhaps influenced by his personal loss, Lincoln joined an impatient public in demanding that the Union army move to crush the Rebels. The man under pressure was Union Brig. Gen. Irvin McDowell, a Washington-based staff officer who had drawn the early assignment to transform thousands of raw recruits into an army.

ᵂᶜᴰ °McDowell's problems were an example of what was wrong with jumping into war. During the Mexican War he had been a staff officer. Prior to the Civil War he had been attached to the adjutant general's office in Washington. He had never led troops into battle and had never issued commands to any group larger than a company. He had no training for commanding an army of thirty-five thousand.•

Regarding the Northern army that was assembling near Washington, Col. William Tecumseh Sherman observed: "No curse could be greater than invasion by a volunteer army. McDowell and all of the generals tried their best. But to say he commanded that army is no such thing. They did as they pleased."

ᴳᵂᴳ °This huge aggregation of civilians who had come into the military seeking glory were not soldiers. McDowell knew that they were not ready for combat, but the Lincoln administration was under political pressure to make something happen. The officers heard the same things everywhere they went. "We've got all these men in uniform. Let's go smite the Rebels. Let's chastise them. Let's crush the rebellion and restore the Union. Let's move now. Move now! Move against Richmond! Move against the Rebels!"•

Reluctantly, McDowell finally followed his orders from Lincoln to march his mob of men into Virginia to end the war. Lincoln tried to encourage McDowell by pointing out, "It is true that you are green. So are the Confederates. You are all green together."

On July 16, 1861, McDowell marched his thirty-five thousand troops toward Manassas Junction. Years later,

A member of the Fire Zouaves, the Eleventh New York, Cpl. Francis E. Brownell was named the Avenger of Ellsworth, his colonel. After Ellsworth was killed by an Alexandria citizen, Brownell shot and bayoneted the assassin. Brownell is wearing the first uniform issued the Eleventh New York: a red fireman's shirt, gray jacket and trousers, and a red kepi with a dark blue band. His embossed fireman's belt reads "Premier." He holds a Springfield rifle with a sword bayonet and stands with his left foot on the flag Ellsworth had removed from the Alexandria inn.

At two o'clock, Tuesday afternoon, July 16, Union Gen. Irvin McDowell reluctantly began moving his army toward Manassas. The undisciplined soldiers frequently stopped to rest, as depicted above (left), or plunder Virginia farms. Some took the time to chase after pigs and bees (to raid their store of honey). Col. William T. Sherman, a brigade commander, sent one of his aides to put a stop to the unruliness. His men defiantly answered the order with, "Tell Colonel Sherman we will get all the water, pigs, and chickens we want." After two days of trudging in the hot July sun, McDowell's army reached Centreville, Virginia—only three miles east of Manassas.

On the morning of July 18 Confederate President Jefferson Davis sent Gen. Joseph E. Johnston a telegram stating that the Union army was closing on Manassas and asking, "if practicable," would he reinforce Beauregard's army. Johnston immediately dispatched his nearly eleven-thousand-man army by train. Along the way they stopped at Bristoe Station (above right) where the women greeted them with shouts, waving handkerchiefs, and refreshments. The first reinforcements arrived near Manassas later that day. By July 21 most of Johnston's army was on the field and had taken part in the battle. The war would be one of the first to use a railroad system to maneuver troops and supplies.

poet and novelist Herman Melville described the volunteers as they set off into the unknown:

> All they feel is this: 'Tis glory,
> A rapture sharp, though transitory,
> Yet lasting in the laureled story.
> So, they clearly go to fight,
> Chatting left and laughing right.
> But some who this blithe mood present
> As in lights and files they bear
> Shall die, ere three days are spent,
> Perish, enlightened by the volleyed glare.

WCD °THE REBEL ARMIES waiting in Virginia were led by Gens. Joseph E. Johnston in the Shenandoah Valley and P. G. T. Beauregard, the hero of Fort Sumter, who was at Manassas. The two armies were connected by a railroad line. By using the rail line between these two halves, either force could be rushed to support the other within a matter of hours. Thus the two armies could double their strength quickly if the need arose.•

Opposite Johnston in the Shenandoah was a small Federal force led by sixty-nine-year-old Union Gen. Robert Patterson. McDowell would be moving from Washington to confront Beauregard at Manassas. The Confederate strategy was simple, but its execution had to be carried out carefully. Johnston would slip away from Patterson and move to support Beauregard, but he would

be prepared to rush back to the Valley should Patterson try to move south.

°McDowell helped the Confederate cause greatly by advancing very slowly, allowing his raw recruits to become accustomed to the march. Placing his men four abreast on a single road meant that the Union column stretched out for ten miles. A single slow regiment in the line could hold up everyone in the column behind it. Nevertheless, McDowell did not press his men. He was terrified of what would happen when they encountered the Confederates. He did not want to execute this campaign because he knew he and his army were not ready.•

It soon became obvious to the young soldiers that they had not trained sufficiently. °They expected a quick march and a quick victory, but none of them had ever walked twenty miles a day carrying forty pounds of gear. The march proved to be a nightmare. They bumped into each other. They would double-time an occasional mile to catch up to the column and then stand in position for an hour, waiting for the rest of the column to catch up to them. The men began eating their packed rations before they even left Washington, so food was running out before they reached the battlefield. The July heat and humidity took their toll on men dressed in ill-fitting

While McDowell's army rested in its camps, the Confederates fortified the area around Manassas Junction. The Fourth South Carolina, brigaded with Wheat's Louisiana Battalion, deployed on the western bank of Bull Run near the Stone Bridge. During the morning hours of July 21 the small brigade, numbering only eleven hundred, detained two Union brigades (nearly seventy-six hundred men), due in no small part to this strong defensive position. The Fourth South Carolina also helped defend Matthews Hill and Henry Hill.

The Confederate leadership perceived that to defend Richmond, they would have to protect the Shenandoah Valley and southeastern Virginia. That strategy made Manassas Junction, approximately twenty-six miles from the Federal capital, a strategic position for WCD *the Confederates. Two railroads intersected here—the Orange and Alexandria and the Manassas Gap—and these railroads linked northeastern Virginia with the Shenandoah Valley and the western and eastern regions of Virginia. In anticipation of the Federal movement against the rail hub, the Confederates had more than a month to prepare their fortifications, which were enhanced later in a second battle at Manassas and sketched above (left).*

At 6:00 A.M., July 21, Union Lt. Peter Hains fired the first shot of the battle, depicted above (right). The shell flew over the Confederate infantrymen and smashed into the Van Pelt house. Hains had been assigned to command an eleven-man crew of a huge 30-pounder Parrott rifled cannon. The piece weighed six thousand pounds and hurled a thirty-three-pound projectile. Men from the Second Wisconsin nicknamed the piece "President Lincoln's Babywaker." Because of its size the crew could not easily move it as the battle lines shifted, thus it was not employed effectively. During the retreat, Hains was forced to render the cannon useless and abandon it.

heavy woolen uniforms. The march was an ordeal for which they were not in the least prepared.•

As the Federal army crept forward, Beauregard, on the banks of Bull Run, anxiously awaited reinforcements. °On the morning of July 18, Beauregard had only eighteen to twenty thousand men to face McDowell's army of thirty-five to thirty-seven thousand men.

Unknown to Beauregard, Johnston had already JHH decoyed Patterson into holding his position. °Patterson, completely fooled, wrote messages to Washington assuring Washington that Johnston's army was still in the Shenandoah Valley. In reality Johnston was marching over the mountains to board the trains that would take his men to join Beauregard at Manassas.•

The Federals suspected something was up at Manassas WCD Junction, but they could not be sure. °All through the day before the main battle, the Union army heard the steam whistles of locomotives coming into Manassas Junction and going out. McDowell's officers believed Beauregard was receiving substantial reinforcements.• It did not matter. McDowell knew he had to attack to satisfy the Washington politicians. Despite misgivings, McDowell issued the final battle order for an attack the next day. As night fell on July 20, soldiers on both sides knew that the dawn would forever change their lives.

"All is hushed and still. As I look up at the starry vault and think of the morrow," wrote Caleb Clark of the Second Ohio Regiment, "I must confess I am a bit homesick." Union Pvt. Edwin S. Barrett recalled: "At two o'clock, one drum sounded through the camp and was repeated through the numerous camps around us. In half an hour, forty thousand men stood ready to battle for the Union."

The battle was not scheduled to begin for hours, yet McDowell had already made his first major mistake. °Night marches were difficult for veteran troops, much less men who had never marched more than five miles in their lives.• McDowell's untrained army had been marching for two days in the heat and dust, and now, without taking time for a night's rest, his men were on the road again. °Many of the Union troops, when they finally reached the battlefield at Bull Run, were exhausted. They had cut their way through the brush when the roads were not wide enough. They were covered with sweat and dirt. Their legs were chafed. Their wool uniforms were sticking to their clammy flesh.• They were in no shape to fight a battle after just a few hours of sleep.

As the dawn turned into day, the soldiers were met with an incredible sight. °Hundreds of civilians had ridden out in their buggies that Sunday, bringing picnic baskets and blankets to spread on the hillsides near the battlefield. The civilians, mostly politicians who had knowledge of the movement, planned to watch as the battle unfolded.• °Those people in their decorative carriages, carrying their lunches, faithfully reflected what the nation expected this war to be like: a picnic.•

The Union first attacked along Bull Run, hoping to keep the Confederates along the creek occupied while the main attack moved farther to the Rebel left. A Confederate looking at the battlefield through a spyglass happened to spot a glint of sunlight off a polished Federal cannon barrel. The warning went up. The Federal plan was to turn the Confederate left flank. Before the meager Confederate forces could be redeployed, ten thousand Federal soldiers attacked at Matthews Hill, overwhelming one thousand Confederates at about 10:00 A.M. The real war had begun. "The air

After the Union divisions crossed Sudley Ford, they passed Sudley Church. Churchgoers were just beginning to gather as wounded Federal soldiers streamed in. The congregation quickly evacuated the area.

A member of the West Point class of 1822, David Hunter (below) had served on the frontier and in the Mexican War. In May 1861 he was made colonel of the Third U.S. Cavalry and then given command of a division. His men led the flanking march and attacked the Confederates near Matthews Hill. During the fighting, Hunter was wounded in the neck but survived.

On the evening of July 19, McDowell sent out revised orders. Hunter's division would lead the main flank attack. Its march, however, was slowed by fallen trees in the road. The division took more than seven hours to advance three miles, and when it did find the battlefield, the division joined the battle piecemeal. Hunter's men fought from 10:00 A.M. to 11:30 A.M. Col. Ambrose Burnside's brigade took position near the Matthews house while Col. Andrew Porter's brigade deployed on Burnside's right flank. After Hunter was wounded, Porter assumed command of the division. During the afternoon battle two of Porter's regiments assaulted Confederate positions on Henry House Hill and failed.

was filled with a medley of sounds: shouts, cheers, commands, oaths, the sharp retort of rifles, groans, and prayers," wrote Arnold Williams of the Second Rhode Island Infantry.

BP   Within minutes the potential horrors of war became real to the men in arms. °What they were most unprepared for was the horror of seeing their friends struck down around them and writhing in agony on the ground. There was nothing glorious about this; it was ghastly. Worse, those struck did not always die a quick death.• They lay there screaming, trying to hold their blood, bones, muscles, and organs inside their bodies.

BP   °Civil War tactics were based on the tactics Napoleon had employed successfully in conquering his enemies: men marching elbow to elbow to fire their muskets in massed volleys. The problem was that Napoleon had fought just after the turn of the century, when the smoothbore musket was the weapon of choice. The smoothbore had an accurate range of just one hundred yards. The rifled musket, which had become the standard military weapon in the 1850s, had an effective range of several hundred yards, yet the generals still marched their men into close quarters with the enemy. Those geometric blocks of flesh and blood that had

served armies so well in the past could now be torn to pieces at a much greater range than the generals realized. Massed fire that might have hit dozens of men in Napoleon's time now felled hundreds.

Moreover, the .58 caliber minié ball was more destructive than anything in Napoleon's time. Named after the Frenchman who invented it, the conical minié ball expanded inside a musket's barrel, gripping the rifling grooves inside, and spinning with more accuracy toward its target. Once it had penetrated a man, the ball would often career around inside his body, shattering bones and tearing vital organs and arteries. So much damage would be done to the bones that amputation was the only answer for a wound in the arm or leg.•

At first the massed fire of the numerically superior Fed-erals worked against the outnumbered Confederates. °The Northerners, for a moment, thought they were victorious. In fact, McDowell arrived on the battlefield with his staff, waving their hats and yelling, "Victory! Victory! Victory!"•

Outnumbered ten to one, °the Confederates on Matthews Hill fought for time, waiting for their reinforce-ments to arrive. They bought ninety minutes with hun-dreds of casualties. McDowell followed those ninety minutes by awarding the Confederates two hours. He

Burnside's brigade (above)—the van-guard of the Union flank attack—was three hours late in arriving on the bat-tlefield. Around 10:00 A.M. he threw his first regiment into the fight. At 10:30 he deployed his second regiment. His remaining units arrived shortly thereafter. Although novices to com-bat, his four regiments stood their ground. Out of 3,700 men, Burnside (below), a West Pointer, lost 58 killed, 177 wounded, and 134 missing.

Wearing gray pants and blue coats, the Second Rhode Island was the first regiment in Burnside's brigade to be deployed on Matthews Hill. Many took cover behind the farm buildings or dropped to the ground.

Barnard E. Bee (below), a native of Charleston, South Carolina, and a West Point graduate, commanded a brigade at Matthews and Henry Hills. Late on July 21, he was shot from his horse while leading the Fourth Alabama and died the next day. He is most noted for giving Thomas Jonathan Jackson his famous nickname, "Stonewall."

simply stopped fighting between noon and 2:00 P.M. That delay helped turn the tide of battle.•

WHILE MCDOWELL was contemplating what to do next, thousands of Joseph E. Johnston's men arrived by railroad. Disembarking at Manassas Junction, the troops marched immediately to the sound of the fighting. McDowell, well behind the Union lines, could not see the Confederate reinforcements arriving. Had he known about them, he might have pushed harder.

Slowly, the Confederates under newly appointed Brig. Gen. Barnard E. Bee retreated from Matthews Hill to nearby Henry House Hill. Still outnumbered, Bee desperately searched for something or someone who could help his men stop the slow-moving Federal tide. °As Bee fell back toward Henry House Hill—named after the elderly and ill Mrs. Henry, who stayed inside her house despite all the bullets and artillery shells raining down in her yard—he galloped up the hill to see what troops, if any, were there to aid him. On the reverse slope of Henry House Hill, Bee, an 1845 graduate of West Point, encountered 1846 West Point graduate Gen. Thomas Jonathan Jackson. Jackson had left the army nearly ten years earlier to become a professor at the Virginia Military Institute. Now he headed a brigade of Virginians into position on Henry House Hill.

Bee said to Jackson, "General, they're pushing us back."

Jackson very calmly replied, "Well, sir, we shall give them the bayonet."

With that reinforcement from Jackson, Bee rode back to his men, who were still reeling in the face of the Union onslaught. Bee shouted to get his men's attention, then pointed up Henry House Hill and shouted above the din of battle: "Look, men! There stands Jackson like a stone wall. Rally behind the Virginians."•

In that moment the legend of Stonewall Jackson was born. The name seemed to fit. °Jackson's personal style was a clenched-jaw determination with a stern power of will to succeed. On a field filled with military innocence on both sides, Jackson's determination, his intentness on winning, his confidence that he was doing God's will, all combined to make him like the wall he was described as being.• Bee's troops rallied around Jackson and his brigade and fortified the hill. Finally Bee's men had something they could cling to as a defense. Bee was shot later in the day, and he died the following day, never realizing his simple observation about a fellow officer would create a legend.

The advancing Union troops probably could not see Jackson's troops, as most of his Confederates were lying prone, hiding in the tall grass on the reverse slope of the hill. Even the greenest Yankee probably recognized the significance of the high ground that Henry House Hill represented. °If the Federals could secure that hill, they could turn the entire Confederate army. From their vantage point in the valley, looking up to the hill, the crest looked

As the Union soldiers withdrew, McDowell ordered Col. Dixon Miles's division to cover the retreat. Although inebriated, Miles was able to deploy his brigades in a line of battle near Centreville. Col. Louis Blenker positioned his German brigade west of the village and repulsed a Rebel cavalry attack in a rear-guard action. While the retreating column was in total disarray, McDowell secured his flanks and rear. Although this drawing depicts Southern infantry attacking the rear guard, there is no evidence that they charged the Union line near Centreville; however, Confederate cavalry did harass the retreating Federals near Cub Run.

79

The drawing on the right depicts a Union Zouave regiment charging up Henry House Hill. From 1:30 to 4:00 P.M. chaos reigned here. Fifteen Federal regiments and thirteen Confederate regiments charged and counterattacked so quickly that the action resembled a whirlpool. Much of the fighting focused around the Henry house and two Union batteries. Adding to the confusion, some Northern regiments wore gray uniforms, creating a distressing dilemma for both Rebels and Yankees alike. The similarity of flags also contributed to the choas.

Long considered one of the pivotal moments of the battle, at 2:30 P.M. Federal batteries under Capt. Charles Griffin (below) and Capt. James Ricketts were ordered to Henry House Hill. Confused about the identity of a body of infantry coming toward them, the artillerymen did not fire. The infantry, however, was the Thirty-third Virginia. With only a few yards between them, the Virginians loosed a fearful volley on the Yankee artillerymen. Griffin escaped, but his guns were captured.

empty except for Bee's retreating men. The Federals smelled victory, and they charged with great enthusiasm. About thirty yards from the top, from behind the brow of the hill, Jackson's brigade rose and delivered a point-blank volley of musketry into the faces of the startled Union soldiers.•

Jackson's volley devastated the Union line and stopped the attack in its tracks. Finally, the grimmest reality of war struck home for the Federals. Union Pvt. Edwin S. Barrett recalled: "There were at least forty men, some with both legs shot off, others with hard flesh wounds. They lay so thick around me that I could hardly step between them, and every step was in blood. Some besought me to kill them and put an end to their agony."

Desperate to keep the momentum of the attack going before more Confederate reinforcements arrived, JJH McDowell brought his cannon forward. °Two artillery batteries rolled to within three hundred yards of Jackson's line. The Virginians hunkered down below the slope of the hill as Union shells whistled harmlessly over their heads. McDowell had hoped to blast a hole through the Confederate line, which was what Napoleon would have done. The major difference was that Napoleon's artillery crews would not have been within range of the enemy's rifles, as McDowell's men were.• Jackson's riflemen targeted the Union batteries. "There was never such a destructive fire. It looked as if every horse and man at that battery just laid down and died right off," recalled Union Lt. William Averell.

The New York Fire Zouaves, the same men who had caroused in Washington, were rushed in to support the artillery, but °they had not paid enough attention in drill to learn how to deploy from a marching column into a line of battle. They stumbled about the field with their officers shouting and cursing as they tried to get the men into some sort of formation in anticipation of the next Confederate volley.•

°Before the firemen could get themselves into position, their lines were broken by Confederate Col. James Ewell Brown "Jeb" Stuart and his First Virginia Cavalry.• Stuart would eventually win fame and a major general's command of the cavalry of the Army of Northern Virginia.

°The Fire Zouaves, those zealous New York firemen who had boasted of their bravery in camp, felt their patriotism drain out of them. Many ran.• The Union batteries were now vulnerable.

With thick smoke from muskets and cannon shrouding the field, the fight became more difficult as the variety of uniforms added to the chaos. Because there was a wide assortment of militia uniforms worn by the men and because the U.S. flag and the First National flag of the Confederacy looked very similar from a distance, °the men had a hard time figuring out who was who on the battlefield.• Blue-coated troops sometimes turned out to be Virginia militia. Gray-clad soldiers were often from Wisconsin.

Confederate cavalry helped turn the tide of battle (above left). By 4:30 P.M. the entire Union army was in full retreat. One Maine private later recalled the withdrawal, "How we traveled! Nobody tired now. Every one for himself, and having a due regard for individuality, each gave a special attention to the rapid momentum of his legs." While many of the men ran, it was a twenty-six-mile journey to the national capital. Once the panic had subsided, most of the soldiers walked or collapsed in Centreville. In the chaos hundreds of troops and Northern civilians were captured. Three colonels and several Yankee politicians were among the captives.

The artist took the liberty of adding a Rebel infantry attack against the Yankees on the bridge over Cub Run (above right). Historically, a Confederate shell struck a wagon and caused it to flip over and block the bridge. Panic seized the Federal soldiers. Men and animals frantically splashed through the small creek. Wagons and artillery pieces crowded together as they forded the shallow water. The tangled mass made an easy target for the Southern artillerymen. Debris and dead Federals littered the area. No infantrymen, however, charged the fleeing Union troops. By 7:00 P.M. the Northerners had crossed the bridge and fled the area.

Approximately sixteen hundred Union prisoners were taken and sent to several Southern locations, such as Castle Pinckney in Charleston, South Carolina. These captives were from the Eleventh, Sixty-ninth, and Seventy-ninth New York. One officer of note held here was Col. Michael Corcoran, commander of the famous Sixty-ninth "Irish" New York regiment. The men adapted quickly to their situation and were treated well. Their casemates were in excellent condition, and they shared the same fare as the guards. The Northerners even taught their captors how to soften their hardtack. One regiment made things a little more homey by displaying a sign in their quarters: "Music Hall—444 Broadway."

It was just such a problem in identifying the opposite side that proved to be the turning point in the battle. Union artillery Capt. Charles Griffin had made his way with two cannon to the far left of Jackson's position. He was in an enviable position to blast down the Confederate battle line when he spotted a regiment in blue bearing down on his position. °He swung his two cannon to face the oncoming threat, which, based on the direction from which they were coming, he believed to be Confederate reinforcements. As he was about to fire, his commanding officer came up to him and ordered him not to fire because the men were Union men. Griffin replied, "I swear to the world those men are Confederates." The commanding officer claimed that they were Griffin's battery supply. Glumly, Griffin watched the blue-coated soldiers level their muskets at his battery to fire a volley. Griffin said later, "That was the end of us."• Griffin had been right, and his commander had been wrong. The blue-clad soldiers were the Thirty-third Virginia Infantry. Later Griffin spotted his commanding officer watering his horse in Bull Run. Griffin rode up to him and asked sarcastically if the man still believed the regiment was a Federal one.

His forces in disarray, McDowell, who had once taught tactics at West Point but who had never led troops in battle, committed one final blunder that sealed his army's defeat. °Instead of attacking by full brigades of several regiments or by divisions of several brigades, he attacked by sending in one regiment at a time. He did not recognize that his tactics were doomed to defeat because those lone Union regiments would be cut up by the defensive fire of several Confederate regiments. McDowell used up the rest of his army without thinking of what he was doing.•

As Union soldiers fell by the hundreds in uncoordinated attacks, more Confederate reinforcements from the Shenandoah Valley poured in to support Beauregard and Jackson. °Every minute of fighting on Henry House Hill saw more Confederate troops arriving on the field. By four o'clock that afternoon, the Yankees had no fresh regiments left to put into the fight.•

Overwhelmed by fresh Confederate troops, the Federals fled the battlefield in final defeat. Even the officers could not hide their despair.

"One of my close comrades was smashed by a solid shot, and what reply could be made to that?" asked a dejected Union officer, Abner R. Small. "Men fell rising and others melted from sight. And we saw the glitter of bayonets coming against our flank. And we heard the order to retire."

°THE EXHAUSTED UNION army fell back from Henry House Hill after fighting for seven hours. The recruits had done all they had been asked to do, but it was not enough. This unforeseen disaster would haunt the Union war effort for months to come,• but the disasters that distinguished the battle of Bull Run were still not over.

°As they fled the battlefield, the retreating rabble of Union troops came upon the frightened group of civilians who had come out in their Sunday best to watch the great battle. The ladies with their parasols and the men in their linen coats and straw hats were now in the Federal army's line of retreat—or flight.•

°Before the civilians could get away in their buggies and carriages, the soldiers, cannon, wagons, caissons, and ambulances came down the road, creating a gigantic traffic jam. Then a fortuitous Confederate artillery shell arched onto the bridge over Bull Run and exploded. A wagon overturned, which completely tied up the bridge, preventing any other traffic from passing.•

°Seeing their escape route cut off was all it took to put McDowell's army, already in a nervous retreat, into a full-scale panic. Men dropped their knapsacks and muskets and ran for their lives. Some jumped into the creek and swam across. They did not stop running until they got all the way back to Washington.• McDowell himself could not stop them.

"We tried to tell them there was no danger, called on them to stop, implored them to stand. We called them cowards, put out our heavy revolvers and threatened to shoot—but all in vain," McDowell lamented.

After being caught up in the retreat, some prominent civilians, such as New York Congressman Alfred Ely, fell

Like many Northern civilians, Congressman Alfred Ely from Rochester, New York, was anxious to see the Confederate army routed. He had traveled to Manassas from Washington earlier in the day to witness their defeat. Ignorant of the Union retreat, Ely remained close to the battlefield. He was captured by two officers from the Eighth South Carolina and taken to their colonel, Ellerbe Boggan Crawford Cash. The redheaded colonel became so enraged at the sight of the politician that his face reddened and he threatened to kill the congressman. Cash was restrained, and Ely was sent to Richmond, where he stayed as a prisoner of war for five months.

GWG captive to the Southerners. Ely was brought before Confederate Col. E. B. C. Cash, who °exploded with a tremendous string of oaths when he realized who he had. Accusing Ely of being one of the politicians who had caused the war, he threatened to kill him and pulled his pistol. The congressman crouched behind a sergeant so the colonel could not get a clear shot at him. It must have been quite a scene: an officer spurring his horse around a civilian crouching behind a sergeant.• The congressman survived and spent the next several months in a Confederate prison.

JJH Meanwhile, remnants of the Union army retreated twenty miles to Washington. °One Confederate wag noted after the battle that it took the Union army four days to get to Bull Run and only twelve hours to get back to Washington.• Those twelve hours were an ordeal. Reeling from exhaustion, awake for as long as thirty hours, the Federals staggered through the night.

"I suffered untold wounds from thirst and fatigue but struggled on, clinging to my gun and cartridge box," remembered Elisha Hunt Rhodes. "Many times, I sat down in the mud, determined to go on no farther, willing to die to end my misery."

As dawn broke on July 22, Union soldiers began to trickle back into the capital. Some looked behind them to see if Confederate troops were following. Luckily for the Union, Confederate President Jefferson Davis had called off a planned pursuit of the Federals back to their

Soldiers wandered into Washington for days after the battle, returning to bars and brothels rather than their camps and exchanging extraordinary tales of their participation at Bull Run. A civilian recognized a Fire Zouave near Washington market and asked, "What the devil are you doing here, got leave of absence?" The Zouave exclaimed, "No, I got the word to 'fall back' at Bull Run, and nobody has told me to halt, so I have kept on retreatin' ever since, and got away here." Within the next several weeks, as a new command structure was imposed in the capital, this undisciplined and frivolous attitude changed.

capital city. Davis recognized that his troops were as tired as the Union's, and he did not want the South to appear to be aggressive by invading Northern territory when it was telling the world that it only wanted to be left alone by an invading North.

°The civilians in Washington were shocked when they got their first look at their returning soldiers: men covered with dirt and mud, many not carrying their weapons, which had been thrown away on the battlefield. Many men were wounded and had hands, heads, and arms bandaged. The panic on their faces had to be the most demoralizing sight that a national capital could encounter. When Lincoln himself saw it, he could only say to another congressman nearby: "It's bad. It's damn bad."•

For a few anxious days Washington was gripped with fear of a Confederate attack. The Rebels, however, were far too disorganized to press their advantage. The capital remained safe, and shame over defeat and retreat gave way to a newfound determination to win at all costs. An embarrassed Lincoln, who had pressed for the battle before his army was ready, was now more determined.

°One of Lincoln's first actions, just a few days after the battle, was to issue a call for five hundred thousand volunteers, followed almost immediately with a call for another five hundred thousand volunteers to serve for three years. This call for a million men showed that Lincoln now had a much better understanding of what he was facing.•

While the North grimly wondered what to do, the South, flushed with victory, at first believed that the war

Traditionally, the photograph above (left) has been captioned Confederate Dead on Matthews Hill. It is now believed that the bodies are posed Federal soldiers. For instance, the soldier in the forefront wears a winter overcoat. No troops at Bull Run would have worn winter clothes in July. The battle for Matthews Hill included at least five stages and lasted from 10:10 A.M. to 11:40 A.M. Nearly 1,054 troops were killed or wounded from the Matthews House to the Stone House.

Two roads intersected the battlefield, Sudley Road and Warrenton Turnpike (above right). The Warrenton Pike ran east and west; the Sudley Road lay north and south. Around 11:30 A.M. the Confederates on Matthews Hill began retreating. Col. Wade Hampton's South Carolina Legion and the Seventh Georgia covered the withdrawal. They deployed on the Warrenton Pike—facing north-northwest—and threw back the Twenty-seventh New York, the Eighth New York Militia, and the Fourteenth Brooklyn. Having shielded the retirement, Hampton's Legion and the Seventh Georgia repositioned on Henry House Hill near the Robinson house.

was over. Euphoria turned to mourning as the population realized that its victorious army had suffered grievous losses and that the North had issued a call for a million-man army.

WCD   °Within a few days after the battle, the newspapers throughout the South published the lists of the boys from that county or that town who had gone to war, fought in the great battle, and who now would not be coming home. It was the first taste the Confederate civilian population had of what the war was going to be like. They had not yet heard the guns themselves and had not yet seen the blood on the battlefields, but in the black and white of newsprint, they could see the cost of the war

JIR   in which they were now engaged.• °Suddenly the romanticism of war had disappeared in the smoke and gore of one battle. The bands that had been playing so gaily were quieter now. The flags that had been flying so beautifully hung lower. This was going to be a stinking war, a war that smelled, a war with blood, a war with death.•

JJH   °After the battle was over, the men saw something that no American had ever seen before and something no American had truly expected from any war: nine hundred dead and more than three thousand wounded and missing. This battle was the emotional signal that this war would be different. It would be fought at a higher, infinitely more awesome and destructive level than anyone had expected.• What these shocked citizens could not

The battle seesawed for two hours near the Henry house, the remains of which are shown at right. Early in the conflict, Capt. James Ricketts's battery unlimbered to the right of the home. From the first floor Rebel soldiers shot at the artillerymen. Ricketts ordered his cannoneers to fire into the house. No one realized Mrs. Judith Henry, two of her children, and a servant girl were cowering upstairs. One shell burst directly in Mrs. Henry's room, wounding her in the neck and side and blowing off part of one foot. She died later that day and was buried near her house. She was eighty-five years old and the only civilian killed during the battle.

know was that the battles would get larger and more deadly. In less than eight months Shiloh would have more than twenty-three thousand casualties. In less than two years Gettysburg would generate more than fifty thousand casualties. When compared to those battles, First Manassas (there would be a Second Manassas on almost the same ground a year later) was small, but it was well remembered by its participants.

"I cannot give you an idea of the terrors of this battle," wrote Jesse Reed of the Eighth South Carolina Regiment. "For ten long hours, it literally rained balls, shells, and other missiles of destruction. The sight of the dead, the cries of the wounded, the thundering noise of battle can never be put on paper. The dead, the dying, and the wounded all mixed up together. Friend and foe embraced in death. Some crying for water. Some praying their last prayers. Some trying to whisper to a friend their last farewell message to their loved ones at home. It was heartrending. I cannot go on any further. Mine eyes are damp with tears."

Never again would Americans so blithely yell for blood. Never again would civilians flock to see their fellow countrymen shoot, stab, and slaughter one another. The young nation had begun to learn the lessons of war, but no one yet imagined what the next four years would bring.

The first Union campaign was a failure. Two days after the battle Lincoln met with Irvin McDowell. Always polite, the president said to him, "I have not lost a particle of confidence in you." By the end of the week, Lincoln had appointed Maj. Gen. George B. McClellan commander of the Division of the Potomac. McDowell was made a corps commander. The two stand in the center of this portrait of the principal generals of the army in August 1861: they are, from left to right, William F. Smith, William B. Franklin, Samuel P. Heintzelman, Andrew Porter, McDowell, McClellan, George McCall, Don Carlos Buell, Louis Blenker, Silas Casey, and Fitz John Porter.

THE *MONITOR* VS. THE *VIRGINIA*

One BATTLE IN MARCH 1862 FOREVER changed the face of naval warfare. It lasted barely four hours, few men died or were wounded, little substantial damage was done to either ship, and neither emerged as the clear-cut victor. Yet the battle between the USS *Monitor* and the CSS *Virginia* proved that the days of wooden fighting ships were over and a new type of fighting ship made of iron and steel would command the open seas.

Before the battle, skeptics called one of the combatants a "tin can on a shingle," the other a "floating barn." During the months in which both ships were being built in their respective shipyards, many believed these radically new ironclad vessels would sink the moment they touched water. Critics predicted the ships' crewmen faced certain death aboard these iron coffins, but the naysayers were wrong. On a spring day in 1862, the USS *Monitor* and the CSS *Virginia*, formerly known as the USS *Merrimack*, met in a mortal test of design and power. For more than four hours the experimental craft pounded each other with round after round, often at point-blank range. The shells ricocheted off their sides, denting the armor, but never penetrated their iron shields. Although neither ship clearly won the desperate battle, this first clash of the ironclads began a revolution in naval warfare.

The sailors engaged in that momentous battle may not have realized that they were changing history, but they did know that they were fighting for their lives. William Keeler, paymaster of the USS *Monitor*, sent detailed letters to his wife about life aboard the ironclad.

WCD	William C. Davis
DH	Dina Hill
EWP	Ernest W. Peterkin
CDR	Colan D. Ratliff
ALR	Armstead L. Robinson

Despite being small and understrength, America's pre–Civil War navy had one of the most modern, expansive naval facilities in the world—the Gosport Navy Yard in Norfolk, Virginia, a portion of which is depicted here.

In one he wrote: "The sounds of the conflict were terrible. The rapid firing of our guns amid the clouds of smoke mingled with the crash of solid shot against our sides and the bursting of shells all around us."

Ashton Ramsey, the acting chief engineer of the Confederate ironclad, had nearly the same experience and recalled: "The roar of the battle above and the thud and vibration of the huge masses of iron being hurled against us, altogether produced a scene and sound to be compared only with the poet's picture of the lower regions."

Although their recollections sound similar, these two men were writing about two very different ships. The *Virginia* was essentially a massive iron fort built on the hull of the wreck of the wooden frigate USS *Merrimack*, a six-year-old, three-thousand-ton ship that had been waiting for new engines when it was scuttled and burned at its Gosport Naval Yard dock in Norfolk, Virginia, by retreating Union soldiers and sailors in April 1861. The hulk was raised by the Confederates, an iron casement was built on the deck, and the new ship was rechristened the CSS *Virginia*. Its purpose was to smash the wooden ships surrounding Norfolk. If that were accomplished, she and others like her would cruise up and down the Atlantic destroying all of the Union's wooden fleet and thwarting the Yankee blockade. In time, or so the Federal politicians worried, one or more *Virginia*-like vessels would be built that could cruise up the Potomac River to bombard Washington itself.

The idea undergirding the ironclad was that it would be equal to ten or more wooden ships. Since an ironclad is just that, wooden ships could not damage it. In the case of the *Virginia*, the Confederates built an iron platform atop an existing wooden hull and installed the heaviest battery the structure could bear—ten huge cannon. The CSS *Virginia* was designed to wreak havoc upon all wooden warships.

The Union's *Monitor* was built to do one thing: stop the *Virginia*. The vessel's design was older than the

Virginia by several years, and it was also more controversial. While the *Virginia* was essentially an iron fort, the *Monitor* looked like a cheese box on a raft. Its iron decks rode just eighteen inches above the waterline. While the *Virginia* carried four guns on each side and one each in the bow and stern, the *Monitor* carried only two guns mounted side by side in a revolving turret.

DH   °The design of the *Monitor* was quite radical. Because the turret could be rotated without moving the ship, the two guns had the same advantage as those on a ship that could fire ten or twelve guns broadside. A vessel like this had never been seen before, and crews had never performed tasks like this crew had to perform.•

As strange looking as both ships were, their meeting CD was inevitable. After the battle of these ironclads, °the world's major navies immediately began planning the construction of ironclad fleets. The admirals of the world had been waiting for the day when wooden ships would be proven obsolete; they knew it had to happen sometime, somewhere. The conjunction of events and technology dictated that this momentous naval event happened in America at Hampton Roads in the form of a battle between the *Monitor* and the *Virginia*.•

The need for armored vessels arose in the early 1800s CDR with the advancement of explosive artillery shells—°huge hollow cannonballs that exploded when they struck a wooden ship. A few bursts of these cannonballs would tear a ship apart.• Over the next half-century, the world's ocean bottom was littered with the hulks of wooden ships that had been bested by other wooden ships that were crewed by men who were better shots with explosive shells.

When Virginia seceded on April 17, 1861, the Union abandoned Gosport and made an attempt to destroy the supplies and ships left behind. Enterprising Confederate troops, however, quickly salvaged what they could, including more than one thousand badly needed cannon and hundreds of rounds of ammunition, in addition to the remains of the USS Merrimack.

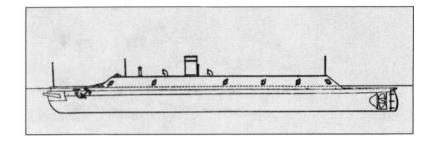

The Virginia *in profile—the sight that struck terror into the Union sailors at Hampton Roads during the morning hours of March 8, 1862. The ram-equipped fore section of the ship is at left, and the aft section containing the ship's propeller and rudder is to the right. Ventilation tubes were placed next to the smokestack, and the gun ports appear as small black dots along the hull. Unlike the* Monitor, *the* Virginia *was equipped with a variety of cannons. Her armament consisted of two 7-inch rifles, two 6-inch rifles, six 9-inch Dahlgren smoothbores, and two 12-inch howitzers. The "point" visible at the top left of the superstructure is the armored pilothouse.*

In 1859 the French built a steamer of conventional design with sides protected by four and a half inches of iron plate. The British followed with the *Warrior,* an iron-cased warship weighing more than nine thousand tons. The U.S. Navy's best effort was poor. The 420-foot *Stevens' Battery* weighed six thousand tons and carried seven guns, but the massive ship was under construction for seven years and never completed. When the Civil War started, the U.S. Navy consisted of only a few warships, most of them old, some of them obsolete, and none of them of iron.

Shortly after the war began, President Lincoln put the navy on notice that it would play a major part in defeating the Confederacy. He planned to strangle the South by blockading its Atlantic and Gulf of Mexico ports, keeping supplies and ammunition from reaching the industry-starved South.

The blockade was a bold plan, and Lincoln anticipated its success since, °for all practical purposes, the Confederacy had no navy. The South even lacked ocean-going merchant vessels that could be converted into fighting ships. Whatever force the Rebels could put on the water would have to be built from scratch with the resources at hand or purchased in other countries.•

ALR

Construction laborers hustle on the deck of the CSS Virginia *as the vessel sits near completion in a Gosport Naval Yard dry dock. Visible on the ship's prow, just below the waterline, is the iron ram, which was more feared than the ship's cannon. The superstructure—the part of the ship arising from the deck—was protected by a double layer of two-inch-thick iron plates produced at Richmond's Tredegar Iron Works over a period of five months. The armor protected the ship but also gave it a displacement of 4,636 tons, a heavy burden for its feeble steam engines. As a result the* Virginia *could only generate a paltry speed of nine knots.*

With such meager resources, the South was willing to experiment with anything. The Confederates could afford to be bold thinkers because they had nothing to lose. Chief among the innovators was Jefferson Davis's secretary of the navy, Stephen Mallory, a former U.S. senator from Florida who had followed ironclad development in Europe and who recognized its potential for the Southern cause.

"I regard the possession of an iron-armored ship as a matter of the first necessity." Mallory wrote in early 1861. "Such a vessel at this time could traverse the entire coast of the United States, prevent all blockades, and encounter, with fair prospect of success, their entire Navy." Clearly an optimist and a forward thinker compared to the aging, blue-water admirals of the North, Mallory championed the building of ironclads, the outfitting of former merchant vessels as privateers, and the purchase of blockade-runners and armed raiders from overseas manufacturers.

Although initially passed over by the Navy's Ironclad Board in favor of Ericsson's Monitor, *the USS* Galena, *pictured above, was eventually built in Mystic, Connecticut, and launched in February 1862. More conventional than the* Monitor, *the* Galena *was a modified steamship with sides sloped at forty-five-degree angles and covered with iron plates. Her baptism of fire occurred on May 15, 1862, when she sailed up the James River to bombard a Rebel fort on Drewry's Bluff, a two-hundred-foot-high prominence eight miles below Richmond. Severe plunging fire from the fort repeatedly pierced the ship's sides and caused twenty-four casualties among the crew.*

The biggest disaster to befall the Union early in the war facilitated Mallory's dream of outfitting an ironclad and also provided the armaments needed by forts throughout the South. It was the worst case of mismanagement in the history of the U.S. Navy.

For the first three months of 1861, the Union nervously monitored the situation at its Gosport Naval Yard in Norfolk, Virginia, one of the most modern naval facilities in the world, boasting dry docks and machinery for overhauling vessels. It was also the storage area for more than three thousand cannon. Estimates of the base's value ranged as high as $10 million, a tremendous sum in the 1860s. As sectional tensions rose, Northern officials were unsure what to do with Gosport. It certainly could not be moved, and any removal of the cannon to safety in the North would appear provocative since Virginia was still in the Union.

Gosport's commander was Como. Charles McCauley, an old salt who had started his naval career in the War

During his term as Confederate secretary of the navy, Stephen Russell Mallory (above) demonstrated the axiom "Necessity is the mother of invention." Mallory, who had served as a U.S. senator from Florida on the Committee on Naval Affairs before the war, literally created the Rebel navy from scratch, using ingenuity to compensate for the South's material shortcomings. In addition to ironclads like the Virginia, Mallory authorized and approved the use of submarines to harass the Federal blockading fleet and sent agents overseas in search of new naval technologies that might be used on his ships.

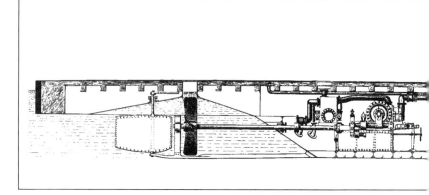

of 1812. He took literally his orders not to agitate the people of Norfolk with any actions that could be interpreted as warlike and made few efforts to defend Gosport, even as Virginia moved toward secession after the attack on Fort Sumter and President Lincoln's call for seventy-five thousand volunteers to invade the seceding states. At one point, McCauley even refused permission for the ships in Gosport to leave because he thought it would insult the people of Norfolk. Not long after that, Virginia seceded from the Union, and Gosport was suddenly in foreign—and enemy—territory.

Finally, another old sailor, Como. Hiram Paulding, was ordered to Norfolk to salvage what he could and destroy the rest. Several ships, including the *Merrimack*, were set on fire and scuttled, and an attempt was made to destroy the cannon. Afterward, the Confederates salvaged at least half of the guns and immediately shipped them to Southern forts in the Carolinas, Tennessee, and Arkansas. Confederate salvagers began appraising the burned hulk of the *Merrimack*, which was lying just below the surface of the water. While the Federals thought they had wrecked the ship, the Confederates saw an opportunity.

WCD   °In a stroke of inspired genius, the Southerners realized that raising the *Merrimack* would trim months off the proposed building schedule. Instead of constructing a ship from scratch, they would build an ironclad on the top of this former Yankee ship.•

The architects of the ironclad were Confederate Lt. John M. Brooke, who was also a designer of a new type

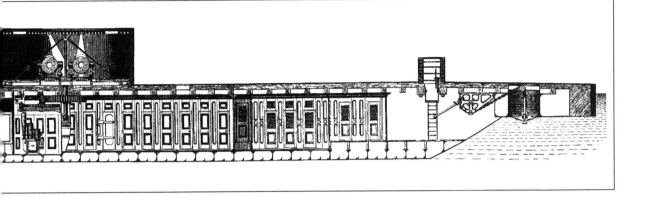

of cannon that would prove useful to the South, and naval contractor John L. Porter. Their design was simple but effective. The iron housing, or casemate, looked something like the roof of a barn built on top of a boat. °The casemate frame was covered with twenty-four inches of solid oak over which two layers of two-inch iron plate were placed, adding four inches of iron to protect the ship's crew and armament.●

The armor was sloped at a thirty-five degree angle to deflect enemy fire. Inside were ten cannon of varying sizes, four on each side, and a pivot gun on each end. All had been cast for the U.S. Navy, and all had been salvaged from captured Gosport.

The cannon, however, were not the most fearsome weapons of the ship when it was modified and renamed *Virginia*. °Greater hope for doing terrible destruction to Yankee ships was placed in the iron ram, or beak, on the prow of the vessel. Placed about a foot and a half below the waterline, the ram was like a massive iron tooth that would be driven into the bowels of an enemy wooden ship. The hole would be too large to plug, and the victim ship would sink.●

Throughout the summer and fall of 1861, more than fifteen hundred workers labored around the clock to complete the vessel. The ship's sides were covered with more than 750 tons of iron plate produced by the Tredegar Ironworks of Richmond,

For novelty, the Monitor equaled and perhaps surpassed the appearance of the Virginia. This improbable-looking ship, seen above in one of Ericsson's blueprints, was little more than a gun turret affixed to a floating platform. Its functional nature lacked the romantic lines of traditional sailing vessels, and those who saw the craft were little impressed. The cross-section engraving of the innovative turret below shows one of the two massive 11-inch Dahlgren smoothbore cannon installed in the revolving structure. Formidable weapons, their shells could have penetrated the Virginia's armor if the Federals had used the 30-pound powder charge recommended for the guns. Eight overlapping one-inch plates shielded the turret, making it impervious to most weaponry of the era.

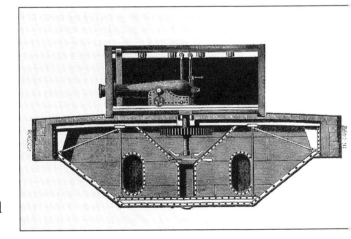

An anxious North first glimpsed the rough image of the Monitor *in the above* Harper's Weekly *illustration. Although the features were distorted, the ungainliness of the vessel could not have been emphasized more. One Union soldier called it a "most ridiculous looking craft" and compared it to a "cheese box . . . on a pumpkin seed."*

The ship's eccentric inventor, John Ericsson (below), proved to be a vital asset to the Union navy despite his irascible nature. After serving in Sweden's navy, he came to America in 1839. The Swede designed the Princeton, *America's first steam-powered warship, but his fortunes suffered when a cannon on this ship exploded, killing several dignitaries, and he was blamed for the accident. It was not until 1861 that Ericsson again submitted a ship design to the Navy Department.*

WCD

WCD

one of the few modern foundries in the South. Strangely, although the *Virginia* was meant to be a weapon that would defeat the North, little was done to keep its construction a secret. Southern newspapers followed the shipbuilding progress in print, much to the satisfaction of Southern readers and the fright of Northerners.

"Her great size, strength, and powerful engines and speed combined with invulnerability secured by the iron casting will make the dispersal or the destruction of the blockading fleet an easy task for her. We hope soon to hear that she is ready to commence her revenging career on the seas," wrote an editor of the *Mobile (Ala.) Register*. He was only partially right. The *Virginia* might have been huge and maybe even invulnerable to the fire of wooden ships, but it did not have "powerful engines." In fact, the ship had been stranded in Gosport for months because its engines were badly in need of an overhaul. Lying in the muddy water for weeks had not improved the vessel's power plant.

THROUGHOUT THE NORTH rumors spread about an iron monster being built by the Confederacy. Panic began to build, both with the public and the government officials charged with conducting the war. °Northern newspapers were full of accounts of this dreadful iron behemoth under construction in the South. The great fear in the North was that this vessel would steam up the Atlantic Coast and bombard Washington and wreak havoc wherever it went.• It was clear that the North had to counter the *Virginia*; the North needed its own ironclad. To that end Secretary of the Navy Gideon Welles established a board to field proposals for a new ship, although the enterprise seemed to have been a low priority at first. The board advertised for bids from contractors for an ironclad with two masts for sail-rigging even though steamships had been around for years. The advertisement was buried in one newspaper beneath an ad for women's clothing.

°Seventeen designs, most of them impractical, were submitted. Several basic designs showed the most

As this illustration (left) reveals, the bulk of the Virginia's mass was below the waterline. The superstructure of the ship that could be seen was like the proverbial tip of the iceberg. The wooden hull was what remained of the burned-out USS Merrimack. Although it lacked armor protection, the hull was crammed with crew quarters, ammunition lockers, coal bunkers, and the steam-driven machinery that powered the vessel.

promise, including one to sheath a conventional warship in iron much like clapboard siding, with one sheet of iron laid partially over the other. This ship even had a name, the *Galena*. Its inventor, Cornelius Bushnell, was told that he should get a second opinion assessing if the *Galena* could support the weight of the armor he suggested.

Bushnell chose to consult with Swedish immigrant inventor John Ericsson of New York. Ericsson was credited with numerous breakthrough inventions, including the screw propeller, but Ericsson hated the navy, and the navy hated him. The hard feelings dated back to 1844, when an experimental cannon, designed by an Ericsson partner, exploded onboard an Ericsson-designed ship, the USS *Princeton*. Among the men killed were the secretary of the navy and the man in charge of purchasing the vessel. Although it was not his fault, the navy blamed Ericsson. Not only did the navy not honor his bill for the design of the ship, naval authorities stole his patent on the screw propeller, adapting it for their ships but never paying for its use.

Ericsson had not set foot in the Navy Department for more than fifteen years when he heard about the search for an ironclad. He sent a letter offering to design one, but the letter was never answered. When Bushnell visited, °in the course of their discussion, Ericsson almost offhandedly asked if he would like to see the design for a virtually impregnable warship made of iron. Ericsson then pulled out a dusty cardboard model of a ship he had designed years earlier. It looked like a round cheese box on a raft. The cheese box was to be a rotating gun

An experienced "salt," Franklin Buchanan (below), the Virginia's commander, had entered the U.S. Navy in 1814. After serving the Confederate navy in an administrative capacity, he was placed in charge of the Chesapeake Bay Squadron in February 1862 and chose the Virginia as his flagship. Wounded during the battle with the Congress (interestingly, Buchanan's brother—McKean—served as an officer on the Congress at the time), Buchanan missed the duel with the Monitor. Later promoted to admiral, Buchanan was placed in charge of the defenses of Mobile Bay, Alabama. He tried unsuccessfully to defend the bay during Union Adm. David Farragut's 1864 attack, although he fought desperately and suffered another injury in the engagement.

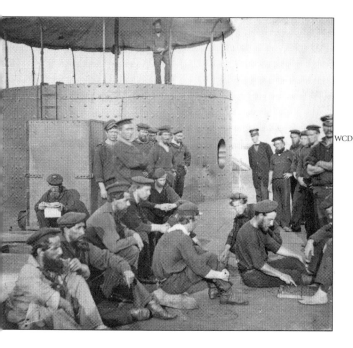

A group of the Monitor's battle-tested "tars," or crewmen, relax on the iron-clad's deck by reading, playing games, or smoking pipes in this photograph taken on July 9, 1862, as the vessel lay at anchor in the James River. Most of these crewmen were probably civilians at the beginning of the conflict, for the U.S. Navy only had 7,600 seamen and 90 ships in 1861. By 1865, however, nearly 133,000 sailors had served on 716 ships for the Union cause, an unprecedented increase fueled by the needs of war. Of additional interest in this photograph is the canvas canopy shading the top of the turret and the gun port visible on the turret's right side.

platform protected by a dome of iron, an innovation he had suggested in 1854 to France's Napoleon III.

Bushnell was immediately impressed, but he knew that Ericsson himself would have a difficult time selling the invention because of his reputation as °an egotistical, annoying, and difficult man whom no one liked• and his history of disputes with the Navy Department. Bushnell asked if he could take Ericsson's design to Washington. In September 1861, Bushnell chose to bypass the navy and went directly to the White House with Ericsson's model. The president, who enjoyed the consideration of new weapons so much that he often tested new rifles himself, was impressed. "All I have to say is what the girl said when she put her foot in the stocking: 'Strikes me there's something in it,'" Lincoln said as he ordered that the model be evaluated by the ironclad board.

The president's recommendation carried little weight with the board, which resisted the unconventional design. Incensed that the navy men had so little imagination, Ericsson went to Washington, a place he had not visited since the explosion in 1844. Showing the confidence and cockiness that had always been his trademark and his downfall, Ericsson demanded, "Gentlemen, after what I have said, I consider it to be your duty to the country to give me an order to build the vessel before I leave this room."

The board finally approved Ericsson's design but buried a clause in the contract that the inventor did not notice. It stipulated that if the vessel did not work out as promised, Ericsson would be personally responsible for refunding all the Federal money spent on developing the ironclad. Construction began on October 25, 1861, on what was called "Ericsson's impregnable battery." Later, near the time it was launched, it acquired the name *Monitor* after Ericsson wrote that he intended the ship to be a monitor on the intentions of Southern politicians.

DH ○The *Monitor* incorporated a number of innovations, including a very shallow draft, because it was designed primarily for river and harbor defense. Speed would not be the vessel's specialty; it made only eight knots. The ship rode very low in the

EWP water,• ○with only eighteen inches of free-board—the distance between the deck and

DH the surface of the water.• ○Virtually all of the vessel was below the water: engines, crew's quarters, officers' quarters, galley, and magazine.• ○The design placed little above the water's surface to shoot at other than the nine-foot-tall turret, which housed two 11-inch Dahlgren cannon, and a small pilothouse forward of the turret from which the captain and the helmsman would guide the ship.• To protect the deck and underwater portions of the vessel even more, an overhanging sheath of armor extended from the deck five feet below the waterline so no cannonball fired into the water could harm it. This also protected the ship from ramming, although with only eighteen inches above the water, a ramming attempt would prob-ably take any assailant completely over the *Monitor*.

What intrigued other designers was the rotating turret, married to the deck of the ship by a close-fitting ring. The idea was that the turret, which could rotate two and a

EWP half times per minute, ○would allow the body of the vessel to take any position, while the turret would be rotated to aim the guns at any target.• The turret was twenty-one feet in diameter with armor eight inches thick. It weighed 120 tons. The cannon were mounted side by side so one could be firing while the other was being reloaded, a five-minute operation. To move the turret, a "donkey engine" would jack it up from the ring, crank it around by meshing teeth on the turret to teeth on the deck, then drop it back into place for firing.

Much to Ericsson's disgust, the navy forced him to use 11-inch diameter cannon instead of the 15-inch guns he wanted, although 11-inch guns were still the largest naval guns afloat. On top of that, it forbade him to charge the cannon with more than fifteen pounds of black powder,

The gun crew of the Virginia is depicted in this inaccurate engraving that appeared in the Illustrated London News. *While the artist shows an orderly and calm atmosphere, in reality the stale, fetid air of the gun deck was dense with smoke and the stench of sweating, toiling gunners who had stripped off their shirts to alleviate the searing heat generated by the ship's boilers. Moreover, the guns depicted here are English-made Arm-strong breech-loading rifles. Fortu-nately for the crew of the* Monitor, *such powerful weapons were not installed on the* Virginia.

The handsome tri-masted frigate USS Cumberland lists heavily to port as she fires a futile blast at the Virginia and begins to slide beneath the waters of Hampton Roads, the first victim of the powerful Confederate ironclad's onslaught. Although some of her four hundred crewmen can be seen leaping from the doomed ship and floating away in lifeboats, others stayed with the vessel, firing salvos until the ship sank. Thus they fulfilled the reported request of Lt. Comdr. George Morris, the ship's captain, to "give them a broadside boys, as she goes!"

half the charge the guns were designed to handle. The old admirals feared that the noise and concussion of such huge cannon and large powder charges would kill the crew. Rather than argue, Ericsson agreed and moved on with the construction of the ship.

To complete this monumental task, Ericsson used the innovative technique of subcontracting. He farmed out the construction to various builders throughout the North and visited the contractors to ensure they were building the ship to his specifications. They were glad he did; Ericsson's penmanship was terrible, and some of his design notes were indecipherable. In just 120 days, the *Monitor* was complete. °It was launched in front of invited guests, some of whom expected the vessel to sink immediately.• A confident Ericsson stood on the deck during the launch. Still, he or someone on Ericsson's staff was not absolutely certain all would go well. A rowboat was nearby to fish the inventor out of the water in the event "Ericsson's Folly," as critics called it, did go straight to the bottom. On January 30, 1862, in Green Point, New York, the *Monitor* slid down the ways exactly as Ericsson had planned.

Rather than congratulate Ericsson, the navy abruptly instructed him to prepare the ship for combat; however, Assistant Secretary of the Navy Gustavus Fox was more encouraging as he told the eccentric inventor, "I congratulate you and trust you will be a success. Hurry her for sea, as the *Merrimack* is nearly ready at Norfolk, and we wish to send her there."

Although Ericsson was the ship's inventor, there were never any plans for him to command the *Monitor* himself. That new duty went to Lt. John Worden, a veteran of the U.S. Navy since 1834. His executive officer was twenty-one-year-old Lt. Samuel Dana Greene, who would command the guns in the turret. Fifty-eight crewmen were given positions on the new ship.

"Dear Anna, yesterday I saw my iron home for the first time," wrote the ship's paymaster, Keeler. "I shall not attempt a description of it now, but you may rest assured your better half will be in no more danger from Rebel compliments than if he were seated at home with you."

ON FEBRUARY 20, Lieutenant Worden received his sailing orders from the secretary of the navy, Gideon Welles: "Proceed with the U.S. steamer *Monitor* under your command to Hampton Roads, Virginia."

Waiting there would be the *Virginia*, finally ready after nine months of construction, three times as long as it took to build the *Monitor*, a fact that reflected the lack of industrial technology that would hamper the South throughout the war. The two ships had nothing in common other than being ironclad. The *Virginia* was 262 feet long, 90 feet longer than the *Monitor*. It was four times heavier, which made the *Virginia*'s weak, cantankerous engines work very hard just to move it. More critically, the Southern ironclad had a draft of twenty-two feet, more than twice that of the *Monitor*. While cruising, her pilot had to be constantly aware of the location of sandbars so the ship would not run aground.

On March 8 the *Virginia* steamed out of Gosport Navy Yard on its maiden voyage. This was not a shakedown cruise. It was time to take back the waters around Norfolk from the Yankee blockaders.

"In an instant, the whole city was in an uproar. Women, children, men on horseback and on foot,

With decks awash in blood, water, tangled rigging, and mangled men and her wooden sides turned into kindling by the guns of the Virginia, *the* Cumberland *begins to sink. Prior to her violent end, the* Cumberland *had enjoyed a productive career in the U.S. Navy. Launched from the Boston Navy Yard in 1842, the frigate had served in the Mediterranean, in the Gulf of Mexico, and off of the coast of Africa before the Civil War. During this period, future Union naval heroes Andrew H. Foote and John A. Dahlgren had served aboard the vessel. After the bombardment of Fort Sumter, the* Cumberland *served in the North Atlantic Blockading Squadron until her sinking on March 8.*

running down towards the river from every conceivable direction shouting: 'The *Merrimack* is going down!'" exclaimed a story in the *Norfolk Daybook* newspaper.

In command was Capt. Franklin Buchanan, a forty-six-year naval veteran who had been the first superintendent of the U.S. Naval Academy in Annapolis. Buchanan had resigned his commission early in the war when he thought Maryland was going to secede from the Union. When it did not, Buchanan tried to get his commission back. Naval Secretary Welles refused, citing Buchanan's wavering loyalty between his state and his nation. Buchanan's executive officer was Lt. Catesby Jones, a naval ordnance expert. Another officer was Lt. John Taylor Wood, the grandson of former President Zachary Taylor. The crew of the *Virginia* numbered 350 men, more than six times what it took to run the *Monitor*, a reflection of the additional sailors needed to crew ten cannon, as opposed to the two on the *Monitor*. Although

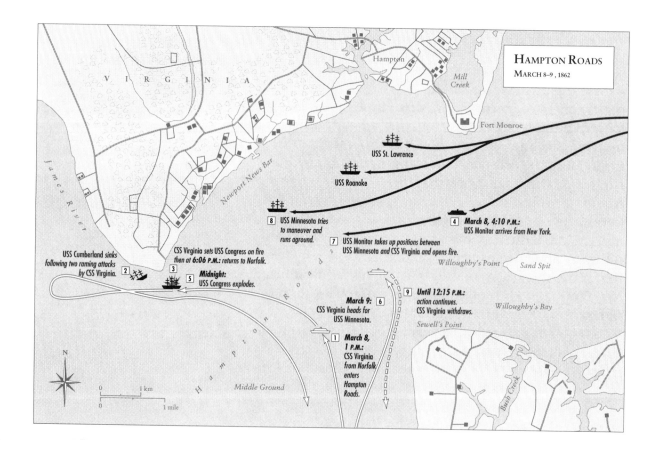

HAMPTON ROADS
MARCH 8–9, 1862

Hampton
Mill Creek
Fort Monroe

USS St. Lawrence

USS Roanoke

VIRGINIA

Newport News Bar

James River

8 USS Minnesota tries to maneuver and runs aground.

4 March 8, 4:10 P.M.: USS Monitor arrives from New York.

7 USS Monitor takes up positions between USS Minnesota and CSS Virginia and opens fire.

Willoughby's Point   Sand Spit

USS Cumberland sinks following two raming attacks by CSS Virginia.

CSS Virginia sets USS Congress on fire then at 6:06 P.M.: returns to Norfolk.

2

3

5 Midnight: USS Congress explodes.

March 9: 6 CSS Virginia heads for USS Minnesota.

9 Until 12:15 P.M.: action continues. CSS Virginia withdraws.

Willoughby's Bay

Sewell's Point

1 March 8, 1 P.M.: CSS Virginia from Norfolk enters Hampton Roads.

N

0   1 km
0   1 mile

Middle Ground

Hampton Roads

Bush Creek

the ship would no doubt be formidable, not everyone was impressed with the *Virginia*.

"From the start we saw that she was slow, not over five knots. She steered so badly that with her great length it took from thirty to forty minutes to turn around. She was as unmanageable as a waterlogged vessel," wrote Wood.

The major problems—too deep of a draft, great weight, and sluggish steering—were not as critical as the *Virginia*'s poor engines. What the Confederates may not have known, and something they could not have done anything about anyway, was that °the engine plants had been designed for only short periods of steaming,• principally when the ship was nearing harbors or during periods of becalming. The *Merrimack* had been a magnificent wooden sailing ship, but it had been a very bad steamship.

In spite of its problems, the *Virginia* headed for Hampton Roads and the blockading Yankee fleet. There was work to do as the captain, bitter toward the Federal navy, explained: "Sailors, in a few minutes you'll have the long-expected opportunity to show your devotion to our cause. Remember that you are about to strike for your country, for your homes, for your wives, and for your children."

The captain made some last-minute additions to the ship. When an officer suggested that the *Virginia* might be boarded, Buchanan had the top and sides of the casement slathered in pig fat so any boarders would slide off.

The Federal fleet knew the *Virginia* was coming long before they could see it. The sailors had heard the rumors about the construction of the giant ship. When they saw a huge plume of black smoke coming down the Elizabeth River, they knew it was time for action. Waiting for the *Virginia* were °four vessels: the *Cumberland, Congress, Minnesota,* and *Roanoke,* which were big, powerful wooden warships. As soon as the *Virginia* came within range of the guns on the Federal fleet, they began to fire at it, but their firing was ineffectual. The Federal cannonballs merely bounced off, thanks to the iron, the angle at which it was mounted, and maybe the addition of the fat from several hundred pigs. The *Virginia* kept coming,

CDR

WCD

John Worden, the Monitor's captain, had been captured by Rebel forces shortly after the war's outbreak and served for seven months in Confederate prisons. After being exchanged, Worden accepted the command of Ericsson's craft and did a commendable job training his crew in the nuances of the experimental vessel. During the engagement on March 8, a well-placed shot blinded Worden as he stood in the Monitor's pilothouse. Although his sight eventually returned, his wounding added to the dramatic nature of the engagement and made him a hero in the North. In July 1862 he was awarded the Thanks of Congress and made a commander in the U.S. Navy. Worden stayed in the navy after the war and retired in 1886 as a rear admiral.

103

With the Cumberland *destroyed, Buchanan turned the* Virginia *toward his next victim, the USS* Congress. *The* Congress *had also been commissioned in 1842, and her forty-eight 32-pound cannon had hurled iron at the enemy during several Mexican War battles. This was a different war, however, and her once-feared broadsides now bounced harmlessly off the iron titan bearing down upon her. As a last desperate measure, the Congress hauled up her anchor and tried to flee, but the ship soon ran aground and was pummeled by the* Virginia's *fire. Before the day ended, 120 crewmen of the* Congress *were dead, and the ship burned to the waterline.*

firing its own guns but obviously aiming to ram the first ship it could find.•

Captain Buchanan chose his first target, the USS *Cumberland.* The ship was a sloop of war, mounting twenty-four cannon, which were rumored to be of the latest rifled design. Buchanan considered those guns a threat, something that might be able to penetrate his armor. The *Cumberland's* sailors knew what they were in for when they saw the ironclad heading their way. The fine shooting of the Confederate cannon crews doomed the ship from the opening rounds.

"The shot and the shell from the *Merrimack* crashed through the wooden sides of the *Cumberland* as if they had been made of paper, carrying huge splinters with them and dealing death and destruction on every hand. The once clean and beautiful deck was slippery with blood, blackened with powder, and looked like a slaughter house," said Charles O'Neil of the *Cumberland.*

The cannon fire was the least of the *Cumberland* crew's problems. "[The *Virginia*] looked like a huge, half-submerged crocodile. At her prow, I could see the iron ram projecting straight forward. It was impossible for our vessel to get out of her way," wrote A. B. Smith of the *Cumberland.*

The *Virginia* drove its iron ram deep into the *Cumberland,* and the wooden ship began to sink immediately. The *Virginia* was also being dragged down because the iron ram had jammed inside the Federal vessel. Finally, the ram broke off, and the *Virginia* pulled away with its most formidable weapon now lost following its first use. Buchanan called out to the acting captain of the *Cumberland,* asking him to strike his colors in surrender. The Union man refused and fought on until the *Cumberland's* hull sank beneath the water, with the tops of its masts sticking out. More than one-third of the *Cumberland's* crew, 121 men, went down with the ship. Observers, both Confederate and Union, said that the *Cumberland's* crew stayed at their cannon and fired right up until the water washed into their barrels. Still flying from one of the masts was an American flag, the colors the captain refused to haul down in defeat. Nevertheless, the mastery of iron ships over wooden vessels had been proven.

WCD ° Once the *Cumberland* was out of the way, the *Virginia* turned its attention to the USS *Congress*, a much more formidable ship, a frigate of fifty guns, which was more than twice the firepower the *Cumberland* had. The *Congress* caught fire from incendiary shells fired at it, and it soon became unmanageable.• The men aboard the *Congress* had seen what had happened to the *Cumberland*, and with the captain dead the crew surrendered. As Confederate escort ships pulled alongside to rescue the crew of the *Congress*, they came under fire from Federal shore batteries and soldiers close enough to the action to take potshots at the ships.

Meanwhile, aboard the *Virginia*, Captain Buchanan left the safety of the iron casement, apparently to get a better look at the Confederates' attempts to rescue the Federals. He went up to the promenade deck where he was wounded by a Federal sharpshooter. Angered that he would be shot during what he considered a humanitarian mission to rescue sailors who might drown, Buchanan relinquished his command to Lt. Catesby Jones with orders to continue the incendiary shelling.

WCD ° Jones saw that his mission was to go after the *Minnesota*, which, in the panic to get away from the *Virginia*, had run aground.• As he took stock of his own vessel, Jones realized that he had some damage and an exhausted crew. Daylight was also fading, making it difficult for the pilots to avoid the shoals and sandbars. Jones decided to return to port and wait until morning to destroy the *Minnesota*.

While the *Virginia* enjoyed its successful first day of combat, the *Monitor* was coming down the coast to meet it, but the voyage was a struggle. Early on the day the *Virginia* had engaged the wooden Union ships, the *Monitor* encountered rough weather. Its low freeboard allowed the seas to wash over the deck, and the vessel began leaking

The stumpy and the graceful representing the future and the past of naval warfare appear in juxtaposition as the Monitor *bobs protectively next to the marooned* Minnesota *after the Yankee ironclad's arrival on March 8. Although the* Minnesota *remained stuck on the sandbar throughout March 9 and suffered additional damage from the* Virginia's *guns, she was eventually refloated and repaired. In the winter of 1864–65 the* Minnesota *took part in the operations that reduced Fort Fisher, closing the port of Wilmington, North Carolina, to Confederate use. She served the U.S. Navy in various capacities until intentionally burned in 1901.*

badly. At one point, water poured down the blower stacks and extinguished the boiler fires. Flooding was so bad in the engine room that there was some thought that the ship might become a death trap.

"The fires burned with a sickly blaze, converting all the air in the engine and fire rooms into carbonic acid gas, a few inhalations of which are sufficient to destroy animal life," wrote Alvin Stimers, a naval engineer assigned to the *Monitor.*

WCD The crew was not taking any chances on the newfangled ship. °Most of them made their way to the upper deck, knowing they did not want to be caught below with the water coming in. The *Monitor* came close to foundering.• Frantic pumping controlled the flooding, and the ship was saved. By 9:00 P.M. on March 8, the evening of the *Virginia*'s first battle, the *Monitor* steamed into Hampton Roads. That afternoon, as they were making their way south, the *Monitor*'s crew had watched what they assumed to be the clouds of cannon smoke coming from Hampton Roads. They knew the *Virginia* was attacking the fleet.

The aftermath of the *Virginia*'s attack was shocking to the *Monitor*'s crew. "We could see the fine old *Congress* burning brightly. Sadly indeed did we feel to think those two fine old vessels had gone to their last homes with so many of their brave crews. Our hearts were so very full, and we vowed vengeance to the *Merrimack*," asserted Lt. Samuel Greene, the *Monitor*'s executive officer.

At 8 A.M. on the morning of March 9 the Virginia *chugged slowly back into Hampton Roads, intent on bludgeoning to death the stranded* Minnesota *before it turned on the other Union ships in the area. The* Monitor, *however, thwarted these plans, and the two ships soon commenced their famous four-hour duel. Xanthus R. Smith, who had served in the Union navy on a traditional wooden warship during the conflict, created the oil painting below of the engagement in 1869. Symbolically, the* Virginia *appears shaded and ominous, surrounded by clouds of dark smoke— depicted by Smith as the incarnation of evil. In contrast, the* Monitor *floats in full sunshine, further illumed by brilliant plumes of white smoke.*

AS MORNING BRIGHTENED on March 9, 1862, the crew of the *Virginia* had no idea that the *Monitor* had arrived the previous night under cover of darkness. The Confederate ironclad steamed confidently into Hampton Roads, its crew secure in the belief that they were invincible since no cannon from any of the wooden ships had penetrated their vessel's armor. The wounds the previous day had come from lucky shots hitting the gun ports and from stray wooden splinters.

The *Virginia*'s crew knew that no traditional warship could harm them. Once they finished with the hard-aground *Minnesota*—a giant wooden target—they planned to move on to the other wooden ships. If they were successful in breaking the blockade at Hampton Roads, Confederate Secretary of the Navy Mallory was already contemplating attacks on Washington and New York City in the belief that if the average Northern citizens saw what the *Virginia* could do, they would demand peace at once.

What the *Virginia*'s crew had not counted on was that the *Minnesota* was no longer defenseless. At its side was the little *Monitor,* poised to do battle against the Confederate giant. The Southerners were surprised to see the little ship pull into view.

"We looked eagerly out over the bay," wrote John Ableston of the *Virginia*. "There was the *Minnesota* lying aground where she had struck the evening before, and near her was the strangest looking craft we had ever seen before." James Rochelle of the CSS *Patrick Henry,* one of the small wooden escort vessels that accompanied the ironclad on its deadly mission, added: "Such a craft the eyes of a seaman never looked upon before. An immense shingle floating on the water with a gigantic cheese box rising from its center. No sails, no wheels, no smokestack, no guns. What could it be?"

°Not only was the *Virginia*'s crew not expecting to see the *Monitor,* they seemed not to have noticed it until the *Monitor* fired its first shot. Through their glasses they saw what some took to be a boiler or part of an engine being

WCD

Like two faceless monsters from the nether regions, the ironclad behemoths steamed toward each other, their hulls at times scraping together as the ships exchanged fearsome volleys. From the slits in the *Monitor's* small pilothouse, visible on the ship's foredeck, Captain Worden tried to observe the progress of the battle through thick clouds of battle smoke. A well-placed shot from the *Virginia* struck the pilothouse while Worden was peering out from the structure, knocking the Union officer blinded and senseless to the floor. Samuel D. Greene then succeeded Worden in command.

As the Virginia *and her escort ships steamed down the James River toward Hampton Roads, the Rebel garrisons of the numerous water batteries lining the watercourse turned out to cheer on their metal-sheathed champion (above). The mere presence of the Confederate ironclad had helped keep such batteries inactive, as the captains of Yankee ships were afraid to sail too far up the James lest they run into the feared vessel. Other Union officials, including Secretary of War Edwin Stanton, were initially so afraid of this innovative ship that plans were made to block the Potomac River with sunken barges to prevent the* Virginia *from shelling Washington. Such plans were cancelled when it was learned the ship could not navigate the shallow Potomac.*

removed from the *Minnesota*. They thought the puff of smoke that was the first shot was the boiler exploding.• "You can see surprise on a ship just the same as you can see it on a human being, and there was surprise all over the *Merrimack*," wrote Peter Truscott of the *Monitor*.

The crew of the *Virginia* was disappointed that they would not be able to finish their mission with the wooden ships, but they were not shocked that this new threat had appeared. "The *Monitor* could not possibly have made her appearance at a more inopportune time," commented Lt. John Taylor Wood on the *Virginia*. The two vessels closed on each other. The crew of the *Monitor* was probably more nervous because this would be the first test of their armor.

Paymaster William Keeler of the *Monitor* remembered: "I experienced a peculiar sensation. I do not think it was fear, but it was different from anything I ever knew before. We were enclosed in what we supposed to be an impenetrable armor. We knew that a powerful foe was about to meet us. Ours was an untried experiment, and our enemy's first fire might make it a coffin for all of us. Everyone was at his post, fixed like a statue. The most profound silence reigned. If there had been a coward heart there, its throb would have been audible, so intense was the stillness."

"The *Merrimack* was quick to reply, returning her rattling broadside, and the battle fairly began. The turrets and other parts of the ship were heavily struck, but the shots did not penetrate," wrote executive officer Samuel Dana Greene of the *Monitor*. "A look of confidence passed over the men's faces, and we believed the *Merrimack* would not repeat the work she had accomplished the day before."

°For two hours the two ships gave each other their undivided attention, with the *Monitor* ignoring the *Virginia*'s wooden ship escort and the *Virginia* ignoring the grounded *Minnesota*. The superiority of the *Monitor*'s engines became immediately apparent as it literally steamed circles around the *Virginia*.• °The Yankee ironclad also had the advantage of its much shallower draft. Thus the Federal helmsman did not have to watch the channels as closely to keep from running aground. Because only the turret had to be moved to bring its guns to bear on the *Virginia*, the *Monitor* could fire quicker. The Southern ironclad, however, had to be maneuvered into position to fire on the *Monitor*.• Maneuvering did not really matter; the two were almost touching sides.

"The fight continued with the exchange of broadsides as fast as the guns could be served and at very short range. The distance between the vessels frequently not more than a few yards," wrote executive officer Green of the *Monitor*.

As the fight wore on, some of the iron plates on the *Virginia* began to crack and the wooden backing splintered. On the *Monitor* the turret was dented, but the iron was holding. The crew of the *Virginia* knew they had met their match.

"The *Monitor* circled around and around us receiving our fire as she went delivering her own. We saw our shells burst into fragments against her turret. I find I can do the *Monitor* as much damage by snapping my finger at her every five minutes," said an exasperated John Ableston on the *Virginia*.

Officers of the Monitor *sit proudly in front of the ship's turret in a photo taken in July 1862. In the front row, from left to right, are Robinson Hands, Albert Campbell, and Edwin V. Gager. Seated behind them are Master Louis N. Stodder, paymaster William Keeler, William Flye, and (at the far right) surgeon Daniel C. Logue. Standing to the rear are George Frederickson, Mark Sunstrom, Lt. Samuel D. Greene, an unidentified visitor, and Isaac Newton.*

Opposite page: The Monitor *won a tactical victory over the* Virginia *by preventing the further destruction of the Union fleet blockading Hampton Roads. This perceived success generated a rampant enthusiasm in the North for similar vessels, a kind of "Monitor fever." Within three weeks of the battle, Ericsson received orders for six enlarged and improved* Monitor-*type vessels and similar orders were placed by the Navy Department with other builders. Some people, however, saw the ironclads as harbingers of man's increasing subservience to machinery. A section of a Herman Melville poem entitled* A Utilitarian View of the Monitor's Fight, *for example, reads: "War yet shall be, but warriors / Are now but operatives; War's made / Less grand than Peace."*

Federal naval officers—one of whom wears a nonregulation wide-brimmed straw hat to shield himself from the scorching southern sun—and sailors pose on the deck of the Monitor, *observing large dents, visible to the left of the gun ports, made in the turret by shells fired from the Virginia's cannons. On the foredeck, part of the armored pilothouse is visible to the left of the sailor standing with his hand on his hip. The Monitor's low freeboard is emphasized by how closely the ship's deck sits to the water of the James River.*

The pig fat that had coated the outside of the *Virginia* began to take its toll on the men within the Confederate ironclad. As each Federal shell struck the side of the *Virginia*, it would heat the fat, making it sizzle and smell. The odor wafted down into the *Virginia*, not helping the atmosphere, which was already filled with the stench of smoke, gunpowder, sweat, and blood. One Federal seaman, close enough to inhale the scorching pig fat, asked a mate what that awful stench was. "The smell of hell," the other Yankee sailor replied.

WCD   °The atmosphere inside the *Virginia* once the battle was underway was like a scene out of Dante's *Inferno*. The guns blazed away. Powder smoke was everywhere. It was incredibly hot. The men of the cannon crews had stripped to the waist, the only way they could combat the heat.•

Aboard the *Monitor,* conditions in the turret were just as bad. °Tremendous noises deafened the gunners as the shots rang off the iron armor. They heard the sound of the *Virginia* firing and the Confederate shells exploding against their own armor as the vessels were at point-blank range during the four-hour battle. The noise and the heat were tremendous. At times the gunners in the turret could not see because the smoke was so thick.•

EWP °Even though the *Monitor* had forced ventilation, it was at least 120 degrees in the turret and even higher in the engine room. The biggest problem, aside from heat exhaustion, was concussion. A gunner who was leaning against the turret bulkhead when a projectile hit it from the outside was knocked out.•

DH   °Despite its tremendous promise, the turret did not work as well as was hoped. It was difficult to begin to rotate it because the donkey engine that controlled it was underpowered. Once the turret started to move, however, it was difficult to stop it. The Union gunners started shooting on the fly, timing their blasts to hit where they thought the *Virginia* was.•

About two hours into the battle, the *Virginia* lost track of its position and ran aground. °Worden, the captain on the *Monitor,* saw this, so he maneuvered his ship into a position from which none of the *Virginia*'s guns could be brought to bear against him. The *Monitor* fired shot after shot into the *Virginia*'s casemate in hopes of cracking the armor. The Southern crew knew they were in trouble.•

"Our situation was critical," wrote acting chief engineer Ashton Ramsey of the *Virginia.* "We had to take our chances. We lashed down the safety valves. Heat quickly burning combustibles into the already raging fires brought the boilers to a pressure that would have been unsafe under ordinary circumstances. The propeller churned the mud and water furiously, but the ship did not stir. It seemed impossible that the boilers could stand the pressure we were crowding upon them. Just as we were beginning to despair, there was a perceptible movement, and the *Merrimack* [even the crew sometimes referred to the ship by its old navy name] slowly dragged herself off the shoal. We were saved."

Unable to seriously damage each other with cannon fire, each ship tried ramming the other, but with little result. Then the *Virginia* fired the single most effective shot of the battle.

Pungent coal smoke wafts across the deck of the Monitor *as sailors prepare their dinner on a portable cookstove assembled on the deck. When the ship hoisted anchor, such stoves could be quickly taken apart for storage below decks. The average sailor, North or South, spent the bulk of his time engaged in such mundane, yet necessary, tasks. Note the African-American sailor squatting in the center of the photo. Unlike the Federal army, which remained segregated throughout the conflict, the U.S. Navy had been integrated before the war, and mixed crews of black and white seamen served aboard many Northern vessels.*

The Virginia's *destruction did not come because of a naval engagement, but was caused by Confederate reverses on land. In early May 1862, Federal troops occupied the strategic city of Norfolk, Virginia, forcing the Rebels to retreat closer to Richmond. An attempt was made to sail the Virginia up the James, but the vessel's deep draft would not allow it to negotiate the shallow sections of the river. Therefore, on May 11, the ship was scuttled, plied with explosives, and blown up by her crew so she would not fall into Northern hands. The Southern navy, in an ironic twist, finally completed the destruction of the* Merrimack *which was botched by the Union at the beginning of the war.*

"A heavy shell struck the pilothouse. A flash of light and a cloud of smoke filled the house. I noticed the Captain stagger and put his hands to his eyes. I ran up to him and asked if he was hurt. 'My eyes,' he said. 'I am blind,'" wrote paymaster Keeler of the *Monitor.* Executive officer Greene hurried from the turret to take over for Worden.

"Gentlemen, I leave it with you. Do what you think best. I cannot see, but do not mind me. Save the *Minnesota,* if you can," Worden gamely called as they took him to sick bay. The blindness was not caused by a shell fragment but some dust knocked loose by the direct hit on the pilothouse. Worden recovered his sight after the battle.

With the wounding of its captain, the *Monitor* pulled back from the battle. °The *Virginia* also pulled back to check itself. Although it was free of the sandbar, the engines were performing poorly. Its ammunition was running low. Two guns were out of commission from being hit by the *Monitor*'s shells. Jones, thinking he had defeated the *Monitor* since it was no longer firing on him, decided to take his ship back into Norfolk. Conversely, seeing the *Virginia* pull out and head back toward its home port, the men on the *Monitor* believed they had driven the *Virginia* away and that the battle was their victory. Each side disengaged thinking it had won.•

"WITH WAVING HANDKERCHIEFS and the wildest shouts of joy, the battle-scarred *Virginia* steamed slowly back to her moorings. No conqueror of ancient Rome ever enjoyed a prouder triumph than that which greeted us," exclaimed R. C. Foote of the *Virginia.*

Meanwhile, Greene of the *Monitor* noted, "Cheer after cheer went up from the frigates and the small craft for the glorious little *Monitor,* and happy, indeed, did we all feel. I was Captain then of the vessel that saved Newport News, Hampton Roads, Fortress Monroe, and perhaps your Northern ports."

°There was no clear victor in the battle of Hampton Roads. The *Monitor* was not penetrated by shot, although there were some dents and some damage to the pilot-house. The *Virginia* apparently lost its smokestack and had a bit more damage than the *Monitor,* but there was no substantial damage to either vessel. Both vessels had accomplished their mission. The *Virginia*'s purpose was to destroy as much of the Federal fleet as it could, which it did the day before meeting the *Monitor.* The *Monitor*'s purpose was to protect the *Minnesota* that morning, which it did successfully.• The question of which ship was victorious has never been resolved.

Some suggest that °the whole purpose of the *Monitor* was to blunt the effort of the *Virginia,* and in succeeding in doing that, the *Monitor* was the victor.• While the *Monitor* did not sink the *Virginia,* it did prevent the *Virginia* from doing the damage it could have done. To that extent, some conclude that the *Monitor* won, if not the battle, possibly the war.

The crews of the two ironclads did not see each other again. °The *Virginia* never again attempted to go out into Hampton Roads to harass the Federal wooden fleet. The vessel steamed out in the next few weeks to challenge the *Monitor* to battle again, but the *Monitor* did not respond. The *Monitor* was there to protect the fleet, so if the *Virginia* did not attack the wooden ships again, the Southern ironclad was essentially nullified.•

Still, the mere presence of the *Virginia* worried the Northern politicians who feared the ironclad would somehow slip past the *Monitor* and steam up the coast. They never realized the ship was as unseaworthy as the *Monitor* and could never actually leave the safety of harbor waters. The Union military men were so afraid of the *Virginia* that its presence helped to delay Gen. George McClellan's campaign against Richmond in the spring and early summer of 1862.

°Neither ship survived their historic meeting for very long. In May 1862 Norfolk fell to the Federals. With the

The Monitor *survived longer than her antagonist, remaining active during the Seven Days' battles and helping to cover Gen. George B. McClellan's army as it left the Virginia peninsula in early August 1862. The ship was then placed on blockade duty in Hampton Roads until December, when it was ordered to proceed to Wilmington, North Carolina, and assist in the Union attack on the crucial port. On December 31, the ship* Rhode Island *was towing the* Monitor *to Wilmington when the vessels were caught in a gale near Cape Hatteras. As this engraving shows, the unseaworthy* Monitor *wallowed in the growing waves of the storm while the* Rhode Island *helplessly watched. The turreted ironclad quickly foundered and went to the bottom with sixteen crewmen unable to reach the salvation offered by the nearby lifeboats.*

An artist's rendering of the wreck of the Monitor *(right) shows the vessel on the ocean floor upside down with the port stern supported by the turret, which is also upside down. The turret is situated so that the two gun ports are beneath the wreck. In 1979 archaeologists found that the floor of the turret had deteriorated and the turret itself was filled with sand. The stern shows significant damage, possibly from a depth charge during World War II. The propeller and shaft have fallen, the midship's bulkhead and the lower hull have collapsed, and the aft sections rest atop the engine and boilers, which are visible through openings in the hull. The starboard side is buried in the sand and believed to be in better shape than the port side. The port armor belt, despite missing a section, seems to be supporting most of the wreck.*

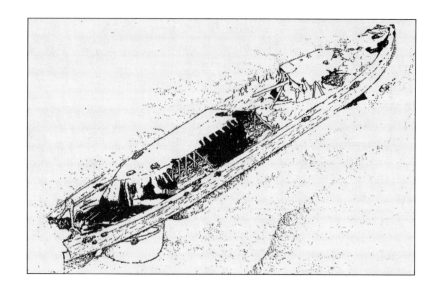

city gone, the Confederacy worried the *Virginia* might be captured and turned against the South. The vessel was too heavy, drawing too much water to get over the sandbars, so the Confederates saw no alternative but to scuttle it. It was sunk in the Elizabeth River, and its superstructure blown up. The *Virginia*, never defeated in battle, was destroyed by its own crew.•

"Still unconquered, we hold down our drooping colors, their laurels all fresh and green, and with mingled pride and grief, gave her to the flames," said a saddened Ashton Ramsey of his ship.

The *Monitor,* its dents treated like badges of honor, remained in Hampton Roads on blockade duty. Late in the summer of 1862, the vessel ventured up the James River for a brief skirmish with Confederate shore batteries at Drewry's Bluff, south of Richmond.

°In December 1862 the *Monitor* was ordered from Hampton Roads to Beaufort, North Carolina, for repairs. From there it was to have been sent to blockade duty in either Charleston or Wilmington, North Carolina. The transfer was risky as the ship would have to get into the open ocean off Cape Hatteras, North Carolina, an area long known as the graveyard of ships because of its treacherous shoals and uncertain weather. The *Monitor,* designed to operate in shallow rivers and bays, was not designed for the ocean. It encountered a gale and sank approximately sixteen miles off the coast of North Car-

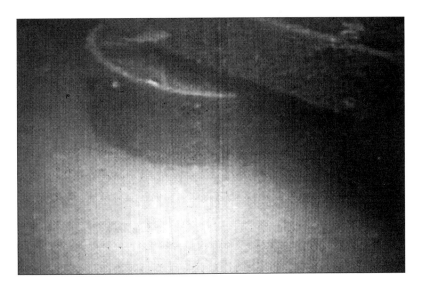

Although both the Virginia and the Monitor suffered ignominious ends, the ruins of the Monitor, once thought lost, were found in 1973 by a team of divers. While proposals have been made to raise the vessel, it is unlikely the ship's battered hull would stand the strain of such an operation.

olina. Sixteen crewmen and the ship mascot, a black cat, were lost at sea. Most of them were swept overboard trying to get into the lifeboats.•

The wreck of the *Monitor* was discovered in 1973. It remains unrecovered, a silent memorial to the men who died. Underwater photographs show that the turret detached as the ship rolled when it went down. The turret now rests under the hull. Tests show that the hull may be too fragile to recover. All the crew members would probably agree with some present-day historians who say the wreck should remain untouched.

"Their names are for history, and so long as we remain a people, so long will the work of the *Monitor* be remembered, and her story told to our children's children. The little cheese box on a raft has made a name for herself, a name that will not soon be forgotten by the American people," wrote Grenville Weeks of the *Monitor*.

Although neither ship survived a year of service, their designs inspired the North, the South, and the entire world to convert their navies from wood to iron. The creation of ironclad vessels to enforce and break the blockade marked the beginning of a new era in maritime warfare. The *Monitor* and *Virginia* were the first vessels in the world to match iron against iron, and every battleship since owes a debt to their revolutionary designs and to the ingenious men who brought them to life.

The first expedition to the site in July and August 1977 recovered the brass navigation lantern below. Although the brass was very fragile, the red fresnel lens suggested this was a signal lamp rather than an interior lamp. It is ironic that the first item recovered from the wreck may be the lamp that one of the survivors described as his last glimpse of the Monitor.

NEW ORLEANS

The BATTLE FOR NEW ORLEANS, Louisiana, was one of the more unusual episodes of the Civil War. First, there was no actual land engagement near the city. The only clash occurred more than seventy miles to the south, along the Mississippi River. While that ten-day action culminated on April 20, 1862, with one of the fiercest naval battles of the war, few men were killed or wounded during the fight. Second, although New Orleans was obviously one of the most vital cities in the South because of its strategic location at the mouth of the Mississippi, the Confederate government in Richmond seemed to give little attention to its defense. Those Southern soldiers and supplies initially posted to defend the area were gradually reassigned to sectors viewed as more critical, making this vital gateway to the rest of the Confederacy vulnerable and allowing it to fall into Federal hands without a single shot being fired.

Early in the war, Northern strategists realized that one of their priorities should be control of the Mississippi River. The key to accomplishing that task was obvious: Capture New Orleans, the largest city of the Confederacy with a population of nearly 170,000. First established by French explorers in 1662 who were following the Mississippi River, then ceded to Spain, and later purchased by the United States, this river city leading to the Gulf of Mexico was accustomed to threats of invasion. During the War of 1812 the townspeople had seen an entire British army virtually destroyed trying to capture it. Now, fifty years later, another war threatened the city.

AWB	Arthur W. Bergeron Jr.
GCC	Glen C. Cangelosi
RC	Raphael Cassimere Jr.
WCD	William C. Davis
PE	Pat Eymard
CGH	Chester G. Hearn
JL	Joe Logsdon
BP	Brian Pohanka

This 1858 photograph was taken from the top of the Customs House, looking up Canal Street, the central avenue of commerce in New Orleans. At the opposite end were the vast wharves stacked high with the commerce of the Mississippi River and the huge cargoes of merchandise offloaded from around the world. In wealth and population, no southern city compared with the Crescent City, but New Orleans was the South's most un-southern city. While the townspeople were outspokenly in favor of slavery, a large segment of the population was foreign to the South and wanted little to do with slaves. In the decade preceding the war, the number of slaves in the city decreased by five thousand; they were replaced mostly by Irish immigrants. This foreign element had stronger commercial ties to the Northeast and overseas and lacked a southern identity.

The people of New Orleans were not eager about the Civil War. Secession was not a popular concept among them, many of whom were transplanted northerners who had come south to make their fortune in shipping. The city's multinational legacy engendered the people to no one in particular, thus the townspeople's true allegiance was largely to themselves. When the war erupted, the people of New Orleans quickly realized how important their city was. "A gloom enveloped our dearly beloved city. My breakin' heart but aches the more when I am prepared to record events which can never fade from my memory," wrote Clara Solomon, a New Orleans diarist in 1862. She did not have long to wait before her sense of impending gloom turned to reality.

RC   °New Orleans before the war was a place of great contrasts. It was home to some of the wealthiest individuals in the South and some of the poorest. It had blacks, whites, Latinos, and Americans who had migrated from other southern states. It had a wealthy free black class, including black slave holders. There were Creole Africans and Creole French. The city was exotic, familiar with the unusual becoming common. Not even war could stop Mardi Gras, a time of riotous celebration that had medieval origins in Catholic countries. Mardi Gras culminated with a party the day before Ash Wednesday that for

a hundred years before the war had included in New Orleans organized parades, private parties, dances, and balls that were by invitation only. The war did not change that.•

The only issue that divided prewar New Orleans was the same that was tearing the rest of the country apart: slavery. While almost half the state of Louisiana was black and most of these were slaves, urban New Orleans was slow to support secession. °Unlike Charleston and most other southern cities, New Orleans had a large population of northern businessmen who relied on the river for their trade. They had slaves, but their business was trade, and anything that interfered with that trade would hurt them economically. Even the large slave owners who raised sugarcane wanted the protection of federal tariffs on foreign sugar, while the rest of the South was against tariffs. There was a widespread suspicion that secession from the Union was a destructive idea for New Orleans. The people of New Orleans would have preferred to sit out the war if they could.•

The sentiments of Louisiana to stay out of the coming unrest were reflected in the presidential election of 1860 when the southern candidate, John C. Breckinridge, received less than 45 percent of the ballots cast in Louisiana and Stephen A. Douglas, the northern candidate, defeated him in the city of New Orleans. Still, the state of Louisiana was a major slaveholding state, and the voters did not want Abraham Lincoln, an Illinois congressman with an antislavery platform, as the sixteenth

South Claiborne Avenue (above left) was lined with the homes of influential outsiders who had come to call New Orleans home. They were businessmen, merchants, craftsmen, and workmen who had moved from the North. They had little use for slaves, but they lacked the numbers needed to stem the rush toward secession.

Another view of Canal Street (above right), this one opposite from that at the top of the previous page, shows the Customs House under construction in 1858 to the far right. The avenue is lined with commercial ventures reflecting a vigorous middle class.

Flatboats carried grain from Illinois and Indiana and whiskey from Kentucky and Tennessee, but the principal export of New Orleans was cotton from Mississippi and Louisiana. Annually the city handled two million bales of cotton. In 1860 port receipts exceeded $185 million, of which 60 percent was cotton, and thirty-three steamship lines served the port. Cotton was in such demand that it usually shipped on the same day it arrived, thus there was little need for warehouses on many wharves.

On January 26, 1861, Louisiana seceded. When the news reached New Orleans, bells rang and people took to the streets. Pelican flags were mounted from the windows of private homes and the roofs of public buildings. For a city with little ill will toward Lincoln, the moment was an opportunity for soirees and general celebration—it was also Mardi Gras.

On January 29 the secession convention delegates moved from Baton Rouge to New Orleans, specifically City Hall (below right). There they chose six representatives to send to Montgomery, Alabama, for the convention that would establish the Confederate States of America.

president of the United States. They believed, as did the rest of the South, that his election would precipitate war.

°The hysteria that followed Lincoln's election made it difficult for anybody to oppose openly the movement toward secession,• and on January 7, 1861, the citizens of Louisiana voted to leave the Union, although the vote to secede carried by a very narrow margin. °The citizens of New Orleans passed the ordinance of secession by the narrow margin of 51 to 49 percent, possibly due to the large numbers of transplanted Yankees.• Once it had seceded, however, New Orleans quickly took up arms to defend the city against Yankee retaliation. °Citizens paraded in the streets and gathered any weapons they could find. Everyone realized that as a port city New Orleans was important to both sides.•

It is worth noting that one of New Orleans's favorite sons helped initiate the war and that soldiers from the area gallantly fought across the South for the next four years. On April 12, 1861, Confederate forces under Gen. Pierre Gustave Toutant Beauregard, a French Creole and a West Point graduate, bombarded the Federal garrison at Fort Sumter in Charleston Harbor. Lt. Gen. Richard Taylor, the son of former president Zachary Taylor and a Louisiana planter, won battles from Virginia to Louisiana and would be the last Confederate general to surrender his army in the field. Other Louisianians played prominent roles in the war. One of the units engaged in the

first major battle of the war, First Manassas, was the First Louisiana Battalion, a hard-fighting, rowdy bunch sometimes called the Louisiana Tigers, who had been recruited from the docks of New Orleans. Fewer than half of these soldiers were native to the United States.

°Immediately after the fall of Fort Sumter, when Lincoln proclaimed a blockade of all Southern seaports to stop the flow of goods in and out of the South, New Orleans knew it would be one of the prime targets of the war.• °It was obvious to Lincoln and other observers that stopping the cotton trade would have an immediate impact on the economy, not only of New Orleans, but of the entire South. Now the very foundation of the South's economy would be in jeopardy if the cotton could not get through the Northern blockade and European money for that cotton could not be brought back.•

The siege of New Orleans began as a naval battle between two Confederate forts and Union gunboats in the lower Mississippi passage, seventy miles south of the city. Union Gen. Benjamin F. Butler described the April 18, 1862, bombardment of the two forts by noting, "My war had never burned brighter. As with all that you have ever seen in life, it was like the breaking up of the universe. The moon and all the stars bursting in the skies." If the Union fleet successfully passed by the forts, it was only a matter of time before New Orleans itself would fall. When that happened, it was believed that the long-term future of the Confederacy would be sealed.

By mid-February 1861 eight new companies had formed in New Orleans. Each adopted its own style of uniform, but none were more colorful than the Zouaves. Tasseled caps, tight-fitting red jackets, and blue pantaloons made up the distinctive uniform modeled after those worn by France's colonial troops from Algeria, which were well known and admired for their fierceness in battle. Some Zouaves were French and Italian veterans of the Italian, Crimea, and African wars, and a few recruits were from the city's jails. The popularity of the Zouaves, bolstered by regular public performances of precision drills, led to the founding of two additional Zouave companies: the Avegno Zouaves and the Tigers (also known as Rob Wheats's Zouaves or Wheats's Tigers). A theater group called The Traveling Zouaves also appeared in New Orleans and drew large crowds. The photograph above is of Gaston Coppens's Zouave Battalion, including a vivandière—a woman attached to a regiment who performed various camp and nursing duties.

121

A critical situation at Fort Pickens, Florida, depleted Louisiana of most of its enthusiastic enlistees in April 1861. As they marched off to Florida, Governor Moore called for more volunteers. Enlistments were slow until Fort Sumter was fired upon on April 12. Recruits for the Confederate army were sent to Camp Walker at the old Metairie racecourse in New Orleans, and the overflow was sent to Camp Lewis (above left), a few miles from New Orleans.

The Washington Artillery (above right) had acted in the seizure of the U.S. arsenal at Baton Rouge prior to Louisiana's secession. Now that war had erupted between North and South, the distinguished unit was sent to Virginia, where it took part in the battle of First Manassas. The meal ticket below is an artifact of the unit.

WCD

BP

°By taking New Orleans, the Union was able to deprive the South of a major port. The Federals were then able to use the city as a base for the move up the Mississippi to split the Confederacy in two. With these two aims accomplished fairly easily, the capture and occupation of New Orleans ranks among the half-dozen most decisive events of the war.•

While the South had lost the battle for New Orleans, the citizens of the Crescent City began a longer battle— not a shooting engagement but a war of intolerance under the ironclad rule of Union forces. °This second battle of New Orleans was not a battle with bullets, but a battle of words, a war of ideas, and a test of wills between the citizens of occupied New Orleans and the occupying Union army. New Orleans's experience in the war was a daily test of survival, a test of a psychological warfare, a test that neither side really won.•

THE FEDERAL BLOCKADE at the mouth of the Mississippi in mid-1861 began almost immediately to strangle trade coming into New Orleans. The city's citizens wondered how long it would be before they were starved into submission. Rumors flew everywhere.

"Every day they hear one-thousand alarming rumors. And their wonder is every morning they're not made prisoners of war during their sleep by an invading army," observed the *New Orleans Picayune* on January 3, 1862.

Crises were rapidly brewing in New Orleans as food and currency became scarce. Some wondered when and if the

RC Confederacy would break the blockade. °Gradually, the blockade began to cause a shortage of goods. Newspapers not only cut down on the size of their paper but also began to reuse older editions. Staples like tea and coffee

PE began to disappear.• °Clara Solomon, a young diarist who lived in the New Orleans area, noted an early abundance of meat and vegetables and produce, but within a couple of months she recorded that her family had only bread and molasses for dinner.• "Everything is so dead. The bakers have suspended baking. And flour is selling at enormous rates. I expect before long we shall all starve," she wrote in early 1862.

President Jefferson Davis moved very slowly to build a strong military defense in the region, and he lost the people's confidence when he assigned men of dubious

BP loyalty to command the city's defenses. °Originally New Orleans had been under the command of Gen. David Twiggs, an elderly veteran of the War of 1812. He was loyal to the South, but he was not sufficiently dynamic to shoulder the job of defending New Orleans against the attack that was coming. Twiggs was replaced with Gen. Mansfield Lovell, a former New York City streets commissioner whose wife was a southerner.• He received a

WB °mixed welcome when he reached New Orleans in late October 1861, because the people were suspicious of where his loyalties might lie.•

BP °Lovell's heart was in protecting the city, but he did not have the support he needed to accomplish that task; he lacked the full cooperation of the Confederate navy. Although he was responsible for the city's defense—and the expected attack would likely come from the river—he did not have command over the Confederate vessels on the Mississippi. Moreover, as the Union army was preparing to attack New Orleans, many of Lovell's troops and guns were ordered away from his command by Richmond for use elsewhere. In effect, the South's largest city was slowly abandoned without any preparations being made for a fight.•

"The city's been almost entirely stripped of everything available. Should you see in the New Orleans papers we

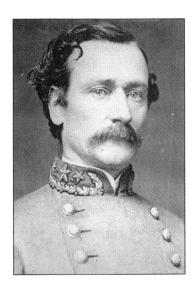

Maj. Gen. Mansfield Lovell (above) was given command of the Confederate troops in and around New Orleans. He had such faith in Forts Jackson and Saint Philip that he discounted the Federal buildup at Ship Island as a "harmless menace."

At the head of the buildup was Capt. David Glasgow Farragut (below). During the briefing on the attack on New Orleans, he was given a list of vessels being outfitted for the task and asked if the number were sufficient. Farragut said that he would run the forts and occupy the town with two-thirds the number.

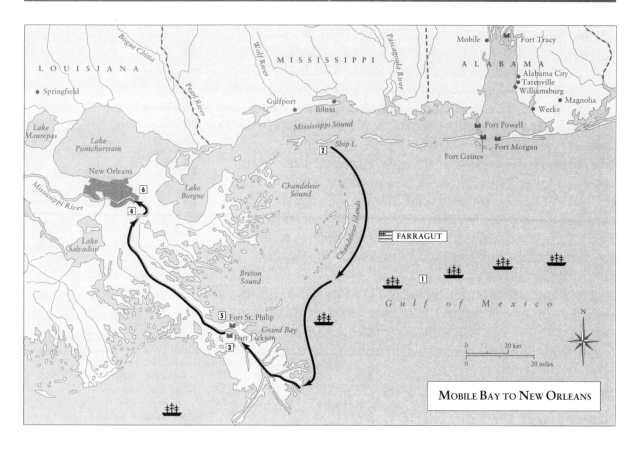

MOBILE BAY TO NEW ORLEANS

[1] **Mid-1861:** *Union blockade established in the Gulf of Mexico and at the headwaters of the Mississippi River.*

[2] **Dec. 1861:** *David G. Farragut and David Dixon Porter organize a massive Federal fleet—seventeen warships and nineteen mortar boats—near Ship Island with the goal of taking New Orleans.*

[3] **Mid-April 1862:** *The fleet approaches Forts Jackson and Saint Philip.* **April 18, Good Friday:** *Porter's mortar boats begin a round-the-clock bombardment.* **April 24, 2 A.M.:** *Farragut's ships make their run past the forts.*

[4] **April 24:** *The Union fleet anchors at New Orleans shortly after sunrise, and Farragut demands the surrender of the city.*

[5] **April 28:** *The garrisons of Forts Jackson and Saint Philip mutiny and surrender.*

[6] **Early May 1862:** *Federal troops under Benjamin F. Butler begin the occupation of New Orleans.*

are well supplied with everything, you may regard it as a ruse," Lovell wrote to Davis in October 1861. Nevertheless, Davis did not answer Lovell's requests for more men and supplies, which is °one of the great mysteries of the Civil War. In fact, Davis did very little to protect New Orleans and the Mississippi although he knew the city and the river were vital to the Confederacy. One reason may have been that he had a false confidence in the two massive masonry fortresses that were downstream from New Orleans, Forts Jackson and Saint Philip.•

These two forts were more than seventy miles south of New Orleans, on opposite sides of the Mississippi River. Built before the War of 1812 to fend off foreign invasion, the fortresses were outdated and in need of repair, but the leaders of the Confederacy must have thought the forts could stop any Union fleet since they had the Mississippi covered with converging fire from two directions.

°It was believed that a small naval force in conjunction with those forts would be sufficient to prevent any

WCD

AWB

Union vessels from coming up the Mississippi River. The Confederate high command did not realize that steam power had made the Union navy vessels much faster than the old sailing vessels the British had used in 1812. The Union ships would be under fire a shorter time than ships formerly were, and therefore it would be much easier to get past the two forts.•

GH   To help the forts °the Confederate navy started to build two ironclads—the *Louisiana* and the *Mississippi.* Ironclads had not yet made their appearance on the rivers, so the Confederates expected to surprise the Federal navy. Both ships were planned to be strong enough to go down-river, break up the blockade, and chase away all Union vessels. Success, however, would depend on whether construction of the ironclads was ever finished.•

The Confederacy began to believe its own propaganda when it assured the citizens of New Orleans that the two forts, with the help of the two ironclads under construction, could easily defend their city. Few plans for the defense of the city even mentioned using soldiers. What the Confederates had not counted on was that the Union navy had its own master plan of attack, carried out by two adoptive brothers—David Dixon Porter and David G. Farragut—that would be able to blunt all of the Confederate plans.

BP   °Porter was one of the most ambitious officers in the U.S. Navy. He had risen through the ranks to captain, then commodore, then admiral in the space of two years, and he had no plans to wait for the blockade to starve New Orleans into surrender. Porter wanted to take the CGH city• °and suggested bringing mortar boats up the river to demolish Forts Jackson and Saint Philip.•

Before Porter could begin his attack, however, Capt. David G. Farragut was given overall command of the operation as flag officer of the naval attack on the two CGH Confederate forts. °Farragut had been adopted at the age of eight by Porter's father, a commodore in the navy at

Comdr. David Dixon Porter proposed the plan of attack for the taking of New Orleans. He suggested that a squadron of mortar boats be towed inland from the Gulf to bombard Forts Jackson and Saint Philip. A fleet of shallow-draft vessels could then run the forts to take New Orleans. Army troops would follow and occupy the forts and the city. When the plan was approved, Porter was placed in command of the mortar squadron, Benjamin F. Butler was to head the army contingent, but overall command of the operation was entrusted to Farragut.

Just south of Forts Saint Philip and Jackson, within range of their cannon, massive iron chains stretched across the river. These were supported by anchored rafts and floating hulks. Any ships attempting to make a run past the forts would be ensnared by this barrier and caught under a deadly cross fire. The link above was part of this defensive obstacle.

The crew of one of Porter's Federal mortar schooners pose around their vessel's twenty-five-thousand-pound weapon, which was capable of hurling thirteen-inch shells almost two and a half miles. At midmorning on April 18 the lead mortar boat opened on Fort Jackson, beginning a rain of iron at the rate of a round every two minutes. The thirteen-man gun crews loaded twenty-pound powder charges, cut fuses, loaded 216-pound shells, and lobbed the iron toward the fort. By the manual, each member of the gun crew stood on tiptoe and held his mouth open to lessen the shock of the discharge and the impact on their eardrums. In shallow water the recoil drove the schooners into the mud, where they stayed for a few moments before popping free. By dusk the Yankee mortars had lobbed more than one thousand shells at the fort, and Porter seemed pleased at the prospect of making good on his goal of reducing the forts within two days.

that time, and he entered naval service at the age of nine when his father placed him on board a vessel. David Porter was born four years after Farragut's adoption, so they knew each other only vaguely as children and had grown up in the navy as rivals.• Actually, Porter felt the rivalry more keenly than his adoptive brother. Farragut was too involved in mastering his vocation and later fighting a war to realize that Porter was talking behind his back.

Chief among the stories Porter helped spread about Farragut was that his brother was too old to command effectively. Farragut was sixty years old when the war began and only twenty-seventh in ranking as captain. Further clouding his future was the fact that he had been born in the South and had married a southerner. Regardless of Porter's criticisms, °giving Farragut a command in 1861 was a risk Lincoln and his secretary of the navy, Gideon Welles, were willing to take. They liked him and believed he was neither too old nor too southern to fight the Confederacy.•

WCD

By December 1861, the two found themselves working together in assembling a massive fleet from Ship Island, a dozen miles off the Mississippi coast in the Gulf of Mexico. It would be the largest American war fleet ever assembled: seventeen warships of varying descriptions

mounting more than 150 cannon. Porter commanded another nineteen vessels, mortar boats, each housing a huge 13-inch mortar designed to throw a heavy explosive shell onto its target. All of these wooden ships were steam driven, either by paddle wheels or screw propellers, so they could go upstream against the Mississippi's current.

WHEN WORD OF the massive fleet reached New Orleans, the city's leaders began worrying in earnest. "The Yankees are comin' in great force. And to cut a long argument short, we have ever merely to repeat the talk. Are we prepared?" fretted the editor of the *New Orleans Crescent* on December 15, 1861. By March 1862 fear filled the streets as rumors spread that the Yankees were within days of invading the city.

°The rumors reflected the citizens' growing sense of unease, paranoia, and panic. They felt left to their own devices, that they were not being protected. They had little trust in General Lovell and his five or six thousand troops.• "Lovell is more and more distrusted. Persons are open and plain in the expression of their opinions of him," wrote diarist Elsie Bragg on March 12, 1862.

By mid-April 1862 Farragut's fleet was nearing its target. He anchored his ships several miles below the forts, and Porter positioned his mortar flotilla to attack

On April 20, seeing that the mortars had done as much damage as they could, Farragut decided to run the forts. Under fire that evening two ships severed the chain that stretched across the river, but Farragut held back in case the mortars might incapacitate the river installations. By April 24, he could wait no longer. That night the fleet moved in three divisions past Jackson and Saint Philip, with the first division focusing its fire on Saint Philip, the second on Jackson, and the third free to aid whichever unit required assistance. In the engraving above, Fort Saint Philip and the Confederate ironclad Louisiana are in the lower left corner; Fort Jackson is in the upper right, drawing fire from the mortar fleet in the far distance. The second division of Farragut's fleet is in the foreground, with the flagship, the Hartford, in the lead.

VCD

Farragut's fleet slid past an improvised blockade of moored hulks as it ran the gauntlet between the two forts. In the painting below by Mauritz Frederik Hendrik de Haas, the Hartford *is attacked by the Confederate ram Manassas. The disabled tug* Mosher *lists dangerously in the right foreground; it was one of eight ships lost that night. The evening attack was dramatically heightened with flashes of cannonfire and the arcing glare of the mortar shells' trajectories. Farragut described the scene "as if the artillery of heaven were playing upon the earth." Another witness commented, "Imagine all the earthquakes in the world, and all the thunder and lightning together in a space of two miles, all going off at once." The night assault proved advantageous to the Federals: during the engagement both forts had their guns elevated too high and could not see the effect of their fire to compensate. Most of Farragut's vessels had no damage to their hulls and little to their masts. Those that came under fire once the sky began to brighten were badly shot up, and three had to turn back.*

the forts. The first phase of the operation was Porter's task, which was to reduce the forts to rubble so Farragut's fleet could pass unmolested.

Aware of the imminent attack, °the Confederate commanders in the two forts were concerned that not enough had been done to ensure a proper defense. Gen. Johnston Kelly Duncan, a Pennsylvanian by birth, knew what it would take to defend the old masonry forts, but he had only five hundred men and eighty cannon. Duncan knew that he needed more cannon, more men, and more ammunition if they were to successfully defend New Orleans.• He would not get them.

In the early morning hours of April 18, Porter's mortars opened up on Fort Jackson and maintained a ten-hour bombardment, lobbing approximately three thousand shells toward the fort. That was just the beginning. °The mortars fired at least one round every ten minutes, and this continued over the next six days. While the mortars were fearsome, they did not do a great deal of damage to the forts or their garrisons.•

°Farragut watched the ineffectual bombardment and on April 23 assumed that the mortars had done as much

damage as they were going to do. He finalized plans to run his fleet between the two forts.•

In the predawn hours of April 24, 1862, Farragut's ships began to run the gauntlet. Under a dark and clear sky, two Union boats broke through a chain barrier across the river, then Farragut's flagship, the *Hartford*, gave the signal for the rest of the fleet to steam ahead. °When the fleet started moving, both forts opened fire. One sailor said that it was like being in the center of a volcano, as if the heavens had opened up and rained down a shower of fire and sparks in the air all around them.•

"Passing the forts was one of the most awful sights and events I ever saw or expect to experience. It seemed as if all the artillery of heaven were flamed upon the earth," observed an amazed Flag Officer Farragut.

°The Confederates tried everything to stop the Union fleet, including setting barges on fire and sending them downriver. One of these flaming barges snagged up against Farragut's flagship, but it was dislodged.•

The fighting seemed fierce to those in the middle of it. "We were struck now on all sides," wrote Signal Officer B. S. Osbourne aboard one of the Union ships. "A shell entered our starboard, exploded the main hatch, killing one man instantly, and wounding several others. Men's faces were covered with powder, black and daubed with blood. It had become like a lot of demons in a wild inferno."

°The next Confederate tactic was to send in some of its own warships, including the ironclad ram CSS *Manassas*, an ugly, iron-plated, former Northern ice breaker mounting one cannon. The ship looked like a half-submerged cigar with a smokestack and had to be aimed so its cannon could be fired. The ungainly vessel ran aground and was destroyed. Nothing seemed capable of stopping the Union fleet.•

The Confederate tug Mosher *pushed a fire raft toward the* Hartford. *While trying to outmaneuver the raft, the Union vessel ran aground on a muddy flat under the guns of Saint Philip. The Mosher then succeeded in ramming the raft against the Federal flagship's hull. Farragut ordered a gun crew to open fire on "that rascally little tug." While others fought the fire, he turned to see his signal officer with his coat over his head uncapping shells and said, "Come, Mr. Osbon, this is no time for praying." The officer responded, "Flag officer, if you'll wait a second, you'll get the quickest answer to prayer you ever heard of," and rolled the twenty-pound shells over the side and onto the burning raft below, blowing a hole in it. The gun crew sank the tug with two shots, the raft drifted away, and fire crews doused the flames aboard* Hartford.

At times the sound of the battle around the forts could be heard in New Orleans. The Confederate commander, Lovell, had only three thousand men, most of whom were untrained. He met with Mayor John Monroe and indicated that the threat of Farragut's shelling the town far outweighed the effectiveness of any resistance he could offer. For that reason, he had no choice but to withdraw. On the rainy afternoon of April 25 the Union fleet arrived (above left), greeted by flames along the wharves, which many sailors took as a sign that the Southerners had torched the city.

CGH

Farragut dispatched Capt. Theodorus Bailey and Lt. George H. Perkins to demand the peaceful surrender of the town. The two officers were greeted by a hostile vocal mob at the Laurel Street wharf (above right). Amid cries of "Hurrah for Jeff Davis" and "Kill them," Bailey asked where he might meet Mayor Monroe. Perkins later reported: "As we advanced the mob followed us in a very excited state. They gave three cheers for Jeff Davis and Beauregard and three groans for Lincoln. Then they began to throw things at us, and shout, 'Hang them! Hang them!' We both thought we were in a bad fix, but there was nothing for us to do, but just go on."

WCD

The two Confederate ironclads in which President Davis had put so much faith were far from completion when the Union attack came. The half-built *Louisiana* was towed in front of Fort Saint Philip to act as a floating gun platform, but it did little damage to the Union vessels.

°Dawn rose before the Federal fleet had cleared the forts. The daylight made the ships better targets, so the last three Union ships turned around rather than risk being sunk.•

In three and a half hours, fourteen of seventeen warships had successfully passed the forts. Farragut counted only 37 dead and 147 wounded. The Confederates lost fewer than 100 dead in the forts and the warships that tried to stop the fleet. Considering the tonnage of shells fired, it was a remarkably safe battle on both sides. The way was now open for Farragut to seize New Orleans.

°Farragut's message to Porter that he was on his way to the city upset Porter, who thought that Farragut should have stayed in the area to help mop up the forts. Farragut, however, had other tasks ahead of him. Once his fleet was past the forts, the forts no longer mattered.• An angry Porter, anxious to share in the capture of New Orleans, followed orders and continued to bombard the forts while the citizens of New Orleans waited to see what would happen to their city.

The actual capture of the city was anticlimactic. Once the Federal fleet had passed the forts, New Orleans had no other defenses, no major forts of its own. The Confederate troops abandoned the city. When that news reached

Forts Jackson and Saint Philip, the garrisons at both forts mutinied and both fell without much more bloodshed. There was little for the civilians to do but surrender without a fight.

THE OCCUPYING YANKEES believed the siege was over with the fall of the forts, but while the men in the city seemed ready to give up, the women of New Orleans had not yet begun to fight. The press had not yielded entirely, either. "The hour is rapidly approaching whether or not New Orleans will be a conquered city. The issue is now to do or die. Who will be so craven as to fault it?" wrote the editor of *True Delta* on April 19, 1862.

GCC °Farragut's fleet anchored near the French Quarter. He sent just two hundred soldiers under the command of one captain, Theordis Bailey, to accept the city's surrender, and they had to navigate through an angry mob in the streets to meet with the city council. The soldiers anticipated problems by half-cocking their rifles, but Bailey calmly walked to city hall and demanded surrender.•

AWB °Mayor John Monroe replied that he had no authority to surrender the city and that the Federals would need to talk to General Lovell or one of his subordinates. Yet Lovell and his troops had evacuated New Orleans; there was no one to whom the Federals could submit their demands other than the civilian authorities.•

Farragut rejected the suggestion that he find Lovell. He told the council to surrender within forty-eight hours or his ships would open fire. The mayor, however, remained somewhat defiant. "I beg you to understand that the people of New Orleans, while unable at this moment to prevent you from occupying this city, do not transfer their allegiance from the government," he said.

The city held fast for two days but finally surrendered when it learned that the soldiers in the forts had given up. Southern observers knew that a strategic disaster had occurred, essentially without anyone firing a shot in

Bailey and Perkins walked to City Hall with the mob in tow. About every third man had a weapon. They were cordially but coldly received at City Hall, where Mayor Monroe indicated he did not have the authority to surrender the city since it was under martial law. General Lovell was summoned, and he vowed not to surrender, claiming to have fifteen thousand troops under arms. Finally, he said that he would withdraw and leave the matter of the surrender to the mayor and his council. Monroe said that Farragut would have his answer the next morning. The stalemate continued until Forts Saint Philip and Jackson surrendered and occupation troops under Benjamin Butler arrived.

On the morning of April 26, Farragut sent a detachment of marines from the Hartford to receive the city's answer. Meanwhile, a group of marines from the Pensacola went to the former U.S. Mint and raised the Stars and Stripes. A crowd gathered to jeer them and the flag, and after the Federals had left the area, William B. Mumford (near right), a gambler by trade, tore the flag down. The mob paraded it through town with a fife-and-drum accompaniment then shredded the banner in front of City Hall and hurled the bits at the Union negotiators. When Farragut met with Butler just days after the incident, the general said, "I will make an example of that fellow by hanging him." Mumford was apprehended and, despite the pleas of his wife (far right), hanged. Below are a piece of the shredded flag and a part of the rope used to hang the unfortunate gambler.

defense of the city. From her home in Charleston, diarist Mary Chesnut wrote, "New Orleans is gone. And with it the Confederacy. Are we not cut in two?"

In the meantime, Farragut began to restore order to New Orleans. He insisted that the city recognize the Federal government and ordered the lowering of all Louisiana state flags and the raising of the Stars and Stripes over all government buildings. In response °a mob marched on the U.S. Mint, climbed the walls, and tore down the U.S. flag. One of the leaders, William B. Mumford, tore the banner to bits. That single defiant act set the stage for the arrival of Maj. Gen. Benjamin F. Butler and eighteen thousand Federal troops on May 1.• Butler used the incident to assert his martial authority over New Orleans. He announced, "I find the city under the dominion of the mob. They shall fear the stripes if they do not revere the stars of our banner!" Farragut had conquered New Orleans by sea, but it was now Butler's turn to conquer its citizens on land.

°Butler was arguably the ugliest general of the Civil War. He was cockeyed, with one eye looking off in another direction. He was portly, balding, and looked something like a walrus. Visually, he was a very unsympathetic man, and he had a temperament that in some ways matched his appearance. He was nonetheless a brilliant politician from Massachusetts who probably had

Maj. Gen. Benjamin F. Butler (far left) was the first military governor of New Orleans. He arrived in May 1862, after the surrender of the two forts, and moved quickly to banish or imprison Southern activists and confiscate their property. His iron-fisted rule had many practical benefits—looting and destruction were rare—but his implementation of politically delicate policies—such as according blacks equal status with whites under the law—made him controversial. Butler was so reviled by the people of New Orleans that he was caricatured relentlessly. In the image at the near left he is depicted as a hyena, and the spoon alludes to the most notorious sobriquet Butler endured—"Spoons"—an allusion to his alleged penchant for stealing silverware from wealthy homeowners. Below are several spoons purported to have been stolen by Butler and a bank receipt for spoons credited to Butler's account.

dreams of exploiting a successful military reputation for higher office. There is no question that he was devoted to the idea of the Union.•

BP °Butler may have been the Union general most hated by Southerners, but he did not shirk from that. He and his staff entered the city on foot at the head of eighteen thousand troops. On all sides the people cursed, shouted, and shook their fists, displaying their absolute hatred for this occupying army.•

Butler immediately imposed martial law, censored newspapers, and ordered a successful manhunt for Mumford, the man who had torn down the U.S. flag from the

BP mint. °Mobs rallied in the streets in support of Mumford, his wife, and their child. Mumford's wife begged for her husband's release, but Butler viewed the situation as a test of wills. If Mumford were not hanged, Butler would have given in to the mob. So Mumford was taken to the gallows that had been erected in the shadow of the mint and hanged under the flag he had torn down. There was no last-minute reprieve.•

The execution sparked an immediate war of words against the Union occupiers. Leading the attack, probably because they could not take up arms and because they did not think Butler would do anything to them, were the Rebel belles of New Orleans. Julia LeGrande, one of the enraged women, noted: "The whole city was the

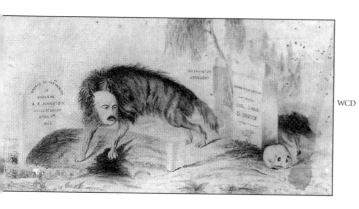

The caricatures of Butler went on end-lessly. Above, he was depicted as a hyena and a desecrater. Yet Southern-ers were not alone in their frustrations with Butler. He incurred no small amount of contempt from his col-leagues in the campaign for New Orleans. First, he was critical of Porter once Butler's troops occupied Forts Jackson and Saint Philip, claiming that little damage had been done by Porter's mortars. Second, to his wife (below) Butler confided, "I deem wholly an unmilitary proceeding on [Farragut's] part to run off and leave forts behind him unredeemed, but such is the race for the glory of capturing New Orleans . . . that thus we go." Farragut, however, was more generous to Butler in according him an equal share in the credit for taking the Southern port.

scene of wild confusion. The women only did not seem afraid. They were all in favor of resistance, no matter how hopeless."

°The reaction of the women of New Orleans was not uncommon. Women were often the most ardent Confederates because they could not fight, but they could urge their men to fight. The women were also more exposed to the hardships at home while the men were on the battlefields. In New Orleans the women refused to speak to Union soldiers. If an officer approached a woman on the sidewalk, she walked to the other side of the street. Women would place a fan to their faces or turn away from the soldiers. They would pull their hoop skirts aside so that their clothing would not even touch a dirty Yankee. In some cases they spat on them.• Sometimes they did worse.

°There were several incidents reported to Butler of women's emptying their chamber pots—portable toi-lets—onto the heads of the soldiers below them. One woman, Anne LeRoux, wore a secession flag on her cloth-ing, an incident that almost incited a riot that endan-gered the life of a young Federal soldier.• Incensed by the treatment his troops were receiving, Butler issued General Orders No. 28, better known as the "Woman's Order," which firmly established his image in the South.

°More than anything else he did in the course of the Civil War, Butler would be remembered and vilified in the South for the Woman's Order. This order stated that women in the city who showed rudeness or impertinence or gave insult to Federal officers and soldiers would be considered by Butler's administration as "women of the street" or "women of the city, plying their trade." Essen-tially, they would be regarded as prostitutes. This was a humiliating slap in the face especially to middle-class and upper-crust New Orleans women. It had the effect Butler intended, ending much of the rude behavior.•

Butler made examples of several women. One woman was heard laughing inside her house while a Federal sol-dier's funeral procession was passing outside. Although

she claimed she was laughing at her daughter's birthday party, the woman was arrested and imprisoned.

Butler was soon dubbed "Beast Butler" and carica-
BP tured in newspapers across the country. °He was hated by the South, but Butler thrived on that attention because the people who hated him were the people he was trying to defeat.•

GCC Butler also °instituted the Confiscation Act, which allowed him to seize property owned by the Confederate state and by all Confederate officers. This act granted the occupation army license to enter private houses to seize valuables. This resulted in Butler's nickname "Spoons"•
BP °because it was alleged that he had amassed a vast collection of stolen silverware. The stories are difficult to prove and may not have been true, but they made good stories for Southerners and added to the caricature and scorn that was directed against him.•

Although the citizens would not admit it, Butler did institute policies to help New Orleans. He quarantined ships coming into port, which prevented the spread of yellow fever, and he provided food for the poor. He wanted to combat his image problems so that he did not appear to be a complete beast. That would not play well back in Massachusetts. "I was always a friend of Southern rights," he pronounced in 1862, "but an enemy of Southern wrongs."

DURING HIS REIGN in New Orleans, Butler took up the cause of black freedom, which angered the cotton aris-

Butler ordered that all persons living in New Orleans take an oath of allegiance to the Union or be expelled (above left). Steadfast Southerners could leave and face starvation or acquiese and enjoy the things that were still good about New Orleans. Although not as controversial as some of his other acts, Butler's military government assessed taxes on the wealthy to feed the poor (above right). The Lincoln administration acted to recall him in December 1862.

135

**Head-Quarters, Department of the Gulf,
New Orleans, May 15, 1862.**

General Orders, No. 28.

As the Officers and Soldiers of the United States have been subject to repeated insults from the women calling themselves ladies of New Orleans, in return for the most scrupulous non-interference and courtesy on our part, it is ordered that hereafter when any Female shall, by word, gesture, or movement, insult or show contempt for any officer or soldier of the United States, she shall be regarded and held liable to be treated as a woman of the town plying her avocation.

By command of Maj.-Gen. BUTLER,
GEORGE C. STRONG,
A. A. G. Chief of Staff.

The hostility of the population did not subside with the surrender of the city and the raising of the Stars and Stripes. Butler's troops were subjected to numerous slights and insults, not that they did not mirror similar behavior toward the Southerners. The general, however, was infuriated when he heard of chamber pots being emptied from balconies on his men. To squelch the civil contempt he authorized the most notorious edict promulgated by his administration—General Orders, No. 28 (above). WCD

BP tocrats. °Initially, his position on slavery had been quite ambivalent, but once he saw former slaves with lash marks on their backs and heard the horror stories of slave life, his opinions were transformed. Earlier in the war, one of the first things Butler had done when he was serving in Virginia was to declare runaway slaves to be "contraband of war." He did not consider them free people but the captured property of the United States. It was not the same as giving slaves their freedom, but he used the South's own view of African Americans as property as a means of getting the slaves out of the clutches of their owners.•

Fugitive slaves reacted to Butler by offering their services to the Union army. Some of the first to respond were free blacks who were former members of the state militia, called the Native Guards, who had once offered to sign up with the Confederate army to fight the invading Yankees, but their help had been refused.

°The free blacks had wanted to enlist in the Confederate army because they were Southerners first. As free blacks they had a stake in the Southern economy, and some of them even owned slaves. When the Yankees came, however, they realized that the Confederacy was doomed, and they shifted their loyalties and offered their services to the Union instead.•

AWB °Butler quickly seized on the idea of arming blacks and allowed the men to re-form their regiments to be incorporated into the Union army. He met some resistance from the government in Washington, which was not convinced of blacks' fighting abilities, but the regiment was formed nonetheless. The First and Third Regiments Louisiana Native Guards were involved in the first major assault by black soldiers in the Federal army in May 1863 at Port Hudson, Louisiana.• Butler, however, was not there to lead them. In December 1862 he was replaced by Maj. Gen. Nathaniel Banks, another political general from Massachusetts. Butler, who had restored

order to New Orleans, had become so unpopular in the city that he could no longer accomplish much except to maintain the peace. As the controversial general sailed away from the New Orleans dock, few tears were shed by the city's citizens. "There was not one 'Hurrah.' Not one sympathizing cry. I wonder if he felt it," wrote a satisfied Julia LeGrande.

With Butler gone, Banks and Lincoln used occupied Louisiana to incorporate a plan for early Reconstruction, particularly in New Orleans with its educated and wealthy free black population, many of whom had pur-

RC chased their freedom before the war. °They had organized their own schools, but they had never really assimilated into the culture. They had no civil rights and

WCD could not vote.• °Lincoln saw Louisiana as a proving ground where he could test his hopes for the eventual reconstruction of the entire South by drawing free blacks into society and making loyal Americans once again out

RC of Southerners.• °The free blacks in New Orleans, however, demanded more than simple freedom; many had had that before the war. They wanted citizenship rights on an equal basis with everybody, something Lincoln was not yet prepared to give.• "A strange error in a society in which prejudice weighed equally against all those who had African blood in their veins, no matter how small the amount," wrote P. S. Pitchback in 1863.

A Northern cartoon above illustrates the temper of the times before and after the announcement of General Orders, No. 28. On the left, two "ladies" of New Orleans spit on Union soldiers encountered on the street. On the right, the same ladies carry themselves with more dignity in the exchange of pleasantries. While Butler was reviled across the South for his provocative assertion that women who acted in the previous manner were women "of the town plying [their] avocation," no one was ever arrested under the terms of this law.

Freedom came for the slaves in occupied Confederate states in 1863 with Lincoln's Emancipation Proclamation; however, black suffrage would have to wait. Although the war brought promising social change early to New Orleans, by the end of the bloody conflict Louisiana was left in economic and social despair. "The ravages of both armies of the last two years leaves us all in a very exhausted and ruined condition. And I anticipate much suffering," wrote one Louisiana planter after the war. He was right.

WCD °In the end, the credit for the Union capture of New Orleans did not have to go solely to Farragut and Porter. It should be shared with Confederate President Davis and the Richmond government who never appreciated the danger New Orleans faced. Davis realized his mistake after it was too late, but he never admitted it.• For the North, taking New Orleans divided the Confederacy and paved the way for an eventual Union victory. For the South, the loss of New Orleans, the Confederacy's largest city, was both a stunning blow to its ability to carry on the war and to its morale. The citizens of New Orleans survived four years of Union occupation although they were left with a mixed legacy of hope and bitterness.

RC °The occupation of New Orleans left a legacy of emancipation for the large slave population in and around the city. It left a legacy of humiliation and defeat for the largely white population who could not undo the

Life in New Orleans for the remainder of the war went on in the way it had before the war. There were unpleasantries about being an occupied city, but the occupation army was not overtly hostile, and a common heritage made the celebration of such universal occasions as George Washington's birthday in 1864 (right) as festive in the city as it was in Washington, New York, or Richmond.

fact that New Orleans, Louisiana, and the Confederacy as a whole had been defeated. Psychologically there have been generations of people in New Orleans who could never live down that they surrendered to the North without even firing a shot.•

°The city of New Orleans and the structures themselves came out much better than its citizens. The invader's cannonballs never exploded among the lovely old houses, warehouses, and factories. All survived the war, which was not true in many other large Southern cities. New Orleans went ahead with the business of being New Orleans, which is what New Orleanians always have and always will do.• "New Orleans was a sad, sad blow. And has affected me bitterly . . . bitterly. But I am getting over it," wrote an optimistic Stephen R. Maury in 1865.

While Butler went on to a kind of ignominy in New Orleans, Farragut's star continued to rise. After seizing the Crescent City, Farragut's fleet participated in the siege against Vicksburg until the city fell in 1863. In August 1863 he began preparations for an assault on Mobile Bay, which he executed successfully a year later—his greatest victory which also facilitated his promotion to vice admiral. The battle is depicted above by William H. Overend in An August Morning with Farragut. *The admiral leans dramatically into the fury of the battle as the ironclad* Tennessee *brushes alongside.*

ANTIETAM

°*Narrow* MEANDERING ANTIE-
tam Creek will forever stand out in American history for
loss of life. It was the bloodiest single day in American
history with casualties of more than twenty-four thousand men killed, wounded, or captured. The number of
casualties at Antietam exceeded the total of American
dead in the country's three earlier wars—the Revolution,
the War of 1812, and the Mexican War.• °This staggering
loss of life was graphically illustrated for the country•
°because photographers immortalized the scenes of
twisted Confederate dead along the Hagerstown Pike
and in the Sunken Road. They captured the brutality of
warfare and displayed it to Americans who had never
before seen such sights.•

Because it was a significant battle fought in Maryland,
a border state, rather than in Virginia, Louisiana, or Tennessee, Northerners seemed to pay much more attention
to Antietam. The eyewitness accounts of what their men
saw was sobering. "I hope that I may never see such a
sight again. The dead were thicker here than I had seen
them anywhere else," was how Union Lt. Tully McCrea
described the horror of the battle.

As the epic engagement was concluding, a reporter for
the *New York Times* submitted this account: "The combined forces of the enemy, under Jackson, Lee, Longstreet
and the whole Rebel set, have made a stand near Sharpsburg, and all day long, from five o'clock in the morning
until now—8 o'clock P.M.—have been contesting with the
Union Army under McClellan. Nothing, I'm sure, can
compare with this day's fight. Neither in its colossal

WCD	William C. Davis
GWG	Gary W. Gallagher
JMM	James M. McPherson
BP	Brian Pohanka
JIR	James I. Robertson Jr.

141

On Thursday, September 4, the Army of Northern Virginia began crossing the Potomac near White's Ford (above left). Bands played "Maryland, My Maryland," and the men cheerfully splashed through the waist-deep water. Johann August Heinrich Heros von Borcke, a Prussian in the Confederate cavalry, wrote, "There were few moments, perhaps, from the beginning to the close of the war, of excitement more intense, of exhilaration more delightful." Some soldiers were disappointed that the moment did not last longer, for they all needed a good bath.

Artist Alfred R. Waud sketched the scene above (right) and wrote a vivid description of Jeb Stuart's troopers: "They seemed to be of considerable social standing, that is, most of them . . . so to speak, and not irreverently; for they were not only as a body handsome, athletic men, but generally polite and agreeable in manner. With the exception of the officers, there was little else but homespun among them, light drab-gray or butternut color, the drab predominating; although there were so many varieties of dress, half-citizen, half-military, that they could scarcely be said to have a uniform."

proportions nor in the bloody character of the struggle. Many a poor fellow will lie in the cold, damp earth tonight and pray for death to relieve him of his sufferings." Henry Kyd Douglas, a member of Stonewall Jackson's staff, observed: "It was a fearful day. One I am not likely ever to forget. Mars was striking iron fire. Time moving with leaden heels."

The bloodiest day in the Civil War goes by two names: Antietam in the North and Sharpsburg in the South. By either name it refers to a contest between George B. McClellan and Robert E. Lee that eventually elevated the underpinnings of the war to a higher moral ground. After the fighting at Antietam, the North no longer viewed the war as a campaign to preserve an abstract idea called the Union, but one to free people from bondage.

Antietam was a battle where seemingly simple features of the landscape took on historically significant names that would live through the ages: °the North Woods, the Miller Cornfield, the West Woods, the East Woods, the Dunker Church, the Mumma Farm. These were all immortalized by the slaughter that took place at Antietam. When they are mentioned, there is little doubt that the subject is Antietam.•

When the battle of Antietam occurred in September 1862, the war had been going on for more than a year. The pomp and bluster of those politicians who had predicted a short war had long since given way to a hail of minié balls and canister shot. The April 6–7, 1862, battle of Shiloh, Tennessee, five months earlier, had shocked the nation with its twenty-three thousand casualties and had disappointed the South when a second-day defeat followed a sweeping first-day victory. The surrender of the South's largest city, New Orleans, on April 25, had shown the Confederacy how vulnerable it could be to superior forces. Although the South had been unable to organize a strong defense in the West in Tennessee, Mississippi, and Louisiana, the course of the war had shifted in Virginia, the eastern theater of the conflict.

As poor as the situation was in the West, in early 1862 the situation was dire in the East. A Union army had marched within sight of the spires of Richmond. It was then that command of the Confederate army was entrusted to Lee. During the three short summer months of 1862, his soldiers lashed out at two Union armies in Virginia. McClellan was repulsed from the Virginia peninsula between the York and James Rivers, and John Pope's army was crushed at the battle of Second Manassas (or Second Bull Run).

JIR °Few incidents in military history compare with Lee's accomplishments during these one hundred days. Lee orchestrated a complete reversal of Southern fortunes, ridding Virginia of all Federal forces and leading his army to the banks of the Potomac, almost within sight of the unfinished Capitol dome. There he contemplated an invasion of the North.•

For Abraham Lincoln the situation was grave. Despite the good war news in the West, the Northern public focused on what was happening in Virginia. They saw

Work on building a dome for the Capitol in Washington began in 1853 under the watchful eye of Franklin Pierce's secretary of war, Jefferson Davis. It was not completed by the beginning of the war, but Lincoln ordered that construction of the dome be continued, symbolizing the continuation of the Federal government. When Robert E. Lee's legions moved into Maryland, they were almost within sight of the unfinished dome. News of the Southern invasion caused panic throughout the capital, and the many forts that ringed the district were manned to capacity.

An 1842 graduate of West Point, John Pope (above) had first seen combat in the Mexican War. In March 1862 he was given command of the Army of Virginia and immediately alienated his men by criticizing them for past losses stating, "I have come to you from the West, where we have always seen the backs of our enemies." Pope arrogantly believed he could take on Lee and Jackson but was instead soundly defeated at the battle of Second Bull Run. He was relieved of command on September 2 and replaced by George B. McClellan, who had commanded the Army of the Potomac earlier.

Harpers Ferry (right) was fifty miles from Washington, D.C. Lee ordered Stonewall Jackson to capture the town, hoping to shift his supply lines from east of the Blue Ridge Mountains to the Shenandoah Valley. The Federal garrison at Harpers Ferry was commanded by Col. Dixon Miles, who on September 15 concluded that he was outnumbered and that resistance was futile. Before an official surrender could be arranged, a Confederate battery fired on an area occupied by Miles and his officers. The shell struck the colonel and nearly severed his left leg; he died the next day.

that the Rebel army was in a position to threaten Washington itself. Some Northerners imagined that Lee would soon reclaim his home at Arlington. Everyone in the North and the South believed Lee was just one victory from winning the war. If he vanquished just one more Union general or sent one more Union army scurrying back to Washington, politicians were theorizing that the Congress would be willing to let the South go in peace.

°In September 1862 the South had a great opportunity to gain a negotiated settlement. After the Union armies opposing them had suffered two consecutive major defeats and fallen into disarray, many believed that one more Confederate victory might dissolve the Federal will to fight.•

°Pope's Army of Virginia, which had been defeated at Second Bull Run, and McClellan's Army of the Potomac, which had retreated from Virginia's peninsula, were jumbled together in Washington, waiting for a leader to show them the way.• Recognizing this vacuum of leadership, °Lincoln was at a loss for what to do. Pope had been completely discredited. His men would never march under him again. On the other hand, Lincoln was frustrated by McClellan's tendency to consolidate numbers rather than strike when an opportunity was presented. McClellan had dallied interminably on the peninsula and had been slow to reinforce Pope. McClellan had for-

merly had total control over all the Union armies, but Lincoln had taken that from him in the failed experiment with Pope. Now, most of the cabinet advised the president to dismiss McClellan from the army.

Lincoln, however, decided to take a chance on McClellan once more. He gave him a vote of confidence—such as it was. Pope was sent off to fight Indians in Minnesota, and McClellan was chosen to be the Union's general in the East to fight the Confederacy.•

McClellan had been politicking diligently to regain his command, but he was hardly gracious when Lincoln returned the Army of the Potomac to him. "Last night, I received a dispatch from [General in Chief Henry W.] Halleck begging me to help him out of a scrape and take command here. Of course, I could not refuse, so I came over this morning mad as a march hare and had a pretty plain talk with him and Abe. The President expressed the opinion that the trouble now impending could be overcome better by me than anyone else. I only consent to take it for my country's sake, and with the humble hope that God has called me to it," McClellan pronounced in a letter to his wife on September 2, 1862. Although McClellan's troops adored him, the general's lack of respect for the president was notorious. The most outrageous example had transpired several months earlier when the president called on the general's residence for a meeting and was informed that the McClellans were attending a wedding. Lincoln chose to wait, but when the general and his wife returned home, the couple ignored their visitor and went upstairs. Moments later the president was told that McClellan had retired for the evening.

McClellan may not have known it, but Lincoln, a hands-on manager when it came to the war effort, was going to watch McClellan's performance more closely this time. He was also going to take note of the general's subordinates. While Lincoln had but one choice in McClellan at this critical hour, another general might emerge in the coming months. Lincoln went with the best choice at the moment, but he knew he would probably have to replace McClellan when the general's weaknesses surfaced again.

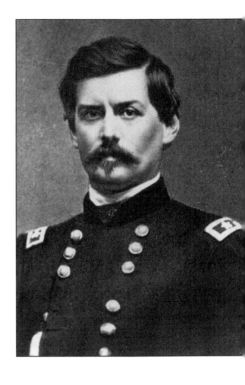

McClellan was a prodigy. He graduated second in his class from West Point in 1846 and went on to serve in Mexico. He was viewed as a gifted officer and joined the American observers in the Crimea. When the Civil War broke out he was given command of volunteers in western Virginia, and his successes there opened the door for elevation to command of the Union army following the disaster at First Manassas. McClellan created an army and then floundered on his seaborne invasion of Virginia. He withdrew only after a significant part of his army was reassigned to Pope, but when Pope failed, Lincoln turned to McClellan to defeat the Southern invaders. When his soldiers heard of his return, a veteran wrote, "The effect of this man's presence upon the Army of the Potomac—in sunshine or rain, in darkness or in daylight, in victory or defeat—was electrical, and too wonderful to make it worth while attempting to give a reason for it."

Lee seemed invulnerable after the battle of Second Manassas, and the Union army was in disarray. When McClellan resumed command, he reinstilled confidence within the men and reorganized the army. Again they were drilled into looking and acting like soldiers, much like the photograph above. Pope was sent to Minnesota to quell an Indian uprising, and McClellan marched northwest with eighty-five thousand men to find the Army of Northern Virginia.

"He has acted badly in this matter, but we must use what tools we have. There is no man in the army who can man these fortifications and lick these troops of ours into shape half as well as he. If he can't fight himself, he excels in making others ready to fight," the president explained on September 5, 1862.

No one in the country, not even the Confederates, doubted McClellan's ability to organize and inspire the Union army, but there were many doubters on both sides who questioned if "Little Mac" could match "Marse Robert" on the battlefield. Lee and McClellan were two entirely different men.

JMM °Lee was a quiet gentleman who concealed within that demeanor the heart of a gambler. He was willing to take enormous risks with the lives of his men to achieve success. McClellan was more flamboyant, even allowing himself to be compared to and called "the Young Napoleon." To fulfill the analogy, McClellan was fond of Napoleonic phrases and gestures, but while Napoleon was a gambler much like Lee, McClellan had the heart of a chicken.•

ON SEPTEMBER 3, 1862—the day after Lincoln rehired McClellan to lead the Union army—Lee wrote to Confederate President Jefferson Davis to suggest an invasion of the North: "Mr. President, the present seems to be the most propitious time since the commencement of the war for the Confederate Army to enter Maryland."

Lee's plan followed common military strategy. °He knew that he could not sit back and rest on the laurels of the victories he had achieved over the summer. It seemed logical to take the war into the enemy's camp for the first time, to lead the Army of Northern Virginia across the Potomac and invade the North.• He thought he might go as far as Philadelphia before swinging down on Washington.

°There were a number of reasons to support a Northern invasion. The Southern public, shocked at the destruction the Union army brought on the Southern civilians, was clamoring for it. The off-year elections in the North were only two months away, and Lee and other Southerners believed a Confederate victory in the North might sway those elections enough to bring about demands for peace. Strategically, Lee could only go in one direction. If he moved east or west or south, he would be giving up land that had been dearly bought with Southern blood. It would seem like a setback to his

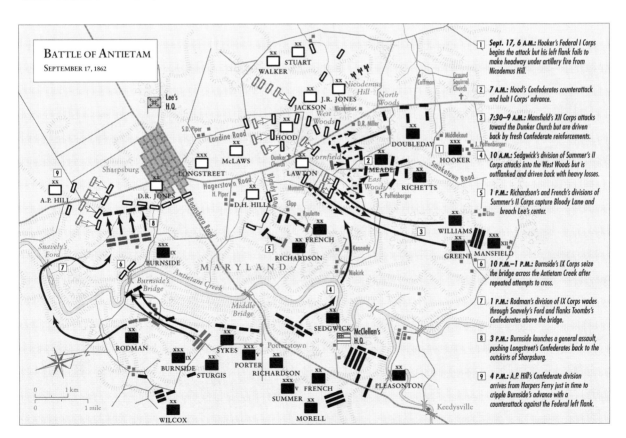

BATTLE OF ANTIETAM
SEPTEMBER 17, 1862

1. **Sept. 17, 6 A.M.:** Hooker's Federal I Corps begins the attack but his left flank fails to make headway under artillery fire from Nicodemus Hill.

2. **7 A.M.:** Hood's Confederates counterattack and halt I Corps' advance.

3. **7:30–9 A.M.:** Mansfield's XII Corps attacks toward the Dunker Church but are driven back by fresh Confederate reinforcements.

4. **10 A.M.:** Sedgwick's division of Summer's II Corps attacks into the West Woods but is outflanked and driven back with heavy losses.

5. **1 P.M.:** Richardson's and French's divisions of Summer's II Corps capture Bloody Lane and breach Lee's center.

6. **10 P.M.–1 P.M.:** Burnside's IX Corps seize the bridge across the Antietam Creek after repeated attempts to cross.

7. **1 P.M.:** Rodman's division of IX Corps wades through Snavely's Ford and flanks Toombs's Confederates above the bridge.

8. **3 P.M.:** Burnside launches a general assault, pushing Longstreet's Confederates back to the outskirts of Sharpsburg.

9. **4 P.M.:** A.P. Hill's Confederate division arrives from Harpers Ferry just in time to cripple Burnside's advance with a counterattack against the Federal left flank.

Col. William T. Wofford commanded the famous Texas Brigade at Antietam, consisting of three Texas regiments, one Georgia unit, and one South Carolina unit. In the morning hours the brigade entered the Cornfield and encountered the Union's Iron Brigade—soldiers from Wisconsin, Indiana, and Michigan who had just recently earned the nickname during fighting at South Mountain. Wofford later described the combat in the Cornfield: "The men and officers were gallantly shooting down the gunners, and for a moment silenced them. At this the enemy's fire was most terrific, their first line of infantry having been driven back to their guns, which now opened a furious fire, together with their second line of infantry." Out of 2,332, the Texas Brigade lost 72 killed and 400 wounded.

men. Going north was the only logical direction to move. On a more practical side, Northern Virginia itself had been so ravaged by both armies that Lee wanted to take the war away from that region for a while to give Virginia's farmers a chance to bring in the late summer harvest as best they could. In Lee's mind the farmers of Pennsylvania would have plenty of food for his soldiers. Politically, Europe was still debating recognition of the Confederacy, and a victory on Northern soil would make the Southern cause seem more credible.

Finally, a Southern invasion of the border state of Maryland posed a delicate issue. Both Lee and Davis had high hopes that the presence of the Army of Northern Virginia in Maryland would bring Marylanders to the Confederacy's colors. In their view, Lee would liberate Maryland from the yoke of Northern oppression. Lee imagined his ranks would swell with new recruits once the men of Maryland saw that the South was winning the war.

The time seemed right for invasion. The only problem Lee foresaw was that his army was not in the best condition to march hundreds of miles into enemy territory. °The Army of Northern Virginia, victorious though it was, was in rather sad shape in early September. Battlefield losses, wounds, sickness, exhaustion, starvation, and exposure had reduced the army to about forty thousand troops, roughly two-thirds of its former strength.•

°The Confederate army that crossed the Potomac into Maryland was ragged, worn, and weary from battle after battle over the last few months. Thousands of exhausted men fell out along the wayside as stragglers; they just could not keep up the pace of a march bent on invasion. As the men neared the Potomac River, which divided North from South, they perked up as they realized they were about to carry the war to the North. As they stripped off their trousers and tied their accoutrements to their muskets to wade across, the regimental bands played "Maryland, My Maryland," a year-old song commemorating the clash between Southern sympathizers and Union troops in Baltimore. Lee's army was filled with hope.•

While the morale of the Southern army improved, Lincoln became concerned when news of this Rebel invasion of Maryland reached the War Department in Washington. °A range of issues were in Lincoln's mind as the Confederate invasion unfolded, some of which matched the Confederate goals. He feared European recognition of the Confederacy, which could lead to an alliance and possibly a world war. The Northern president was also considering a move that the South had not anticipated: emancipation of the slaves.•

°Lincoln had already made up his mind in July 1862 that he wanted to issue what he called the Emancipation Proclamation. He told his cabinet that the document was ready, but he needed a significant Union victory to announce it. If he announced it after a victory, the document would have some moral and material force. If he announced it after a defeat, it would appear as a desperate measure. He needed a victory.• While Lincoln waited for a decisive victory to free the slaves, the Northern press called for immediate emancipation.

Col. William H. Irwin rashly and carelessly threw his five regiments— the Seventh Maine, the Twentieth, Thirty-third, Forty-ninth, and Seventy-seventh New York—toward the Dunker Church and afterward was accused of being drunk during the battle. The brigade attacked and repulsed the Third Arkansas and Twenty-seventh North Carolina, driving the Southerners from their positions and gaining possession of the Dunker Church area. Confederates positioned in the West Woods, however, attacked Irwin's brigade and forced the Federals to retreat and reform just east of the Dunker Church at a cost of 342 casualties.

JMM   °In August 1862 Horace Greeley, the editor of the North's leading newspaper, the *New York Tribune,* published an editorial called "The Prayer of 20 Millions" in which Greeley claimed that twenty million Northerners were demanding some decisive action against slavery that would weaken the Confederacy and add to the moral force of the Union cause.•

GWG   °Lincoln could not ignore Greeley, a man who shaped the opinions of voters. Nevertheless, Greeley was one of the great cranks of the nineteenth century with a strong opinion on everything pertaining to the war, although he lacked military experience himself.•

JMM   °The U.S. president took the unusual step of responding to Greeley's editorial with a public letter that was published in the *New York Tribune* on August 22, 1862. "My preeminent purpose in this war," Lincoln wrote, "is to save the Union."• He then went on to explain, "If I could save the Union without freeing any slave, I would do it; if I could save it by freeing all the slaves, I would do it; and if I could save it by freeing some and leaving others alone, I would also do that."

The Confederate Army of Northern Virginia knew little about Northern politicians and their plans for the country. All they knew on September 5, 1862, was that they were on Union soil for the first time in the war.

"We crossed the Potomac at White's Ford, a few miles below Leesburg, and started forward in the direction of

During the morning phase of the battle, Gen. Joseph E. Hooker ordered Abner Doubleday's and James Ricketts' divisions to attack the Confederate position near the Dunker Church. George Meade's division acted as reserves. Maj. Rufus Dawes participated in this fighting and recalled the scene: "Forward is the word. The men are loading and firing with demoniacal fury and shouting and laughing hysterically . . . the whole field . . . is covered with rebels fleeing. . . . Great numbers are shot while climbing over the high post and rail fences. . . . We push on over the open fields half way to the little church."

Frederick, Maryland. The passage of the river by the troops, marching in fours—well closed up, shouting, laughing, singing—with a brass band in front playing 'Maryland, My Maryland,' was a spirited scene," recalled Henry Kyd Douglas.

°Upon crossing the Potomac, Lee issued a proclamation to the citizens of Maryland: "We have come to liberate you from Union tyranny." Being a proud, loyal Southern gentleman, Lee assumed that all Southerners, including Marylanders, would join him.• He made few mistakes during his three-year career as general of the Army of Northern Virginia, but this was one of them. °As his soldiers moved toward Frederick, or Fredericktown, as it was often called then, they were received well by some of the Union citizens, but many more turned their backs on the Confederates, even shouting insults as the Confederates marched by.• "Come on! Come on! Yeah, that's right! March on! March on! You going to all end up dead!" one onlooker called out.

°It was not the kind of reception the Army of Northern Virginia expected.• They were in a Southern slave state. Yet the Confederate soldiers were stunned to find they were not welcome.

On the Union side, word of the Confederate invasion galvanized the men behind their newly reappointed and popular leader, McClellan. Rid of Pope and back under the man who had trained them, the Union army marched

Prior to the war Capt. James Hope of the Second Vermont was a landscape artist. In the above and four additional paintings, he depicted grotesque scenes of the battle. In the foreground are Confederate artillerymen nearly cut in two. This scene shows the advance of Maj. Gen. John Sedgwick's division. As several Federal regiments entered the West Woods (upper left corner), Rebel reinforcements sent a devastating volley into their ranks. A sergeant in the First Georgia remembered, "You could hear laughing, cursing, yelling and the groans of the wounded and dying."

from Washington to meet the Rebel threat. Their resolve found expression in the words of Capt. David Hunter Strother: "This move must be the ruin of the rebellion since to suppose they can conquer the United States is absurd. They must then perish by their own movement."

WHILE LEE'S ARMY tried to recruit the men of Maryland for an eventual attack into Pennsylvania, °one of the most fortuitous twists for the Union of the entire war occurred.°

°Lee suspected McClellan would be hesitant to blunt the Confederate invasion, so he considered a number of objectives that had to be accomplished before his army could push into Pennsylvania. Chief among them was taking the town of Harpers Ferry, Virginia, at the confluence of the Shenandoah and Potomac Rivers.° In the town was a major Federal supply depot holding stores of war matériel and forage. °If Lee ignored Harpers Ferry, the Federal garrison of twelve to thirteen thousand troops would be to his rear, a dangerous potential Yankee staging area to entrap him on the wrong side of the Potomac.°

On Tuesday, September 9, the Southern commander revealed a daring plan to his generals. From Frederick, Lee issued Special Orders No. 191 that detailed Stonewall Jackson and more than half the Rebel force, twenty-six brigades, to seize the arsenal at Harpers Ferry. The rest of the army would remain with Lee to march north toward Pennsylvania.

Lee's plan was bold and almost unprecedented. In enemy territory with a large enemy force in pursuit, he divided his army °into five different units so it could surround Harpers Ferry. He did so in the face of McClellan's army, which was intact and at least twice as large as Lee's entire force. The Southern commander counted on McClellan's slowness and timidity to keep him at bay so the Federal commander would never discover just how scattered the Army of Northern Virginia was. Lee gambled, but his understanding of McClellan's generalship made it a worthwhile risk.•

Lee did not anticipate, however, that a copy of his battle orders, which detailed the splitting of his army, would fall into the hands of McClellan himself. Yet that happened because of a bureaucratic blunder.

°Each division commander had been given a copy of the orders.• James Longstreet thought the order so secret that he allegedly ate his copy. Stonewall Jackson made a copy of the order for his brother-in-law, Maj. Gen. Daniel Harvey Hill. One of Lee's staff officers, not knowing of Jackson's copy, made a second copy for Hill, which ended up in the hands of one of Hill's staff officers. Knowing that Hill had a copy, this officer may have considered the second copy a war souvenir. °He used it as a wrapper for three cigars, but somehow the three cigars fell to the ground in Frederick. The extra copy of Special Orders No. 191, the most secret paper in all of

For decades this photograph was believed to show a portion of the Antietam battlefield while the battle was being fought. In recent years that contention has been challenged. The smoke in the upper right corner is most likely from Union campfires and not from gun powder. Furthermore, the artillery battery in the distance is not waiting to go into battle. The reserve artillery units on the day of the conflict were deployed near McClellan's headquarters, which is not in the picture. The man in the foreground probably posed for the photographer, who was Alexander Gardner. It was he who miscaptioned the image as "View of the Battle-field . . . on day of battle."

Confederates from Brig. Gen. William E. Starke's Louisiana brigade battle behind the fence along the Hagerstown Turnpike. A Southern journalist witnessed the conflict in this area and wrote: "The fire now became fearful and incessant, [and] merged into a tumultuous chorus that made the earth tremble. The discharge of musketry sounded upon the ear like the rolling of a thousand distant drums." At one moment the two lines came within thirty yards of each other. Starke's unit was caught in a deadly cross fire and retreated to the West Woods. A Federal infantryman ran toward the First Louisiana flag, which lay in the road, and was cut down by seven bullets.

the South, lay in a Maryland field, waiting to be found by the enemy.•

JMM °Two soldiers of an Indiana regiment resting in a field near Frederick found the three cigars and the paper wrapped around them. Finding three cigars is something a soldier might pray for, so the two men anticipated a good smoke. Just before lighting up, one of the men, a sergeant, glanced at the paper, which started with the phrase "Headquarters of the Army of Northern Virginia."•

BP °Realizing the importance of the paper, the soldiers took the document and the cigars to their commander, who confiscated the cigars as well. The lost order went up the chain of command to McClellan himself.• The handwriting of Lee's staff officer was verified by a prewar acquaintance serving on McClellan's staff. To the best of his knowledge, the Federal commander knew that the order was authentic.

BP °On September 13, McClellan held in his hands a golden opportunity. The single sheet of paper detailed the whole Confederate battle plan. He knew his enemy had divided his army into several smaller units. He knew where these units had been sent and when they were supposed to rejoin.• Any other general would have used the plans to attack Lee immediately, while he was most vulnerable, but McClellan was not any other general.

BP °With his own army massed near Frederick, all that lay between McClellan and the portion of the Confederate army with Lee at its head were a few gaps through South Mountain, Maryland. If McClellan could move his army over the mountain and strike at Lee's scattered command, he could destroy the Confederates before the pieces rejoined.•

WCD °McClellan informed Washington, "I have come into possession of information that gives me these plans."• To the officers on his staff, he said, "Here is a paper with which, if I cannot whip Bobby Lee, I will be willing to go home!"

WCD °Even though he had the tremendous advantage of knowing what Lee was doing, McClellan did little to

take advantage of this knowledge. Instead of moving on Lee's dispersed army, McClellan called for more men: "I'm still not strong enough to take on Lee."• At that time, however, he probably had at least three times as many men as Lee's central corps. Even after the fragments of the Army of Northern Virginia reunited, Lee had only forty thousand men to face McClellan's ninety thousand.

°The Union commander was beneficiary of the greatest security leak in American military history, but he reacted to it with the timidity of a newborn calf trying to walk.• Instead of moving toward Lee that night, McClellan waited until the morning of September 14 to make his move. Luckily for Lee, the Southern commander either learned or deduced that McClellan knew the Confederate battle plan. Some sources claim that a Maryland civilian who had been in McClellan's camp when the lost order was delivered had made his way to Lee's lines to warn the general. °Whether or not Lee knew that McClellan had knowledge of his order, Lee did know within a day that McClellan was moving toward the passes more rapidly than he normally would. He knew McClellan was pursuing him, and the handful of Confederate soldiers holding the mountain gaps on South Mountain certainly knew they would be the first to engage the Yankee army.• °The columns of ninety thousand blueclad soldiers snaking across the Middletown

After the Federal infantrymen successfully crossed Burnside's Bridge they drove the defending Confederates through the fields and advanced toward Sharpsburg. A member of the Ninth New York Zouaves wrote, "The whole landscape for an instant turned slightly red. . . . The truth is, when bullets are whacking against tree trunks and solid shot are cracking skulls like eggshells, the consuming passion in the breast of the average man is to get out of the way. Between the physical fear of going forward and the moral fear of turning back, there is a predicament of exceptional awkwardness from which a hidden hole in the ground would be a wonderfully welcome outlet."

Confederate sharpshooters fired from behind a stone wall as Federal infantry attempted to cross the bridge, which was later named after the Federal commander on the scene, Ambrose E. Burnside. The troops could have waded across the creek, but the Union officers were fixated on charging across the small stone structure. Finally, Col. Edward Ferrero's brigade was given the responsibility of taking the bridge. The colonel yelled out to two of this regiments, "It is General Burnside's especial request that the two 51st's take that bridge. Will you do it?" A Pennsylvanian yelled out, "Will you give us our whiskey, Colonel, if we make it?" (As a disciplinary act, the soldiers' whiskey ration was being withheld.) "Yes, by God," Ferrero replied. With that, the Fifty-first New York and Fifty-first Pennsylvania captured the bridge.

Valley and heading toward South Mountain were an awesome sight.•

Lee reacted quickly and sent a brigade of infantry to hold the main path through South Mountain. Their only immediate support came from Jeb Stuart's cavalry.

°On the crest at Turner's Gap, Gen. Daniel H. Hill bore most of the responsibility for the defense of South Mountain. Watching the oncoming blue wave, he knew that his men could not stop the juggernaut rolling toward them.• Lee rushed more men to three widely separated gaps, but the Rebels could only check, not stop, the Yankee advance.

°Bitter fighting lasted five or six hours on ground so steep that bodies toppled down the mountainside. One Union general—Jesse L. Reno—and one Confederate general—Samuel Garland Jr.—were killed as the Army of the Potomac threw itself against a small Confederate force on top of South Mountain. Finally, the overwhelming numbers of the Federals prevailed, and McClellan seized the summit of South Mountain.•

More than four thousand soldiers were killed or wounded in the fight. That night Lee retreated to

Antietam Creek, near the town of Sharpsburg. He expected worse to follow as his army still had not reformed itself. McClellan, however, continued to brood that he did not have enough men to give a good fight to the supposedly much larger Confederate army.

JIR °Anyone but McClellan would have immediately pressed forward, gone down South Mountain while there were still hours of daylight, and attacked Lee when he knew the Confederate army was still divided. Instead, McClellan sat atop South Mountain. From the mountaintop, rather than on a contested battlefield, McClellan watched the Confederate army consolidate.•

The next morning, September 15, Lee contemplated retreat. With his back to the Potomac, he feared his small part of the army might be trapped, but McClellan did not advance. Then Lee received news that Harpers Ferry had surrendered and that Stonewall Jackson was marching to his rescue with all but A. P. Hill's light division. Looking over the rolling Antietam Valley, Lee told his lieutenants, "We will make our stand on those hills." His plan for the invasion of Pennsylvania was now shattered; his only hope was to preserve the Army of Northern Virginia to fight another day.

WG °Lee followed up his greatest gamble of the war by staying on the field to fight McClellan. He knew of McClellan's reluctance to fight and likely thought he could defeat the Northern commander on the battlefield by frightening him. He believed that McClellan lacked the moral fiber to stand up to him. On the other hand, Lee's army was outnumbered, in enemy territory, and backed against the wide Potomac River. Fighting would be a great risk.

Lee, however, did not want to concede defeat without some kind of a confrontation. Militarily, it might have been a poor decision to fight rather than retreat, but fighting was part of Lee's makeup.•

"In his address to the people of Maryland, General Lee had almost pledged that his army would not give up that

The Boonesborough Pike crossed the Antietam Creek via the Burnside Bridge. This crossing was also known as the middle bridge. In the distance is Joshua Newcomer's farm. The ridge in the background was the first line established by the Confederates on September 15. The first Federal unit to reach this bridge was the Fifth New Hampshire. McClellan then ordered Brig. Gen. George Sykes's division of the Fifth Corps to take the bridge and prevent the Southern army from burning it. Lee was not ready to do battle, and he pulled his line back toward Sharpsburg. The bridge was taken intact.

On the morning of September 16, 1862, McClellan cautiously deployed his army on the east side of Antietam Creek. A Federal signal corps detachment was sent to Elk Ridge, known locally as Red Hill. At the time of the battle this log observation platform had not been built. Signal men had to climb the trees and observe the Confederate army from a perched position. A flagman in the branches below relayed the enemy's movements to McClellan's headquarters about two miles away at the Pry House. This photograph was taken by Gardner in September or October 1862.

state without a struggle," wrote Henry Kyd Douglas. If he could win on Maryland's soil, it would be of incalculable benefit to his army and the cause of the South. Whatever his reasons, he determined to stake his outnumbered army against McClellan's and to take his chances.

SEPTEMBER 17, 1862, dawned in the valley of the Antietam, an ancestral home of the Delaware Indians. Near the Confederate line stood a church built by a German sect called Dunkers, because they baptized their brethren in the creek. They were opposed to war of any kind, but they could not stop what was about to happen near the small town of Sharpsburg, °a quiet, sleepy village in western Maryland surrounded by hills to the north and to the east.• °At the time of the Civil War, there were about thirteen hundred residents, primarily farmers, many of German descent.•

°Lee's engineering eye immediately saw that the hilly topography would offer a good defensive position, and angled his left flank toward the Potomac River. He then ran his line in a semicircle facing north and east around the village of Sharpsburg and south along the banks of Antietam Creek. He used the hills and the water as natural defensive obstacles that would force the Federals to come to him. It was as good a defensive position as Lee probably could have found in that part of the country, and it was just the type of ground an army outnumbered nearly two to one should have.•

Lee watched as McClellan positioned his men for battle. McClellan's plan was simple: attack Lee's left, center, and right with three equal parts of the army while holding the fourth part in reserve. It was simple, and had it been effectively carried out, any one of the three parts of Lee's line could have failed, giving the Federals a breach through which they could pour reserves. It was a good battle plan that McClellan and his subordinates would not make work.

°The first advance that McClellan tried was from the north at dawn, against the Confederate left flank. The troops of Maj. Gen. Joseph Hooker started forward, heading south from the North Woods through Farmer Miller's Cornfield toward an objective the Federals

could see: the whitewashed Dunker Church resting beyond the cornfield.•

°Throughout most of the morning some of the heaviest fighting yet seen in the war took place in this small cornfield. Heavily outnumbered, the Confederates under Stonewall Jackson stood and countercharged against several charges by Hooker's Federals.•

°During the battle senior officers threw themselves personally into the melee to try to maintain the momentum or to try to hold their ground. It became a seesaw battle back and forth with terrible, terrible losses on both sides.• °The corn was cut down by bullets and artillery, and bodies covered so much of the ground that it was said after the fighting was over that a person could walk through that forty-acre cornfield and never touch the ground.

After the armies had exhausted themselves in that sector of the battlefield during the morning, the fighting shifted to the center of the Confederate line. There the Confederates waited in a farm lane southeast of the Dunker Church. Decades of use had caused the road to sink below the surface of the adjacent land, and it was known as the Sunken Lane or Sunken Road. The Confederates used this farm road as a ready-made rifle pit from which they could fire on Federals attacking from the exposed hillsides.•

°If the fighting in the Cornfield was bad, the battle for the Sunken Road was even worse. The roadway soon acquired another nickname: Bloody Lane. There, out-

Capt. Joseph E. Knap's battery (above left) was assigned to the Twelfth Corps and fought along the Smoketown Road between the East and West Woods. This unit was engaged around 7:30 A.M. Later in the morning a section from his battery was ordered to take position on the left of Brig. Gen. George S. Greene's brigade. This view was taken just south of the Smoketown Road. Battery E was more fortunate than other Federal units; it counted one killed, six wounded, and one missing. This photograph was taken September 19 on the battlefield.

The photograph above (right) was taken by Gardner around September 20. At the time of the battle, Dr. Anson Hurd had accompanied the Fourteenth Indiana to the front lines. As the fighting intensified, the doctor moved his operations back about a mile and a quarter from the main division hospital. The doctor was then assigned to help care for wounded Confederates near Otho J. Smith's farm. Records show that about 1,396 wounded men from both sides were treated at this site. While helping the injured, Hurd was also suffering from rheumatism, asthma, piles, and chronic diarrhea. Due to his ill health he was forced to retire three months later in late December 1862.

159

In early July 1862 President Lincoln began work on the Emancipation Proclamation. One witness remembered watching the president: "[H]e did not write much at once. He would study between times and when he made up his mind he would put down a line or two." In late July he read a draft to his cabinet (right). The proclamation declared all slaves in the states then in rebellion to be free on January 1, 1863. By linking the Union cause with emancipation, the president took the war to a higher moral plane at the risk of losing unqualified support in the North from those who would not fight to free slaves. His advisers counseled him to not announce the proclamation until the North had won a substantial battle, otherwise it would seem like a desperate political measure.

numbered Confederates, mostly North Carolinians and Alabamians, stood and held against numerous Yankee charges. The brave men of the Union Second Corps charged time after time after time, strewing the landscape with their own dead.● Some of the worst casualties were suffered by the famous New York Irish Brigade. They attacked shouting a battle cry in their native Gaelic, which, translated, meant "Clear the Way!"●

BP   °The Sunken Road was a formidable Confederate position, but the Union troops pinned down in front of it fired back, which meant that anybody moving toward the Sunken Road or trying to move out of the Sunken Road made a good target. The Confederate defenders crowded down into the road itself, and that later had tragic repercussions.●

After suffering terrible losses, troops of the Second Corps finally broke through the Bloody Lane when a mistaken order pulled a Confederate unit out of the trench. Union soldiers poured into the hole, and they were able to start shooting down the Confederate line, turning the Sunken Road into a slaughter pen from which the Confederates had no escape.

GWG   °The Federals finally punched through the center of the Confederate line, and the way to Sharpsburg lay open. Gen. Israel Richardson, one of the Union division commanders who had achieved that breakthrough, begged McClellan to follow up on this success and push through to Sharpsburg to divide Lee's army in two. McClellan, who was observing the fighting from his headquarters at the Pry House, within sight of the Sunken Road, refused to exploit the Union break-through.● He did not know how many men Lee had, and he did not want to endanger the Union soldiers who were trying to take advantage of the breakthrough. Richardson, the man who could have launched an attack on Lee himself, was cut down by artillery fire. He would linger in a battlefield hospital for more than two months before dying.

°As usual, McClellan had estimated that he was facing twice as many enemy troops as he actually was, and so he did not take advantage of his breakthrough. Instead, the battle shifted to the southern end of the battlefield, to a stone bridge over Antietam Creek.●

°The fight for the bridge—later called Burnside's Bridge for Maj. Gen. Ambrose Burnside whose men attacked it—was the scene of great bravery on both sides. A few hundred Georgia sharpshooters held the heights across from the bridge, and their accurate, fast shooting keep several thousand Federals at bay.

The fighting here illustrated how out of touch McClellan was and how inept some of his subordinates were, including Burnside.● McClellan had ordered Burnside to cross the Antietam and gain a foothold on the western bank. Burnside's men could have waded across the shal-

This view looks northwest along Hall Street and was taken either on September 21 or 22. Sharpsburg, founded in 1763, was a small rural town in Maryland. When Lee's army deployed just west of Antietam Creek, many residents fled the village and others hid in their basements. At least one civilian was killed during the fighting. When the residents returned to their homes they found dead and wounded Confederates throughout the town and thousands of dead and wounded from both armies littering their farms and the surrounding countryside.

161

This photograph was taken two days after the battle. In the background is the West Woods. To the right of the dead soldier a grave with a makeshift marker can be seen. The grave is that of twenty-two-year-old First Lt. John A. Clark, Company D, Seventh Michigan. Clark's family later claimed his remains and reburied him in Woodlawn Cemetery, Monroe, Michigan. The unburied Southerner is believed to have been either a Louisiana or North Carolina soldier.

low creek, but Burnside became obsessed with taking the bridge itself rather than crossing the creek. Again and again his men tried to cross the bridge, but the Georgians covering it from the hill behind repulsed every effort. Finally, Union troops, promised a ration of whiskey if they stormed across and secured a position, overwhelmed the Confederates. There, on the west side of the creek, Burnside halted to collect his command, and Lee shifted more troops to save the Rebel right flank.

JIR   °It was on this portion of the battle-field that one of the dramatic moments of the battle happened that afternoon. General Lee himself rode over to send a Virginia artillery battery back into action. As he was giving directions, one of the young gunners—his face blackened by powder and gun smoke—walked up to Lee, saluted, and said, "General, are you going to send us in again?" Lee looked at the young lad for a puzzled moment then finally recognized him as his own son, nineteen-year-old Robert E. Lee Jr. The general smiled lovingly at his son and replied: "Yes, my son. You all must do what you can to help drive these people back."•

McClellan's left wing was now on the other side of Antietam Creek and most of his forces were poised to strike at Lee's exhausted army, which was trying to regroup

JIR outside of Sharpsburg. °The climactic moment was supposed to come in the afternoon, when Burnside launched a massive attack against the Confederate right flank. Lee had shifted men back and forth and back and forth until his ranks were extremely thin. The Southern commander feared that this assault by Burnside would break the right flank.• Both Lee and Burnside likely believed this last assault would end the battle and maybe the war.

BP   °Burnside moved his men forward in a grand sweeping advance. He did not seem to notice another blue-clad column marching toward him. If he did, Burnside likely assumed they were more Federals because of their blue uniforms. They were not. The troops coming toward the Federals were A. P. Hill's light division, some of whom were wearing captured Federal uniforms from Harpers Ferry. Having finished paroling the prisoners at Harpers Ferry and cleaning up after the surrender there, Hill had marched his men steadily for more than ten hours to reach the battlefield. They arrived just in time to deliver two devastating volleys into Burnside's unsuspecting men.•

Shouting a defiant Rebel yell, Hill's men slammed into the exposed Union flank. Seeing this, McClellan imagined this was just the first wave of Confederate reinforcements joining the battle. Rather than press his attack he decided to halt and hold his ground. The battle was over.

°At the end of the day, 13,000 Union troops and 10,700 Confederate troops had been killed, wounded, or were missing. The sun set on a scene of carnage unparalleled in the American Civil War.• °The veterans in the Army of the Potomac and the veterans in the Army of Northern Virginia were accustomed to war, but few of those soldiers were prepared for what happened at Antietam Creek.•

Stonewall Jackson's aide Henry Kyd Douglas described what he saw in those twilight moments: "It was a dreadful scene. The dead and dying lay thick on the field like harvest sheaths. The pitiable cries for water and pleas for help were much more horrible to listen to than the deadliest sounds of battle. Silent were the dead and motionless, but here and there were raised stiff arms. Heads made a last effort to lift themselves from the ground. Prayers were mingled with oaths, and midnight hid all distinction between blue and gray."

ON THURSDAY, SEPTEMBER 18, 1862, there was little fighting, and several white flags were honored to allow for burial details to begin the work of interment. Both armies stood defiant, waiting for the other to attack. Neither did.

During the battle Brig. Gen. Roswell S. Ripley's, Brig. Gen. Alfred H. Colquitt's, and Brig. Gen. Samuel Garland's brigades occupied this area with Alabama, North Carolina, and Georgia regiments. Throughout the conflict the Confederates sustained heavy casualties from artillery fire. Approximately twenty-five bodies lie just southeast of the Smoketown Road on the Mumma Farm. According to the custom of the period, the side that held the battlefield at the end of the fighting had the unceremonious task of burying the dead. Unidentified enemy dead were usually buried in long trenches.

The Hagerstown Pike is on the other side of the fence (above left); the small road to the left is a farm lane. Only one Southern brigade deployed behind this fence along the pike, Brig. Gen. William Starke's Louisiana unit. Starke's men fought against the Union's Iron Brigade. Out of 650 present, 70 were killed and 204 were wounded. The Tenth Louisiana lost its heaviest casualties along the rail fence.

The Sunken Road (above right) was a well-worn farm road that provided a natural rifle pit for two brigades of D. H. Hill's men. It was the center of Lee's defensive line and the scene of some of the fiercest fighting of the day. Beginning at about 10 A.M. and for the next four hours, wave after wave of Federals from the Second Corps assaulted the position before finally breaking through. What had once been a natural defensive position for the Southerners then became a slaughter pen. Estimates of casualties at the Sunken Road were three thousand Union soldiers and twenty-five hundred Confederates, reason enough for the old road to become known as Bloody Lane. After the battle, as the photograph above shows, a Yankee officer claimed the roadway was filled with enough bodies that he could walk down the lane without touching the ground.

GWG

McClellan, who had missed an extraordinary opportunity to destroy the Confederate army, believed that he had won a great victory. Writing to his wife, he exulted: "The spectacle yesterday was the grandest I could conceive of. Nothing could be more sublime. Those on whose judgement I rely tell me that I fought the battle splendidly, and that it was a masterpiece of art."

While the Federal commander congratulated himself, Lee took advantage of nightfall to begin the retreat back across the Potomac and into Virginia. McClellan failed to pursue him immediately or to engage the Confederates as they crossed the river. Since the Confederate invasion had been repulsed and Union soldiers occupied the battlefield, he believed he had accomplished his task.

°When McClellan failed to mount a vigorous pursuit, some of his men turned bitter. They had lost so many comrades, and now they were letting the Rebel army get away. No one, however, was more disappointed at Lee's escape than Lincoln,• who even visited the general's camp to urge him to pursue and engage Lee again.

On September 19 photographer Alexander Gardner also arrived from Washington, D.C. He found no glory on the battlefield, just the wreckage of war, which he photographed. Officers directed him to some of the more gory spots.

Union Capt. David Hunter Strother described the battlefield that Gardner found: "In the bloody cornfield,

Burying the dead was one of the worst tasks a soldier had to endure. The dead seen here are possibly from either Gibbon's or Patrick's Union brigades. One Federal infantryman who survived the conflict contemplated what this fight had meant: "I felt, as never so strongly before, how utterly absurd in the face of high Heaven is this whole game of war, relieved only from contempt and ridicule by its tragic accompaniments. . . . Within a space of four square miles lay two thousand men, some stiff and stark, looking with visionless eyes up into the pitying heavens."

lay two or three hundred festering bodies, nearly all of them Rebels. Heads and faces hideously swelled, covered with dust until they looked like clods. Killed during the charge and flight, their attitudes were wild and frightful. In a lane, hollowed out and affording some protection, the dead lay in heaps. The line was a quarter of a mile in length, and they were close enough to touch each other. In front of this was another line along a fence row. There were at least a thousand Rebel dead in this field. This exceeds all the slaughter I have yet seen."

JMM °When Gardner's photographs were exhibited in Mathew Brady's studio in New York City a month after the battle, thousands of people saw them. They were shocked. War was no longer glorious, no longer romantic, no longer heroic.•

The battle at Antietam was not the grand victory that Lincoln wanted, but he would take what he could get. On Monday, September 22, 1862, he announced his plans for the Emancipation Proclamation, which would become effective January 1, 1863.

BP °Lincoln knew that Antietam was not a decisive victory, but he was pleased that McClellan's army had thwarted Lee and held on to Maryland. The North had won a victory of sorts, so the Yankee president used the perception of victory as the opportunity to sign the Emancipation Proclamation to carry the war to the higher moral plane of freeing the slaves:• "On the first day of January in the year of Our Lord one thousand eight hundred and sixty-three, all persons held as slaves within any state or a designated part of a state, the people whereof shall then be in rebellion against the United States, shall be then thence forward and forever

JMM free." °The fight was now for both the Union and free-

GWG dom.• °The Emancipation Proclamation changed the entire focus of the Civil War; the entire fabric of Southern society was at stake.•

Although Lee's army had been severely bloodied at Antietam, the Maryland campaign was not entirely a failure. The Shenandoah Valley farmers brought in crops to feed the Rebel cause that winter. Europe did not recognize the Confederacy, and Maryland did not join it, but for one brief moment that autumn, the state of Virginia had peace.

Two days after the November elections, McClellan was relieved of command, primarily because he failed to follow up on his victory at Antietam. Despite "Little Mac's" enduring popularity with his soldiers, Lincoln had begged him for weeks to attack a weakened Lee, but McClellan refused, citing the need for his own army to recover. Lincoln sarcastically dubbed the Army of the Potomac "McClellan's bodyguard." More than twenty thousand men of the Army of the Potomac had been

The men seated from left to right are: Pvt. Robert J. Morgan, Lt. Frederick W. Owen, Lt. Aaron Jerome, and Lt. Edward Pierce. Pierce transferred to the signal corps in 1861. At the age of twenty-four he aided in overseeing a signal station near the North Woods. Jerome and Pierce served at Gettysburg and were stationed on Little Round Top. They are holding flags that were used in semaphore. The black men are probably the officers' servants.

Weeks after the battle Lincoln traveled by train to visit McClellan and try to convince him to pursue Lee's army. Along the way the president was greeted and cheered in Frederick, Maryland, which was recorded in the engraving to the left. The general waited nineteen days after Lincoln's visit before he started after the Confederate force. Lincoln relieved McClellan of command. The president later said to his secretary, John Hay, "I determined to make the test. If he let them get away I would remove him. He did so and I relieved him."

held in reserve during the battle. Had McClellan exploited the breakthrough at the center of the Confederate line, the war might have ended there.

WCD   °Despite all the enthusiasm and the euphoria of the early days of the war, when people North and South thought it would last for a summer and be glorious, there were thoughtful, insightful men like Lee, Lincoln, Davis, and others who realized that the issue of decades was not going to be settled in a war of weeks.• Lincoln offered little consolation when he observed, "God wills this contest and wills that it shall not end yet. He could give the final victory to either side, any day. Yet the contest proceeds."

JIR   °The battle of Antietam will forever be one of the great and meaningful battles in American history. At the same time, it would be hard to find a more mismanaged battle than the one McClellan mismanaged here.• In 1862 the population of the United States and the Confederacy was about thirty-four million. It has been estimated that one out of every twenty people knew someone who was killed or wounded at Antietam. By any measure of human decency, the Civil War should have ended at Antietam, but in the months ahead other battles showed that the war could still offer even more terrible carnage.

FREDERICKSBURG

The SECOND YEAR OF THE CIVIL WAR
had taken a great toll on the armies of both the North
and the South. Union Maj. Gen. George B. McClellan had
spent all spring slogging through the swamps of Virginia's
peninsula only to be repulsed and retreat shortly after his
army caught sight of the church spires of Richmond. By
late summer, Gen. Robert E. Lee, the new commander of
the main Confederate army, the Army of Northern Virginia, had routed another Union army under Maj. Gen.
John Pope at the battle of Second Manassas, twenty-five
miles south of Washington, D.C. Then came the battle of
Antietam in mid-September, when Lee was forced to
abort his first invasion of the North by an army commanded again by McClellan. In the early winter months
of 1862, the Union seemed poised for victory.

The Federal forces were rested and reequipped. They
were ready to launch a second drive to Richmond. At the
halfway point between Washington and Richmond was
the colonial-era town of Fredericksburg, Virginia. At first
glance on a map, the town appears to be just a stop on
the road to Richmond, but it was to become the next
great proving ground for the superiority of the Union
army. A series of blunders and delays here left the Federal
soldiers devastated and demoralized. At Fredericksburg
the Rebel forces found new hope, and at Fredericksburg
the Union soldier began to doubt the ability of his military commanders, his political leaders, and his moral
cause to restore the Union.

This was evidenced in the soldiers' letters home. For
example, Henry Hastings Curran of the 146th New York

WCD	William C. Davis
GWG	Gary W. Gallagher
AWG	A. Wilson Greene
JMM	James M. McPherson
FO	Frank O'Reilly
DP	Donald Pfanz
BP	Brian Pohanka

Halfway between Washington and Richmond, Fredericksburg, Virginia, was founded in the 1700s. Most of George Washington's childhood was spent near the town, and James Monroe began his law practice in this small village. During the Civil War it attained military significance because it was on the main road that connected the two capitals. Strategically, Fredericksburg was built on the banks of the Rappahannock River, which was navigable all the way to Richmond. Additionally, a rail line ran nearby and provided the quickest route to the Confederate capital.

wrote: "Dear Mother, the fearful battle of Fredericksburg is over. The slaughter is terrible. The result is disastrous. Until we have good generals, it is useless to fight battles. Our real loss is far greater than reported in the newspapers." There is little doubt that Curran's feelings reflected those of the entire Union army.

The battle of Fredericksburg was marked by delays, confusion, and uncertainty on the part of Union commanders that resulted in a heavy death toll among the men who fought in the field. On the other side, historians credit Confederate commanders with luring Federal forces onto ground that was perfect for one thing—killing an attacking army. Fredericksburg was distinguished by both the defensive genius of the Confederates and the offensive blunders of the Federals.

BP °The Fredericksburg battlefield witnessed as much bravery and dedication on the part of the fighting men as any in the Civil War. It was also one of the most tragic and useless because it was a battle that did not have to

GWG happen.• °In a war filled with brutal images, Fredericksburg offers the most brutal: thousands of Union soldiers facing almost certain death or disability against heavily fortified Confederates.•

The soldiers who were there never forgot what they witnessed. Capt. D. P. Conyngham, the historian of the Irish Brigade, which launched one of the bloodiest and most futile assaults, recalled: "The Rebel position was unassailable. It was a perfect slaughter path and column after column was broken against it. It was not a battle. It was a wholesale slaughter of human beings sacrificed to the blind ambition and incapacity of some parties."

Conyngham's bitter observations show why °Fredericksburg has become one of the most compelling of the battles of the war. It was one of the true milestones of the Civil War, marking one of the most resounding Confederate victories won by Lee's Army of Northern Virginia. At the same time, it was one of the most disastrous moments during the Lincoln administration.•

Fredericksburg was a picturesque colonial village. This photograph of Princess Anne Street shows two of the three steeples for which it was known. The closest is the steeple of the brick courthouse, and the steeple in the center is that of Saint George's Episcopal Church. The third steeple, which is not visible, was that of the Baptist church. Although deserted in this image, this street was filled with cheering townspeople when Robert E. Lee and his entourage entered Fredericksburg on November 20.

The cause of the battle of Fredericksburg can be traced back to September 1862, when McClellan turned back the Rebel forces at Antietam, near the town of Sharpsburg, Maryland. He had frustrated Lee's invasion of the North, but instead of pursuing and crushing the weakened and battered Confederate army, McClellan allowed Lee to escape. Nearly two months after the battle, the Union general was still resting and resupplying his army on the Maryland countryside, refusing to pursue Lee, who was back in Virginia.

°McClellan's unwillingness to press Lee was in character with the way he had commanded the Army of the Potomac throughout the war. He was a very cautious man who wanted the situation to be just so before he would risk anything. He always saw reasons why he should not take the initiative, not attack. It was part of his military personality to go slow; thus he simply played his hand as best he could by camping his army in Union territory rather than marching into enemy territory.•

Abraham Lincoln was frustrated by McClellan's reticence to take action. At one point he charged the general with a "case of the slows." Nonetheless, Lincoln tried to keep his comments and actions against McClellan in check. The troops loved this general, and McClellan's strong Democratic political allies kept the president off balance.

171

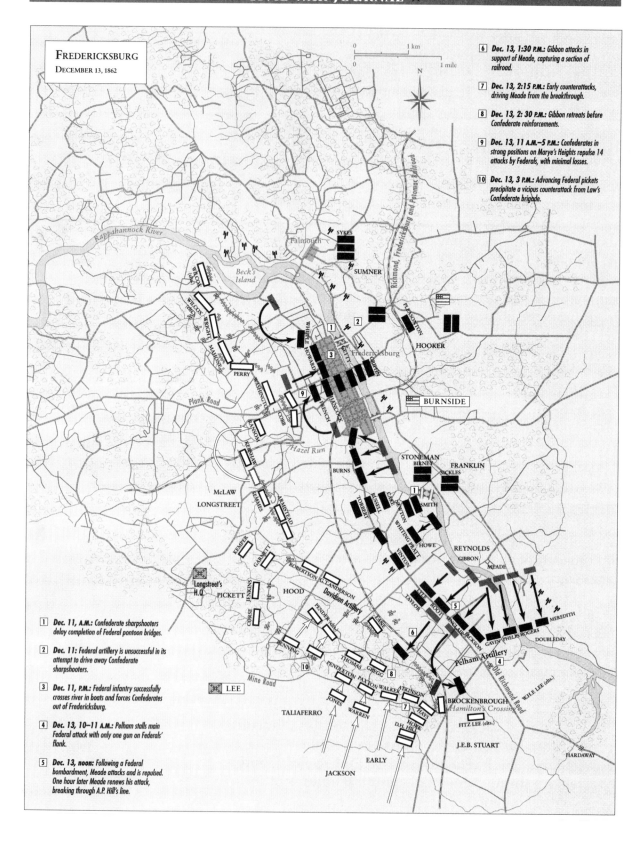

FREDERICKSBURG
DECEMBER 13, 1862

0   1 km
0   1 mile

N

6 *Dec. 13, 1:30 P.M.:* Gibbon attacks in support of Meade, capturing a section of railroad.

7 *Dec. 13, 2:15 P.M.:* Early counterattacks, driving Meade from the breakthrough.

8 *Dec. 13, 2: 30 P.M.:* Gibbon retreats before Confederate reinforcements.

9 *Dec. 13, 11 A.M.–5 P.M.:* Confederates in strong positions on Marye's Heights repulse 14 attacks by Federals, with minimal losses.

10 *Dec. 13, 3 P.M.:* Advancing Federal pickets precipitate a vicious counterattack from Law's Confederate brigade.

Rappahannock River

Beck's Island

Falmouth

SYKES

SUMNER

Richmond, Fredericksburg and Potomac Railroad

WILCOX

WILCOX   WRIGHT   MAHONE

PERRY

WHIPPLE   HOWARD

BETTY

1   **2**

PLEASONTON

HOOKER

Fredericksburg

3

GRIFFIN

HANCOCK

9

FRENCH

WASHINGTON   COBB

Plank Road

RANSOM

KERSHAW

Hazel Run

BURNSIDE

BURNS

STONEMAN   BIRNEY

FRANKLIN

SICKLES

McLAW

LONGSTREET

SEMMES

ARMISTEAD

TORBERT   RUSSELL   CAKE   NEWTON   SMITH   **1**

HOWE

WHITING   PRATT

REYNOLDS

GIBBON

MEADE

KEMPER   GARNETT

ROBERTSON   G.T. ANDERSON

VINTON

TAYLOR

THE ROOT   ST. CLAIR JACKSON

5

GAVIN   PHELPS   ROGERS

DOUBLEDAY

MEREDITH

Longstreet's H.Q.

PICKETT   JENKINS

COOKE

HOOD

Davidson Artillery

PENDER

LEASE

6

Pelham Artillery

4

W.H.F. LEE (elts.)

Old Richmond Road

LEE

BENNING

LAW

PENDLETON   THOMAS   GREGG

PAXTON   WALKER   ATKINSON

8

Mine Road

10

JONES   WARREN

7   HAYS

HOTE

D.H. HILL

BROCKENBROUGH
Hamilton's Crossing

FITZ LEE (elts.)

TALIAFERRO

J.E.B. STUART

HARDAWAY

EARLY

JACKSON

1 *Dec. 11, A.M.:* Confederate sharpshooters delay completion of Federal pontoon bridges.

2 *Dec. 11:* Federal artillery is unsuccessful in its attempt to drive away Confederate sharpshooters.

3 *Dec. 11, P.M.:* Federal infantry successfully crosses river in boats and forces Confederates out of Fredericksburg.

4 *Dec. 13, 10–11 A.M.:* Pelham stalls main Federal attack with only one gun on Federals' flank.

5 *Dec. 13, noon:* Following a Federal bombardment, Meade attacks and is repulsed. One hour later Meade renews his attack, breaking through A.P. Hill's line.

Although McClellan finally crossed the river and began marching south, Lincoln took action. In November 1862 he relieved McClellan of command. That, however, did not solve the problem. °Lincoln had to select a successor. From the president's perspective, the awful fact was there were not many candidates. Few Union generals in the East had shown any potential for winning battles. The list was short, but one potential commander was Maj. Gen. Ambrose Everett Burnside.•

Thirty-eight-year-old Burnside had done well in early 1862, winning small battles at Roanoke Island, New Bern, and Fort Macon, all along the coast of North Carolina. He was noted for his prewar invention of a breech-loading carbine. The affable Rhode Islander was mostly well liked by his peers, but some of his detractors thought him obstinate and unimaginative. At least one woman thought that way of him too, leaving him at the wedding altar at the last minute. To the Lincoln administration Burnside seemed like a good candidate for the job of leading the Union army to Richmond.

°Burnside was a stalwart, rather dashing-looking man. Although bald on top, he grew his side whiskers thick and bushy, a look that has survived today in the term "sideburns." His clothing was unostentatious, but he always wore a high-crowned hat that every soldier recognized.•

Like McClellan, Burnside knew the power of image. Once while his army was in transit on naval transports fighting a days-long storm off the coast of North Carolina, Burnside chose as his flagship the smallest ship in the fleet. He spent the daylight hours on deck, wearing his distinctive hat so his soldiers could see that their commander was not afraid of the ocean.

Burnside was personally unsure if he had the capability to command. Twice before, Lincoln had asked him to head the Army of the Potomac, but both times Burnside had refused. Besides his own misgivings, Burnside

The Union army had a new commander at its head on November 7, 1862. Reluctantly, Ambrose E. Burnside accepted command of the Army of the Potomac after Lincoln relieved George B. McClellan of the post. His acceptance was not rooted in ambition but in the knowledge that if he rejected the offer, the next candidate was Joseph E. Hooker, an officer whom Burnside detested. An 1847 graduate of West Point, Burnside ranked eighteenth in a class of thirty-eight. He was inclined to be innovative, but his greatest problem was a lack of confidence. He knew that he had to defeat Lee decisively, and so he proposed a winter campaign that first targeted Fredericksburg and then Richmond. It was a bold strategy requiring the precise coordination of men and supplies. The intricacies of that plan, however, led to its undoing. While the army waited for equipment, Lee had time to discern Burnside's target and gather his army for the assault.

Federal engineers started work on pontoon bridges across the Rappahannock during the early hours of December 11. At dawn Confederate infantry from the town and artillery from the heights began harassing the engineers, and so Burnside ordered his artillery to open on the town and drive the Southerners from the city (above left). Those civilians who had not fled the city cowered in their basements during an hour-long barrage that succeeded in silencing the Southerners briefly. Yet when the barrage was lifted, the sharpshooters opened again on the engineers, forcing them to seek cover. The cycle continued throughout the morning, with the Federals increasing the number of guns firing on the town. By noon they had turned one hundred guns to bear on Fredericksburg and reduced it to rubble. The guns fell silent around 2:30 when the artillerists admitted they could not dislodge the tenacious Confederates. Troops would be needed to accomplish that.

The huge cannonade ignited several fires within the city (above right). On December 11 and 12 Federal infantry crossed the river in boats and entered the town to engage the Confederates harassing the engineers. Of the devastation visited upon the town, one Federal commented, "When all the time-honored associations belonging to Fredericksburg were remembered, . . . we could not wish that such a fate had overtaken this old town. . . . [but considering] the bitterness of the present, there was a subdued satisfaction as the angry flames, approaching from different directions, threatened to leave the doomed city a mass of ruins."

WCD

enjoyed a long friendship with fellow West Point graduate McClellan, so he was reluctant to replace his old friend. This reluctance emerged later as a reoccurring theme in Burnside's life.

°One story told about Burnside was that when he was born, he did not immediately start breathing. The attending physician had to tickle the newborn's nose with a feather to make him sneeze so he would take a breath. The story was frequently recalled when Burnside as a man and as a general was reluctant to act.•

What might have pushed Burnside to accept Lincoln's third offer of command was the shameless politicking for the job conducted by Maj. Gen. Joseph E. Hooker, who saw Burnside as his chief rival and had criticized his military capability privately and in public. Finally, with McClellan's blessing, on November 7, 1862, Burnside took command of the Army of the Potomac. At the time it was composed of 130,000 troops encamped over the twenty miles between Manassas Junction and Waterloo, Virginia.

Burnside now moved south with surprising swiftness that initially impressed observers. "Burnside reorganized the army into three grand divisions. The right wing was commanded by General [Edwin V.] Sumner. The center by Hooker, and the left wing by General [William B.] Franklin. No commander during the war had a more difficult task than Burnside, or a problem more perplexing," one editor for the *Boston Journal* observed.

Lincoln did not waste any time in pressing Burnside to move toward Richmond. Although it was traditional for armies to cease campaigning during the cold, snowy, wet winters, Lincoln made it clear he did not want to wait for spring. There would be no winter quarters for the Army of the Potomac.

To supply his mammoth force with rations and matériel, Burnside needed access to a river and a railroad. The only place to get both on the way to Richmond and to get across the Rappahannock River was at Fredericksburg.

°Burnside decided to launch a lightning assault. If his army moved quickly, he calculated that he could march to Falmouth, on the north bank of the Rappahannock, across from Fredericksburg. Pontoon boats would be there, awaiting the army, and these would be used to erect temporary bridges across the river. He would cross his army over to Fredericksburg and move down the line of the Richmond, Frederick, and Potomac Railroad, directly toward the Confederate capital. If everything happened according to his timetable, Burnside would virtually steal a march on Lee, whose army would still be in winter quarters west of Fredericksburg. It was a good plan that required precise coordination from the War Department and the general in chief, Henry W. Halleck, who would have to ensure that the pontoon boats arrived in advance of the army.•

Everything depended on those boats being at the river when Burnside's army appeared. The logistics depended upon Halleck, who liked his nickname of

To squelch the Southern sharpshooters, Federal troops had to be dispatched across the river in boats. Col. Norman J. Hall headed volunteers from the Seventh Michigan, the Nineteenth and Twentieth Massachusetts, and the Eighty-ninth New York in the crossing. Despite a constant fire, all the volunteers save one touched ashore. They rushed into the first street they saw and within minutes had taken thirty prisoners and cleared the areas nearest the bridge work. Reinforcements arrived and the Federals moved into the town itself, which the Rebel troops grudgingly relinquished street by street. In perfect order, the Confederates eventually withdrew to the safety of the stone wall at the foot of Marye's Heights.

There were three separate river crossings, one for each of the so-called grand divisions in Burnside's reorganized army. Little significant resistance was offered at the downstream crossing in contrast to the sixteen hundred Mississippians under William Barksdale who invested the town and repeatedly drove off the bridge-building engineers shown above. Barksdale's mission was to impede the central division from entering Fredericksburg for as long as he could, and his men bought the better part of a day for their comrades before retiring to Marye's Heights themselves.

Lee had chosen not to make much of a battle of the river crossings. The Southern commander had seen that the town itself was under the guns of the enemy and that "no effectual opposition could be offered to the construction of the bridges or the passage of the river, without exposing our troops to the destructive fire of [Yankee artillery.]" Instead, Lee was content to have the enemy come to him on ground of his choosing, and the Confederate army occupied a particularly strong position at the heights.

WCD

"Old Brains," thinking it was an accurate description of his strategic abilities.

Bureaucracy prevailed, however, and Halleck failed miserably at gathering the boats, much less in coordinating their arrival with Burnside's army. °When Burnside arrived at the north bank of the Rappahannock, he found no pontoon boats waiting for him and no way to get across the river. This first blunder was a result of Halleck's dithering in Washington, and a chain of events then commenced that led a few days later to one of the worst debacles in American military history.•

The boats arrived ten days later than Burnside had expected. During the time the Union army waited on the north bank of the Rappahannock, they watched Confederate troops entrenching on the south side. When they first arrived, the Yankee troops could have stormed across the river. During the delay the Confederates increased daily in numbers and in strength. Lee, who had been surprised by the swiftness of Burnside's first movements, was catching up and trying to mass his troops in front of the Federals.

The pontoon fiasco had cost the Federal army its jump on the Rebels, and Burnside could no longer enter into Fredericksburg uncontested. For two weeks the Federal commander considered other river crossings, but the Confederates continued to reinforce the high ground behind the river, thus limiting his options. The grand army's morale was slipping as Federal troops waited for their inhibited commander to make a decision. Their greatest fear was that Burnside would decide to attack the enemy entrenched on the high ground, the worst military scenario any army could face.

°When he had first taken command, the Union soldiers had high regard for Burnside. It was not until they got to Fredericksburg and saw the heights behind the city where more and more Confederate troops made their appearance that the misgivings began to set in.•

With the pontoons finally on hand and more than one hundred thousand Union soldiers waiting to prove themselves in combat, Burnside met with his officers on December 10, 1862, to tell them of his plan to cross the Rappahannock directly into Fredericksburg. It was chilling in its simplicity.

When the orders were written up, Burnside noted: "I think now that the enemy will be more surprised by a crossing immediately in our front than in any other part of the river. The importance and details of the plan seem to be well understood by the grand division commanders, and we hope to succeed." He proposed no maneuvering, no attempts at fooling the Confederates with false attacks elsewhere, no flank crossings of the river at undefended points on the river. Instead, he proposed that his entire army cross an open river several hundred feet below and in full view of the entire Army of Northern Virginia. Burnside might have been the only man in the army who believed his bold plan would work.

Col. Edward E. Cross of the Fifth New Hampshire recalled: "The pontoon bridges were to be put down that night. Franklin was to cross three miles below and turn the right wing of the enemy. Sumner was to attack the center and left. Hooker was to be held ready to strike where the occasion offered. Such was the plan. As God is my witness, it seemed to my heart that it was to be a failure. I had the sense we were marching to disaster." With the river still in front of them and three days to go before the largest land battle in the history of the United States, the delays and blunders had only begun.

BY DECEMBER 10 Lee's Army of Northern Virginia, 72,000 strong, was converging on Fredericksburg. Across the Rappahannock River, it faced the 116,000 men of Burnside's

The assault on the Confederate sharp-shooters took time, a commodity Lee treasured and Burnside seemed to fritter away. Once the Federals had moved troops across the Rappahannock, they had to scale the riverbank to get into the town. The volunteers from the Seventh Michigan were the first to enter the town and engage Barksdale's men, but they were pinned down quickly and needed reinforcements badly. The Massachusetts men were obliging, and the sweep of the town began.

Army of the Potomac. Never before or since in U.S. history have so many armed men faced each other on this continent in anticipated combat.

The town of Fredericksburg was caught between the two armies, and the civilian population of the loyal Southern city evacuated the area. The departure of the refugees was a sad scene that troubled the leaders of Lee's army. James Longstreet noted: "Many were destitute and had nowhere to go. But yielding to the cruel necessities of war, they turned their back on the town, forced to seek shelter in the woods and brave the icy nights to escape the approaching assaults from the Federal Army."

The Union soldiers surveyed the Confederate works across the river and saw that Lee had made the most of the delay. °The Southern commander's training as a military engineer and his tactical mind enhanced his ability to react to the situation and to take advantage of natural defenses. He positioned his army to react wherever Burnside's forces appeared.•

Behind Fredericksburg and to the southeast was a long wooded ridge called Marye's Heights, a natural defensive position. Longstreet's division was placed here. In organizing his artillery to cover the ground in front of him, Longstreet assured Lee that "a chicken could not live on that ground when we open up on it." Stonewall Jackson's troops were deployed outside of town, along another ridge miles down the river. Jeb Stuart's cavalry guarded the flanks.

Although he was less than a half mile away and could clearly see the Confederate defenses as they were being prepared, Burnside remained strangely calm. "Oh, I know where Lee's forces are, and I expect to surprise him. I expect to cross and occupy the hills before Lee can bring anything serious against me," the Federal commander said.

As the time for battle neared, Burnside's thinking and communication became uncertain. His grand division leaders had been told where to cross, but details beyond that were unavailable. Before dawn on December 11, only the pontoon builders were sure of their mission. Engineers were told to erect five bridges in a few hours, which would allow more than one hundred thousand men and artillery to cross.

What Burnside did not know was that Lee wanted the Union army to cross the Rappahannock. He could not damage them if they stayed on the north side. Lee was so confidant that his defensive position was unassailable that he wanted Burnside to follow through with his plan. As a master tactician, the Southern commander knew that he had to offer some form of resistance. Lacking that, the Union army might grow suspicious about crossing the river and would alter its plans.

°Lee posted a brigade of Mississippi troops under Brig. Gen. William Barksdale in the town to resist the crossing. Burnside's engineers began their work around 3:00 A.M. By dawn they had the bridges about two-thirds complete. As the rising sun began to dissipate the early morning fog, Barksdale's men opened fire on the Federal engineers,• °which forced the work to stop.•

Burnside ordered a massive bombardment of the town to rid his engineers of Barksdale's sharpshooters. Within two hours the Federal artillery on Stafford Heights hurled five thousand shells into Fredericksburg, devastating the properties along the riverfront.

A correspondent of the *Boston Journal* observed: "The air became thick with murky clouds. The earth shook beneath the terrific explosions of the shells which went crashing into the houses, battering down the walls, splintering doors, ripping up floors." Idle Union soldiers along the north bank of the Rappahannock marveled at the destruction. "The bombardment was terrific and seemed ridiculously disproportionate to the enemy therein. Like an elephant attacking a mosquito," wrote Union Pvt. Warren Lee Goss.

Overwhelmed near the riverbank, Barksdale's infantrymen (above) retreated stubbornly from one building to the next, taking advantage of anything that offered them cover from which to harass the Northerners. Although the Yankees rejoiced at capturing the city, sixteen hundred Confederate "hornets"—to use James Longstreet's nickname for the Mississippians—had thwarted the Federal advance for almost a day. Even after the Southerners had abandoned the city, Burnside did not press for any advantage or seek to assault the Rebels at the stone wall.

JMM

With the riverbank cleared of Rebel sharpshooters, the men of the Twentieth Massachusetts found themselves in some of the first street fighting of the war. Having accomplished his mission, Barksdale ordered his Mississippians to fall back slowly. One of the officers of the rear guard, Lt. Lane Brandon, however, learned that the unit attacking him was led by a former classmate. He counterattacked and was actually pushing the Federals and his former colleague back. Brandon was arrested for violating orders, and his unit retreated.

During the bombardment, Barksdale's Confederates took refuge in the rubble. When the shelling stopped and the smoke cleared, they emerged unscathed and called on a Florida regiment for support. When the Federal engineers resumed their work, they once again drew heavy fire from the Southerners. Burnside's chief of artillery, Brig. Gen. Henry Hunt, suggested an amphibious assault to land troops on the south side of the river and drive the Rebel sharpshooters back.

°Two Massachusetts regiments and a Michigan regiment volunteered. They rowed across in pontoon boats, under fire all the way, then engaged in street-to-street fighting to drive out the Confederates. Both sides took heavy casualties in one of the few examples of house-to-house fighting in the Civil BP War.• °Because the soldiers were trained to fight in the open in large formations, this kind of urban warfare was new and added to the terror of combat. As the Federals moved into the town, they found themselves in a maze of streets and were regularly caught in cross fires. Death was behind every building and every window and behind every tree and every wall.•

Future Supreme Court Justice Oliver Wendell Holmes Jr. recalled the brutal street fighting and the valor of a comrade in the Twentieth Massachusetts, a young Harvard graduate, Capt. Henry Abbot. "I will never forget the awful spectacle of this advance in the streets of Fredericksburg. If you had seen him with his indifferent carriage and sword swinging from his finger like a cane, you would never have suspected in less than sixty seconds he would become the focus of a hidden and annihilating fire. He was moving on in obedience to superior command to certain and useless death," wrote Holmes.

Finally, after just the right amount of resistance, the Rebels fell back to their main position at Marye's Heights. They took shelter behind what would become the symbol of Fredericksburg's stubborn resistance, a long stone wall that fronted a sunken road. Lee was not yet quite ready to defend this position. He was still moving

After ridding the town of Confederate sharpshooters and while awaiting the movement of the army into Fredericksburg, the Yankees began plundering the town. The civilian evacuation left the city wide open for the invaders. What the soldiers could not use, they destroyed. They smashed windows and pottery and stripped every pantry of anything edible. Because the winter of 1862 was particularly harsh, they burned the furniture for firewood. They drank all the liquor and roamed through the streets in search of plunder. Some donned female attire. The whole affair took on a carnival-like atmosphere. There was no military discipline among them. For a deluded night they sang, danced, and forgot about the seriousness of war. Some commanders tried to stop the looting and placed guards on the bridges to prevent any loot from making its way back to camp. Piles of confiscated goods grew around the bridgeheads, but when the fighting began again, the contraband mysteriously disappeared.

Jackson's troops closer to enforce the Confederate stronghold, and only one division of Longstreet's corps was nearby. It was near dark when the Yankees secured the town of Fredericksburg on December 11.

Burnside took stock of the situation and liked what he saw. Two pontoon bridges were complete, one directly to the town and another slightly downriver. He could finally cross his army. True to form, however, Burnside hesitated, although he had exactly what he needed to attack. °Throughout the campaign, Burnside repeatedly demonstrated inflexibility and an inability to adapt to changing situations or to alter his plans accordingly. He threw away a great opportunity on the night of December 11.•

°Burnside's army did not cross the Rappahannock River that night, which would have placed it in position to make an attack early on December 12. Had Burnside done so, he would have caught Lee with at least a portion of the Confederate army still not on the battlefield.•

The following day was instead marred by more Federal delay, confusion, pondering, and miscommunication. Restless, bored Union troops, knowing that they might not survive many more hours in Fredericksburg, used the time to pillage the shell-damaged city. They rationalized the town owed it to them before they marched into what one witness would later call "the jaws of death."

181

Confederate Maj. John Pelham had attended West Point and had resigned his appointment just two weeks prior to his graduation. At the age of twenty-four he was at the head of Jeb Stuart's horse artillery. Within the Rebel army he was known as the "Boy Major," and for his bravery at Fredericksburg, Lee dubbed him "the gallant Pelham." He was aggressive and innovative on the battlefield, earning the respect of both Confederates and Federals. Just three months after the battle of Fredericksburg Pelham was mortally wounded at Kelly's Ford. Stuart, the bold Confederate cavalier, wept loudly over the body of his young protégé.

WHILE THE UNION troops foraged through the town, their officers did little to control them. °The men made flapjacks on the stoves of the abandoned homes and got drunk on the wine and applejack they found in the cellars. The breakdown in discipline took on a carnival atmosphere,• but that soon turned to a horror show as souvenir hunting became wholesale looting and destruction. Although some soldiers were ashamed to see what their army was doing, they and their officers could do little to stop the rampaging horde. °The soldiers smashed mirrors, danced on pianos, tore books out of libraries, broke vases, and destroyed what had not already been smashed by the artillery. It was the most disgraceful episode in which the Army of the Potomac ever took part.• While the generals planned how to destroy Lee's army, the soldiers destroyed the town. "Nothing seemed to be revered. Houses torn to pieces. The city was given up entirely to sack," wrote Maj. George Macy of the Twentieth Massachusetts.

Lee watched the destruction as his engineers continued building his defenses. Although he was saddened to see the destruction of the old city, he knew that Burnside's army would soon pay for the delay in attacking him. Lee's bemused officers, knowing what lay in store for any attacker, had time to think about the coming battle. A master of defensive fighting who recognized the strength of the Confederate position, Longstreet noted, "The Federals carefully matured their plans for advance and attack."

Burnside did not recognize that his delays were endangering his army. °By failing to cross the river on the night of December 11 and by using all of the next day to make the crossing, Burnside gave Lee another full day to refine his defensive preparations.• In effect, Burnside had completely changed his earlier strategy of rapidly marching against Lee to keep him from having time to set up a defense. Now the Federal commander was giving Lee all the time he needed.

Several of Burnside's officers recognized the desperate situation in which he had placed the army. "Burnside persisted in crossing the river after all hope of a surprise had faded away. And now we must fight under great disadvantages," wrote Maj. Gen. William F. Smith, a division commander assigned to attack Jackson's troops farther down the river.

Most of the Union general officers felt the Confederate position on the high ground was impossible to penetrate, but Burnside insisted his plan for a frontal assault was sound. He assigned Franklin, who had graduated at the head of the West Point class of 1843, to attack Jackson's troops opposite the Union left while Sumner's men attacked through the town toward Marye's Heights on the right. Hooker's men would wait in reserve to pour through any openings made by Franklin and Sumner.

After meeting with his officers to convey his plan, Burnside rode back to headquarters past his anxious troops. Every soldier seemed to know what lay ahead of him. °It must have been an awesome spectacle for thousands of soldiers to be in such a confined space as the narrow streets of Fredericksburg, but witnesses said it was deathly quiet. The soldiers just looked at each other, knowing that some of them would not be there after the next day.•

When Union Gen. George Gordon Meade prepared to launch an attack on the Confederate right, Pelham noticed that the Federals' left flank was exposed. The young Alabama officer brought up two guns, unlimbered them only four hundred yards from the advancing Yankee infantry, and fired shot and shell, causing the lead brigade to falter. One of Pelham's guns was disabled quickly by Union artillery, but the major continued to move his remaining gun into different positions and fire into the oncoming Federals. At one point thirty-two Federal cannon focused on this lone unit. Stuart sent word that Pelham could withdraw as he saw fit, but the confident artillerist responded, "Tell the General I can hold my ground." He did not fall back until his ammunition was exhausted. He had stalled the enemy's advance for almost an hour. Lee saw Pelham's action and reportedly remarked, "It is glorious to see such courage in one so young."

About six hundred yards outside of Fredericksburg, James Longstreet's corps had deployed on a commanding ridge known as Marye's Heights (right). In front of the ridge twenty-five hundred Rebels stood in a sunken road behind a four-foot stone wall. Behind them were about five thousand infantry and several batteries. The ground in front of this position was narrow, allowing only one Union brigade at a time to assault the heights. Longstreet's chief of artillery, Col. Edward P. Alexander, reported to his commander, "We cover that ground now so well that we will comb it as with a fine-tooth comb. A chicken could not live on that field when we open on it."

Burnside arose early on the morning of December 13 to dispatch written confirmation of his orders. Franklin's directive arrived late. On top of that, Franklin—a meticulous, by-the-book military engineer—was confused by the order. While he had previously understood that his men were to make the main assault, Burnside's orders were notably passive, even vague. The orders called for Franklin to use at least a division in the attack; there seemed to be no mention of an all-out assault. In Franklin's literal reading of the order, Burnside had told him not to commit all his resources in the attack. °Instead of using sixty thousand men, the order implied that he should use just four thousand. Confused by the wording of the orders and the small numbers of troops referenced in the orders, Franklin decided to do exactly what the order instructed rather than seek clarification. If Burnside wanted a four-thousand-man division to make the attack against Jackson's corps of at least thirty thousand men, that is what would happen.•

Around noon on December 13 Brig. Gen. William H. French's division was the first to assault the heights. His men came within 125 yards of the stone wall when it encountered a sheet of fire from behind the stone wall. Hundreds of Union soldiers fell with each volley. A few men came as close as 40 yards of the wall, but the rest fell back or took refuge behind the dead comrades who fell in front of them. Those who could retreated. In a little more than thirty minutes, a third of the attacking force lay dead or wounded on the ground before the stone wall.

Maj. Gen. George Gordon Meade, a grizzled, mean-tempered Pennsylvanian, was chosen to spearhead the attack. As soon as Meade's division moved up, it was fired on by one of Jeb Stuart's artillerists, twenty-four-year-old Maj. John Pelham, who had resigned from West Point in April 1861, just weeks before he would have graduated. With Stuart's permission Pelham had galloped out in front of the Confederate lines, to the skirmish line, and there opened fire down Meade's line. The young gunner, who commanded only two cannon, soon found himself the target of Yankee artillery. Pelham and his two gun crews maintained their poise and continued to fire on Meade's division despite several orders to retreat. The young major risked not only death from opposing Federal cannon fire, but also court-martial for refusing to follow the orders of a general officer. To one such order Pelham curtly replied, "Tell General Stuart I can hold my ground."•

Pelham continued to shift his guns to elude the Federal gunners, who were under the impression they were fighting an entire section of Confederate artillery rather than just two guns being rapidly pulled from one part of the battlefield to another. Only after he had exhausted his ammunition did Pelham finally hitch up his guns and return to the Confederate lines. Pelham's two cannon had held up Meade's division and all of Franklin's fifty thousand men for more than two hours. The man Lee called "the gallant Pelham" would live only three more months; he was killed while participating in a cavalry charge near Culpeper, Virginia—he had joined the charge on a lark. At least three different women, each claiming to be his fiancée, mourned the young Alabama officer.

Meade's men were again ravaged by Confederate artillery as they began to advance the second time. Finally a thunderous explosion provided enough confusion for Meade's division to break through the Confederate line. Bad directions from Burnside and Franklin, however, sent the Union division down the wrong road

The Marye house (above) marked the center of the Confederate position on the heights. Brig. Gen. Thomas Cobb's Georgians occupied the sunken road behind the stone wall just below the house. Cobb positioned his men in two ranks; one was to fire and then step back to reload while the second rank fired. On his left flank a trench extended the line and was manned by Brig. Gen. Robert Ransom's Twenty-fourth North Carolina. All together, about two thousand men were behind the stone wall, with seven thousand in reserve. Cobb and Ransom were also supported by fourteen cannon placed near the house.

Prior to the first onslaught Longstreet had feared that the trenches at the north end of the line might be compromised and suggested that Cobb fall back if such should happen. To an aide Cobb said, "Well, if they wait for me to fall back, they will wait a long time."

Lee's troops suffered twelve hundred casualties on these heights; Burnside lost seven thousand killed or wounded. Cobb was one of the Southern casualties, felled by a shell fragment that struck him in the thigh and severed an artery. He bled to death as surgeons frantically worked on him.

On the Federal left, Meade's division had broken through the Rebel line but retreated when he failed to receive reinforcement. The Confederates, under Stonewall Jackson, then counterattacked. Twenty-four-year-old Union Col. Charles Collis, seen above holding the U.S. flag, led his Zouave regiment—the 114th Pennsylvania—to meet this assault and prevent the total collapse of the left side of the Federal line. The officer pinned under his horse in the left foreground is Brig. Gen. John Robinson. Both men survived, and Collis was awarded the Medal of Honor for his actions.

The fighting in this sector was a draw; after the last shot had been fired, the lines were largely in the same position as they had been at the start. Burnside had lost 4,800 men, and Lee had suffered 3,400 casualties. The Federal commander called for a renewed assault, but William B. Franklin's grand division was disheartened and demoralized by the aborted breakthrough. Franklin refused to issue the order and in so doing likely avoided the annihilation Edwin V. Sumner's grand division endured at the stone wall.

and they ran straight into the veteran troops of Confederate Lt. Gen. A. P. Hill.

GWG °Hill had left a large, boggy marsh undefended, creating a gap about six hundred yards long in the Confederate line. By chance the Union men under Meade hit that gap. Rushing forward, they captured several hundred Confederates.•

South Carolina troops under forty-eight-year-old Brig. Gen. Maxcy Gregg were positioned near Meade's break-

BP through. °One of the three signers of South Carolina's Ordinance of Secession who became generals, Gregg was well read, literate, and a dabbler in science and astronomy. He was also slightly deaf, but he was a fighter.•

Gregg's Confederates, who were not expecting a fight so quickly in the battle, had stacked their arms. They were as surprised as Meade's soldiers to encounter one another. Gregg assumed the Union soldiers were after Rebel forces protruding from the front and feared there were friendly

GWG troops in the line of fire, so he °told his men not to fire. Shortly thereafter he took a musket ball to the spine and died two days later. His men, however, rallied to plug the momentary break in the Confederate line.• Now the Union men began to feel the effect of allowing Lee to bring all of his forces to bear at Fredericksburg.

"Our men were soon after attacked in heavy force. And wholly without support, they were driven back. All that we gained at so fearful a cost is lost," said Jacob Heffelfinger of the Seventh Pennsylvania Reserves.

With the momentary hole in the Confederate line sealed, a critical opportunity for the Federals had

186

passed. °Moreover, Meade learned that Franklin would not support him. Meade's men had seized the ridge as they were supposed to, but Franklin made no move to reinforce them. Overwhelmed, Meade's men started back toward the river.• The Union's one real chance at Fredericksburg had been lost. °If Franklin had exploited Meade's breakthrough by sending the fifty thousand men under his command through that hole, there might have been some chance for success on that sector of the battlefield.•

In Meade's breakthrough, Confederate and Federal casualties were equal. That fight was over by 2:00 P.M. An impatient Burnside, however, ordered Sumner to attack Marye's Heights, and the great battle of Fredericksburg began in bloody earnest. History would not remember much about the near success on the Union left; it would concentrate instead on the disaster on the Union right and center.

During the next seven hours, brigade after brigade attacked the Confederates en-sconced behind the stone wall at Marye's Heights. Before the fight-ing ended at nightfall, Rebel rifle-men had cut down more than eight thousand Yankee soldiers. None of the Northerners even touched the fieldstones of the wall.

Thomas Francis Galwey of the Eighth Ohio Volunteers recalled: "Line after line our men advance in magnificent order. Poor glorious fellows shaking good-bye to us with their hats. They reach a point within a stone's throw of the wall, no farther. They try to go beyond, but are slaughtered. Nothing could advance farther and live."

THE DEVASTATING SPECTACLE that took place in front of the Confed-erate stone wall would not abate. Union and Confederate flags

Meanwhile, at the stone wall, the second wave of the Federal assault by Hancock's division was thrown back. A third assault was mounted by Brig. Gen. Thomas Meagher's Irish Brigade. The men had placed green sprigs in their caps as a mark of their heritage. Ironically, the portion of the Confederate line before them was held by Irishmen of the Twenty-fourth Georgia. Upon seeing their country-men's green emblems, one of the Georgians muttered, "What a pity. Here comes Meagher's fellows." The Confederate Irish devastated the onrushing Federal Irish. Capt. D. P. Conyngham, the Irish Brigade's histo-rian, recalled the murderous fire opening great gaps in the rank and bodies piling on top of one another. "It was a wholesale slaughter of human beings," he summarized. Meagher lost 545 men in the attack.

The view above (left) from behind the stone wall offers a perspective on the Confederate position. Here Georgia and North Carolina infantrymen fired volley after volley into the waves of Federal troops attempting to take the heights. James Longstreet observed, "At each attack, the slaughter was so great that by the time the third attack was repulsed the ground was so thickly strewn with dead that the bodies seriously impeded the approach of the Federals." Lee was concerned with the massive numbers of men still waiting to attack, but Longstreet confidently added, "If you put every man now on the other side of the Potomac on that field to approach me . . . and give me plenty of ammunition, I will kill them all before they reach my line." In spite of his confidence, Longstreet moved two regiments from the ridge to join Thomas R. R. Cobb's Georgians at the stone wall. It was during this reinforcement that Cobb was mortally wounded while standing beneath the tree near the farthest house in the photograph above (right). Joseph Kershaw succeeded Cobb in command. With the new reinforcements, he positioned his men in four ranks and increased his firepower, which Kershaw described as "the most rapid and continuous I have ever witnessed."

waved through the smoke. Bayonets flashed as endless Federal lines pressed forward over the bodies of their fallen comrades. Both armies witnessed the gallant display of battle and the foul reality of death.

The generals knew it would be like that. Early on December 13 the Union Second Corps commander, Maj. Gen. Darius Couch, assigned the first attack on Marye's Heights to Brig. Gen. William H. French's division. By midmorning uneasy troops stood in the streets of Fredericksburg awaiting orders to attack Marye's Heights. Only six hundred yards separated the Union troops from the Confederates, but in between lay an open plain that sloped gently upward to the stone wall.

Brig. Gen. Nathan Kimball, a trained medical doctor, led the assault. The Confederates were amazed to watch the wave of light blue coming at them—the light blue of the long woolen winter overcoats worn by the Federals over their dark blue uniforms.

"What a magnificent sight. Long lines following one another like some huge serpent. Nearer and nearer the enemy advances and now they are within range and we give it to them. Volley after volley, great gaps appear," wrote Confederate Lt. William Miller Owen of the Washington Artillery of New Orleans.

As they approached the wall, Kimball's men were immediately fired upon by the Confederate artillery from Marye's Heights. °Kimball saw his men being

DP

disheartened and demoralized, so he galloped in front of them and shouted: "Cheer up, my hearties. Cheer up! This is something you must all get used to. This brigade has never been whipped. Do not let it be whipped today." At that point he led his troops forward. They ran to within 150 yards of the Confederate position when at least two thousand Confederate rifles opened fire on them.•

Soldiers under Brig. Gen. Thomas R. Cobb, a fiery secessionist and talented lawyer, had risen up from behind the protection of the stone wall. The withering fire from Cobb's men stopped Kimball's men in their tracks. The survivors started to fall back.

"The din was awful. The destruction terrible. Nothing human could withstand this terrible and destructive fire," recalled Union Pvt. Warren Lee Goss.

Another brigade from French's division and then another advanced on Marye's Heights. None came closer than seventy-five yards of the stone wall before being ripped by a sheet of flame from Cobb's riflemen. General Couch next ordered up the division of Brig. Gen. Winfield Scott Hancock, whose advanced brigade also fell before the stone wall. Although the men waiting their turns at assault could see the death and destruction in front of them, few ran.

AWG °The motivation for fighting during the Civil War would be called peer pressure today. Civil War units were almost always recruited from specific towns or counties, so if a soldier showed cowardice in the battle, he would not only let down the men with whom he had been

The scars on Fredericksburg lasted for the remainder of the war. Federal artillery had thrown at least five thousand shells into the town itself on the first day (below left) when the goal was to dislodge the sharpshooters from their cover. Later, during the assaults on Marye's Heights, Union artillery had tried to punch holes in the Confederate line, but were ineffective. The homes on the plains between the town and the heights (above) took a beating. Walls fell in, great holes were made, and chimneys collapsed. General Lee watched the terrible bombardment and was angry that the enemy would fire on civilians. As he saw the flames rise from the town he stated: "These people delight to destroy the weak, and those who can make no defense. It just suits them." Yankee artillery was not entirely to blame, however. Some of the homes on the plains afforded cover to the Federals advancing on Marye's Heights, and Confederate artillerists had no choice but to fire on the structures.

By the early afternoon of December 13 the Federal line was exhausted. Frustrated by Jackson on the left and mauled by Longstreet on the right, the Army of the Potomac stalled. Burnside, however, was never more sure of himself and stubbornly refused to reconsider his plan of battle (below). He ordered Franklin to renew the attack on Jackson and then called for Maj. Gen. Joseph E. Hooker to bring up his grand division, which was being held in reserve on the other side of the Rappahannock. As his men crossed the river, Hooker set out to investigate the situation and returned to Burnside's headquarters convinced that another assault would be a "useless waste of life." Nevertheless, the commander was obstinate and ordered another attack. Hooker sent in Andrew Humphrey's Third Division, and when it was driven back at nightfall he discontinued the fighting, saying that he "had lost as many men as his orders required." Overall, seven Union divisions, approximately thirty thousand men, tried to take the heights and failed.

sharing all sorts of trials, but he would also embarrass his family, neighbors, and friends at home.•

One of the most courageous attacks against the stone wall was made by the Irish Brigade, five regiments of men of Irish descent, many of them Irish immigrants who had flocked to Philadelphia, New York, and Boston to answer the call sent out by Brig. Gen. Thomas Meagher, an Irish-born officer who had been banished from his native country for advocating independence from England. He inspired his men with calls for devotion to the United States that had taken them in and for the love of their native Ireland.• The Twenty-eighth Massachusetts marched under a bright green battle flag showing a harp, a traditional musical instrument of Ireland. Before their charge at Marye's Heights, each member of the Irish Brigade placed a sprig of boxwood in his cap to remind him of his Irish heritage. It was the last act of love many of the men would perform.

"See that number of brave fellows now stretched in their gore, who an hour ago were the personification of life and strength and manners. They will never march again," wrote Capt. D. P. Conyngham, historian of the Irish Brigade. Meagher lost 535 men at the stone wall. While the charge of the Irish Brigade was noteworthy, at least five other brigades suffered even greater casualties. Thousands of dead and wounded Yankee soldiers lay on the field. The wounded, unable to leave the field without drawing fire, pressed themselves to the ground and fired on the Confederates behind the wall. Many built barricades and breastworks from the lifeless bodies of their comrades.

Cobb, the Confederate lawyer who taught himself to be a soldier, was shot in the thigh as he paced behind the wall, encouraging his men. He bled to death in a field hospital within sight of the house where his parents were married.

The Confederates watched with astonishment as the Federal soldiers continued their

futile advances. One of Lee's staff officers, Maj. Walter Taylor, observed: "The whole line of blue bristling with glittering bayonets moved steadily forward. The eye takes in the whole panorama at a glance. Men hold their breath and realize that war is indeed as glorious as it is terrible."

°The battle of Fredericksburg was a magnificent affair, played out on a huge stage in numbers approximating two hundred thousand strong. There was a single moment during the battle that summed up warfare itself. Lee had been watching the Federal troops rush toward his lines and then, just as quickly, fall back. He turned to one of his staff and remarked, "It is well that war is so terrible, else we should grow too fond of it." That was the kind of majesty that could be seen from the winning side in Fredericksburg, but the comment also spoke to the terrible brutality and the horrible waste of war.•

Wasteful though the Federal assaults were, they continued. Maj. Gen. Oliver O. Howard, who had lost his arm earlier in the war, commanded the third division hurled against the stone wall. It too was decimated one brigade at a time. °As the day went on, the carnage increased. Burnside had lost five thousand troops in two hours' time, but it did not occur to him to stop the assaults.• Despite horrific losses, Burnside insisted on continuing the assault. Hooker's division was brought up late in the day.

The most notable of the last assaults on Marye's Heights was led by Brig. Gen. Andrew A. Humphreys. Soldiers who had charged the wall earlier and failed tried to stop this assault. °They reached up to grab the pant legs of Humphreys's soldiers as they went toward what these wounded survivors viewed as certain death. Humphreys's soldiers shook off those friendly hands of brotherly interference. They knew they had to try to reach the wall, even though they already knew it was impossible to take.•

Not one Federal soldier made it to the stone wall. The last attack of the day was made by Col. Rush Hawkins's colorfully

Along with Longstreet, second from the right below, and several other officers, General Lee watched the terrible slaughter in front of Marye's Heights. At one point he was concerned that the Federals would break through and said to Longstreet, "General, they are massing very heavily and will break your line, I am afraid." All attempts to break through at Marye's Heights, however, were repulsed. Viewing the human wreckage in front of the heights, the Confederate commander commented to the officers around him, "It is well that war is so terrible, else we should grow too fond of it."

As night fell on the battlefield, there was little talk of a counterattack. Jackson tried to attack on the right side of the line, but his men were thrown back when they came under the guns of Yankee artillery. Lee had known at the outset that his position was a strong defensive line but that it offered little chance for counterattack. He anticipated that Burnside would continue the attack the next day, but the two armies only stared at each other for two days.

Gen. Andrew Humphreys's division was the last to assault Marye's Heights. Humphreys (above) said to his staff, "Gentlemen, I shall lead the charge. I presume, of course, you will wish to ride with me." His lead brigade was shot down like the others, and he realized that he would make little headway if his men paused to take aim and fire their weapons. He ordered his men not to load their rifles but only to fix bayonets. Again with a mad rush the Federal troops ran toward the wall. They were allowed within fifty yards of the barrier before the four ranks of Southerners opened fire. Even the Confederates recognized the insanity. As one Southerner took in the sight of the onrushing Union infantry, he shouted, "Ye Gods! It is no longer a battle, it is a butchery." The Federals fell back again.

DP clad Zouaves as the sun was setting. °One of the advancing soldiers said that he wished he could get up and kick the sun down because he knew that only night would bring an end to the slaughter.•

When nighttime came, thousands of men were still pinned to the ground, unable to move toward the town and safety without attracting the fire of Confederates. They kept from freezing that night by stripping the clothes from their own dead; they kept from getting shot themselves by using the bodies of the dead as shields. There were plenty of bodies from which to pick—approximately eight thousand Federals lay before the stone wall.

Capt. John Ames of the Eleventh U.S. Infantry remembered: "Almost an army lay about us and scattered back over the plain to die, groveling on the ground or fallen in the mire is dreadful indeed. The pallid faces looked ghastly by the fog light. The new bright blue overcoats only made the sight the ghastlier."

"IT WAS A night of dreadful suffering. Many died of wounds and exposure, and as fast as men died, they stiffened in the wintry air," wrote an agonized Union Gen. Darius Couch.

Couch was not the only man troubled by the suffering of the Federal wounded. As the sun rose on December 14, Confederate Sgt. Richard Kirkland of South Carolina could no longer stand the cries of the Federals on the slopes. He first asked permission to climb over the wall to take them water. He was refused because Federal snipers were trying to keep the Confederates pinned WCD down behind the wall. Ignoring his orders, °Kirkland gathered some canteens and went over the wall anyway. Unarmed, he crawled among the Yankee wounded to give them water. Men on both sides saw him, and both sides held their fire. An informal truce on one part of the field held as Kirkland crawled from man to man, ministering to the wounded. For his brave act, Kirkland was called "the angel of Marye's Heights."• The next year, twenty-year-old Kirkland was killed at Chickamauga.

To the shocked surprise of his generals, Burnside wanted to renew the attack on Marye's Heights and to personally lead his old Ninth Corps into battle. Burnside's officers had no desire to renew the assault. They dissuaded him, but some of them privately believed the battle had affected Burnside's mind. The general seemed to constantly point toward Marye's Heights and mutter about "those men out there," meaning the thousands of Federals he had ordered to their deaths. Two days later the Federal army retreated back across to the north side of the Rappahannock. This time Lee let them go. He did not pursue them, just as McClellan had not pursued him in September. The Federal army was defeated, Lee thought, perhaps for good.

"There was universal despondency. Gloom pervaded every rank. On the other hand, the Rebels were very jubilant and believed the southern Confederacy would be acknowledged and the fighting over in another month," wrote Union Pvt. Warren Lee Goss.

Burnside tried to redeem himself in mid-January by marching his army several miles above Fredericksburg in an effort to move against the Confederate rear. This time the weather turned against him, and rain began to fall as his army left camp. °His artillery sank in mud up to the axles and beyond. Mules sank up to their bodies in the freezing mud. The whole army lurched and reeled through the rain and the sleet.• A march that should have taken no more than a few hours took two days out and two days back to camp. It became known as the Mud March, another Burnside disaster.

"It was the general opinion among us that the whole piece was a blunder. As far as we could see, it was worse than a blunder," wrote W. H. Spiller, Third Division, Ninth Army Corps. The Mud March was more than a blunder, it was a deadly mistake. Soldiers died of exhaustion and exposure to the mud, cold, and rain. Some regiments stopped listing causes of death, and clerks simply wrote "Died at Falmouth." With this last disaster, Burnside lost the confidence of his officers and the army. Several generals

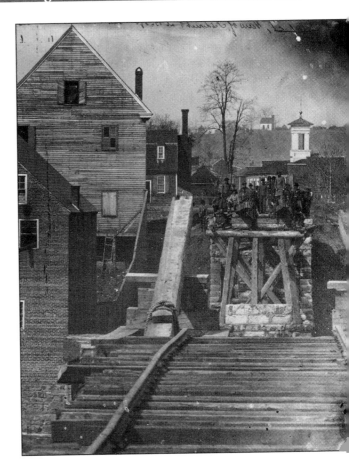

On December 15 a truce was arranged for burial parties to attend to the corpse-strewn plains around Fredericksburg. During a fierce thunderstorm that night, the Federals withdrew from the town and retreated across the river, cutting loose the pontoons and taking them up. For several months Rebs and Yanks glared at each other across the Rappahannock. One such moment was captured above by photographer A. J. Russell who set up his camera at the end of the destroyed railroad trestle. The obliging town defenders would have to fight from the heights five months later, but Fredericksburg would not be the primary target that time, for the Federals would be concentrated near the crossroads of Chancellorsville.

The Federal defeat at Fredericksburg in December 1862 left soldiers and officers disheartened. To compound the low morale, Burnside tried to press a second campaign against Lee. He proposed to outflank Lee behind Fredericksburg, but this time politics and the weather proved to be his greatest adversaries. He had tried to initiate the campaign in late December but was recalled to Washington when two of his generals voiced concerns to Lincoln that the plan was faulty. After gaining the president's approval, Burnside set out with the army on January 20. Four days of torrential rain turned roads into mud and fields into quagmires. Wagons sank to their wheel hubs, horses and mules sank to their bellies, and exhausted soldiers slipped, floundered, and fell. There was no dry place to make camp, no wood to start fires and make coffee. Rebels on the other side of the river held up signs ridiculing the cold, wet Federal army. Burnside tried three times to march out of Washington, and three times he returned. When the storm passed, the army was too exhausted to try again, and the campaign—called the Mud March—was canceled.

JMM

AWG

staged a mutiny by going to Washington to urge the president to replace him. Hooker was again eager for the job.

°Lincoln sympathized with Burnside because he felt that part of the general's problem was Hooker's plotting behind his back and saying that the army could never succeed under Burnside. Lincoln was not pleased with Hooker's politicking, but at the time, Hooker was the most likely candidate to succeed Burnside.

A great general should be able to improvise, to make the right kinds of decisions under the stress of the initial plan's coming apart, but Burnside lacked that capacity. When his initial plans fizzled, he was not able to adapt. He was not flexible. Burnside had confessed those shortcomings to Lincoln earlier, but it took Fredericksburg to prove them.•

Although he took the blame for the battle, Burnside also tried to spread the blame. °Chief among those he singled out was Franklin, who misunderstood or intentionally placed the most conservative interpretation on the orders he received from Burnside. Franklin had attacked Jackson's line with far fewer men than he had under his command.• Had he rushed headlong with his entire force, he might have broken through and been on Lee's flank.

On January 25, 1863, Burnside was replaced by Hooker. In March, Burnside was given a desk job, but by the fall of 1863 he was back on the battlefield in the West. Following the war he was three times elected governor of Rhode Island, and in 1874 he became a U.S. senator.

Hooker, who badly wanted command of the Army of the Potomac, kept it only five months. He was soundly defeated by Lee at Chancellorsville in May 1863.

The fiasco at Fredericksburg was more than a military defeat. It almost caused the dissolution of the Union army. Thousands of demoralized men simply started FO marching home; however, °those who remained in the ranks and stayed with the army became stronger and developed a new resolve to see the war through, to win back their honor. They were no longer under the illusion that the war was rapidly ending. After Fredericksburg they knew it would be a long, drawn-out affair.•

WCD °Following the battle of Fredericksburg, the desperately difficult year of 1862 came to an end. North and South were both very nearly exhausted by it. The two sides needed a winter season to rest, to recoup, to get ready for what was to come. The next year, 1863, was to be one major contest after another. It would be the defining year of the war.•

The conflict along the Rappahannock represented a horrific loss for the Union and one of the most one-sided victories the Confederates enjoyed. Yet despite tremendous sacrifices on both sides, little was gained. Thousands of lives were wasted, and the morale of the Union army reached its nadir. Rarely in the Civil War did futility and disaster so completely intertwine as they did on the field at Fredericksburg.

CHARLESTON

BOTH SIDES, CHARLESTON, SOUTH Carolina, was the city that best symbolized the Confederacy. The North saw it as the hated seedbed of rebellion. The South saw it as the courageous citadel that finally brought forth action after years of Northern tyranny. Because of its symbolic importance, Charleston was shelled and besieged for four long years. Soldiers and civilians alike were drawn into the battle where the weapons ranged from bayonets to submarines. The outcome seesawed until the very last days of the war.

Charleston was nothing if not defiant. In the early days of the war, its leaders issued a proclamation reading: "It is hereby resolved that Charleston should be defended at any cost. We would prefer the entire city in ruins to surrender." With those words the city leaders threw down the gauntlet to the surrounding Yankees. In the end, the people of Charleston would not have to choose: they would have both.

It was fitting that Charleston would be the flash point for the war. No city more symbolized the South, and no city fought harder to maintain its traditions. While this made Charlestonians proud, it also made the city an irresistible target for the North once the war began.

JIR   °The city was the past incarnate, a place where time seemed to stand still. Charlestonians cherished their way of life, and they were not about to tolerate its being changed, especially by Yankees.° Charleston had no fondness for Yankees. During the decades before the Civil War, the city had been a hotbed of anti-Northern feeling. State and city leaders often threatened to leave the

WCD	William C. Davis
GWG	Gary W. Gallagher
JMM	James M. McPherson
BP	Brian Pohanka
JIR	James I. Robertson Jr.
SRW	Stephen R. Wise

A crowd gathered at City Hall in Charleston (above left) when news of Lincoln's election was announced. The Republican's victory was viewed as a declaration of war against the South because of Lincoln's opposition to slavery. The Charleston Mercury *called the Republican president "the beau ideal of a relentless, dogged, free-soil Border Ruffian, a vulgar mobocrat and a Southern hater."*

Charleston celebrated on November 10 when the General Assembly called for a secession convention. Robert Barnwell Rhett, editor of the Mercury, *announced, "The tea has been thrown overboard—the revolution of 1860 has been initiated."*

On December 18, 1860, the secession convention convened in Charleston (above right) having previously met in Columbia, South Carolina. A threat of smallpox had caused the change of venue. Almost all of the 169 delegates were slaveholders, including 5 former governors, 40 former state senators, 100 former state representatives, 12 churchmen, and 10 lawyers. They met for two days, and on December 20 they voted to secede from the Union. The Ordinance of Secession was signed that evening at Institute Hall, which allowed a large public audience to witness the event. The signing lasted two hours.

WCD Union. Thus °the city was viewed throughout the South and the North as the place where secession was fathered.• Charlestonians needed to look no farther than the grave of John C. Calhoun to remind them of that heritage. Calhoun, twice the nation's vice president, had first talked of leaving the Union in a Charleston house in the 1830s.

It was in this city during the summer of 1860 that the Democratic Party fractured and talk of the South's leaving the Union became more real. By December the talk had turned to action, leading to the Ordinance of Secession, which was signed in Charleston on December 20, 1860, barely a month after Abraham Lincoln's election. The election of a president from an antislavery party indicated to the Carolinians that the North was actively threatening the cotton-growing South, which needed slaves to harvest its crops. The resultant ordinance was a one-page document that took South Carolina out of the Union.

Secession was motivated as much socially as it was JMM politically. °In 1860 approximately 60 percent of South Carolina's population was black and enslaved. This disparity led the whites to believe that they were sitting on a powder keg that the Yankees were constantly threatening to touch off with their talk of abolition. Carolinians were afraid slave insurrections would destroy the South and

cause the slaves to rise up and slit the throats of their former owners.•

Charlestonians also believed their genteel society was superior to that of the money-hungry North. °They believed their lifestyle was correct and that the industrialized North had dehumanized its society. Charlestonians viewed the South as the keepers of the proper culture.•

Charleston was a cultural center for the South and the region's second largest city—after New Orleans. It was a °thriving port, which made it strategically important to the South during the war. Charleston was a key point where goods such as cotton could leave the country and where war matériel or other goods could enter.•

The view of Charleston above is placid, hardly indicative of the mood of 1860. The housetop view at the bottom right is dominated by the Citadel. Citadel cadets had manned a battery on Morris Island and had fired the first shots of the war on a supply ship when it approached Fort Sumter in January 1861.

Some of the first Yankee prisoners of the war were kept at Castle Pinckney, in the harbor. When that facility began to overflow, Union POWs were moved into the old jail house (bottom left). Southern strategists believed that keeping prisoners in the city would spare it from shelling. They were wrong, but Union gunners avoided those buildings that were known to house their comrades.

As the scene of the opening salvo of the war, Charleston suffered the war's longest siege. In the summer of 1861 a Federal armada began sinking old ships in the harbor channel (above). Incoming vessels had to run the gauntlet and risk either capture or running aground. Many Europeans were outraged and viewed this blockade as an act against civilians. The stone fleet tactic failed, however, as the ancient vessels sank into the thick mud of the harbor bottom.

After secession in December 1860, Charleston's pride and anti-Northern feelings escalated, thanks to the fact that WCD °Charleston had more than its share of hotheads, such as Robert Barnwell Rhett Sr., a newspaper publisher who had first used the term *Confederacy* in an editorial calling for the slave-holding states to form a confederation of states that would leave the Union. Rhett and his supporters who pushed for secession were very anxious to bring about the confrontation with the North.•

Other Charlestonians, however, like James L. Petigru, one of the state's most prominent lawyers and a slave holder himself, believed the fever for independence was overdone. °Petigru snarled, "It will never work! South Carolina is too small for a republic and too large for an insane asylum."•

The hotheads, however, won the day. As tensions increased in the city, the Federal garrison at Fort Moultrie on Sullivan's Island abandoned that installation in late December 1860 as indefensible and moved to Fort Sumter in Charleston Harbor. The city leaders were livid and demanded the soldiers relinquish the fort and leave the state. Finally, the South decided to bombard them into submission on April 12, 1861, and within two days the Union troops under Maj. Robert Anderson surrendered. The war had begun.

JIR °The feeling in Charleston was one of joy, excitement, and grandeur. Something mighty had been accomplished. South Carolina had won its independence again as it had done in the 1700s against the English.•

BP °Beneath the confidence of the most determined secessionists, however, lay the thought that the North would want vengeance because of this humiliation at Sumter.• They were right.

JMM °Losing Fort Sumter galvanized the Northern people into a paroxysm of war fever and united them in their determination to fight a war to preserve the Union.•

The siege of Charleston began on April 7, 1863, when a flotilla of ironclads under Samuel F. Du Pont steamed into Charleston Harbor and opened fire (left). Du Pont was a reluctant warrior, doubting that the ironclads could successfully press an attack of this nature. Nevertheless, under pressure from Washington, he was forced to engage the forts. The affair was an embarrassment for the navy. The monitors' limited maneuverability combined with the Confederates' well-placed artillery at Forts Sumter, Wagner, and Moultrie forced the vessels to withdraw. During two and a half hours, the Southerners fired 2,200 rounds to the Federals' 139 shots. John Ericsson, the architect of the monitors, had warned the Navy Department, "A single shot may sink a ship while a hundred rounds cannot silence a fort." Du Pont was recalled.

To the Confederates' credit, the right man was in the right place at the right time in Charleston, namely, P. G. T. Beauregard (below). Beginning in August 1862 he strengthened the city's defenses and the surrounding forts, and the thoroughness of those preparations were the basis for the "warm reception" he promised Du Pont when word arrived of the approaching Yankee monitors.

Retaliation came swiftly. Lincoln immediately ordered that Charleston's lifeline, its harbor, be blockaded. °If the port could be closed, Confederate supplies would be constricted. The South would strangle if all of its ports could be shut down.•

The first move to close Charleston's port came in June 1861 when the North requisitioned some ancient whaling ships, filled the hulls with granite, sailed them to Charleston, and then sank the worm-eaten vessels in the Charleston shipping channels. With obstructions in the channels, blockade-running ships might run aground and possibly sink. It seemed like a good idea. "At least one cursed rat hole has been closed," reported the *New York Herald* in December 1861.

This attack on the port itself, rather than against military targets, sparked international outrage. °It angered the British and French diplomats based in Charleston because they interpreted this action as an act of war against the people rather than the Confederate government or military.• "Among the crimes of mankind it would be difficult to find one more atrocious than this of Washington," sniffed an editorial writer for the *Times* of London.

The outrage did not last long, however. The stone fleet blockade failed to close down the channels. °The ships were so heavy and the mud at the bottom of Charleston Harbor was so thick that the ships continued sinking until they sank out of sight. Some of the ships came apart under the pounding of the tides and some of the granite was caught up in the tides and used naturally to

Quincy A. Gillmore (above), an 1849 graduate of West Point, had demonstrated the effectiveness of rifled cannon by demolishing Fort Pulaski in Savannah, Georgia. That achievement earned him a general's star and a reputation as perhaps the best engineer in the Union army. Gillmore came to South Carolina in June 1863 to head the Department of the South in joint operations with the Federal navy to capture Charleston. He proposed and executed a three-step strategy to accomplish that goal: (1) the capture of Fort (or Battery) Wagner, (2) the reduction of Fort Sumter, and (3) the naval occupation of the harbor. The successful execution of those steps occupied the army and navy for the remainder of the war.

To take Fort Wagner the Federals created miles of siege works, earthworks, and trenches. The men seen to the right demonstrate a rolling sap—a wicker basket—that shielded the diggers from fire. By such means Union engineers positioned their largest artillery closer to Wagner and within range of the other Charleston forts. Once the guns were in place, the Federals could bombard any target in the harbor and also lob shells into Charleston itself.

scour the channels, making them even deeper. On paper the stone fleet had seemed worthwhile. Instead, it was a hilarious failure.•

Washington switched to a more conventional blockade, placing warships in the shipping lanes. The Confederates responded by running the blockade with specially outfitted ships. The risk in blockade-running was great, but so were the profits of success. Hence the Yankee blockade did not work very well, either, as eight out of every ten blockade-runners succeeded in avoiding capture. °The South was able to export approximately one million bales of cotton in return for which it received six hundred thousand muskets and five hundred thousand shoes.• Charlestonians particularly excelled at the blockade-running enterprise.

The success of the blockade-runners could be traced to the fact that they were specially built. °Painted in camouflage colors so they would not be seen against the blue of the ocean, the vessels' masts were hinged so they could be dropped to the deck.• Their smokestacks could telescope to lower the line of the ship. They also burned clean coal, thus reducing the amount of smoke they produced at sea.

The blockade-runners were among the very few vessels the Confederacy had since, when the war began, it had no shipbuilding industry. The South had almost no warships to counter the Yankee blockade on a military

basis, so the blockade-runners were designed to outrun the Federal ships.

°The lack of a Confederate navy pointed to one more difference between North and South. The North had a vast commercial fleet, including whaling ships and cargo ships, that routinely sailed the Atlantic. The South was not a maritime nation at all. The area had always depended on Northern ships to carry its imports as well as its exports. As the South had never developed a shipbuilding industry, the only warships of the Confederacy were those that were captured from Union naval bases.•

To help raise a navy, the women of Charleston °created "Ladies' Gunboat Societies," which sponsored fairs where the women sold handmade items for the patriotic purpose of raising money to build gunboats.• Charleston's ladies raised funds for two ironclad gunboats—the *Chicora* and the *Palmetto State*—but neither was very effective. °Their engines were cranky. Their steering was bad. They were too heavy and too slow. In the end, the two ships spent most of their short careers moored to a Charleston wharf.•

While the ladies were helping the navy, a local slave did just the opposite. One day while the slave crew for a Confederate dispatch ship, the *Planter*, was resting, the ship's pilot, a slave named Robert Smalls, playfully put on the captain's straw hat and imitated the distinctive way the captain stood on the prow of his boat. The rest

At dawn on August 17, 1863, Gillmore concentrated his long-range artillery on Fort Sumter, beginning one of the fiercest bombarments in history. His gunners fired on the harbor fort for seven days without interruption. The eight breaching batteries were named for officers who had died in battle and famous Union generals. The Confederate gunners tried to respond, but Beauregard realized the fort was no match for the Union batteries. On August 23, the Southerners ceased firing. The next day Gillmore reported, "Fort Sumter is today a shapeless and harmless mass of ruins," but the fort was hardly harmless as the Federals discovered later. The Haas and Peale photograph here shows the three 100-pounder Parrot rifles of Battery Rosecrans on Morris Island.

Fort Moultrie on Sullivan's Island overlooked the northeast side of the harbor entrance. After the bombardment of Sumter was lifted, stores and ammunition were sent here. The greater symbolism of the harbor fort—Sumter was the installation from which the Federals had been expelled by force in April 1861—spared Moultrie the brunt of the Union onslaught. During the bombardment's hiatus, C. W. Chapman painted the above relatively calm scene at Moultrie in September 1863 as part of a series of harbor studies for Beauregard, all of which carried a suggestion of endurance and defiance.

of the crew kidded Smalls, telling him he looked just like the captain. That gave Smalls an idea.

On the night of May 13, 1862, Smalls and the crew boarded the ship and cast off as if they were on a regular trip. Smalls put on the captain's hat and stood in the prow of the ship with his back turned to the shore so no JMM one could see that he was black. °Because he knew the recognition signals to blow on the ship's whistle, he was able to steer the ship past Fort Sumter as he would normally. The fort's sentries and cannon crews paid little attention to the ship.• They expected to see it; they just did not know it was commandeered by slaves.

WCD °Once Smalls was outside the channel and past the Rebel forts, the crew took down the Confederate flag and ran up a white sheet of surrender. They surrendered to GWG the Yankee fleet• °and received tremendous newspaper coverage in the North because their acts were seen as examples of slaves' seizing an opportunity to achieve their freedom. The act also demonstrated that slaves were willing to fight for their freedom if necessary.•

Smalls was allowed to captain the *Planter* for the Union for the rest of the war, taking it on raids up rivers and creeks he had come to know so well all his life. After the war he became a congressman from South Carolina. One of his major accomplishments was the transformation of a small naval coaling station into a major military base: the U.S. Marine Corps training depot on Parris Island, South Carolina.

While Smalls had been able to get his ship out of Charleston, it was still impossible to get a Federal ship into the harbor. In November 1861 a huge Union fleet

The 1863 photograph to the left shows a group of Charlestonians, some of whom are boys, constituting a home company at Fort Pemberton on James Island, possibly Company I of the Palmetto Battery, Charleston Light Artillery. The Stono River is in the background. The large rivers of the area were a weakness in the defense of the city because they allowed Federal ships numerous approaches to the city that were difficult to protect. Perhaps the greatest mistake of the Confederates was the abandonment of Cole's Island at the Stono River Inlet, which ultimately allowed Union forces to occupy Folly Island and subsequently Morris Island. Extensive batteries were therefore erected by the Southerners on James and Sullivan's Islands, and batteries were also constructed east and west of Fort Moultrie. The effectiveness of the James Island batteries contributed to the Rebel success at the battle of Secessionville in June 1862 and led the Northerners to abandon any further attempts at the overland conquest of Charleston.

captured Port Royal, fifty miles south of Charleston. With the Federals investing that area, it would be a perfect assembly point for action against Charleston, and Charlestonians knew it. "There is great terror here. And no preparation. I regard the city in hourly peril," wrote Jacob Sherman in his diary.

THE NORTH'S FIRST attempt to take Charleston was by land. The target was Secessionville, a plantation community on James Island, twelve miles southeast of the city. The community received its name, not because of Southern politics, but because young farmers had gone there to break away from their elders.

In June 1862, without orders, an overconfident Union Brig. Gen. William Benham led six thousand men against a Confederate fort defended by only five hundred. Before they could reach the fort, °Benham's men began to fall out from heat exhaustion. Not thinking, the general ordered whiskey rations given to these men, which doubled the number of men reporting themselves as exhausted. The whole column fell apart.•

By the time Benham could order a frontal assault, the outnumbered Rebels were °waiting with a huge cannon that tore a wide swath through the Federals. The screams of the men cut down by that one cannon blast carried above the sound of the gunfire.• Benham was forced to retreat °with heavy losses. He was charged

The Confederate garrison at Sumter had had quiet duty for the two years between the taking of the fort and Gillmore's bombardment. As part of Beauregard's strengthening of the Charleston defenses, he sought heavier guns for the forts. Living conditions, however, deteriorated for the 320 Southern infantrymen. Gunners even slept near their cannon, which C. W. Chapman chose to depict above. A second major bombardment began on October 26 and continued through December 6. One night shortly after the shelling began, 13 soldiers of the Charleston Washington Light Infantry were killed when their barracks was struck. In December a powder magazaine exploded, creating an inferno and killing 11 men. When the fire was extinguished, the fort commander ordered the band to the parapet to boost morale. They played "Dixie," and when the sound carried to the Yankee gunners on Morris Island, they ceased firing and even cheered the fort's defenders.

with mismanagement and with being drunk and nearly lost his military career as a result.•

JIR   °The failure at Secessionville should have sent a signal to the North that, despite its heavy preponderance in numbers, it could not win by sheer strength alone. That lesson would go unlearned for a good while to come.•

Washington fell back on its naval power to try to capture Charleston. Standing by in Port Royal was the Union's fleet of new ironclad warships, called monitors after the original Union ironclad that had fought the Confederate ironclad CSS *Virginia.*

WCD   °The Federal secretary of the navy, Gideon Welles, was a good politician, but he knew little about naval vessels. The monitors had been constructed, but no one really knew how to use them.• Among their leading critics was the man commanding them, Adm. Samuel Du Pont, an

JIR   old aristocrat from Delaware. °Du Pont was out of step with the times, preferring wooden ships to ironclads. Someone once said he would have been a greater commander at Trafalgar, a British naval victory over Napoleon, than he was at Charleston.•

Du Pont had little faith that the newfangled monitors could take Charleston. "Something always breaks," he said. He was right about that, and as it turned out, right about his suspicions of the new ships.

WCD   °No one had used monitors in an attack against stationary fortifications. Du Pont did not want to attack Fort Sumter and the other Confederate forts, but he received orders from Washington to do so.• He feared leading his nine warships into Charleston Harbor, which was superbly defended on all sides. "Charleston's defenses are like a porcupine hide with the quills turned inside out," Du Pont said.

Those defenses, which had originally been used to force Union-held Fort Sumter to surrender, were the brainchild of the region's flamboyant Confederate com-

WCD   mander, °Pierre Gustave Toutant Beauregard. A short Creole dandy who began coloring his hair once it began

This photograph of the first breach in Sumter's wall was taken by Charleston photographer George S. Cook on September 8, 1863. The opening was probably made by one of the Morris Island batteries. The other batteries concentrated on it for the rest of the day, widening it. The Federals tried to exploit the opening by launching a small-boat attack by marines. The Yankee seaman had expected to find the fort vacant, but the attack failed and 125 Northerners were taken as prisoners. Even though the fort was in process of becoming rubble and some of the garrison lacked sufficient shelter, Beauregard warned his Federal counterparts, "The ruins of the fort will be defended to the last extremity."

to turn gray, the general was once described as hardly tall enough for his name. Although he had his critics, he was well known as an engineer.•

°Beauregard used his engineering skills to perfect a system of fortifications around Charleston that would bring tremendous fire to bear on any Union naval force that tried to enter the harbor.• °His batteries could deliver intensely concentrated fire, perhaps as intensely as existed anywhere in the world at that time.• Nevertheless, in April 1863 the reluctant Du Pont steamed into the harbor.

Although the monitors were supposedly impervious to shells, °the ironclads were slow sitting ducks that made great targets. When the Rebels' shells struck them in just the wrong place, the ships could be knocked out of action.• °In the course of a few hours the Confederates fired more than two thousand rounds, and almost five hundred hit Du Pont's ironclads, an exceptional display of marksmanship. In that same period of time, the ironclads fired fewer than two hundred shots of their own and did no damage whatever to Charleston's fortifications.• The wounded fleet withdrew. One ironclad sank, and Du Pont decided not to try again.

Washington was furious. "After all our great preparations, a fight of thirty minutes and the loss of one man satisfied the admiral," exclaimed an angry secretary of the navy.

Gillmore's guns gradually reduced Sumter to rubble. The parade ground was littered with wood, shattered barrels, and bits of brick and mortar. The garrison found shelter under cover of the gorge or within the splinter-proof blindage at its base. Considering the amount of shot and shell hurled at the fort, there were few casualties. During the first shelling sixteen Confederates were injured—one man was killed, two were seriously wounded, and thirteen were slightly wounded. Under cover of darkness the Southerners tried reinforcing the exterior of the gorge with thousands of sand bags. Only one of the fort's five walls retained a distinguishable appearance. The rest looked like a rocky hillside. Gaps in the wall were patched with palmetto barricades and reinforced with dirt- and rubble-filled baskets. Charleston photographer George S. Cook documented the damage inflicted by the Yankee batteries in the photographs below.

JIR Du Pont was sent into retirement by officials in Washington °who were not aware of everyday military affairs, especially the complicated, unusual affairs that were part of the siege of Charleston.• The North had tried to take Charleston separately by land and sea—and had failed. Next it tried a combined army-navy effort.

AFTER TWO YEARS of war the Union forces still had no foothold in Charleston. The next operation was a massive assault against Morris Island at the entrance to Charleston Harbor. Once used as a hospital cemetery, the island was known to the locals as Coffin Island. The name soon proved horribly accurate.

The man who chose Morris Island for this showdown in the summer of 1863 was Union Brig. Gen. Quincy A. Gillmore, a military engineer and an artillery expert whose rifled cannon had earlier subjugated Fort Pulaski in Savannah, Georgia, proving that brick forts were obso-

BP lete. Having experienced that success, °Gillmore became like Beauregard, that is, he was quite full of himself. He had a great deal of self-confidence, perhaps more than was healthy.

Gillmore viewed the attack on Morris Island as a personal contest with Beauregard. Gillmore was a West

Point–educated engineer,• too, but his self-confidence was dangerous to his men, because °like many other generals, he had not led troops in the field. His expertise was in artillery tactics. When he began to issue orders prior to the assault on Morris Island, his soldiers began to have second thoughts about him.•

His plan was simple. He would attack Battery Wagner, also called Fort Wagner, a sand fortification at the top of Morris Island within sight of Fort Sumter. Once Wagner was captured, Gillmore could then attack Sumter. Once he had taken Sumter, he could take the city.

On July 10, 1863, Union troops stormed ashore on Morris Island, led by dashing Brig. Gen. George C. Strong. °As his boats neared the shore, Strong decided that he would be the first one in the water to lead his men to the beach. As the boat slowed, Strong jumped in the water and disappeared from sight. After a while his hat bobbed to the surface, and his men jumped in and rescued him. The boats had not reached the shore; they had reached an outer shelf.• °Strong managed to get ashore minus his boots and much of his equipment, but he commandeered a mule that he came across and led his men on muleback up the beach. His soldiers were cheering, firing, and shouting as they swept the Confederate defenders back to Wagner.• The taking of Morris Island seemed to be going well for the Federals; the hard part was seemingly over.

°This early success in occupying most of Morris Island may have boosted Gillmore's confidence and that of his officers that Battery Wagner would fall quickly• since it was defended by only thirteen hundred men. The next day Gillmore ordered his infantry to take it.

°The Yankees swept forward just as the Confederates opened fire. Almost immediately the front ranks of the Union troops were mowed down. The Confederates stood firm and counterattacked. Strong was forced to retreat from the ramparts of the fort.•

On the morning of September 8, 1863, George Cook took his camera to Sumter's parapet and captured this image of three Union ironclads firing on Fort Moultrie. The three ships the day before had thrown 152 shots at the Sullivan's Island fort, and during the engagement one of the vessels, the Weehawken, ran aground. On September 8 Confederate gunners fired on this exposed and stranded ironclad. The vessel, of course, returned fire, and a shell struck the muzzle of an 8-inch Columbiad positioned at Fort Moultrie and ricocheted into some shell boxes. The explosion killed sixteen men and wounded twelve others. With the help of other Federal ships the Weehawken made its escape. For his part, Cook's movement on the parapet drew the attention of some Union lookouts, and they opened fire on Sumter as a Confederate officer demanded Cook leave the wall.

The bombardment of Charleston began at the order of President Lincoln. The first shell fired at the city by Gillmore's gunners exploded on Pinckney Street at 1:30 A.M. on August 29. Life in the city thereafter was totally disrupted. Entire sections of town became deserted, and schools and churches closed. The lower part of the city was shelled regularly, and buildings and homes were flattened. Downtown Charleston was abandoned. On Christmas Day 1863, the Federals continued to fire into the city, using church steeples as targets.

In November 1863 the Confederate president, Jefferson Davis, visited Charleston despite the shelling. From the portico of City Hall he addressed the people and said that it would be better to leave the city a "heap of ruins" rather than "prey for Yankee spoils." The crowd chanted back at him in agreement, "Ruins! Ruins!" True to their word, that was all that remained of several parts of the city by the end of the war.

Union overconfidence in their sheer numbers had again proven costly. Gillmore now decided to pound Wagner to pieces with artillery before charging again. The tactic had worked with Pulaski near Savannah, but Wagner was made of sand, not bricks.

JMM   °Gillmore had proven artillery could knock down a brick fort, but throwing a rifled artillery shell at a sand fort was like punching a pillow.• For a week the Union's land and naval guns rained thousands of shells on Wagner, where the Rebel soldiers huddled below ground in timber-reinforced bombproofs, buried deep under the sand. While they were protected from the Union shells, the situation was horrific for the Confederates.

SRW   °Eight hundred to a thousand men were cramped into a forty-by-one-hundred-foot bombproof. They had no idea what was going on outside. Worse, the garrison's hospital was also inside the bombproof, and the healthy men were forced to watch while their wounded comrades' arms and legs were amputated and then tossed into a pile in the same room.•

Amid the chaos one Southern officer, Maj. David Ramsey, took unusual steps to calm his men. °He left the bombproof, set up a camp chair in the sand, and proceeded to read a newspaper as the shells went off around

BP

210

him. He laughed and bantered with his men. By his example, he inspired them with confidence and courage in the face of the bombardment.•

.w The Rebel soldiers survived the shelling almost intact. The Union troops who had °watched the bombardment thought that no one could possibly survive that onslaught and believed they would just walk in and occupy Wagner.•

Gillmore ordered an attack that would take place after .w dark, but not everyone shared his confidence. °Col. Haldimand S. Putnam, commander of the Second Brigade, said, "We are being led into Wagner like a flock of sheep."•

BP °At the vanguard of this assault was the Fifty-fourth Massachusetts, the first African-American regiment raised in the North. Although the men were tired and had gone without food for hours, their young colonel, Robert Gould Shaw, was determined that this night he would prove conclusively that black men could fight.•

As before, the Union troops had to approach the Con-federate bastion along a narrow beach bordered by sea IR and swamp. °They then had to charge across about a quarter of a mile of open beach.• The Rebels were wait-ing for them.

G °The bombardment had done significant damage to neither the heavy guns nor the defenders in the fort. The

George Cook's September 8, 1863, visit to Fort Sumter resulted in this remarkable photograph. He was there while the fort was under fire and cre-ated an incredible record of Sumter and its garrison under siege. Cook had just positioned his camera for a picture of the devastated parade ground when a shell believed to be from the Wee-hawken exploded just as he exposed the plate. The breach in the wall can be seen left of center.

Confederates simply manned their artillery and rifle pits and cut down the Federals as they approached the fort.• It was easy shooting for the Confederates. Once the Yankees reached the fort by running along the narrow beach, they then had to run through wooden obstacles called abatis, then through a flooded moat, then up the steep sand walls of the fort. It was virtually impossible to do, but the Federals tried.

SRW ○The first three regiments that attacked Battery Wagner were decimated. Although a handful of men got inside the fort and the first African American to win the Medal of Honor actually planted the flag on top of the ramparts, the Fifty-fourth lost nearly 40 percent of its strength. The Forty-eighth New York lost more than 50 BP percent.• ○The fighting was a grim and deadly celebration for the Confederates, who had a "carnival of death," as one survivor called it.•

The reluctant Colonel Putnam had been holding his men back, but finally he charged. When his men made it over the top of the fort and Union victory seemed within his grasp, Putnam sent a message to Gillmore for rein-BP forcements. ○No help came. Some of the messengers were killed, thus Gillmore might not have understood how close the battle was to becoming a Union victory. Instead, he seemed to decide that enough lives had been wasted.•

When the Union troops fighting to stay in the fort BP realized they had been forsaken by their general, ○some

The shelling of the city caused those who could to flee Charleston for Columbia or the upcountry. Those who could not leave the city relocated north of Calhoun Street, which seemed to be the limit of the Union artillery. There were few military casualties, but the number of civilian fatalities is disputed. One town chronicler wrote: "By 1864, the town presented the most extraordinary appearance. The whole life and business of the place were crowded into the few squares above Calhoun Street, and along the Ashley [River], where the hospitals and the prisoners were and the shells did not reach. . . . To pass from this bustling, crowded scene to the lower part of town was . . . like going from life to death."

ran for their lives back through the flooded moat, back down the beach. Others surrendered. Many were killed where they stood. The battle dissipated in the darkness, but the rest of the night was filled with the screams of the wounded, of the men drowning in the moat, and of the men begging for help.•

°When the casualties were totaled, the figures were so one-sided as to be almost unbelievable. As many as 174 Confederates were lost while 1,515 Union soldiers were killed, wounded, or missing.• Among the dead were more than 100 Federal officers, including Putnam, who might have won the battle had he not been stranded. Strong was dead, too, and Shaw died with his troops. The Confederates buried Shaw with his men rather than send his body back through the lines.

°Gillmore must be faulted for the way he ordered the attack with no battle plan and no timetable. The men were not given ladders or boards for crossing the moat or climbing the heights to get into the fort itself, even though Gillmore, an engineer, knew these obstacles were in place. The men were simply told to go forward.•

The Federal commander, however, was not discouraged. He began a third attempt to take Wagner by laying siege. This time he intended to advance slowly on the

On September 8, 1863, the evening following the first breach in the wall of Fort Sumter, a joint army-navy assault was launched against the installation. The naval commander, John A. Dahlgren, believed the constant pounding had softened the fort's defenses to the point that his marines could easily occupy it. He told Comdr. Thomas Stevens, who was to lead the attack, "You have only to go in and take possession, you will find nothing but a corporal's guard." Dahlgren dispatched a force of 25 boats and 400 sailors and marines for the harbor bastion.

At 1 A.M. Maj. Stephen Elliot Jr., Sumter's commander, saw a line of barges advancing toward the northeastern angle and viewed a second moving toward the southeastern angle. His men did not fire on the assault force until the first boats had landed, and then their only weapons were small arms and makeshift hand grenades. The Southern defenders even threw bricks loosened by the bombardment at the Federals. Gillmore held back on sending the army contingent, assessing the scene as hopeless. The attack was over in twenty minutes. Not one Rebel was injured; the Yankees lost 125 captured.

John A. Dahlgren succeeded Samuel F. Du Pont as commander of Federal naval forces in South Carolina. He had made his reputation as a developer of naval ordnance, and that in itself gave him the basis for a good partnership with Gillmore. Following the failed attempt to storm Sumter, Dahlgren's command occupied itself with adding its guns to the army bombardment and screening the harbor as part of the Northern blockade. He next suggested an amphibious assault in January 1865 as William T. Sherman's army entered the Carolinas, but Sherman considered the proposed target—Fort Moultrie—as insignificant compared to the taking of Charleston itself.

fort by digging a network of trenches, an engineering technique with which he was comfortable. °It was a risky undertaking for the soldiers, because if they showed their heads above the trench, they were fired upon. Sharpshooters on both sides targeted everything that moved.•

Siege living conditions for both armies were terrible. The water was unsafe, and food was scarce. °The summer of 1863 was a typical southern summer with not even a hint of an ocean breeze to cool the camps that were just dozens of yards from the sea. Both during the day and at night, the heat was stifling and the humidity terrible. Insects drove men to near madness.•

Worst of all, the trench diggers would occasionally uncover fallen comrades. °The stench was awful. They could not rebury the men, so they simply used the bodies with the sandbags to construct earthworks.• After two months of digging, the Federals were within a few yards of Wagner. From there they launched the third assault, and this time they took the fort. It was, however, a hollow victory. The Confederates had abandoned Wagner the night before. They too had had enough of Wagner. °A Georgia soldier marching out spoke for his compatriots when he said, "I ain't no feared of hell after I been at Fort Wagner."•

Morris Island was finally taken, but at a dreadful cost. Clara Barton, who later founded the American Red Cross, wrote this epitaph for the island: "The thousand little sand hills are a thousand headstones. And the restless ocean waves sing an eternal requiem to the gallant dead who sleep beside."

WITH MORRIS ISLAND now his, Gillmore now turned his attention and his guns on Fort Sumter, less than a mile away. It was from this same area, now under Union control, that the first shot of the Civil War had been fired by a Confederate battery at the then Union-held fort. °Both strategically and symbolically, Fort Sumter remained important to the Confederates and to the

Charlestonians, who day after day viewed it in the harbor bravely flying the Confederate flag in spite of every Yankee effort to destroy it.•

Gillmore fired as many as a thousand shells a day at the fort on the man-made island for weeks on end. The three-story fort soon became a one-story fort and a pile of rubble. As the bricks were blasted into dust, the fort's commander, Confederate Col. Alfred Rhett, son of Robert Barnwell Rhett Sr., the man who had longed for the war, exclaimed, "They have ruined my beautiful fort!"

The brick walls may have shattered, but the soldiers inside the fort survived by building new shelters from the sand and rubble. °They lived like rats, but that description was offered by someone in a very positive sense, because the men burrowed under the ground and came out only when necessary. They resumed their own firing when they had the chance to do so.•

Gillmore, seeing the shattered walls and believing Sumter defenseless, issued Beauregard an ultimatum. °He called for the surrender of Fort Sumter or else he would open fire on the city itself. Beauregard refused, whereupon Gillmore brought up a huge Parrott rifled cannon and opened fire on Charleston.•

This huge gun, nicknamed the Swamp Angel, was placed on Morris Island within range of the city. Just mounting the gun was an engineering achievement, one of the rare times when Gillmore did something right in Charleston. °The Federals drove pillars deep into the swamp muck of the island so that they could erect a platform that would hold the weight of this heavy gun.• It fired incendiary shells on the city until one of the shells exploded prematurely inside the barrel, destroying the cannon before it could destroy Charleston.

°Gillmore was one of the first generals to make civilians legitimate targets of war. At that time such action was certainly beyond the accepted norms of war. In the Civil War, however, all previously accepted norms were challenged.• °Gillmore wanted revenge against

The Beacon House on Morris Island was used as an artillery observation post by both sides, which led to its being targeted and ventillated. This image and the two on the next two pages are three of the more than forty photographs taken by Haas and Peale of Morris Island and Hilton Head in mid-1863, creating a chronicle of sorts of the Gillmore era.

The tenacity of the Confederates in Charleston and the determination of the Federal army and navy created a stalemate. Thousands of shells had been hurled into the city and its fortifications, and though buildings were scarred and neighborhoods leveled, the Northern troops could do nothing to wrest the Southerners from Charleston. Washington concluded that the city had proved to be the best protected on the coast and that the continued bombardment would be a waste of effort and matériel. Frustration following the second bombardment of Charleston led Gillmore to request reassignment. He was not alone in leaving the area. Yankee troops and ships were dispersed among other operations from northern Virginia to Texas as additional troops were required. The Confederates did likewise.

215

A part of the Haas and Peale portfolio, an orderly delivers a message to a colonel on Folly Island in a scene posed for the cameramen. While the officer is in his formal uniform, the men in the neighboring tent are not as taken with the moment.

Folly Island was near Morris and James Islands and had been used as a base of operation for the taking of Morris Island. At one time Folly had hosted twelve thousand Federal troops. In 1864, as both sides moved troops to more critical areas along the battle front, Union forces on Folly were ordered to keep the Confederates on James Island engaged so that none could be withdrawn to reinforce Lee in Virginia.

Charleston for the blood of his soldiers that had seeped into the sands of Morris Island.•

No city in the country had ever experienced what

BP Charleston would experience. °Without any warning other than the roar of a shell overhead, citizens on the city's streets might be killed by Federal artillery. The Union shelling was indiscriminate. It might hit a child, a woman, a slave. The victims might be killed by the shell

JMM itself or by a collapsing porch or a falling chimney.• °The shelling became counterproductive in some ways because Gillmore was denounced as a monster. His name became infamous, and the shelling galvanized the civilian population to angry, determined resistance.•

Charlestonians did their best to ignore the shelling and the increasingly effective Union blockade of the

WCD harbor. °They never let their spirits lag. They continued their social lives just as they had in the days before the war. The difference was that now their coffee was made from burnt chicory. If they drank whiskey, it might have

BP been distilled from pine boughs rather than from corn.• °They still believed they were civilized people willing to continue to conduct themselves in that fashion even if they were besieged by Yankee vandals who wanted to destroy them.•

JMM The blockade forced Charlestonians to become ever more resourceful in helping to supply the war effort. °They saved the contents of chamber pots to be leached for saltpeter, an essential component of gunpowder. People

While Haas and Peale photographed several of Gillmore's batteries, all of which convey a kind of orderly, routine sameness, this image of an upset 300-pounder Parrott in Battery Brown hints at the risks faced by artillerists. During the bombardment of Charleston these weapons were fired at intervals of no less than fifteen minutes to avoid overheating the pieces. As destructive as a shell could be once it was launched from one of these cannon, an exploding shell while still in the tube could eliminate an entire gun crew.

throughout the South melted down church bells so that the brass and bronze could be used to cast cannon.•

Although Gillmore was carrying out his threat to wage war on the city, Beauregard still refused to surrender Sumter. The Federals therefore decided to take the fort by force, believing it to be almost helpless. That was another Yankee mistake. °The Northerners still clung to the idea that superior numbers meant they could win any battle. Defeat after defeat had not changed their minds about their invincibility.•

The idea of assaulting Fort Sumter was so popular that two Union attacks were planned independently of each other. Gillmore wanted to lead an army raid on Sumter, and the naval commander, John Dahlgren, who had replaced Du Pont, wanted to lead a navy raid.

°As might be expected, the army general and the navy admiral argued over the attack. Gillmore and Dahlgren both realized that whoever took Fort Sumter would become an instant hero.• Both planned separate amphibious assaults on Sumter, but Dahlgren's got there first.

°Dahlgren had based much of his attack on the element of surprise and on false information that the fort was virtually abandoned. The attack, however, was no surprise. The Southerners knew the Federals were coming, and there were plenty of men waiting to turn back the attacking Yankee seamen.• The Confederates hit them with grenades, gunshot, and cannon fire. The Union quickly lost more than a hundred men,

217

The Confederates were not content to endure Gillmore's bombardments but chose to strike back in novel ways, particularly with torpedo boats and submarines. The first submarine-type vessel was the David, *which was semi-submersible and carried a torpedo attached to a thirty-foot-long pole. On October 5–6, 1863, the* David *attacked the USS* New Ironsides *(below) and severely damaged it, although the Federal vessel remained on blockade duty.*

The first submarine to sink a ship was the H. L. Hunley, which was conceived in New Orleans, constructed in Mobile, and encountered the enemy in Charleston. The vessel was built from a boiler, carried a torpedo at the tip of a spar, and was manually powered by eight crewmen. Three crews were lost during test dives, including the inventor, H. L. Hunley.

On February 17, 1864, the Hunley *attacked the USS* Housatonic, *exploding its torpedo between the ship's main and mizzen masts. The Yankee blockader sank within minutes. Nothing was seen of the* Hunley *afterward. Years later its wreckage was found near that of the* Housatonic.

C. W. Chapman included a painting of the Confederate craft as part of his harbor series (above right). It is shown on a wharf at Mount Pleasant, near Charleston Harbor. Some called the vessel "Fish" or "Porpoise" for obvious reasons.

while the Confederates lost none. Gillmore saw the futility of Dahlgren's assault and did not proceed with his own.

Gillmore gave up trying to take Sumter directly. Instead, he pressed Dahlgren to make a full naval thrust toward Charleston. Dahlgren, however, refused, not wanting to follow Du Pont into early retirement. °Dahlgren could not take it upon himself to lose a monitor. To do so or, even worse, to lose a monitor to the Confederacy would ruin his career and conceivably turn the tide of the war, at least along the coastal area.•

While Dahlgren knew the harbor was well protected by forts and mines, he had not yet encountered a new mystery weapon, a submarine called the *H. L. Hunley* after its inventor, Horace Hunley of Alabama. First tested in Mobile and then shipped to Charleston to try to break the blockade, °the vessel could submerge completely under water. The trouble was that sometimes it did not resurface. Made from an old boiler, it looked like an iron coffin. Inside, eight men huddled in a fetid, damp, dank, close atmosphere to turn a hand crank that operated its propeller.•

Three times the submarine had sunk and drowned its crew, including Hunley. Somehow, a fourth crew was found, and the machine was finally put to a real combat test. In February 1864 a torpedo was mounted on the *Hunley*'s front spar,

and its crew rammed the *Housatonic,* a Union vessel blockading Charleston Harbor. °The Yankee ship went down, but unfortunately again for the Confederate crew, so did the *H. L. Hunley.* Although the *Hunley* was not seen again until 1997, it had carried out the first successful submarine attack in history.

Eventually it was neither naval battles nor artillery shells that decided the battle for Charleston. °Despite all the efforts of Gillmore, the blockade, Du Pont, and Dahlgren, it was William T. Sherman who forced Charleston's fall. In November 1864, Sherman, whose Union army had been burning and ravaging Georgia, reached Savannah, just south of Charleston.

°Sherman had acquired a horrible reputation during his campaign through Georgia, and Charlestonians were apprehensive that this redheaded general who was rather free with matches might appear at any time to burn their city to the ground. Sherman did not give them any reason to feel secure.

"The whole army is burning with an insatiable desire to reap vengeance on South Carolina. I almost tremble at her fate," said Sherman in January 1865, just before he crossed the Savannah River into South Carolina. After nearly four years of resistance, Charleston was about to meet its destiny.

THE CITY'S WORST nightmare—Sherman and his sixty-three-thousand-man army of burners and pillagers—pushed north from Savannah early in 1865. At first he

Fort Sumter, the largest fort in Charleston Harbor, sustained two years of near constant bombardment. It had been reduced to a pile of rubble, but the Confederates defended it to the last. Since the beginning, its granite, brick, and masonry had been a symbol to both sides, a prize each wanted and willingly died to attain.

On the morning of February 17, 1865, the fort's garrison raised a brand-new flag. That evening they lowered it for the last time. The defense of the fort was over. When no flag was raised the following morning, a small group of Federals rowed to the fort and found it deserted. They then rowed to Charleston and found the Confederate army had abandoned the city. The siege of Charleston was over.

219

When the Federal army occupied Charleston on February 18, 1865, it found the entire town in ruins (above left). The lower half of the city was uninhabited. Debris from the demolition of war matériel littered the neighborhoods. A major fire was burning through the town, sparked by the Confederates as they abandoned the city and torched the Ashley River bridge. Roving mobs looted what they could. Explosions rocked the town from the detonation of an ammunition magazine on Sullivan's Island and the destruction of the last of the Rebel gunboats. The first troops to enter the city, the Twenty-first U.S. Colored Troops, helped to extinguish the fire and restore order.

Hundreds of shells and guns were confiscated and stockpiled at The Citadel, which was now a Federal fort. The pieces above (right) were collected and later displayed in Northern museums or taken by Yankee soldiers as souvenirs.

JIR appeared headed for Charleston, but °Sherman played it brilliantly. He feinted a movement to the west, toward Augusta, Georgia, then he feinted to the east, toward Charleston. The Confederates, unsure which was the real target, rushed reinforcements to both cities. Sherman, meanwhile, just marched straight north, between the two towns, cutting all lines of communication as he went.• He was headed for Columbia, the capital of the state that had launched secession, not the city that had WCD started it. The target did not really matter. °Once a large enemy army was in the South Carolina heartland, less than a few days' march from Charleston, the city itself became virtually untenable. Its railroad connections to the west were cut off, leaving only one way out, retreat to the north. Although no enemy was in sight, the city could be taken any time. All that was required was Sherman's deciding he wanted it.•

Beauregard realized he could not save the city, but he could save his soldiers. In February 1865, despite the protest of the soldiers themselves, the Confederate army evacuated Charleston.

Just as they had been throughout the war, the Union army was duped by the Confederates. One evening the Federals watched a new Confederate flag being raised over Fort Sumter. They did not think much about it. The

next morning when the flag was not there, they grew suspicious. A handful of soldiers rowed out to Sumter and found it had been abandoned during the night. They then rowed to Charleston and discovered that its garrison had also left. °The Union forces that had been besieging Charleston for so long could now march in and take it without firing a shot.•

°Before the Confederates abandoned Charleston, they set fire to anything that might be of value to the Federals.• How much was left that was of value was debatable. Two years of Federal shelling had destroyed much of the lower part of the city that was within the range of Yankee artillery on Morris Island.

°When Union forces marched into Charleston following the Confederate withdrawal, they were confronted with hundreds of fires, which they put out. Most of the white population hid themselves in their homes while the large black population came out in enormous jubilee and celebration to greet the Union troops.• Ironically, among the first Union troops to march into the city were U.S. Colored Troops, black units dressed in Federal blue. The queen city of the Confederacy, the most defiant population in the South, succumbed to black troops marching in its streets, being welcomed as liberators by the former slave population.

McLeish's Vulcan Iron Works (above left) was able to return to business in the midst of the ruins. Its sign is decorated with various war souvenirs—an anchor, a signal gun, and an anvil-like locomotive spring. The looting, meanwhile, continued for months. A visiting Northern journalist in September 1865 described the town as "a city of ruins, of desolation, of vacant houses, of widowed women, of rotting wharves, of deserted warehouses, of weed-wild gardens, of miles of grass-grown streets, of acres of pitiful and voiceful barrenness."

Few landmarks survived the war, but the Mills House (above right), which was home to P. G. T. Beauregard, was one of the few. The devastation surrounding the hotel was not the result of Federal gunners but of the great fire of December 11, 1861, which damaged 540 acres and destroyed 575 homes. Interestingly, Robert E. Lee and his staff were in Charleston that night, staying at the Mills House. He and some of his officers went to the roof to assess the extent of the fire and saw more than a third of the city in flames.

Most of the photographs taken in Charleston after the war show unrepaired damage caused by the 1861 fire, not the Union bombardment. They were widely disseminated, however, as graphic evidence of the repercussions of rebellion.

Long one of the most exclusive neighborhoods in Charleston, this street near the Battery is dominated by a wrecked gun mount, destroyed during the Confederate retreat from the city. Broken carriages and damaged cannon littered the waterfront when the Union army began its occupation. One visitor noted, "The splendid houses are all deserted, the glass in the windows broken, the walls dilapidated, the columns toppled over . . . arches demolished, mantels shattered, while fragments, great and small, of every description strew the floors. . . . But where are the owners of these estates—where are they? . . . [T]hey are fugitives and vagabonds, wandering up and down the interior mountains and plantations." All was not lost, however, for the visitor. "Upon some houses, we found placards to the following effect: 'To be occupied by the owner, who has taken the oath of allegiance to the United States.'" It was the beginning of Reconstruction.

City fathers who had breathed easier when the Union troops saved Charleston from fire were now forced to watch the Federals begin looting it for themselves. WCD °Family silver was stolen. Family paintings were vandalized. Buildings were covered with graffiti. Iron grates were torn down. Fences were torn down. What had not been trashed by Federal shells was now being BP finally destroyed by Federal hands.• °It was as if the final vengeance was being taken out on this Rebel stronghold by the Union occupiers. These men were almost as bad as Sherman's men. Charleston was in a state of anarchy that disturbed even Gillmore.•

Few Northern politicians or generals cared what the Charlestonians thought of the ongoing destruction of their city. GWG °There was a sense in the North that if any place should be punished for what happened—punished for the coming of the war and for all of the carnage—it was Charleston, South Carolina.• The city might have been lucky to have remained standing at all. "I hope the place may be destroyed, and a little salt sown upon the site to prevent the growth of future crops of secession," said Maj. Gen. Henry Halleck, the Union army's chief of staff.

The Union crowned its victory at Fort Sumter on April 14, 1865, when Union Brig. Gen. Robert Anderson, who had surrendered the fort exactly four years earlier in 1861, JIR was invited back. °The old Kentucky officer, using the same American flag he had lowered in defeat, raised it anew over Fort Sumter. Except for scattered fighting that would go on for another month, the war symbolically ended that day, although the nation would also recognize April 9, 1865, the day Lee surrendered to Grant at Appomattox Court House, Virginia. The Union was jubilant on April 14, but there was one last tragedy to take place on that day that could be considered part of the war. That night President Lincoln went to Ford's Theater in Washington to see a play. . . .•

The battle for Charleston had lasted four years, but in the end it had little effect on the course of the war. The capture of the city had been more a point of honor for both sides. °Charleston was a symbol rather than a real strategic point that had to be taken. The battle to take the city was a battle of egos between the commanders. It was a test of wills between two engineers, Beauregard and Gillmore, and a test of the willpower of the people to survive constant warfare.•

°Charleston had come full circle. It started the war very confident, believing that one Southerner was worth ten Yankees. As one Southerner claimed, "We'll whip the Yankees using broomsticks!" When the war was over, the man was asked what had happened. He replied, "Well, the damn Yankees didn't use broomsticks."•

°Charleston could be seen as the microcosm of the whole Southern war effort. It exhibited enormous effort, determination, and dedication through much of the war and enjoyed great success against high odds. In the end, the city suffered defeat and ruin and destruction. That was also true of the Confederacy.•

Sherman did eventually make it to Charleston. He came for a brief visit when the war was over, three months after the city had fallen. Looking out over the ashes of the city he said, "Anyone who is not satisfied with war should go and see Charleston. And he will pray louder and deeper than ever that the country be spared any more war."

John P. Hatch (above, seated to the right), an 1845 graduate of West Point, was put in charge of the Union troops occupying Charleston. He did little to control the looting. The situation deteriorated to the point that Quincy Gillmore wrote Hatch telling him that the plundering must stop: "I hear on all sides very discouraging accounts of the state of affairs in Charleston; that no restraint is put on the soldiers; that they pilfer and rob houses at pleasure; that large quantities of valuable furniture, pictures, statuary, mirrors, etc., have mysteriously disappeared." Finally, Gillmore issued an order directing Hatch and his officers to restore the plunder they had stolen. None of the items were ever returned.

223

THE IRON BRIGADE

THE BEGINNING OF THE CIVIL WAR, the Confederates, the majority of whom were reared as hunters in the rural South, confidently predicted that each of them could whip ten Yankees. The assumption was that the Union army was made up of northeastern shopkeepers who had never seen the business end of a musket. These Southerners had not anticipated that they might encounter Northerners raised much like themselves, accustomed to riding, shooting, and fighting in the rural North. They had never encountered men from Wisconsin, Indiana, and Michigan, rugged frontiersmen whose bravery carved a special place among the greatest heroes of the conflict. The Southerners who came up against these hard-fighting westerners would assign them the hard-won epithet "those damned black-hatted fellows," but their fellow Federal soldiers called them the Iron Brigade.

These young men from the West—what would today be considered the Midwest—came to fight in the East full of youthful idealism and convinced that the Union mattered. They were from the farms, the woods, and along the rivers that marked the frontier of America. They were tough, cocky, and stubborn. Some of their leaders decided that such men needed something distinctive to set them apart from other Union soldiers, so they were issued black hats with straight brims and tall crowns. With these hats they marched into battle looking like giants, and no one who saw them ever forgot them.

The stories from the eastern battlefields were filled with descriptions of the achievements of the Iron

WCD	William C. Davis
LH	Lance Herdegen
HM	Howard Madaus
AN	Alan Nolan
BP	Brian Pohanka

On September 21, 1861, the ten companies of the Seventh Wisconsin were mustered in as three-year enlistments, including the two soldiers above who are wearing the 1861 gray uniform of the state militia. The uniform would later be replaced with the blue volunteer outfit, but many of the Badgers were not pleased with the change, maintaining that their state uniforms were of better quality than the Federal issue. Some secretly kept their original gray overcoats. The regiment arrived in Washington on October 1 and was brigaded with the Second and Sixth Wisconsin and Nineteenth Indiana. The men of these four regiments were mostly country boys, and a number had been foreign born—Germans, Irish, and Scandinavians. One regular army officer described these volunteers as "the finest material for soldiers I ever saw."

Brigade, including several firsthand accounts. One of these was written by Rufus Dawes, major of the Sixth Wisconsin Volunteers. Regarding the action at Antietam, he wrote: "Our men on the left loaded and fired with the energy of madmen, and the recklessness of death truly wonderful. Human nature could not long stand such a terribly waist-thick fire. They literally mowed out great gaps in the lines. The isolated squads would rally together and then rush right up to the face of death."

°Dawes was typical of the men of the Iron Brigade. He was an Ohioan living on the frontier in Wisconsin who was caught up in the war from the very first days. He believed in fighting for the most noble of reasons, the abstract sense of preserving the Union and justice. He answered the call• for volunteers shortly after the fall of Fort Sumter. Dawes, however, °should be remembered, not so much for his brave battlefield deeds, but because his postwar writings told the story of his regiment through his own experience in a very personal and honest way. He described the Sixth Wisconsin, a regiment within the Iron Brigade, in such a way that readers today know not only Dawes but his men and comrades as individuals, as real people of flesh and blood.•

Dawes was not the only man who vividly recorded the story of the Iron Brigade. °The brigade included many men in its four regiments—the Second, Sixth, and Seventh Wisconsin and the Nineteenth Indiana—who were literate. Many of these men were prolific diary keepers and letter writers who knew they were part of something special in fighting the war. They wanted a record of their actions as they contributed to this national epic.• Some were quite poetic about their mission.

"A thrill of joy passed through our being when we think we are in a great volunteer army of 1861 and able to raise our hand in defense of this—the purest and best of governments in existence. Rather would we be pierced with the bayonets and bullets of our wicked enemies or our bones to bleach in the Southern clime than turn our face homeward before victory shall have been won," wrote Pvt. Jerome Watrous of the Sixth Wisconsin.

°Two things made the Iron Brigade distinctive. First, it was a tough combat unit. It was the only western unit in the Army of the Potomac at a time when anything west of Ohio was considered the frontier. Consequently, the men in the brigade believed they had something to prove to the eastern units. What made them tougher was that they came from a rural background, making them much more like the Southerners they fought against than the city boys who had joined the Union army from New York, Philadelphia, and Boston.•

°Westerners looked upon themselves as a tougher breed than easterners. The men from Indiana, Wisconsin, and Michigan were pioneers or the sons of pioneers; they were people who had relinquished the comfortable lifestyle of the East for the dangerous and rough life of the frontier. That frontier attitude, which has almost always been held up as a quintessentially American attitude, gave the men of the Iron Brigade the idea that they would show these easterners how to fight.•

"We were the only western soldiers in the entire army," wrote Pvt. Philip Cheek of the Sixth Wisconsin. "And we would have died rather than have dishonored the West. We felt that the eyes of the East were upon us, and that we were the test of the West."

Second, the Iron Brigade was given a distinctive uniform that made the westerners stand out from the other soldiers of the Army of the Potomac. °Their high-crowned, flat-brimmed black hat sometimes had the left brim pinned up on the crown. It was also called a "Hardee" hat, named after William J. Hardee, a prewar regular army officer who had surrendered his commission to accept appointment as a Confederate general. This contrasted with the vast majority of soldiers in the Union army who wore blue forage caps that had only a small leather bill in front. In September 1861 the brigade received dark blue Federal-issue frock coats and dark blue trousers. Yet it was the black hat that was eventually associated with the brigade and became its distinctive trademark.• One of the men wrote: "We have a full blue suit

An Ohioan, Rufus R. Dawes had just graduated from Marietta College and was visiting his father in Juneau County, Wisconsin, when he heard of the fall of Fort Sumter. Gallantry was not lost on the Dawes family; his grandfather was William Dawes, Paul Revere's cohort on the night of April 18, 1775. At the age of twenty-two, Dawes quickly organized a company—the Lemonweir Minute Men—and proceeded to Madison. The unit became Company K of the Sixth Wisconsin. Dawes was elected captain, promoted to full colonel in 1864. and eventually breveted to brigadier general. In 1890 he chronicled his war experience and that of the Iron Brigade in his memoirs, Service with the Sixth Wisconsin Volunteers.

227

Pvt. Frederick Lythson (near right) was a Norwegian immigrant. His family had moved to Madison, Wisconsin, and at the age of nineteen he enlisted. Lythson was among the first soldiers of the Iron Brigade to fight. Assigned to Company H of the Second Wisconsin, he saw combat at the battle of First Manassas (Bull Run) in the brigade commanded by Col. William T. Sherman. In the photograph he is wearing the gray uniform that his unit wore into battle. While engaged on Henry House Hill, the Second was fired upon by Union regiments that mistook them for Confederates. On October 7, 1863, Lythson transferred from the ranks of the Iron Brigade to the Veteran Reserve Corps.

Sgt. John W. Fonda (far right) of Company C of the Sixth Wisconsin was among the first to respond to the call for troops. Along with his father, John H., Fonda enlisted on April 20, 1861. They were from Prairie du Chien, Wisconsin. In the photograph the sergeant also wears Wisconsin's gray state militia uniform.

and a fine black hat nicely trimmed with bugle and plate and ostrich feathers. And you can only distinguish our boys from the regulars by our good looks."

LH °Thus the Iron Brigade represented young America in many ways. While the eastern units from the original colonies of the country represented tradition, the Iron Brigade was from a part of the country that was spreading westward and represented the future. They helped define exactly what it meant to be an American.•

BP °First known as the Western Brigade, the Iron Brigade set out to prove that it was the finest brigade in the Union army. The tough westerners mastered the drill, demonstrated a proficiency in shooting, and learned to follow orders. They relentlessly pursued their new profession as soldiers. They stood up to the finest troops of the Confederacy and suffered horrendous casualties, almost to the extent that they ceased to exist as an organization.• The Iron Brigade earned its reputation with its own blood, suffering higher casualties than any other brigade in the Union army.

"The dread reality of war was before us, and the frightful death upon the cold, hard stones. The mortal suffering and fruitless struggle to send a parting message to a far off home, and the final release and death all enacted in the darkness," observed Dawes.

In a war when soldiers fought side by side and aimed at other soldiers fighting side by side just a few hundred

AN yards away, the Iron Brigade was used differently. °It was called on in unusually tough situations, which the men accepted as a point of pride. They were often used as

LH shock troops.• °The Iron Brigade ultimately became an efficient combat machine since the men had a certain caliber of marksmanship that was part of their frontier background. Like the Southerners, they knew the value of hitting what they aimed at and hitting it the first time. They inflicted tremendous casualties on the Confederates they faced.•

BP °The men of the Iron Brigade knew this sort of work made them targets themselves, but the true heroes were, are, and always will be those able to put aside their own doubts and fears, their own sense of hope on a personal level, for something higher than themselves.

Dawes referred to that sense of heroism when he wrote his wife, "By the blessing of God, I am still alive. We have had continued fighting and hardship since I wrote two days ago beyond what I can describe. I find this morning that I am reported killed in the New York paper. Do not give me up if you see me reported killed. Such things are often mistakes. The end is not yet though, and I cannot avoid, my dear wife, saying that the probabilities of coming out safely are strongly against me."

THE TRIGGER THAT set off this explosion of patriotism in

LH the westerners was °the firing on Fort Sumter, South Carolina. To them this was a strong emotional event because the U.S. flag had been attacked. Wisconsin had won its way into the Union just twelve years earlier, and statehood was important to its people.•

The call for volunteers, therefore, received an enthusiastic response in the West. "History will record of the republic that in the year 1861, her patriotic children rallied around the emblem of the early fathers, and purged the land of the great curse of secession," wrote Capt. Edwin Brown of the Sixth Wisconsin.

At the head of the Western Brigade was Rufus King. He was a New Yorker by birth, and his grandfather had been a delegate to the Continental Congress and the Constitutional Convention and had proposed the resolution banning slavery in the Northwest Territory. Rufus attended Columbia College and graduated from West Point in 1833. He resigned his commission to become a newspaper editor and in 1845 moved to the Wisconsin Territory and settled in Milwaukee. When Fort Sumter fell, King was commissioned a brigadier of volunteers and given command of the Western Brigade. He was perceived as a promising commander in that he was a trained professional possessing some public renown.

Lysander Cutler was the first colonel of the Sixth Wisconsin. He helped obtain the brigade's distinctive uniforms—the oversized frock coat, sky-blue pants, and tall Hardee hats. Rufus Dawes described Cutler as "rugged as a wolf." During the controversy of George B. McClellan's being relieved a second time from command of the army, many officers threatened to resign. Cutler, however, promised to brand any such officer as a coward resigning "in the face of the enemy." There were no resignations from the Western Brigade. Cutler was wounded in the leg at the August 28, 1862, battle of Brawner's Farm. After recovering in November 1862, he was promoted to brigadier general and took command of a brigade. He was wounded again at Globe Tavern, August 21, 1864, and never returned to the field of battle.

The core elements of the Iron Brigade were formed in mid-1861 at Camp Randall in Madison, Wisconsin, and in camps around Washington, D.C. The harsh realities of war that lay before them quickly confronted the men in the ranks as well as their officers. They understood Abraham Lincoln when he said, "Not with politicians, not with Presidents, not with office seekers, but with you is the question—shall the Union and shall the liberties of the country be preserved?" They took this responsibility seriously. Despite Lincoln's call in 1861 for a limited group of volunteers, the response was overwhelming. From Wisconsin and Indiana came eager recruits ready to preserve the Union at all costs.

Dawes was a part of that early impetuous response: "With the proclamation of the President came the announcement that the quota of the state of Wisconsin would be only one small infantry regiment of 780 men. It seemed quite evident that only by prompt action I might secure what was then termed 'the glorious privilege of aiding in crushing the Rebellion.'"

Formed during the fall of 1861, the brigade, which did not have an official name at the time, was comprised of four regiments of infantry drawn from Wisconsin and Indiana and Battery B of the Fourth U.S. Artillery. At the time there was little to distinguish the westerners from any other unit of the Union army other than they were inexperienced and had missed the first major battles of the war.

One of the regular soldiers of the artillery battery, Augustus Buell, described his new brigade: "The detached volunteers of 1861 were all young men fresh from the farms, sawmills, and blacksmith shops. They had been accustomed to hard work for an honest livelihood, respected themselves, valued their reputations, were keenly ambitious about what the folks back home will say, and were ready to fight anything on Earth at any time or in any shape."

Before these new recruits could fight, they had to be trained. For the men of the West, living in tents with thousands of other men was a rude awakening. °When they first entered the mustering camps, they lost their western independence. After a lifetime of following

In August 1861 Lucius Fairchild (far left) was commissioned lieutenant colonel of the Second Wisconsin and promoted to colonel on September 1, 1862. At Gettysburg on July 1, 1863, Fairchild led his regiment into Herbst's Woods on McPherson's Ridge. During the fight a bullet shattered his left arm. His was taken to a field hospital where he was taken prisoner. When the Confederates retreated on July 5, they left Fairchild at Gettysburg. His injury required the amputation of his arm. He was promoted to brigadier general on October 19 but resigned on November 2, 1863. After the war he was elected governor of Wisconsin and served during 1866–72.

Henry A. Morrow (near left) was commissioned colonel of the Twenty-fourth Michigan on August 15, 1862. In October the Twenty-fourth was attached to the Iron Brigade. Its first action was at Fredericksburg, where Morrow admonished his men not to fall back in the face of the veteran regiments of the brigade. Morrow and the Twenty-fourth are most noted for their valiant stand at Gettysburg on July 1. During the battle five color-bearers were shot down. The colonel received a scalp wound and was taken prisoner, but like Fairchild he was left behind when the Confederates retired. When he recovered from his injury, he returned to the regiment on August 7, 1863. The Twenty-fourth suffered an 80 percent casualty rate during the three-day battle. Morrow was wounded three times and breveted three times.

their own impulses and desires, suddenly they had to do what somebody else told them. That was irksome to these young men who were focused on making a name for themselves.•

Despite their initial resistance to military regimen, they found inspiration in the commander of the army, Maj. Gen. George B. McClellan. "The general is a splendid looking man, just in the prime of life. He pronounced our regiment one of the best in material, presence, and bearing. The boys are all carried away with enthusiasm for him," wrote Dawes.

The first commander of the Western Brigade was Brig. Gen. Rufus King, former editor of the *Milwaukee Sentinel and Gazette* and one of the writers of Wisconsin's state constitution. An 1833 graduate of West Point and a university regent, King appeared to be an able leader, but poor military decisions and failing health soon took him from his duties. Brig. Gen. John Gibbon, former commander of Battery B, replaced King in May 1862. Gibbon had grown up in North Carolina and had represented that state at West Point, from which he graduated in 1847. Only he of four brothers stayed with the Union; the rest joined the Confederate army.

WCD   °Gibbon was destined to rise from the very beginning of the war. He eventually went from brigade command to

231

One of West Point's foremost artillerists, John Gibbon was graduated from the academy in 1847. Although a native of North Carolina, Gibbon sided with the Union. In May 1862 he was promoted to brigadier general and given command of the Western Brigade, superceding Rufus King. The soldiers nicknamed him "Boss Soldier," and he commanded the brigade at Second Manassas (Bull Run) and Antietam. At Fredericksburg he led the Second Division, First Corps, and was severely wounded. He returned in March 1863 and was given command of the Second Division, Second Corps. During the battle of Gettysburg this division defended Cemetery Ridge. He was wounded in the left shoulder during Pickett's Charge.

commanding a full corps in the Army of the Potomac.• His upbringing in North Carolina and his brothers' loyalties to their state, however, generated Union suspicions that he was a Southerner at heart, an outsider at best. Gibbon had other problems, at least with the common men of his brigade who called him "the boss soldier." Not accepted at first since he was not one of them, Gibbon had to earn the respect of the stubborn westerners. "Men who had been working hard all their lives for a purpose could see no use in pacing up and down doing nothing. Often I would ride by a sentinel without any attention being paid to me whatsoever," wrote an exasperated Gibbon.

Yet as important as discipline and respect were to Gibbon, he was no martinet. When soldiers performed their duties well, he implemented a number of rewards that helped win him some respect, but resentment over constant drilling continued. Pvt. Jerome Watrous of the Sixth Wisconsin noted: "My, my how the boys dislike John Gibbon. They had enlisted to fight for their country not to wear themselves out at drilling and marching around." Gibbon was a soldier. They were not, when he took them. He knew what was before them. He knew how much they needed the discipline.

BP °Drill and discipline were part of training men to think not as individuals but as part of a unit—marching, fighting, maneuvering elbow to elbow to get to the point where a soldier would leave his best friend or his father or his brother lying on the battlefield and push on with a dwindling but still tightly packed bloc of men. That was the essence of Civil War drill. That was the kind of action the drill was intended to produce.•

During rare moments when the soldiers were at rest, they found camaraderie and diversion in what Rufus Dawes called "the ever present curse of camp life—

AN cards." °According to the mainline Protestant churches of the nineteenth century, card playing was a sin. These men knew that their families and loved ones considered it as such, but they played cards anyway. Just before a battle, they would throw their cards away because they did not want to be killed with cards in their possession.•

As the men fell into the rhythm of camp life, a number of rivalries developed among the regiments. They were often expressed with colorful nicknames like "the Pet Babies," "the Calico Boys," "the Huckleberries," and "the Swamp Hogs."

The Second Wisconsin received special notice °because of its limited combat experience at the battle of First Bull Run. It had been brigaded with three New York regiments under Col. William T. Sherman. The men of the Second lorded that fact over the rest of the recruits, whom they called "fresh fish." Naturally, the other regiments resented that air of superiority. One of the ways they got back at the Second was to joke about their clothing, particularly their tattered trousers, which gave them the sobriquet "Raggedy Ass Second."•

It was the need for uniforms that helped create the image of the Western Brigade. A number of new uniforms were procured by Col. Lysander Cutler, who was acting commander prior to Gibbon. Although he was fifty-three years old, Cutler was described by Rufus Dawes as "rugged as a wolf." He was tough on his men, but he cared about their welfare. Instead of the standard-issue nine-button shapeless "sack coats" and

Rufus King, standing in the middle with no hat, is shown here with five staff officers. On October 15, 1861, King's brigade became part of Gen. Irvin McDowell's division. One Wisconsin soldier described King as "Bland and genial, a plain, common man, [who] will listen to the complaint of a private as soon as he will to a colonel." The next year King was promoted to division commander. He led his division at the battle of Second Manassas (Bull Run) and was relieved of command after the battle for reasons of health.

233

Solomon Meredith was born in Guilford County, North Carolina, and at the age of nineteen moved to Indiana. At the outbreak of the war, Gov. Oliver P. Morton of Indiana selected Meredith to command the Nineteenth Indiana. On October 6, 1862, he replaced Brig. Gen. John Gibbon as the Iron Brigade's commander. Gibbon had voiced reservations about Meredith's ability, believing that political maneuvering had facilitated Meredith's rank more than ability. Gibbon, however, was alone in this opinion. No other officer in the brigade was critical of Meredith, and the comments of the rank-and-file were universally friendly. He went on to lead the brigade at Chancellorsville and Gettysburg. On the first day at Gettysburg, the brigade suffered nearly 886 killed and wounded and 266 missing, a total of 1,152 out of 1,800 engaged. Meredith was severely wounded as well but recovered from his injury.

forage caps that were common issue for Union regiments, he acquired distinctive oversized frock coats and the tall-crowned Hardee hats for the regiments. °His requisition said "for the comfort of the troops." He did what he could to protect the men of his command from the sun by finding the broad-brimmed hats.•

Later Gibbon saw an opportunity to create an image for the brigade by using clothing. He made the Hardee hat a standard issue. Fully dressed, the hat had a gold eagle stick pin holding up the right brim, a red circle on the front indicating the First Corps, and sometimes even ostrich feathers as decorations. One of Gibbon's other suggestions was not as popular. He tried to outfit the men with white canvas gaiters, or leggings. Unfortunately these tended to trap heat around a soldier's ankles. Gibbon did not take it kindly when he discovered a pair of leggings attached to his horse's legs, but he also realized that the men did not like them.

The more proficient the men of the Western Brigade became at drilling, the more boring camp life became. While the troops hid their true feelings of loneliness behind humor, only letters from home provided comfort. "We indulge in one of the sweetest pleasures in the heart of man. We dream of our homes and souls which we hold dear. We clamp them to our bosoms," wrote Pvt. Ludolph Longheny of the Seventh Wisconsin.

As much as the soldiers dreamed of home, they wanted to be respected by the folks back home, and they also wanted to be respected by the other regiments. The westerners eventually won that respect by fighting a battle much more vicious than they ever expected.

AFTER A YEAR of training, as the summer of 1862 drew to a close, the men of the Western Brigade finally had their chance to prove themselves. Within a few short weeks they earned the nickname, but at a cost that was staggering. "Beyond a doubt, it was this year of preparation that brought the Iron Brigade to a high standard of efficiency for battle service," wrote Dawes.

On August 26, 1862, Stonewall Jackson's Second Corps of the Army of Northern Virginia attacked and captured a large Union supply depot at Manassas Junction, Virginia, near the site of the battle of First Manassas (Bull Run). All the next day his soldiers ate their fill of Yankee food before burning what they could not carry off. On August 28, the Union Army of Virginia under Maj. Gen. John Pope arrived near Manassas with the intention of catching Jackson off guard. All Pope found, however, were the smoking ruins of the Union supply depot. That showed how little Pope knew of Jackson, who always seemed to know what his enemy was doing. Pope started marching his army toward Centreville, all the while looking for Jackson, who was waiting for him. At the head of the Union column was the mostly untested—except for the Second Wisconsin— Western Brigade.

CD They were near Groveton, Virginia, at Brawner's Farm, and had °been marching for hours on a hot Northern Virginia summer day, when they were attacked suddenly on their flank from an old railroad embankment. On that height were two Confederate divisions, which meant the brigade was outnumbered about three to one.• For the next two hours Jackson's veterans and Gibbon's green troops fought each other from a distance that rarely exceeded one hundred yards.

"The Rebels had rallied, and in a line lapping ours both ways, there burst from the dark wood volley after volley by battalion that more than crashed in a manner not surpassed in any action I have seen," wrote Dawes.

CD °The Western Brigade had almost everything going against it: It was in a valley with the enemy on the high ground, it was outnumbered, and it was inexperienced. Still, despite those odds, when the westerners started to fire back, they dug their heels in and they did not budge.•

The fighting was intense and personal, involving men of all ranks. Two Confederate generals, Isaac Trimble and Richard Ewell, were severely wounded, but both survived.

BP °The success under fire of the Western Brigade at the battle of Brawner's Farm proved not only to the army as a whole but to the men themselves that the previous year of drilling had paid off. After that first tremendous bloodletting, they were finally veterans. That meant they could be relied upon in future battles. That also meant

Cpl. Cornelius Wheeler joined Company I of the Second Wisconsin on May 20, 1861, at the age of twenty. To his friends he was known as "Corney." He rose from private to first lieutenant, and he commanded Company I on the return home. Wheeler fought in every battle in which the regiment participated and was never wounded. He recalled one near miss near the Lutheran Seminary at Gettysburg: "I was in front of the guns, fooling around with the boys . . . when suddenly George Jencks caught hold of me and yanked me nearly off my feet, and just then a shell went by from one of [the Confederates'] guns."

Pvt. Charles A. Keeler was from Saint Joseph, Michigan. Another early enlistee, he joined Company B of the Sixth Wisconsin on June 11, 1861. He wears the prescribed uniform of the brigade under Gibbon's command. In addition to the distinctive black hat and frock coat, the brigade had also been issued gaiters, or leggings. These were terribly hot, and most of the soldiers refused to wear them. To make a point of the discomfort, some men placed their leggings on Gibbon's horse. While the general was not amused, he conceded the point to the men. Keeler was shot through both thighs on July 1, 1863, near the famous railroad cut at Gettysburg. He survived his wounds and transferred to the Veterans Reserve Corps on January 15, 1864.

they would find themselves plunged again and again into the center of the fighting.•

The Union casualties at Brawner's Farm were enormous—751 men, almost a third of the entire brigade of four regiments. The casualties were worst among the Second Wisconsin, whose colonel, Edgar O'Connor, was killed. Earlier O'Connor had endured doubts about his loyalty to the Union because his wife's family had come from the South. He paid for his convictions with his life, as did hundreds of men in the other regiments.

"Men were falling in the Sixth, but our loss was small compared to that suffered by regiments on the left," recalled Dawes. "I rode along our line and, when near Colonel Cutler, I heard the distinctive sound of the blow that struck him. He gave a convulsive start and clapped his hand on his leg, but he controlled his voice. He said: 'Tell Colonel Bragg to take command. I am shot.'" Cutler survived his wound and the war.

The green brigade had proven itself. No one was prouder than its commander. "It was a regular standup fight during which neither side yielded a foot. My command exhibited in the highest degree the effects of discipline and drill. Officers and men standing up to their work like old soldiers," reported Gibbon.

LH After the engagement at Brawner's Farm, °Gibbon had a love for his regiments, and they finally respected him. They had seen his courage and began to recognize that the discipline he forced on them in camp was important. It held them together and prevented them from falling to harm. Gibbon loved his brigade so much that he was seen weeping for the men who had fallen on the field.•

BP °The westerners had transcended human fears to accomplish something higher, something beyond themselves. Because of their discipline and training they now knew they could go into the vortex of combat time and again and endure, regardless of their casualties.•

For some of the soldiers, even fear itself was a motivator. "The prospects for getting killed were growing bright," confessed Pvt. Albert Young of the Sixth Wisconsin. "And the question I first put to myself was 'Are you a coward?' To this, I without an instant's hesitation answered: 'Yes.' Did I run? I must have been very pale. It

At Falmouth, Virginia, in July 1862, officers from the Second Wisconsin posed for a photographer. They are, from left to right: Lt. J. D. Ruggles, Surgeon A. J. Ward, Maj. Thomas S. Allen (standing), Lt. Col. Lucius Fairchild, Adjutant C. K. Dean (standing), and Col. Edgar O'Connor. After the Second had dismissed their first commanding officers following the debacle at Manassas, they appointed O'Connor as their colonel. He was from Milwaukee and a West Point graduate who had served several years in the prewar army before being admitted to the bar in Wisconsin in 1861. O'Connor assumed command of a dispirited and demoralized regiment. Along with the other officers, he rebuilt the regiment's morale. A month after this photograph was taken, O'Connor was mortally wounded at the battle of Brawner's Farm on August 28, 1862.

seemed as if my blood had stopped circulating. Waves of intense heat flashed in quick succession through my entire being. I trembled so. I could, with difficulty, keep from dropping my musket, but I hung onto it. Again, the question presented itself to me: 'Shall I run?' I answered in the negative, because I was too much of a coward to run. I was too cowardly to endure being called 'a coward' by my comrades if I survived."

The Western Brigade, sometimes called the Black Hat Brigade, had earned the acceptance of the Union army, but it would not get a chance to rest on its laurels or even to rest at all. Two weeks later the brigade was engaged at the battle of South Mountain, Maryland. It was a battle between a small Confederate force from the Army of Northern Virginia that was holding three mountain passes and the Union Army of the Potomac that had to get through those passes to get at the rest of Robert E. Lee's army. The Southerners held the high ground, and any Union attack would have to go uphill. The Black Hats again took tremendous casualties, losing 318 men, or 25 percent of all engaged, but the brigade also inflicted heavy damage on the Rebels, and this time they gained a tactical advantage by pushing the Confederates out of a strategic position. Union officers watching this fighting suggested the nickname that remained with the brigade for the remainder of the war.

°The exact origin of the term *Iron Brigade* varies among historians. Most accounts say that the Union

The photograph to the right is of several noncommissioned officers of Company E of the Second Wisconsin. The majority of men in Company E were from Oshkosh. Many were lumbermen, farmers, and boatmen. They had adopted the nickname "Oshkosh Volunteers." The company was mustered in on June 11, 1861, for a three-year enlistment. At Camp Randall, Madison, one soldier wrote, "Our boys stayed quietly in their quarters, read their Testaments, looked at the pictures of their absent loved ones, and tried to keep comfortable." One newspaper account, however, reported that the men attacked a brewery. Another complained that drunken soldiers were roaming the streets at night and smashing things. To the citizens' relief the regiment left for Washington on June 20, 1861. At Fredericksburg in December 1862, Company E was part of the volunteer group that crossed the Rappahannock to push Confederate sharpshooters back and enable the Federal engineers to finish erecting pontoon bridges for the army's entrance into the river town.

army commander, McClellan, witnessed their performance and asked Maj. Gen. Joseph Hooker what unit of the First Corps that was. When Hooker answered that it was the Western Brigade, he added that "they had stood like iron." McClellan agreed, saying: "Yes, indeed. Iron they were." The Federal commander later wrote, "Ever after that, I always referred to them as the Iron Brigade."• He also noted, "General Gibbon, in his delicate moment, handled his brigade with as much precision and coolness as if on parade, and the bravery of his troops could not be excelled."

The newly named brigade still did not have a chance to rest. Inexperienced troops on August 28, they had now lost heavily in two battles in just over two weeks. Three days after the devastating battle of South Mountain, on September 17, 1862, the Iron Brigade marched into yet another bloody fight along Antietam Creek in southern Maryland.

AN   °The battle of Antietam was the worst single day of the war. It had the highest casualties of any single day during the entire Civil War, and the Iron Brigade was a part of the fighting from the beginning, charging from the West Woods across Miller's Cornfield on the northern part of the battlefield. The brigade did not succeed in conquering the higher ground at the Dunker Church beyond the Cornfield, which was the Federal objective. Taking that ground eventually took many brigades, with the Cornfield changing hands seven or eight times during

the day. When the fighting was over, the field was carpeted with so many dead that a soldier could walk across it without touching the ground. Many of the dead in the Cornfield were from the Iron Brigade.•

Antietam was ultimately ranked as a Union victory but at a human cost that could never justify its military achievement. The Iron Brigade lost another 42 percent, or 348 men.

"My dear mother, I have come safely through two more terrible engagements with the enemy. That at South Mountain and the great battle of yesterday—Antietam. Our splendid regiment is almost destroyed. We have had nearly 400 men killed and wounded in the battle. The men have stood like iron," wrote Dawes.

THE IRON BRIGADE was so depleted after just three battles
LH that it had to be reinforced. °Gibbon had developed such a high regard for his western regiments and knew that the men had such a natural bond with each other that he asked McClellan, a West Point classmate, to assign any new western regiments coming to the Army of the Potomac to his Iron Brigade.• The Federal commander was inclined to grant Gibbon's request, and on October 8, 1862, the Iron Brigade was reinforced with the Twenty-fourth Michigan Volunteers. "General McClellan made this promise because he knows of no better place where a new regiment can learn how to fight," wrote Gibbon.

This photograph of Company I's street in the camp of the Seventh Wisconsin may have been taken in the fall of 1862. The Seventh consisted of men from Grant, Columbia, Rock, and Chippewa Counties, which were mostly rural areas. The regiment had received its baptism by fire at Brawner's Farm where it sustained a 40 percent casualty rate. At Gettysburg it suffered a 52 percent casualty rate. Col. John Mansfield of the Seventh remembered his men's "cool indifference to danger and long continued and stubborn resistance, resulting from hard-earned experience and thorough discipline."

239

This photograph of the Second Wisconsin headquarters staff was taken at Arlington Heights in the spring of 1862. Seated at the table, from left to right, are Col. Edgar O'Connor, Lt. Col. Lucius Fairchild, Maj. Thomas S. Allen, and surgeon A. J. Ward.

Capt. Edward S. Bragg (below) headed Company E of the Sixth Wisconsin. Prior to the war he had been a delegate for Stephen Douglas at the Democratic National Conventions held at Charleston, South Carolina, and Baltimore, Maryland. Bragg was an extremely bright man but not well versed in military tactics. Nevertheless, he steadily ascended the ranks to brigadier general. He commanded the Sixth at South Mountain, Antietam, Second Manassas, Fredericksburg, Chancellorsville, and Gettysburg and was wounded at Antietam and later incapacitated when kicked by a horse.

The Twenty-fourth had a colorful history prior to its arrival in the eastern theater. °There had been a great war rally in the city of Detroit that was broken up by Southern sympathizers and protesters. The city fathers of Detroit were so embarrassed by this action that they decided to raise an extra regiment for the war effort. This regiment was the Twenty-fourth, a regiment that was raised in pride• and commanded by Judge Henry Morrow.

"I am going to the field. I invite you to go with me," Morrow promised. "I will look after you in health and in sickness. My influence will be exerted to procure for you the comforts of life, and I will lead you where you will see the enemy. We shall together share the triumph, or together mingle our dust upon the common fields."

Although they were westerners as tough as their neighbors from Wisconsin and Indiana, the Michiganders' entry into the Iron Brigade was difficult. "Our suits were new. Theirs were army worn. Our colonel extolled our qualities, but the brigade was silent, not a cheer. A pretty cool reception, we thought. We had come out to reinforce them and supposed they would be glad to see us," wrote a puzzled Pvt. Orson B. Curtis of the Twenty-fourth Michigan.

While they had once been fresh fish themselves and had only seen three battles in nearly two years of existence, the veterans of the Iron Brigade knew that membership in the brigade could only be won on the field of battle.

AN ○The Twenty-fourth Michigan was first engaged on December 13, 1862, at Fredericksburg, two months after joining the Iron Brigade. As they were crossing the Rappahannock River, Colonel Morrow reminded his soldiers that they had to earn the respect of the Iron Brigade veterans, saying: "Be careful, men! Those Wisconsin soldiers are watching you!"•

Among the onlookers, Dawes expressed his appraisal of the newcomers, noting, "No soldiers ever faced fire more bravely, and they showed themselves of a fiber worthy to be woven into the woof of the Iron Brigade."

Afterward, Orson Curtis observed: "Previous to the late battle, the older regiments of the Iron Brigade refused all sociability with our regiment, regarding us with aversion and studiously keeping out of our camp. But our noble conduct on this occasion, entirely destroyed this exclusiveness, and the greatest cordiality ever after prevailed."

The addition of the Twenty-fourth Michigan was not the only change in the Iron Brigade in late 1862. There was also a change in leadership. On November 4, 1862, Gibbon had been promoted to divisional command. Although the westerners had once hated him, Gibbon was now missed.

"His administration of the command left a lasting impression for good upon the character and military tone of the brigade, and his splendid personal bravery upon the field of battle was an inspiration," wrote Dawes.

Gibbon still had strong feelings for his men and he wanted to ensure their welfare by choosing his successor, but his recommendation was ignored. Col. Henry Morrow was given temporary command, followed by Brig. Gen. Solomon Meredith of the Nineteenth Indiana, who had been severely wounded at Groveton.

CD ○Although he had been around since the founding of the brigade, Meredith was not a professional soldier

Capt. Charles H. Ford headed Company H of the Sixth Wisconsin. He enlisted from Trempealeau, Wisconsin, in June 1861 and rose through the ranks, becoming an officer in December 1861. Rufus Dawes described him as over six feet tall and noted that "his soldierly bearing was very fine." During the Gettysburg campaign Ford served on the staff of Brig. Gen. James Wadsworth, and Dawes noted also that the general "would have none but efficient men around him."

On the first day at Gettysburg, as one of the first Federal units to arrive on the battlefield, the Iron Brigade smashed into the Confederate line near McPherson's Ridge. The Sixth Wisconsin was held in reserve. On the brigade's right the Union line collapsed. Rufus Dawes was ordered to reestablish the line by charging with the Sixth Wisconsin. The Confederates, the Fifty-fifth Carolina, deployed in a railroad bed. Dawes remembered there was a terrible melee for the Confederate flag. "Corporal Eggleston . . . sprang forward to seize it, and was shot dead. . . . Private Anderson, of his company . . . swung aloft his musket and . . . split the skull of the rebel who had shot young Eggleston." The Confederate flag was finally seized by another Wisconsinite.

like Gibbon. In fact, many of the men in the brigade did not want Meredith as their commander. A prewar legislator and U.S. marshal, he was seen by many men as a politician. Some thought he was actively politicking to get promotion and get command of the brigade.•

Gibbon was frustrated with the selection. "To relieve a competent colonel and put that fine body of men in the charge of an incompetent brigadier general was a step which excited not only my indignation, but my apprehensions," he wrote.

The Iron Brigade faced other changes in leadership as well. McClellan, beloved as he was by the army, was relieved of his command. This was a tremendous blow to the men, who nearly worshiped him. °Lacking a sense of the big picture, the men felt that the government had made a serious mistake. Not only were rank-and-file private soldiers upset, but Gibbon was also a supporter of McClellan. He felt that McClellan was a superb soldier, and he was infuriated when Lincoln removed him.•

Some of the officers of the Iron Brigade talked of resigning, but common sense prevailed, and their anger

soon cooled down. "The army stands by the old flag. The American soldier is true to his country, true to his comrades, and resolved to fight the rebellion to the bitter end—no difference who commands. I am not a McClellan man, a Burnside man, a Hooker man. I am for the man that leads us to fight the Rebs on any terms he can get," wrote Capt. Henry Young of the Seventh Wisconsin.

The Iron Brigade stayed in the army and continued to drill for the sake of the Union. It trained for the battle of Gettysburg, where most of its men met their tragic destiny.

"I HAD A chance to do a good thing this morning, and it gave me pleasure," remembered Dawes. "One of our men was sent to me under guard to be dealt with for sleeping on his picket post, for which, when in the presence of the enemy, the penalty is death. The poor fellow was sadly frightened, but with a sharp lecture and warning, I released him from arrest. His demonstration of gratitude was quite affecting. He will remember the lieutenant colonel commanding the Sixth as long as he lives. Poor fellow. His life was short. He fell dead eight days afterward in the charge on the railroad cut at Gettysburg."

By June 24, 1863, Dawes had been promoted to lieutenant colonel of the Sixth Wisconsin Volunteers. He and his men were about to march into the twilight of the Iron Brigade's history. By late June 1863 Union cavalry reconnaissance had indicated Lee was pressing his army northward toward Pennsylvania. With the Iron Brigade at the head of the First Corps of the Union army as it headed north to meet the challenge, the Federal troops acknowledged the reputation of the men in the black hats.

"Loud cheers were frequently given when some particular regiment or brigade passed by, and as the great Western or Iron Brigade passed, looking like giants with their tall black hats, they were greeted with hardy cheers. And giants they were in action. I look back and see that famed body of troops marching full of life and spirit with steady steps," wrote Capt. C. A. Stevens of Berdan's Sharpshooters.

Not all was glory, however. Many men were tired of war. After a severe interrogation, a young private from the Nineteenth Indiana admitted he had donned

Nineteen-year-old William E. Strong commanded Company F of the Second Wisconsin at the battle of First Manassas. He vividly recalled his men's coolness just before the regiment charged up Henry House Hill: "[T]he boys had a great deal of sport, laughing and joking among themselves." During the retreat Strong collapsed out of physical exhaustion. His men helped him back to Washington. After the battle he prophesied, "To the relatives and friends of those who are gone, I can say only one word: They are the first to suffer, the first to realize the realities of this unholy war."

The devastation of the Iron Brigade on the Pennsylvania countryside led to the demise as well of its distinctive western makeup. On the march south in pursuit of Lee's Confederates, a new regiment, the 167th Pennsylvania, was added to the tattered remnant of the brigade. The pride in the old unit led to the creation of the above logo, representing each regiment in the original brigade.

Confederate clothing while guarding some Rebel prisoners. The soldier hoped that with his deception, he would avoid further risk on the battlefield. He was gravely mistaken. He was quickly court-martialed and sentenced to death.

LH   °The story of the execution of the Indiana soldier showed just how far down the road these innocent young men, these farm boys of Wisconsin and Indiana, had gone to become real soldiers. They were focused upon the idea of ending the war. They had a mentality of getting the job done no matter how many were killed.• They had no patience when one of their own cracked under the strain.

The Iron Brigade found its final spot of glory in the Civil War in the early hours of the largest battle of the war. It was the leading brigade of the First Corps, the first infantry troops to arrive to help the dismounted cavalry
WCD defend the town of Gettysburg on °July 1, 1863. For several hours that afternoon, all that stood between Lee's army and Gettysburg and Cemetery Hill and Cemetery Ridge was the Iron Brigade and one or two associated units. Hopelessly outnumbered, the Iron Brigade had no choice but to stand and fight and die.•

There were many instances of sacrifice that day, especially fighting for the colors. The Twenty-fourth Michigan, the newcomers, mixed their blood with Iron Brigade honor in a stand-up fight against the Twenty-sixth North Carolina. For more than an hour, these two regiments of farm boys fired at each other from a distance of less than thirty yards.•

LH   °Colonel Morrow played a key role in the tragic story of the color-bearers of the Twenty-fourth Michigan. The color-bearers were repeatedly shot down. Each time Morrow would pick up the flag until another young man rushed forward to take it. Morrow finally took the flag and himself went down wounded. Ironically, the commander of the Twenty-sixth North Carolina, Col. Henry Burgwyn, was mortally wounded keeping his colors from falling to the ground. The two regiments literally destroyed each other. At the same time the rest of the Iron Brigade was being shot to pieces just yards away.•

CD °Time after time, throughout the day, advancing Confederate lines threatened to overlap the brigade's flanks—to take them on the front, the left, and the right, and perhaps even the rear if they were not careful. The Black Hats had no choice but to fall back, but when they fell back they did so with order.•

AN °The climactic event for Dawes and the Sixth Wisconsin occurred at the railroad cut, an otherwise insignificant section of railroad at the bottom of a hill. Dawes's regiment and the Iron Brigade color guard, which he was also leading, were directed there to keep the Confederates from coming up the railroad cut and getting in the rear of the brigade. Dawes ordered a charge.•

"The only commands I gave, as we advanced, were 'Align on the colors! Close up on the colors!' The regiment was being so broken up that this order alone could hold the body together," remembered Dawes.

When the national flag went down, Dawes swiftly picked it up only to be relieved a moment later by a member of the color guard. As his line approached the railroad cut, they came upon the Confederate flag of the Second Mississippi Infantry. "A heroic ambition to capture it overtook the men," remembered Dawes.

Although outnumbered, the suddenness and fierce determination of the Wisconsin charge caught the Rebels off balance, and they surrendered. The Iron Brigade won on that particular part of the battlefield that day. Ironically, the westerners saved the lives of some Confederates as well when they refused to deliver a volley into the helpless Confederates. That action showed that the men of the Iron Brigade had character. "The coolness, self-possession, and discipline which held back our men from pouring in a general volley saved a hundred lives of the enemy. And, as my mind goes back to the fearful excitement of the moment, I marvel at it," wrote Dawes.

Inscribed on the flag of the Iron Brigade are the names of the battles in which the men participated and the Latin phrase, e pluribus unum—Out of many, one. Five regiments—Second, Seventh, and Sixth Wisconsin, Nineteenth Indiana, and the Twenty-fourth Michigan—made up the Iron Brigade. They participated in some of the bloodiest conflicts in the eastern theater, but the first day at Gettysburg saw the virtual annihilation of the brigade with its losing about 80 percent of its men.

One of the last official acts of any unit of the Iron Brigade was the Twenty-fourth Michigan's role as military escort in the May 4, 1865, funeral of Abraham Lincoln in Springfield, Illinois. It was the largest procession anyone had ever seen in the region. Although it had rained the day before, the afternoon of the interment was stiffling hot, and the route through Springfield to the cemetery was not short. The long walk was accompanied by music and the muffled beat of drums marking the step of the procession. The morbidity of the occasion was balanced nineteen days later when the Twenty-fourth rejoined the Iron Brigade's other units for the Grand Review in Washington, a final fanfare before being mustered out.

The bravery, skill, and passion of the Iron Brigade enabled the Federals to hold their position while waiting for the rest of the army. It was held at a considerable cost. The commander of the First Corps, Maj. Gen. John Reynolds, died while trying to place the regiments in line to meet the Confederates. Over the following two days, the Union army would win the battle of Gettysburg, but the Iron Brigade lost almost 80 percent of its men.

BP ∘Gettysburg essentially annihilated the Iron Brigade that once was. Its losses on July 1 left behind a shadow of what it had been. Its losses were so severe that there were no more western troops to fill out the ranks. The men who were left were absorbed into other units, including those made up of easterners. When that happened, the Iron Brigade entered the realm of legend.•

"It would require many pages to justly recount the heroic deeds of all," remembered Dawes. "But one incident is so touching in its character that it should be preserved. Corp. James Kelly of Company B turned from the ranks and stepped beside me as we moved hurriedly forward on the charge. He pulled open his woolen shirt, and the mark that a deadly minié ball had entered his breast was visible. He said: 'Colonel, won't you please write to my folks that I died a soldier?'"

One year after the Iron Brigade's devastation at Gettysburg, Dawes resigned and went home. He was forever torn with guilt that he had lived while his comrades had fallen, but with the publication of his journal he made good on his promise. The Iron Brigade would always be remembered as a fighting unit of westerners. It essentially ceased to exist on July 1, 1863. Gettysburg was the unit's fourth—and last—battle.

Although the name continued to be used, the Iron Brigade lost its original western character when eastern regiments were added to the brigade. Battle losses led to the disbanding of the Second Wisconsin in July 1864. The Sixth and Seventh Wisconsin served until the end of the war, fighting at the Wilderness, Spotsylvania, North Anna, Cold Harbor, Petersburg, Five Forks, and Appomattox. Both regiments took part in the Grand Review at Washington after the war.

The Nineteenth Indiana fought with the Second Corps from Bristoe Station to Petersburg. Battle losses reduced its size until it was absorbed by the Twentieth Indiana in October 1864 and ceased to have a regimental identity.

The Twenty-fourth Michigan fought at the Wilderness, Spotsylvania, North Anna, and Cold Harbor. Its losses were so heavy that it could muster only 120 men on June 18, 1864, for the assault on Petersburg. The Twenty-fourth was withdrawn from the field in February 1865. Its last official act was to serve as the military escort for Lincoln's funeral procession as it moved through Springfield.

At the 1881 reunion of the Iron Brigade in Milwaukee, Gens. Lucius Fairchild, Edward Bragg, and John Gibbon posed for a photographer. Fairchild had been governor of Wisconsin and then devoted himself to veterans affairs. Bragg too had sought public office, serving four terms in Congress. Gibbon, however, had remained in the army and served on the frontier. He also became an author, writing several books, including The Artillerist's Manual *and* Personal Recollections of the Civil War.

GETTYSBURG: THE BATTLE

At THE END OF JUNE 1863, LEE'S ARMY of Northern Virginia had pushed north through Maryland and into Pennsylvania, an invasion whereby Lee hoped, at best, to capture a major Northern city or, at least, feed his army from the harvest-rich land of the North. The Union Army of the Potomac, which had been soundly defeated by Lee just one month before at Chancellorsville, Virginia, gamely marched north, following the Confederates. Although numerically superior, well equipped, and better fed, the Union army was leery of the seemingly invincible Rebel soldiers who splashed across the Potomac River and then moved quickly through the Cumberland Valley toward the Pennsylvania capital of Harrisburg.

What the Yankees did not know was that the Southerners were hungry, their shoes well worn, and their bodies weary. Lee's army needed supplies, and the bountiful summer harvest in Pennsylvania would fill stomachs, haversacks, and supply wagons. Finding shoes for an army of mostly barefoot soldiers, however, posed a different problem. Thus many Confederates were anxious to investigate a rumor that the Yanks had storehouses of shoes in a small town on the way to Harrisburg. The town, where five major thoroughfares met, was Gettysburg.

On the last day of June 1863, a Confederate brigade scouting ahead of the main body of Lee's army approached Gettysburg, expecting to find it defenseless or possibly protected by a unit of state militia. If militia were the only force that had to be faced, then finding,

WCD	William C. Davis
GWG	Gary W. Gallagher
KGH	Kathy George Harrison
RKK	Robert K. Krick
BP	Brian Pohanka

Confederate Maj. Gen. Jeb Stuart had successfully screened the northern movement of Robert E. Lee's Army of Northern Virginia, and on the night of June 27 the cavalry commander and three of his brigades crossed the Potomac River near Rowser's Ford. Stuart knew that the Northern Army of the Potomac was on the march and heading northward. He realized he had to rejoin Lt. Gen. Richard Ewell's corps, but Stuart was cut off from the main Confederate force, and out of contact with Lee. His absence was one of the precipitating factors in the collision of the two armies at Gettysburg.

capturing, and distributing shoes to needy Confederates would be a brief question of time.

Instead, on a ridge west of the town, the Confederates saw Union cavalrymen supported by artillery, men who looked nothing like the ragtag militia units common to small towns. The Southern commander, Brig. Gen. James Johnston Pettigrew, suspected what he had seen was a forward unit of the Army of the Potomac, which he had been told was still in Virginia. He felt that it would be a grave error to engage these cavalrymen. Lee had ordered his subordinates "not to bring on a general engagement" until the entire army was up and ready to fight.

GWG °Pettigrew's infantry would never have gone near Get-
WCD tysburg had Jeb Stuart's cavalry been on the scene.• °Up to this time Lee had made wonderful use of Stuart's cavalry, which was supposed to be the eyes and ears of the infantry, and Stuart had responded by always keeping Lee informed on where the main Union force was. Lee had tremendous faith in Stuart and had once said that Stuart had never given him a false piece of intelligence. As Lee marched into Pennsylvania, he sent Stuart away from the main body of his army so that he could gather more intelligence while still being close enough to coordinate with Lee's attack. Under most conditions, Stuart would have kept in constant contact with Lee by couriers. In this instance, however, instead of staying in touch with Lee, Stuart went off on a cavalry raid deep into Pennsylvania. He did not bring back the intelligence Lee needed, specif-

ically, the position of the Union army. Lee did not know that the Union army had crossed the Potomac.•

Without Stuart's horsemen, Lee had no idea if the Federals in Gettysburg were cavalry, as Pettigrew suspected, or militia. He had no idea how many Union regiments, brigades, divisions, or even corps were in the area. He had no idea of his comparative strength as opposed to the Union force against him. All of this was critical information he needed before he could move to attack the enemy, continue his march north, or halt and await attack. Lee himself did not bring on the battle at Gettysburg. That was done for him, against orders, by Maj. Gen. Henry Heth, Pettigrew's division commander, who moved to support his advance guard.

Forced to do battle before he had the information he needed, Lee threw what forces he had at Gen. John Buford's Union troopers and arriving units of the Union First and Eleventh Corps. By the end of the day, the commander of the Federal army, Maj. Gen. George Gordon Meade, was concentrating all his soldiers at Gettysburg. The largest battle ever fought on American soil was underway.

WG °Many thousands of men were involved on both sides, and tens of thousands were killed, wounded, or missing. At first the Confederates had the upper hand, and over the course of the first day they made the most of their good fortune.•

Overwhelmed by surprise attacks on their flanks by large numbers of Southern reinforcements, the Union force had retreated and regrouped along the hills and ridges south of town by the end of the afternoon on July 1. °On the night of July 1 through the early morning hours of July 2, the Federals deployed along a strong ridge line and along the hills, from Culp's Hill on the right, or north end of the ridge, behind the town and toward the wooded hills called the Round Tops on their left flank, south of Gettysburg.• The longest ridge

Carlisle, Pennsylvania, was not unlike Gettysburg except that twice during the summer of 1863 the town had been visited by Confederates. In late June a Georgia brigade from Richard Ewell's Second Corps camped on the lawn of Dickinson College while Ewell requisitioned fifty thousand dollars' worth of medicines and provisions. On July 1 Confederate cavalry deployed to the east of town and demanded its surrender, threatening to shell the area. The Union commander recently arrived on the scene sent word back, "Shell away." Rebel artillerymen opened fire, but before they could claim the town, the cavalry received orders to move toward Gettysburg.

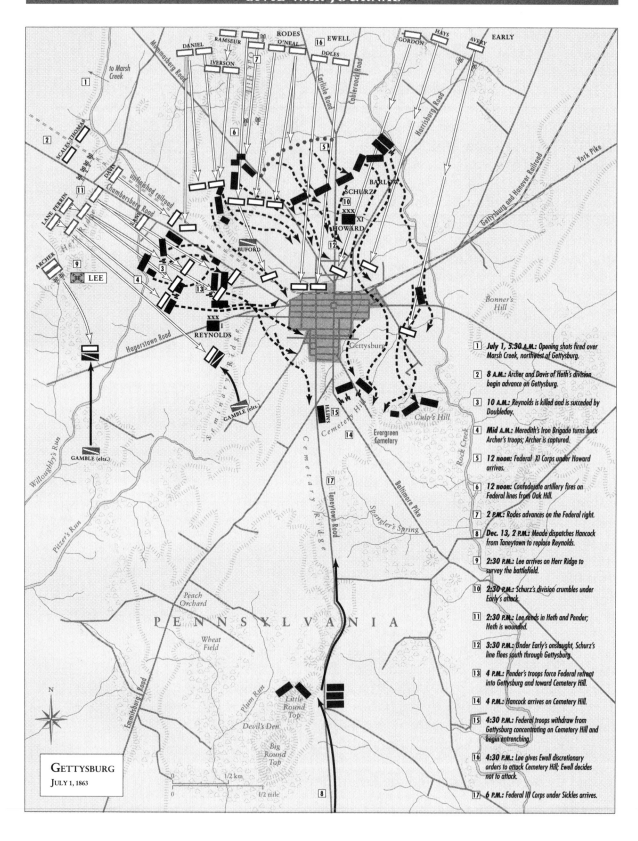

GETTYSBURG
JULY 1, 1863

1 **July 1, 5:30 A.M.:** Opening shots fired over Marsh Creek, northwest of Gettysburg.

2 **8 A.M.:** Archer and Davis of Heth's division begin advance on Gettysburg.

3 **10 A.M.:** Reynolds is killed and is succeded by Doubleday.

4 **Mid A.M.:** Meredith's Iron Brigade turns back Archer's troops; Archer is captured.

5 **12 noon:** Federal XI Corps under Howard arrives.

6 **12 noon:** Confederate artillery fires on Federal lines from Oak Hill.

7 **2 P.M.:** Rodes advances on the Federal right.

8 **Dec. 13, 2 P.M.:** Meade dispatches Hancock from Taneytown to replace Reynolds.

9 **2:30 P.M.:** Lee arrives on Herr Ridge to survey the battlefield.

10 **2:30 P.M.:** Schurz's division crumbles under Early's attack.

11 **2:30 P.M.:** Lee sends in Heth and Pender; Heth is wounded.

12 **3:30 P.M.:** Under Early's onslaught, Schurz's line flees south through Gettysburg.

13 **4 P.M.:** Pender's troops force Federal retreat into Gettysburg and toward Cemetery Hill.

14 **4 P.M.:** Hancock arrives on Cemetery Hill.

15 **4:30 P.M.:** Federal troops withdraw from Gettysburg concentrating on Cemetery Hill and begin entrenching.

16 **4:30 P.M.:** Lee gives Ewell discretionary orders to attack Cemetery Hill; Ewell decides not to attack.

17 **6 P.M.:** Federal III Corps under Sickles arrives.

Under Brig. Gen. John Buford's guidance Union cavalry deployed about a mile west of Gettysburg near McPherson's Ridge. Using trees, fences, or lying prone for cover, the outnumbered cavalrymen (left) hindered the approaching Confederates for approximately three hours. The troopers were using breech-loading carbines that gave them a faster rate of fire than the Confederate infantry's muzzle-loading muskets. The Southerners gained ground slowly. Just as the cavalrymen were about to be overwhelmed, two Union infantry brigades hit the Confederates. Buford's delaying action is one of the most significant and often overlooked contributions to the Northern victory at Gettysburg.

Opposite Buford's troopers was Henry Heth's division, an element of A. P. Hill's Third Corps. On June 30, Heth (below) and Hill had been warned that there was a well-trained Union force near Gettysburg, but both men believed the troops were local militia. Heth requested permission to take his unit into town the next day; Hill voiced no objections. Although under orders not to get involved in an engagement, Heth's men nevertheless became embroiled in an escalating altercation. The two sides fought for approximately eight hours. In the end the Union army retreated to the higher ground southeast of town. Nearly thirteen thousand soldiers were killed or wounded on July 1.

between the two hills went by a name that would prove prophetic. Since it commenced at the town's cemetery, it was known as Cemetery Ridge.

°If each day of the three days at Gettysburg were taken by itself, July 1, 1863, was one of the most resounding victories in the history of Lee's Army of Northern Virginia.• His army had beaten the Federals all along their front and had pushed them from the field. Although the ground was not of his choosing, °Lee believed that he had to have his decisive battle there. He was engaged with the enemy, which was before him in a concentrated position, and Lee needed to take advantage of the momentum that had developed on the first day to close with the Federals.• As he had the previous September when his planned invasion of Pennsylvania had been stopped at Sharpsburg, Maryland, Lee knew he had no choice but to fight on Northern soil.

Lee's men pursued the retreating Federals up Cemetery Hill until darkness fell, ending the fighting for the day. Some fault Confederate Lt. Gen. Richard Ewell, in command of the troops who had won that part of the battlefield, for not continuing his attack into the evening and pursuing the Federals over and past the high ground to the east of Gettysburg. Instead, he stopped the attack at darkness, leaving the Union army to consolidate its position on the high ground. That evening the camps of the two armies were less than a mile apart. During that first day only the most forward divisions of both armies had

fought each other. Throughout the night the main bodies of both armies arrived on the field.

GWG

At dawn on July 2, Lee tried a new strategy. °He decided to pursue the offensive on the second day by applying pressure against both extremities of the Union line: against the right flank on Culp's Hill and the left flank near the Round Tops. He hoped to find a weakness he could exploit to push the Federals from the good defensive ground they occupied.•

Ewell—an odd, birdlike, irritable, one-legged man who had been given command of the Confederate Second Corps upon the death of Stonewall Jackson in May—was to renew his attack on the northern end of the Union line at Culp's Hill. The southern end was to be attacked by Lee's First Corps under Lt. Gen. James Longstreet, whom Lee called "my old war horse." Longstreet delayed the attack for many hours while he sought a weak point in the solid Yankee line. Incredibly, Union Maj. Gen. Daniel E. Sickles, commander of the Union Third Corps facing Longstreet, ordered a bold maneuver. Failing to advise Meade, instead of holding his ground, Sickles sent his men forward, to some high ground at a peach orchard along the Emmitsburg road. Now, instead of forcing the Confederates to come to them, Sickles's men were stretched along a vulnerable salient.

"The struggle was almost hand to hand. There was no wavering or shadow of turning. It seemed as if the last

Sometime after 6 P.M. on July 2, four Confederate brigades smashed through the Union line on the Emmitsburg road. Union Maj. Gen. Winfield Hancock rode along Cemetery Ridge ordering up reinforcements. One regiment he came upon was the First Minnesota (right). The general yelled to its colonel, William Colvill Jr., "Advance, Colonel, and take those colors." Colvill ordered a charge, and his small regiment of 262 men dashed into an Alabama brigade numbering 1,700. With the help of Union artillery, and other infantry units, the First Minnesota repulsed the Alabama brigade. The price was high for the Minnesotans; out of 262 men, 215 lay among the dead and wounded.

man would find his allotted ounce of lead," wrote Capt. George Terrell of the Seventeenth Maine Infantry. The battle in the Peach Orchard and the nearby Wheat Field was so close that one Union colonel was killed by a Confederate bayonet, supposedly the only regimental commander to die by the rarely used weapon during the entire war.

The Rebels broke through Sickles's exposed force. Sickles himself went down with a wound to his leg, which would later be amputated. The Confederates pushed to the Wheat Field and gained a foothold at a jumble of giant boulders called the Devil's Den. From there, an Alabama regiment and a Texas regiment stormed the Union defenses on Little Round Top. The Union right flank was in jeopardy. Anchoring this position was a little-tested regiment, the Twentieth Maine, under Col. Joshua Lawrence Chamberlain, a college professor who had taken a sabbatical from teaching to join the army. His handful of men was the only force preventing the Confederates from getting a foothold on the Union line from which they could enfilade the Federal positions.

The fighting between the Alabama and the Maine men was savage. "The rifles were aimed with deadly precision upon the brave forms before them, and thus, the

The two panels above are from the Paul Philippotaux cyclorama of Pickett's Charge. In the left panel, Winfield Scott Hancock can be seen at the far right, directing the Federal effort. He had arrived at Gettysburg on the first day of the battle to assess the situation for George Gordon Meade, the Union commander. His opinion led to the decision to fight here and not fall back.

The photograph below has traditionally been misidentified as Federal casualties from the first day. Lately, the area has been identified as Rose Woods, and the soldiers are either Georgians or South Carolinians killed in the early evening of July 2.

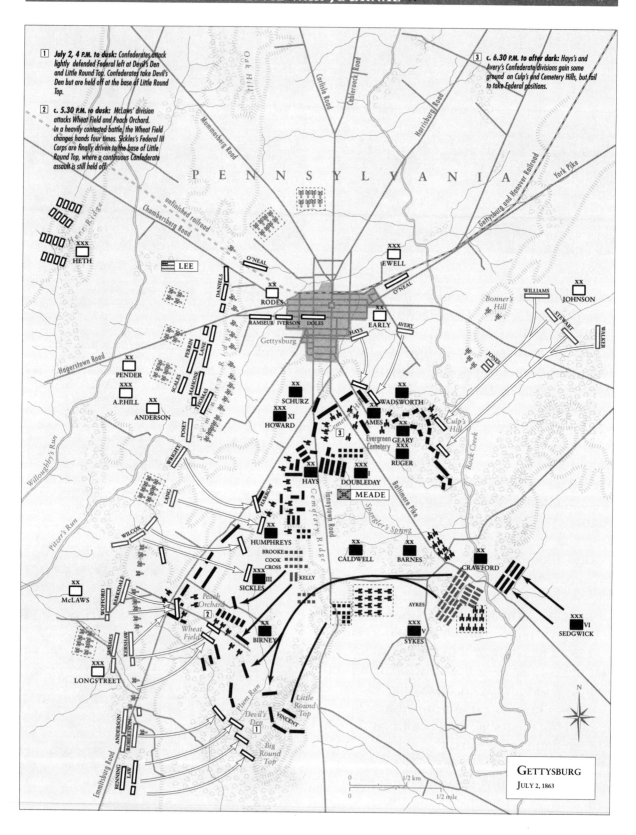

1 July 2, 4 P.M. to dusk: Confederates attack lightly defended Federal left at Devil's Den and Little Round Top. Confederates take Devil's Den but are held off at the base of Little Round Top.

2 c. 5.30 P.M. to dusk: McLaws' division attacks Wheat Field and Peach Orchard. In a heavily contested battle, the Wheat Field changes hands four times. Sickles's Federal III Corps are finally driven to the base of Little Round Top, where a continuous Confederate assault is still held off.

3 c. 6.30 P.M. to after dark: Hays's and Avery's Confederate divisions gain some ground on Culp's and Cemetery Hills, but fail to take Federal positions.

PENNSYLVANIA

GETTYSBURG
JULY 2, 1863

work went on, and many a Federal and Confederate bit the dust. Oh, how fast they went down!" wrote Pvt. Theodore Gerrish of the Twentieth Maine.

The impressions were just as memorable on the Confederate side. "My dead and wounded were nearly as great in number as those still on duty. They literally covered the ground. The blood stood in puddles in some places on the rocks. The ground was soaked with the blood of as brave men as ever fell on the red field of battle," wrote Col. William Oates of the Fifteenth Alabama Infantry.

At great cost Little Round Top stayed in Union hands. Farther north, however, a number of Confederates nearly broke through on Cemetery Ridge, but they were not supported. Unable to hold the line by themselves, the Rebels were forced back, and the Federal soldiers returned to their line.

Two miles to the north, at Culp's Hill, Ewell's Confederates were also beaten back. One of the Confederate dead somewhere on the hill was Wesley Culp. His parents owned the hill, and he had played on its slopes as a child. Although his parents searched for him, they never found his body.

KHK °At the end of the second day, Lee was faced with a stalemate along his whole front. The small gains he had

The painting below by James Walker depicts the massive assault made by A. P. Hill's Third Corps on July 1. After a short respite during the afternoon hours, the Confederates renewed their attack. The Southern divisions pushed through McPherson's Wood and finally secured McPherson's Ridge. Hill's Corps of twenty-two thousand men fought Reynold's First Corps of twelve thousand. The Northerners contested every inch of ground. Seen in the foreground are men from the Fourteenth Brooklyn, nicknamed the "Red Legged Devils" because of their red pants.

Prior to the battle of Gettysburg, John F. Reynolds had been offered command of the Army of the Potomac and he declined. On July 1 he was in charge of the left wing of the Union army. Arriving ahead of his infantry, Reynolds accessed the position Buford had chosen and decided to fight on that ground. The general then rode back to direct his two lead brigades. As Reynolds moved the Iron Brigade into Herbst's Woods (McPherson's Woods) a bullet struck him in the head and killed him instantly (above left). He was forty-three years old.

After a hard fight on July 1, Capt. Greenleaf T. Stevens's Fifth Maine Battery was deployed on a small knoll just east of Cemetery Hill. The battery was composed of six Napoleon smoothbore guns and was supported by the Iron Brigade. At dusk on July 2 a North Carolina brigade and Louisiana brigade swept up east Cemetery Hill. Earlier in the day the Union artillerymen had measured the ranges to several key points. When the Confederates attacked, the artillery fire they encountered devastated their ranks.

made were not decisive. Despite losing a tremendous number of men, the Confederates had failed to dislodge the Union army from its position on either flank. Lee had to decide what to do next: stay and fight another day or retreat back to Virginia. After considering the situation all night, Lee devised a battle plan for the next day.•

Lee's soldiers awaited his decision. "All retired early to rest, little dreaming that upon such a lovely eve, such awful morning should arise. Brave, happy souls, little do you anticipate the horrors of the next twenty-four hours," wrote Corp. David Johnston of the Seventh Virginia Infantry.

BP °IT WAS CLEAR by the dawn of the third day that the fight, bloody and dramatic as it had been, had been indecisive. The fighting had not resolved who was going to carry the field.•

WCD °If Lee did not press forward, his second invasion of the North would end without achieving anything. If he attacked, he would have either dramatic results or he would wreck his army. The third day would be decisive for one side or the other.•

By the morning of July 3, Meade's Union army had reinforced its positions along Cemetery Ridge. The line took the shape of a fish hook nearly three miles long, with the hook curving around Culp's Hill on the north and the shank running the length of Cemetery Ridge and ending at Little Round Top. The Union held the high ground. Lee's army was gathered a mile away, across the

Emmitsburg road, in the woods along Seminary Ridge, named for the Lutheran seminary on the west side of the town. Between the two armies was a mile of open ground, pastures and fields with little more than occasional swales to shield anything and anyone from sight.

BP On the Union side, °Cemetery Ridge was not a very commanding physical feature, hardly more than a low rise. Nonetheless, it did provide a position from which the Federals could command the large open space over to Seminary Ridge, where the Confederates were formed. Along much of Cemetery Ridge ran a low stone wall, not much more than knee high, but it provided some protection for the Yankee troops who had sought cover behind it. The men strengthened the position by piling up fence rails or whatever they could scrape up from the earth with their bayonets, tin plates, and bare hands.•

GWG °Lee's original plan was to drive the Federals from their strong position by getting his corps commanders to attack the Union flanks simultaneously before daylight. Ewell would again attack the north end of the line while Longstreet would strike the south.• It was virtually the same plan as had been tried on the second day, but this time Lee had Stuart's cavalry.

Stuart, like a wayward son, had finally appeared on the battlefield and reported to Lee. The Southern commander, controlling his anger, calmly told his cavalry commander that although he had failed in his duty to be the eyes of his army, he now needed him and his horsemen to win the battle.

KGH °Ewell attacked before daylight on the third day, but Longstreet was not ready. His men were in battle formation for six to seven hours without firing a shot while Ewell's men were counterattacked and lost the initiative. Lee looked to Longstreet and felt disappointment that one of his most trustworthy generals had failed him.•

GWG °As a defensive tactician, Longstreet did not want to follow Lee's orders because he believed the attack was a bad idea. Longstreet wanted to put Meade in a position

Timothy O'Sullivan, one of Alexander Gardner's photographers, took this photo either July 5 or 6. Knowing that Gardner and his men had shot several photographs on the first-day field, an editor noticed the black, broad-brimmed hat covering a face of one of the bodies. Aware that the Iron Brigade had worn similar hats, he concluded that these soldiers were from the Twenty-fourth Michigan. Recent research suggests that these soldiers were probably Georgians killed on July 2 near Rose Woods.

259

where he would have to attack the Confederates,• just as Lee had forced Ambrose Burnside to attack him at Fredericksburg the previous December. The Union army had been slaughtered attacking the high ground, something Longstreet feared would happen if his men tried attacking the Federals on their high ground.

GWG °When Lee found out that Longstreet had stalled the attack, he was upset, but he hid his anger. He heard the fighting on the north end of the Union line, so he knew his original plan for simultaneous pressure against both ends of the Union line would no longer work.• While Lee planned his next step, the fighting at the north end KGH died down. He learned that °Ewell had yielded the field since he had been fighting unsupported for seven hours. Lee now knew that he had to change his carefully crafted plans from the night before.•

The Southern commander gathered his corps and division commanders. Instead of pulling back and marching around the Union army's flank toward a major northern city, as Longstreet hoped Lee would do, Lee proposed an all-out assault on the center of the Union line. He had tried both flanks over the previous two days. Now, on the third day, he proposed striking the Union center in the belief that all of the Union army's reserves had been sent to the flanks.

On the evening of July 2 Brig. Gen. Harry Hays and Col. Isaac Avery led two Confederate brigades in an attack on east Cemetery Hill. Hays's Louisiana Tigers and Avery's North Carolina brigade smashed through the first Union line. The Confederates then swept up the hill toward Capt. R. Bruce Ricketts's Pennsylvania battery. The artillerists defended their guns with handspikes, rammers, stones, and pistols. In the darkness a reinforcing Federal brigade came within a few yards of the Louisiana troops and fired a devastating volley.

GWG   °The idea was for a long Confederate line to punch a hole through the Federal lines at the center. If the line were breached on Cemetery Ridge, Lee would then pour in reinforcements to move both north against that fragment of the Union army and south against that part. He would divide the Union army and break its communications. He would be on the flank of each part of the Union army and in a very strong position to wreak havoc in both directions.•

Longstreet listened in silent dismay when he heard that his corps would lead the attack. Participating in the assault would be three divisions: one under Brig. Gen. James Johnston Pettigrew made up mostly of North Carolinians, one under Maj. Gen. Isaac Trimble of Maryland, and a third division made up of Virginians, who would bear the weight of the attack, under the command of Maj. Gen. George Pickett. Pickett's men were fresh, having arrived on the battlefield late on the second day. Together there were more than twelve thousand men in the three divisions.

Longstreet's opinion of the plan shocked Lee. He later claimed that he told his commanding general, "No twelve thousand men alive can take that ridge." Deep down, Lee might have believed him, but he would send twelve thousand men onto the field to try.

None of the divisional commanders knew the others very well. Pettigrew was a brilliant lawyer and author, fluent in six languages. He had commanded the South

The painting above (left) shows George G. Meade's headquarters during the cannonade that preceded Pickett's Charge. The scene is part of the impressive cyclorama painted by Paul Philippoteaux. Meade arrived in Gettysburg about 1 A.M. on July 2. He made his headquarters in the home of Mrs. Leida Leister; the owner had departed at the beginning of the battle. In the massive artillery duel on the third day, many Confederate shells overshot the Federal infantry on Cemetery Ridge. Consequently, the Leister house was severely damaged. The owner later recalled "dead horses [polluted] my spring, so I had to have my well dug."

Above (right) the caissons and limber chests of the First Rhode Island Battery A are positioned several yards behind the battery during the July 3 cannonade. As the Confederate infantry swept over Alonzo Cushing's guns, Capt. William A. Arnold of Battery A ordered his cannon out by piece. One New York journalist remembered "ghastly heaps of dead men" and noted that "the wounded are like the withered leaves of autumn." Lt. Gulien Weir's Battery C, Fifth U.S. Artillery replaced Arnold's unit.

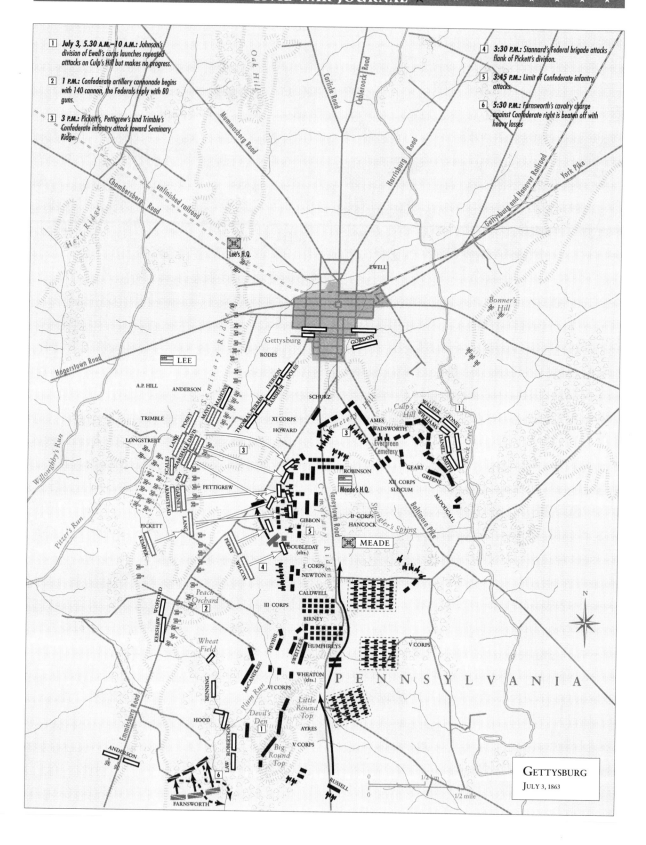

1. **July 3, 5.30 A.M.–10 A.M.:** Johnson's division of Ewell's corps launches repeated attacks on Culp's Hill but makes no progress.

2. **1 P.M.:** Confederate artillery cannonade begins with 140 cannon, the Federals reply with 80 guns.

3. **3 P.M.:** Pickett's, Pettigrew's and Trimble's Confederate infantry attack toward Seminary Ridge.

4. **3:30 P.M.:** Stannard's Federal brigade attacks flank of Pickett's division.

5. **3:45 P.M.:** Limit of Confederate infantry attacks.

6. **5:30 P.M.:** Farnsworth's cavalry charge against Confederate right is beaten off with heavy losses.

GETTYSBURG
JULY 3, 1863

Carolina militia that had captured Castle Pinckney in Charleston Harbor, the first Federal property taken from the Union after the state had seceded in December 1860.

Trimble was a sixty-one-year-old West Point graduate who had been severely wounded at Second Manassas but had returned to the battlefield.

WG °Pickett was a very romantic if odd-looking figure. He wore his hair in long, perfumed ringlets. Some claimed he could be smelled before he was seen because of the amount of oil in his hair. He had the air of a perpetual adolescent, and he was certainly not the brightest officer in Lee's army. He had graduated last in his class at West Point and never demonstrated great aptitude as a commander of a division.• He owed his rank mainly to his birthright as a Virginian in the Army of Northern Virginia. His division of six thousand Virginians was divided into three brigades commanded by Brig. Gens. Richard Garnett, James Kemper, and Lewis Armistead.

;WG °Armistead came from an old military family with ancestors who had fought gallantly in earlier American wars. He had served for twenty-four years in the prewar army, resigning only after Virginia left the Union. He was posted in Los Angeles when his state seceded.• During his service, Armistead had become close friends with another officer, Winfield Scott Hancock, a Pennsylvanian. When Armistead left to fight for the South, Hancock

Around 2 P.M. on July 2, Daniel E. Sickles (above) disobeyed orders and moved his Third Corps to the Emmitsburg road, Peach Orchard, Wheatfield, and Devil's Den area. Before Meade could rectify this move, the Confederates attacked. Immediately Meade directed reinforcements to the scene. Sickles lost a leg and about two-thirds of his command in the attack, but he had dissipated the Southern threat and the Rebels fell back.

In this scene from the Philippotaux cyclorama, Union reinforcements—the Nineteenth Massachusetts and the Forty-second New York—charge into The Angle to hurl back the Confederate breakthrough. The painting was first unveiled in Boston, displayed in a circular building specifically built for this rendition of Pickett's Charge. A reporter from the Boston Herald *wrote, "It tells, and in the most vivid manner possible, the whole story of that dreadful afternoon."*

263

During the fighting at Devil's Den Maj. James Cromwell of the 124th New York suggested a charge to his colonel, Augustus Van Horne Ellis. The colonel shook his head no and told the major to go back to his post. The First Texas approached within yards of the regiment. Cromwell again asked permission to engage; Ellis refused. Cromwell then had his horse brought up and mounted the saddle. Cromwell called out to a fellow officer, "The men must see us today!" Ellis finally ordered the charge; both the colonel and major were killed in the action that followed.

stayed in the Union army. The two friends last saw each other at a party in the Hancock home in Los Angeles. Now, three years later at Gettysburg, Hancock was a major general in command of the Union corps defending Cemetery Ridge. His guns were aimed at his old friend Armistead.

GWG   °Lee's final plan was as simple as his earlier plans had been. He would prepare the ground for the assault with a heavy bombardment against the Union line in the hope that this bombardment would disable the Union artillery and wreak havoc among the infantry behind the stone wall. Col. Edward Porter Alexander, the most gifted artillerist in the Confederacy at the time, was put in charge of this bombardment. His instructions were to blast the Federals, to watch for the effect of his fire, and when he perceived that the Union line had been disrupted, to send word to Longstreet to launch the attack.•

Alexander pounded the Union positions with the largest cannonade seen on the American continent. More than 140 cannon fired on the Union positions for more than two hours, but the vast majority of his rounds overshot the Federal position. "The shells would seem to stop

and hang suspended in the air an instant, and then vanish in fire and smoke and noise. We saw the missiles tear and plow the ground," recalled Lt. Frank Haskell of Hancock's Second Corps.

BP °To boost the morale of his men, Hancock rode the length of his line at Cemetery Ridge. As the men hunkered down and hugged the earth, they glanced up and saw their knightly commander who seemed oblivious to the shell fire. By that heroic gesture, Hancock was able to pass on a bit of his own courage to his embattled soldiers. One of Hancock's staff officers later remarked, "One felt safe when near him."• Warned that he was endangering himself needlessly, Hancock replied, "Sometimes the life of a corps commander does not count."

WG On the Confederate side, °Alexander faced an increasingly difficult task in directing his bombardment against the Union batteries on Cemetery Ridge. The problem was he did not have a deep target. The Federal cannon were mounted in a straight, narrow line, and Porter was shooting directly at them. There was not much tolerance in terms of firing high or low.•

BP °It soon became apparent to the Union troops that most of the Confederate shells were going overhead. Alexander's gunners, blinded by the smoke generated by both sides, overshot the Union line. Most of their shells struck the reverse slope of Cemetery Ridge. The Yankee artillery was commanded by Brig. Gen. Henry J. Hunt, a superb artillerist and organizer who had forged the Union artillery into the finest single branch of service in the Union army. Hunt responded to the Confederate cannonade, exploiting his advantage of having his guns mounted on higher ground, particularly on the Round Tops. For two hours the sides maintained the cannonade.•

"The atmosphere was rent and broken by the rush and crash of projectiles: solid shot, shrieking, bursting shells. The sun, but a few moments before so brilliant, was now darkened. Through this smoky darkness came the missiles of death. It was as if we were placed where we were for target practice for the Union batteries," wrote Corp. David Johnston of the Seventh Virginia Infantry.

At the age of thirty-nine Winfield Scott Hancock commanded the Second Corps of the Army of the Potomac. He had arrived on the battlefield in advance of Meade to assess the situation and recommended that the army fight there or find some more suitable field for battle. Hancock's determination that the Federals held a strong defensive position led Meade to hold on and pursue the battle after the substantial losses of the first day. Hancock had an ability to bring order into the most chaotic situations, and this was nowhere more true than it was at Gettysburg. Rattled Union troops took heart at the mere sight of Hancock on the battlefield.

As perhaps the turning point of the battle, Col. Joshua Lawrence Chamberlain led the Twentieth Maine in a bayonet charge down Little Round Top. The colonel later recalled: "It was imperative to strike before we were struck by this overwhelming force in a hand-to-hand fight, which we could not probably have withstood or survived. At that crisis, I ordered the bayonet. The word was enough. It ran like fire along the line, from man to man, and rose into a shout." At least 270 Alabama and Maine soldiers were killed or wounded in this area, but the Federals denied the Round Tops to the Southerners, solidifying the Union position and preventing a flanking move.

°It was hard to see anything once the cannonade began.• After two hours Alexander knew the time had come to attack. "The enemy's fire suddenly began to slacken, and their guns in the cemetery limbered up and vacated the position. If he does not run fresh batteries in there in five minutes, this is our fight," he reported.

°Alexander communicated this to Longstreet and suggested he launch his attack immediately. Longstreet had tried to put the burden of ordering the assault on Alexander, but Alexander was a colonel of artillery and not a corps commander like Longstreet, so he refused to make the decision for Longstreet. It was Longstreet's job to order the assault.• The men meanwhile waited for someone to give the order.

"Yes, great big, stout-hearted men prayed, loudly, too, and they were in earnest, for if men ever have need of the care and protection of our heavenly Father, it was now," Corporal Johnston remembered.

AFTER STRIKING AT the Union army for two days, Lee was determined and confident that Longstreet's assault on the

266

center would destroy the Yankees. From their positions along Seminary Ridge, eleven brigades of infantry, including Pickett's three brigades of Virginians, received the order to advance. Twelve thousand Rebel soldiers were ready to march into immortality in what has come to be known as Pickett's Charge, but the general who would have to order the charge was not ready to send his men to what he considered certain death.

"I do not want to make this charge. I do not see how it can succeed. I would not make it now, but that General Lee has ordered it and is expecting it," said Longstreet.

°It was evident to all his officers that Longstreet did not like the idea of the frontal assault on Cemetery Hill. He was so sure of its failure and so sad at knowing it would go on that he would not actually give the order to Pickett to make the assault. When Pickett came to him and asked, "Do we go forward, General?" Longstreet could not say a word. He simply dropped his head to his chest and raised his hand. Pickett took that as the order to attack.• The assault that has come to symbolize the Confederacy's last great chance of winning was launched without an official order being issued.

Pickett rode to his brigade commanders—Kemper, Garnett, and Armistead—and passed the word to the anxious men. "I have no orders to give you, but I advise you to head across those fields as quick as you can, for in my opinion, you are going to catch hell," he said.

°When the order came to form and move forward to the edge of the woods, all of the soldiers knew what was coming. They were silent because they could see across that mile of open ground to the other side. They knew they were going to be marching toward thousands of Yankee guns.•

"To the brave soldier going into battle, knowing he must go, the moment seemed to lengthen," recalled Corporal Johnston, who fought under Pickett's command. "This feeling is not born of his love for fighting, but rather realizing, if it must be done, it were well if it were done quickly."

°The men looked left and right to make sure that their friends, brothers, fathers, all the boys they had known growing up were still with them. They drew courage from seeing the faces of others they knew. They looked ahead.

Jeb Stuart's confederate cavalry arrived late in the evening of July 2. His role in the Southern defeat at Gettysburg has been debated since then. Some blame him entirely for the defeat; others believe he was merely a scapegoat.

They felt their fear. They felt everything that soldiers at all times feel.● Pettigrew and Trimble spoke words of encouragement to their men, much the same as Pickett shouted to his. "Up men and to your posts. Don't forget today that you are from Old Virginia!" were the last instructions Pickett offered his men.

Under a blazing sun at just after 1:00 P.M. on July 3, 1863, the twelve thousand Confederates began to march into the open field. Pettigrew's division was on the north, Trimble's men in the center, and Pickett's to the south. The plan was to converge the divisions on a portion of the Union line that was clearly visible. It was a little stand of trees that was more than a mile away from the Confederate lines.

°The Civil War soldier was trained to fight in neat, orderly formations elbow to elbow. This style of fighting was designed to keep the regiments, the brigades, and the divisions intact and in formation, to bring them forward en masse. When gaps were made by enemy fire, troops would plug the holes. When close enough, the combined regiments would deliver their fire upon the enemy. It was a great testimony to the discipline of the Confederate soldier that every Union soldier who

In one of the most famous battery stands at Gettysburg, Capt. John Bigelow and his Ninth Massachusetts battery fought near the Trostle farm. Bigelow clearly recalled, "I then saw Confederates swarming in on our right flank . . . the horses were down; overhead the air was alive with missiles." He then gave the order to retreat, but it was too late. South Carolinians and the Twenty-first Mississippi captured four of their guns. Bigelow was shot in the side and hand; Lt. Christopher Erickson was killed. Bigelow reported losing eighty-eight horses in one day's fighting. On July 3 the two remaining guns and their crews helped repulse Pickett's Charge.

BP

With four Confederate brigades sweeping down on Cemetery Ridge, Hancock directed the First Minnesota to charge one of the brigades. The word rang out along the line and the Minnesotans ran headlong into the Alabama unit. The Confederates engulfed the Minnesota men, but Union artillery poured shot and shell into the intermingled ranks. With the help of several other Federal regiments and batteries, the Southerners were thrown back to Seminary Ridge.

recorded his experience on July 3, 1863, remarked on how precise and how superbly disciplined the oncoming Confederate soldiers were.•

"Out in front of us, an undulating field filled almost as far as the eye could reach, with a long, low, gray line creeping towards us, barely fringed with flame. For a few moments, the whole line seemed to waver, but came steadily on," marveled Augustus Buell, a Union artilleryman.

⁰The Yankee line on Cemetery Ridge went dead still. The oncoming Confederates projected the most grand, most imposing, and probably most terrifying sight any of these men had ever seen. For a while many of them simply stared in wonder as the Confederate line slowly, steadily marched toward them. Even after the Yankee artillery opened up and began cutting huge gaps in the lines, the Southerners did not stop marching. They kept coming closer and closer. It was a tremendously intimidating scene for the Union soldiers behind the stone wall.•

⁰Hardly a Union soldier along that wall on Cemetery Ridge on July 3 expected to get out unscathed or to hurl back that attack.• At the same time the Confederates did not necessarily expect to succeed, but they hoped their onslaught would intimidate the Yankees and possibly effect a breakthrough.

"The fatal field was before us. Where I marched, the division of the Federals flashed into view. As we

269

In one of the most heroic and over-looked moments in the battle of Gettysburg, Brig. Gen. George S. Greene and his small brigade of 1,350 men defended the Union right flank from 7:30 until 9 P.M. Nearly 4,000 Confederates assaulted Greene's position. Well entrenched and utilizing numerous natural barriers, the Northerners held the right flank. Although the Southerners captured many Federal entrenchments, darkness caused the Rebel generals to call off the engagement until morning. At dawn the battle resumed, but the Yankees were reinforced and held the right flank. Overall casualties on Culp's Hill numbered at least 2,700 men.

Brig. Gen. James Lawson Kemper was at the head of his brigade in the infamous Pickett's Charge. During the assault he fell from his horse, shot through the body, the bullet exiting near his groin. Seriously wounded, he was left behind during the Southern retreat. He was captured and three months later exchanged; he never again saw field duty.

came in sight, there seemed to be a restlessness and excitement along the enemy line, which encouraged some of us to hope they would not make a stubborn resistance," said Lt. George Finley of the Fifty-sixth Virginia Infantry.

With his hat on the tip of his sword, Armistead marched into battle with his brigade. He too had words of encouragement for his men. Col. Rawley Martin of the Fifty-third Virginia Infantry recalled, "Armistead, as was his custom on going into battle, said: 'Men, remember your wives, your mothers, your sisters, and your sweethearts.' Such an appeal would have made these men assault the ramparts of the infernal regions."

Armistead's men followed directly behind Kemper's brigade. Kemper's men were out in front, with Garnett's brigade to their left. Garnett, even though he knew he made a clear target for Federal riflemen, led his men from horseback. He was one of the few men on horseback on the field.

BP   °Garnett's integrity had been questioned by Stonewall Jackson, who had accused him of incompetence during the battle of Kernstown in March 1862 in the Shenandoah Valley. This had jeopardized and almost ruined Garnett's career, and it had also hurt his pride. While many speculated that Garnett rode as some sort of death wish to prove his courage, the truth was that the same horse had kicked him earlier in the week. The brigade commander could barely walk, but he would not send his men onto the field without him and urged his fellow Virginians forward.•

"The whole column is now within sight, coming down the slope with steady step and superb alignment," wrote Pvt. Randolph Shotwell of the Eighth Virginia Infantry. "The rustle of thousands of feet amid the stubble stirs a cloud of dust like the spray at the prow of a vessel. The flags flutter and snap. The sunlight flashes from the officer's sword. Low words of command are heard, and thus, in perfect order, this gallant array of gallant men marches straight down in the Valley of Death. Two armies for a moment look on, apparently spellbound. Then the spell is broken by the crack of one hundred guns trained upon the advancing troops. Shot, shells, spherical case, shrapnel, and canister, thousands of deadly missiles racing through the air to thin our ranks."

°Smoke was everywhere, making it very difficult for these men to see or to have any real perception of just how big the attack was as the two lines were about to close.• The three divisions of Confederates covered the distance to the Union line steadily, resting once in a swale. As they crossed the Emmitsburg Road, they had to climb over and knock down a wooden fence, which slowed their progress. They maintained their focus on the clump of trees and a sharp turn in the stone wall known as the Angle.

The Union fire intensified as the men climbed over the wooden fence. One Pennsylvania soldier forever remembered something he saw the North Carolinians do

Around 8 P.M. on July 2, Brig. Gen. Harry Hays's Louisiana brigade and Col. Isaac Avery's North Carolina brigade broke through the Union line on East Cemetery Hill. Near the Federal cannon atop the hill a great melee ensued. One Confederate colonel recalled: "[O]ne of our color-bearers jumps on a gun and displays his flag. He was instantly killed. But the flag was seized by an Irishman, who, with a wild shout, sprang upon the gun, [but] he too was shot down." About 625 Confederate and Union soldiers were killed or wounded in this struggle.

In the morning before Pickett's Charge, the Confederate First Maryland Battalion joined in the third assault that day against Culp's Hill at the far right of the Union line. The Marylanders had barely begun their advance when they came under a continuous fire. Their lines were thinned quickly, including officers and even the battalion mascot, a small dog. The survivors fell back to the woods to assess the damage: 50 percent casualties—56 killed, 118 wounded, and 15 missing.

as they neared his portion of the wall. As the Union men cocked their muskets, the Tar Heel farmers heard the action. They pulled their hats down over their heads and leaned forward. The Pennsylvanian, a farmer, knew that the Carolinians, also farmers, were instinctively preparing for a hail storm such as might catch them in the field. This time they were expecting a storm of lead.

"Men are being mowed down with every step, and men are stepping into their places," remembered Sgt. Patrick Delacey of the 143d Pennsylvania Volunteers. "There is no dismay, no wavering. It grows in magnificence as death's sting waxes stronger. Now they are double-quick stride, and we answer their spur with more shot and shell."

°When Garnett's and Kemper's brigades stalled, torn to pieces in front of the stone wall while the men returned fire with the Union troops behind the wall, Armistead's brigade, which had been in the second line, came pushing forward through the chaos in front of them.• "As steady as ever, the gallant Armistead still in lead, his hat working down the blade of his sword, the point having gone through it. He seemed to be as cool as if on a drill," wrote Lt. John H. Lewis of the Ninth Virginia Infantry.

Armistead's men heard his voice over the din. "Come on, boys! Give 'em the cold steel!" he shouted as he neared the stone wall.

A Union newspaperman described the terror he witnessed: "Our men are shot with Rebel muskets touching their breasts. A fierce encounter takes place. Great God, the line at the stone wall gives way!"

THE CONFEDERATES MARCHED on. "On swept the column over ground covered with dead and dying men. Mother Earth seemed to be on fire, the smoke dense, suffocating, the sun shut out, flames blazing on every side. Friend could hardly be distinguished from foe," wrote Capt. Henry Owen of the Eighteenth Virginia Infantry.

BP °Armistead gained the wall and urged his men forward. They began firing into the Union troops. For the next few minutes there was a desperate standoff at the Angle. Men were firing into each other at almost point-blank range, neither side willing to give way.• A few yards farther north, past the Angle, a few dozen North Carolinians made it to the wall before they were cut down. The fighting was growing more desperate, but the number of Confederates available to break through was dwindling.

Even though he was wounded during the Confederate bombardment, Union Lt. Alonzo Cushing, a young West Pointer commanding a Federal artillery battery, stayed with his cannon in the Angle as Armistead's men swarmed toward his position.

BP °Despite terrible wounds, Cushing stuck by his guns. As the Confederate rush began, his battery released its last salvos and canister shot and Cushing went down, struck by a minié ball that killed him instantly. At that same moment, troops of the Seventy-first Pennsylvania, along the wall near the Angle, began to give way, and a hole opened up. It was into this gap that Armistead's men advanced.•

The Confederacy's chance, perhaps its last chance, to win the battle of Gettysburg was the hole opening at the Angle, but men on both sides were dying to fill it. "Death

George Pickett had graduated at the bottom of his class at West Point in 1846. At Gettysburg he and his men were anxious to prove themselves in battle. They suffered 67 percent casualties. After the failed attack, Lee told Pickett to move his division to the rear of Seminary Ridge in case of a Federal counterattack. Pickett bowed his head and said, "General Lee, I have no division now."

Richard B. Garnett was an 1841 graduate of West Point and led the Stonewall Brigade. Stonewall Jackson accused him of cowardice during the Valley campaign of 1862, and Garnett was anxious to prove the general wrong. He led one of Pickett's brigades on horseback and was killed.

Two artillerists, one Confederate, one Federal, played interesting roles on the afternoon of July 3. Edward Porter Alexander (above) was James Longstreet's head of artillery. He tried to soften the Union middle in a two-hour bombardment, but most of his shells overshot their target. Alonzo Cushing (below) participated in the repulse of the Rebels at Cemetery Ridge. During Alexander's cannonade four of Cushing's guns were rendered useless. Already severely wounded, the lieutenant placed his two remaining cannon near the Angle. He was shot down during Pickett's Charge.

is holding a high carnival," said Lt. John H. Lewis of the Eighth Virginia Infantry. "Death lurks in every foot of space. Men fall in heaps, still fighting, bleeding, dying."

Brig. Gen. Alexander Webb, commanding a brigade of four Pennsylvania regiments, would not surrender his ground at the Angle. °When he saw the Seventy-first Pennsylvania give way and the Sixty-ninth Pennsylvania being engulfed by the Confederates coming over the wall, he went back to the Seventy-second Pennsylvania, a regiment of so-called Fire Zouaves, firemen from Philadelphia. Webb urged them forward to plug the gap that was opening up as Armistead came over the wall. The firemen refused to advance. In disgust, Webb went to where the Sixty-ninth Pennsylvania still held the wall and continued the battle for the Angle. The Sixty-ninth was almost entirely surrounded in front of the little copse of trees—but there they held. As other troops gave way, the Sixty-ninth was a rock that helped to stop that Confederate attack and hold the stone wall. Its ranks were being annihilated, but the Sixty-ninth stood its ground. Webb, who had been grazed by a Rebel bullet, later received the Medal of Honor for his bravery in defending the Angle.•

Pettigrew's North Carolinians and Pickett's Virginians needed more men to hold the wall, but they would get none. Lee had planned to send reinforcements only when the wall was forcefully breached.

"Many an anxious eye was cast back to the hill from which we came in the hope of seeing supports near at hand. And more than once, I heard the despairing cry: 'Why don't they come?' But no help came," recalled Col. Joseph Mayo of the Third Virginia Infantry.

Union General Hancock galloped the length of the line, sending more troops against the oncoming Rebels. °Col. Arthur Devereaux of the Nineteenth Massachusetts stepped in front of Hancock's horse and asked, "General, shouldn't we get in there?" pointing toward where Armistead's men were gaining the wall.

"Get in there pretty goddamned quick," Hancock snapped in reply.

Without another order, the Massachusetts men rushed toward the hole that was opening along the wall. Hancock continued down the line to Gen. Joseph Stannard's

Vermont brigade and urged them to flank the enemy right. At that moment, Hancock's saddle was struck by a bullet that carried a nail into his thigh. He reeled in the saddle and was helped to the ground. As the men scrambled to get a tourniquet for him, Hancock said, "I do not wish to be removed from this field until the issue is decided." He was not about to be carried from that battlefield until he saw the Confederates retreating.•

A few hundred yards from the fallen Hancock, Armistead and about two hundred of his men were engaged in hand-to-hand fighting with the Yankee defenders. Armistead moved forward and placed a hand on one of Cushing's abandoned cannon. It was there that Pickett lost his most gallant brigade commander. °Armistead was grievously wounded and fell near one of the guns. He gave a Masonic symbol of distress that was answered by one of Hancock's staff officers, a young captain named Henry Bingham, who did what he could to ease Armistead's suffering. Armistead inquired about Hancock, and Bingham told him that Hancock had also been wounded. On hearing that, Armistead asked for forgiveness. Some Northerners took these words to be a repudiation of

In the Thulstrup painting below, the dominant character is that of Hancock in the left foreground directing an artillery limber toward the small stone wall sheltering the center of the Union line. Hancock was wounded during Pickett's Charge, taking a nail from his saddle—dislodged by a bullet—and the bullet into his thigh. That evening he reported to Meade: "I arrived just in time to put a small battalion of infantry in the place occupied by those two batteries. . . . I did not leave the field till the victory was entirely secured and the enemy no longer in sight. . . . I had to break the line to attack the enemy in flank on my right, where the enemy was most persistent after the front attack was repelled. Not a rebel was in sight upright when I left."

P. F. Rothermel was commissioned by the state of Pennsylvania to portray Pickett's Charge. To aid the viewer in grasping the dramatic scene being played out, the artist omitted the enormous amount of smoke that engulfed the entire area. There was so much smoke that men from the Sixty-ninth and Seventy-first Pennsylvania, deployed near the stone wall at the Angle, found Confederate rifles pressed blindly against their chests; the men's clothes were burned from the gun powder. The Sixty-ninth's historian recounted the melee. "[Hugh] Bradley, of this company [D], a powerful man, was using his piece as a club very effectively, but was overpowered by numbers and had his skull crushed by a blow from a musket in the hands of a rebel." Rothermel chose to portray Meade on horseback to the far left although the general did not appear at the scene of battle until after the Confederates had been thrown back. While the artist no doubt included him as a favorite son of the Keystone State, the central image is that of an ordinary soldier, albeit one whose bright undershirt would have surely drawn fatal fire. Interestingly, all the men seem to favor one another.

Armistead's allegiance to the Confederacy, but most believe this most determined and gallant Confederate soldier was instead apologizing to Hancock for his wound, believing it was a Virginian who had struck down his old friend.

Farther down the wall, just to the south of the breakthrough at the Angle, a determined group of Confederates also managed to breach the wall and enter the interior of the Union line. They did not get quite as far as Armistead's men, but this little band made a rush toward some Union guns that had come into position on the ridge. This battery was commanded by Andrew Cowan, who ordered his men to load with double canister—a projectile that spewed deadly iron balls when fired. Cowan waited until the Confederates were within fifteen paces of his guns. As General Hunt, the Union artillery commander sitting on his horse behind Cowan's battery, fired his revolver into the Confederates and yelled, "See 'em? See 'em?" Cowan gave the command to fire. When the smoke cleared there were no living soldiers left in front of them. The dozens of Confederates who had crossed the wall lay heaped in death and agony in front of Cowan's battery. There were no more breakthroughs at the wall.•

The attack, usually called Pickett's Charge rather than the more descriptive Pettigrew-Pickett-Trimble Assault, had failed. "They are gone; fleeing over the field, broken,

Southern commander Robert E. Lee had gambled everything he had and thrown a massive punch at the Union line on Cemetery Ridge. He was aggressive and pugnacious to the end. Edward Porter Alexander described him after the failed assault: "Gen. Lee rode up, entirely unattended. He expected Meade to follow the fugitives . . . & he intended, himself, to have a hand in rallying them, & in the fight which would follow. He had the combative instinct in him as strongly developed as any man living." Lee spoke to most of the fugitives saying, "Form your ranks again when you get back to cover. We want all good men to hold together now. It was all my fault this time."

shattered, thrown into confusion by the remorseless fire. Their lines have disappeared like a straw in the candle's flame. The ground is thick with the dead, and the wounded are like the withered leaves of Autumn," wrote Charles Coffin, a Union journalist.

°Incredibly, of the twelve thousand Confederates who went forward, six thousand managed to return to their lines in some degree of safety, although a great many of them carried Yankee lead with them. The charge was one of the most terrifying experiences these men would ever have. It was one thing to go forward in the face of the enemy; it was another to return to their lines and see the demoralizing wreckage of war: the dead, the wounded crying for help, and unidentifiable parts of men who had been blown to bits by the Union artillery.•

Many men felt the kind of horror that led Lt. James Whitehead of the Fifty-third Virginia Infantry to write: "The awful groans of the wounded and dying, pleading for water and help, all comes crowding into my mind. I do pray the good Lord I may never witness such a scene again."

°Gen. Alexander Hays, who commanded the Union division on the right flank during the attack, took a Confederate battle flag that had been captured and trailed it behind his horse, humiliating the Confederates who could see what he was doing. To the cheers of his men, he

A wrecked ammunition chest for a light 12-pounder gun and one of the horses that pulled it litter the field. In the Union army six cannon made up a battery; four cannon usually comprised a Confederate battery. Overall at least seventy-two horses were needed for each Federal battery, and they were a primary target to assaulting troops whose first goal was to incapacitate the battery. Approximately five thousand horses and mules were killed at Gettysburg. Visitors to the battlefield long afterward recalled the nauseous odors of decaying humans and animals. The local militia was given the unceremonious task of burying the horses.

rode up and down the lines as they all yelled: "Remember Harpers Ferry!" One of their brigades had been captured at Harpers Ferry in 1862 and now took advantage of their turn to gloat.•

WCD °Meade was relieved. He had just stopped the greatest threat to the North ever mounted by the Confederates. He was reported to have shouted a "Hurrah!" which for him was about as much gloating as he would do.•

Union Lt. Jesse Young concluded the battle was over, but nobody knew it. "The survivors in the two armies were waiting to see what would come on the morrow, when suddenly a band of music began to play in the rear of the Union line of battle. Down the valley, up the hill, and over the field into the ears of wounded and dying men, and beyond our line into the bivouac of the beaten enemy, the tune was borne on the evening breezes. 'Home Sweet Home' was the tender air," remembered Young. "The next morning was the Fourth of July, but it seemed, at the time to those who were at Gettysburg, a somber and terrible national anniversary, with the indescribable horrors of the field before the eye in every direction."

THE CONFEDERATE GENERAL whose name would forever be linked with the attack could not believe what had happened to his division. More than half of his men had been killed or wounded. "It is all over now. Your soldier lives and mourns, and but for you my darling, he would rather be back there with his dead to sleep for all time in an unknown grave," Pickett wrote to his fiancée. There have been some people who question if Pickett ever got close enough to the combat to chance a grave.

GWG °There was a debate among Southerners after the war, particularly North Carolinians, about where Pickett had been during the charge. Some suggested that the fact that he was not wounded meant he had not really acted in an honorable or gallant way during the assault. Pettigrew had been wounded. Trimble had been wounded so severely in his bad leg that Yankee surgeons amputated it before sending him to prison. Armistead had been killed. Garnett had been killed. Kemper had been wounded so badly that no one expected him to live. (He survived to become a governor of Virginia.) Why was Pickett not wounded? The answer that some officers gave was that Pickett had headed toward the rear or had hidden behind a barn near the road. Some charged that neither Pickett nor his staff could be found during the assault to ask for orders. The implication was obvious. They had hidden somewhere, leaving their brigade commanders and the other two divisions to fend for themselves during the assault.

Many historians have rejected the insinuations that Pickett had not done his duty during the assault. They asserted that Pickett, as a division commander, should not have been in the front of his men, that he should have been in the rear where he could direct the activities of his division.•

Pickett himself blamed Lee for the destruction of his command. Immediately after the attack, Lee told him to look after his division should the Federals launch a counterattack. A dazed Pickett could only answer that he had no division left. Many years later, after an uneasy postwar meeting with his former commander, Pickett referred to Lee as "that old man who wrecked my division."

In three days the Army of Northern Virginia lost nearly twenty-eight thousand men at Gettysburg. Lee accepted that he alone, not his army, was to blame for the defeat. He waited a day for a Federal counterattack. When none came, he successfully moved his army back across the Potomac, headed to Virginia. Lee never formally analyzed his loss as so many historians have.

KK °One of the great lost opportunities at Gettysburg was the failure of the Confederates to bring converging artillery fire on the Federal position—a tactic that allows artillery to fire from two different directions at the same point. This maneuver relieves gunners from worrying about elevation, allowing them to fire straight ahead; if

Photographed by Alexander Gardner in the days following the battle, this individual fell in the Slaughter Pen at the base of Big Round Top on July 2. Approximately two hundred Rebels were killed or wounded in this area; Col. William F. Perry's Forty-fourth and Col. James L. Sheffield's Forty-eighth Alabama and the Second Georgia fought in these rocks. Perry recalled that when the two Alabama regiments descended from Big Round Top, "As the line emerged from the woods into the open space . . . a sheet of flame burst from the rocks less than a hundred yards away."

In the late afternoon of July 3, four cannon from Lt. Charles Hazlett's Battery D, Fifth U.S. Artillery, were pulled up Little Round Top. The guns could not be fired effectively to the immediate front; instead the cannon were used to hit the Confederates in and around Devil's Den and the Wheat Field. During the fighting Hazlett was killed and command passed to Lt. Benjamin Rittenhouse. In the distance can be seen the Pennsylvania Reserves that charged across the Valley of Death and struck Longstreet's corps on Houck's Ridge.

they fire long, they still hit something farther down the line. The Confederates never brought converging fire on the Federal positions at Gettysburg, but the Federals had that advantage when they placed their guns on the high ground at the Round Tops.•

Since the Rebel artillery fired across at the Union line, most of their shells overshot the Yankees. °Porter's bombardment, which Lee was counting on, did virtually nothing to assist the charge that followed.•

Other analysts point out that °Lee did not lose because he failed to place his cannon properly; Lee lost because the Army of the Potomac performed well and was commanded capably by a general on the other side. Lee did not whip himself; Meade defeated him.•

Although relieved to hear of Meade's victory, Lincoln was disappointed that the retreating Rebels were not pursued and destroyed. The same thing had happened the previous September after the battle of Antietam, when McClellan had failed to pursue Lee. Now Meade had won at Gettysburg, but he too failed to pursue Lee. Meade even offered the same excuse McClellan had: the Army of the Potomac had suffered great losses and was not capable of launching a counterattack. In the fight for that Pennsylvania farmland, Meade had lost nearly a quarter of his army—twenty-three thousand men killed, wounded, or captured.

°Gettysburg has become an enduring symbol of the fortitude, courage, determination, and idealism of the men who fought and died there for what they believed to be right. The men who gave so much during this war must be remembered, not as monuments of bronze and granite, but as people of flesh and blood who suffered, died, and risked everything on that ground. If the nation were to forget these men and their sacrifices and forget the ground on which they fought and bled, then the country would lose something of itself.•

°The stakes were never higher than they were during the Civil War: whether or not the nation would remain a united nation, whether or not parts of it would remain a slave society. There simply are no larger questions over which human beings fight.• The answer to these questions was forged over four years of war, and the beginning of that answer began to take shape at Gettysburg.

The survivors of the Army of Northern Virginia retreated south from Gettysburg. During the next two years of the war, Lee never again had the opportunity or the strength to mount a major offensive. The road through Gettysburg that was to guide Lee's army to victory led instead to Appomattox Court House.

Four days after the battle, July 7, the Army of the Potomac began pursuing Lee's army. Most of Meade's soldiers made a hard march of between fifteen and twenty miles over soggy roads. One corps commander reported that his men, some of them barefooted, made a twenty-nine-mile hike to Walkersville, Maryland. Edwin Forbes depicted these men (above) near another Maryland town, Emmitsburg. Torrential rains made the roads almost impassable, and this slowed the Northern soldiers' progress.

GETTYSBURG: THE CIVILIANS

There WAS NOTHING REMARKABLE about Gettysburg, Pennsylvania, until July 1863. It was a simple farming community, much like thousands of other towns throughout the country. If anything made it special, it was that nine roads intersected at the center of town, giving it excellent transportation in all directions.

On the last day of June 1863, the peaceful town of Gettysburg was trapped between two armies totaling almost 160,000 men. Unprepared for the carnage of battle, the citizens of Gettysburg were plunged into the nightmare of war.

Gettysburg was a thriving town of twenty-four hundred in 1863 when Union Maj. Gen. George Gordon Meade and his Army of the Potomac met and fought Confederate Gen. Robert E. Lee's Army of Northern Virginia for three days of the bloodiest fighting of the Civil War. When the fighting was done, these two hard-marching armies disappeared as quickly as they had appeared, leaving behind nearly thirty thousand dead and wounded soldiers. The citizens' story of what happened during that frightful battle and its aftermath has rarely been told except by themselves in their own words.

"We knew that with every explosion and the scream of each shell human beings were hurried through excruciating pain into another world. And that many more were torn and mangled and lying in torment worse than death, no able to extend relief. The thought made me very sad and feel that if it was God's will I would rather be taken away than remain to see the misery that

TC	Tina Cappetta
GAC	Gregory A. Coco
WAF	William A. Frassanito
CG	Charles Glatfelter
BP	Brian Pohanka
JAS	Jacob A. Sheads
WGW	William G. Williams

The sketch above (left) is one of the earliest depictions of the town of Gettysburg. Drawn around 1843 it shows a peaceful country town and depicts a somewhat carefree existence. The rural and urban combined pleasantly to offer the townspeople the benefits of both lifestyles.

The Forney farm (above right) was typical of the family enterprises that ringed the countryside. Farmers tended such staples as corn and wheat, supplemented by various fruit orchards. These were the first areas encountered by the Confederates, and they welcomed themselves to the produce and more. James Longstreet's chief of artillery, Edward Porter Alexander, told the story of an anguished farmer who refused him water, saying, "No! Dere ain't no water! De well is done pump dry! And just look at dis porch vere dey been! And see dere vere dey tramples down dat wheat! Mein Gott! Mein Gott! I'se heard of de horrors of war before but I never see what dey was till now!"

WGW

would follow," wrote Sarah Broadhead on July 3, 1863, the day the battle ended.

Neither the Federals nor the Confederates had intended to fight at Gettysburg. Rather, the town was simply on the road to the site of a battle that never happened. In late June 1863, Lee led his army into Pennsylvania toward the state capital, Harrisburg. His objective was to find food and supplies for his army.

°Lee wanted to move the war out of Virginia's Shenandoah Valley, the breadbasket of the state, which had been devastated by Union raids and various battles.• He looked longingly at the Yankee farms of Pennsylvania. War had not touched them at all, and the bulk of the Union army was in Virginia licking its wounds from several consecutive defeats inflicted by Lee.

Moving with the characteristic swiftness that had almost always worked to his advantage on the battlefield, Lee moved into Maryland and Pennsylvania so audaciously that the Union army lost track of his whereabouts. The Federal cavalry was at a loss to find the Confederate army of more than sixty thousand men. When the horse soldiers did discover Lee's crossing of the Potomac, word was passed back to Meade, the newly appointed commander of the Army of the Potomac, who had replaced Maj. Gen. Joseph Hooker on June 28. Hooker had been soundly beaten by Lee on May 1–3 at Chancellorsville. When Meade received the news of Lee's second invasion of the North, he did not hesitate as Hooker had earlier; he pursued the

Southerners into Pennsylvania, which was also Meade's home state.

BP   °The Confederates had gotten the jump on Meade, but Lee would not be hard to follow. The roads that led through Maryland and into Pennsylvania were covered with a hovering cloud of dust from the thousands of marching feet of the Confederates.• Lee himself was unaware that the Federals had discovered he was no longer in Virginia and were now pursuing him into Pennsylvania.

Fanny Bealer, a Gettysburg resident, was surprised, like Lee, at the sudden appearance of the Union army at the Pennsylvania town: "We thought the bulk of the Union soldiers were far away. And no one dreamed of a

GW   battle being fought in our town." °Nobody planned that a battle should be fought at Gettysburg. It was a mistake brought on by a reading of the map.•

JAS   °Gettysburg had nine roads leading into it, including five major roads, which spread out from the city like the spokes of a wheel.• When Lee learned that the Federals were pursuing him, he looked at a map to find one place where he could quickly concentrate his widely scattered army. All the roads in the area around Harrisburg, where most of his army was, seemed to lead to the small farm town. Lee ordered his corps to concentrate there, but he also told them to wait until they were all together before making any offensive moves.

One division commander, Maj. Gen. Henry Heth, who arrived in Gettysburg on June 30, 1863, did not

The views below were the vistas, looking eastward from Seminary Ridge (left) and from West Middle Street (right), the Confederates had as they pursued the retreating Federals into Gettysburg. Falling back from the open fields west of the town, the Union troops had to negotiate the streets to a predetermined point on Cemetery Hill, marked by the towering tree barely visible in the extreme right of the image at left.

The image of the Globe Inn above is one of four scenic photographs taken of Gettysburg prior to the war, possibly in 1861. The inn was the first brick building erected in the town during the 1790s by the town's founder, James Gettys. According to the proprietor's son, John Wills, on the first day of the battle, the inn did a brisk morning business selling whiskey to Union soldiers. After that, the inn served several meals to Confederate officers who interestingly paid for their food with greenbacks and gold.

In the 1860s Gettysburg was primarily known for its two institutions of higher learning—the Lutheran Theological Seminary (right) and Pennsylvania College (far right, opposite page). The buildings were the most imposing architectural accomplishments of the town. Both were used by Federals and Confederates as observation posts and hospitals. The college was in session at the time of the battle, but classes were quickly dismissed as the sound of gunfire advanced toward the town.

WGW

heed that order. He had heard a rumor about a storehouse of shoes in Gettysburg and entered the town with his division on July 1 to find those shoes, but he drew fire from °an advance Union cavalry brigade guarding the town. With that shot the battle of Gettysburg began.

From dawn until noontime, thousands of men came down the farm roads toward this quiet farming town. The Confederates came from the north and northwest. The Federals came from the south and southeast. All headed toward the battle taking place northwest of Gettysburg.• Confused, frightened townspeople tried to stay out of the way.

"Soon the booming of cannon was heard. Then great clouds of smoke were seen, rising beyond the ridge. The sound became louder and louder, and was now incessant. The troops passing us moved faster. The men had now become excited and urged on their horses," wrote Tillie Pierce, a fifteen-year-old, in her diary.

As the Yankee army slowly yielded the northwestern side of town and moved to new positions to the south

and east, Henry Eister Jacobs noted: "They kept the pace without breaking ranks but they flowed through and out into the battlefield beyond. The human tide had no race speed."

As the soldiers of both sides rushed past the town's residents, °the people were warned to get in their cellars.• Sarah Broadhead recalled: "The time we spent in the cellar seemed long. Listening to the terrific sound of the strife. More terrible sounds never greeted human ears."

By the time the battle began, the town of Gettysburg was populated mostly by women and children. Hundreds of Gettysburg boys had enlisted in the Union army, and many of Gettysburg's fathers, who had seen advance Confederate patrols and had heard telegraphed warnings, had driven their livestock elsewhere and hidden other supplies to preclude their falling into Confederate hands. As the first day's fighting escalated, one Gettysburg resident chose the battlefield over his cellar.

°John Burns, seventy years old at the time, became a citizen hero of Gettysburg. When he heard the

The J. L. Schick storefront marked the southwest corner of the town square. The building was owned by Prof. Martin Stoever of Pennsylvania College; the two top floors were the family residence and the first floor was rented as a dry goods store by John L. Schick. The Stoever family allegedly sheltered twenty wounded Union soldiers from the first day of battle to the last, and other soldiers were hidden in the basement until the Confederates retreated.

WAF Confederates were approaching, this veteran of the War of 1812° °grabbed his old flintlock, donned a dark blue swallowtail coat with bright brass buttons, put on his high silk hat, and started down the Chambersburg Pike, following the sound of gunfire. As the battle progressed during the afternoon, Burns fought with the Seventh Wisconsin of the Iron Brigade, one of the toughest units of the Union army. He was wounded twice, but he kept fighting until finally he was felled by a serious wound in the leg.°

JAS °When Burns was wounded the second time, he threw his gun away because he realized if the Confederates captured him in civilian dress, they would probably execute him as a bushwhacker. He knew the rule that if he wanted to play the part of a soldier, he had to dress the part of a soldier. In the confusion of the retreat of the Union army, Burns made it back to his home where he hid for the rest of the battle.°

WAF °The old man's story was picked up by newspaper reporters after the battle, and he was photographed as a national hero. He became so famous that when Abraham Lincoln attended the dedication ceremonies of the national cemetery the following November, the president JAS asked to meet the old patriot.° °That created the interesting spectacle of Lincoln, the president of the United States, and John Burns, the citizen hero of Gettysburg, walking arm-in-arm up the city streets to attend a political rally in the Presbyterian church.°

Looking north from the town square, or diamond as it was called at the time of the battle, the McClellan House, the oldest hotel in town, stands at the northeast corner of Carlisle Street. The street was lined with store fronts and warehouses, and during the fighting barricades were thrown up by both sides. Interestingly, the two sides did not clash on Carlisle Street during the time in which the Confederates occupied the town or during the retreat.

The Confederates outnumbered the Federals at Gettysburg at the start of the battle. In the late afternoon of July 1, the Union lines defending the ridges north and west of the town began to collapse. °The armies started fighting in the streets. Shells burst and bullets ricocheted off the brick buildings. Wounded horses ran loose. Ambulances and supply wagons toppled over. Barricades were thrown up. Wounded soldiers staggered by, dripping blood in the street. The scene was total bedlam.•

From the relative safety of his home, Henry Eister Jacobs saw what was happening and later reported: "There were twenty-five hundred men made prisoners in the streets before our eyes. Our family took to the cellar, where a window afforded a partial view."

°The civilians had no idea who was coming and who was going. They were caught up in the fog of war that precludes anybody's knowing what is happening.• "In the retreat of the first day, there were more people on the street than I have seen since at any time. The street seemed blocked. In front of our house the crowd seemed so great that I believe I could have walked across the street on the heads of the soldiers," wrote Anna Garlock.

PRIVATE HOMES WERE not immune from invasion. Elias Sheads's home stood alone in an open field on the

After the Confederates captured the town on July 1 they set up a barricade on the pavement on Baltimore Street and manned it with soldiers from Louisiana and Georgia. One man would raise his hat on a stick. After the Federal infantry emptied their rifles the Southerners would stand up and quickly volley back. Sharpshooters also fired from second-story windows. A Rebel remembered there was "a constant rattle of musketry by men stripped to the waist and blackened with powder." Other Confederates, taking a break, lounged on sofas and carpets.

One month prior to the battle of Gettysburg, Company K of the First Pennsylvania Reserves, made up of Adams County men, was photographed at Fairfax Station, Virginia. It was the only unit from the area to fight in the battle. They participated in the charge down Little Round Top on July 2 and suffered seven casualties, only one of whom died from his wounds. After the fighting several of the men slipped out of camp to visit family and friends.

Chambersburg Pike at the western edge of Gettysburg. On the afternoon of July 1, the Union retreat came

WAF toward it. °A group of Union soldiers from the Ninety-seventh New York under the command of Col. Charles Wheelock sought shelter in the Sheadses' home. The house quickly filled with wounded Union soldiers, so when Wheelock entered, he immediately went to the basement. A few moments later Confederate soldiers barged in and began disarming the Union officers. Wheelock fingered his sword, which had been given to him by friends earlier in the war. The sword was a symbol of honor that he did not want to surrender to his Confederate captors.•

JAS °Carrie, one of Sheads's daughters, was with Wheelock when a Confederate demanded his sword. She distracted the Southerner, and when he was not looking, she hid

WAF the sword in the folds of her petticoat.• °Wheelock was forever indebted to her.•

Carrie Sheads and her sisters immediately became nurses to dozens of seriously wounded men. The war had come to the Sheadses' parlor, but it had also taken

JAS their four sons, who were Union soldiers. °The tragedy of the Sheads family was that two sons were killed in action and two others came home but soon died of service-connected disabilities.•

Carrie's sister Louisa married one of her Union army patients, but she too died shortly after the Civil War,

JAS perhaps as a result of working with °formaldehyde as a nurse in the field hospital that occupied their home.

Four brothers and one sister were casualties of war in that one family.●

By the end of the first day's fighting, the Union forces had retreated to Culp's Hill and Cemetery Ridge, just south of town. The town itself was largely occupied by Southern troops. In the midst of battle, the courtesy of the Southerners surprised their unwilling Northern hosts. "During the entire time that Northern and Southern soldiers were in Gettysburg, I never heard a disrespectful word uttered by one to any woman," marveled Salome Sally Stewart. "They were just men, or rather boys. Just like our own boys," added Rosalind Rowen.

During the next two days the Union army at Gettysburg swelled to more than ninety thousand men; the Confederate ranks grew to more than seventy thousand. Before the three-day battle ended, casualties for both sides totaled more than fifty-one thousand. At the end of the first day's fighting alone, eleven thousand Union and Confederate soldiers were either dead on the battlefield, captured, or wounded. The wounded found shelter in makeshift hospitals in the homes and churches of Gettysburg. The battle had barely begun, and the town was already overwhelmed.

BP °Buildings were packed with scores of wounded men, but there were few medical personnel available to treat TC them.● °Some women of Gettysburg took into their own

The two images below are something of a panorama taken from the crest of Seminary Ridge and looking into the town from the west. The road to the right in the photograph below (right) is the Hagerstown Road, which formed the right flank of the Confederate line on the first day. The fences were likely cannibalized for campfires.

During the first day's retreat Union soldiers eluded Southern pursuers by hiding in the homes of the local residents. Col. Charles Wheelock, commander of the Ninety-seventh New York, fled into the Sheads home (above) and down into their basement. A Confederate band raced closely after him; one of the sergeants demanded the colonel's sword, but while one of the Sheads daughters distracted him, another hid the colonel's sword in the folds of her dress. After escaping, the colonel returned to the house and reclaimed his weapon. Another Union private, also captured here, later returned to marry one of the Sheads daughters.

homes as many wounded as they could accommodate. Other women went to the public buildings, such as churches that had been converted into temporary hospitals, and cared for the wounded.•

"We did all we could for the wounded men. Wetting cloths and putting them on the wounds and helping. Every pew was full. Some sitting. Some lying. Some leaning on others. They cut off the legs and arms and threw them out of the windows," recalled a horrified Mary McAllister.

Civil War surgeons used chloroform as an anesthetic, but it was often not effective. Tillie Pierce witnessed numerous operations and remembered: "I saw the wounded throwing themselves wildly about and shrieking with pain while the operation was going on. To the south of the house and just outside of the yard, I noticed a pile of limbs higher than the fence. It was a ghastly sight."

BP The horrible injuries witnessed by the women were caused by the standard °Civil War bullet, a .58-caliber piece of soft lead that tended to lose its shape when it hit a body part. On impact it would expand into a bone-smashing clump. The weight of the bullet and the fact that it was malleable meant that any bones struck by it were completely splintered. Surgeons had no recourse but to amputate the limb.•

GAC °These military doctors operated fifteen hours a day and stood in blood and filth up to their knees with flies buzzing around them. Every ten minutes they amputated a limb. They grew accustomed to that horror.

Later, when women came to see the soldiers, they offered a motherly touch to the hospital. The women might ask the soldiers how they were feeling, change their bandages, mop the sweat from their brows, and clean them up a bit. Such attentions made the men feel human again after going through the torture of being on the doctor's table. They felt wanted. They had a reason to live. The women who nursed the wounded acted as mothers would if these patients had been their own sons.•

"What our soldiers are like in the army, I cannot say. But when they are wounded they all seem perfect gentlemen. So gentle, patient, and kind. And so thankful for any kindness shown them," wrote Sarah Broadhead.

Some of the women no doubt saw in the young faces of the soldiers echoes of their own sons. °Many a town's young men had gone off earlier in the war, when that first flush of patriotism swept the country. There were some units like the First Pennsylvania Reserves and the Eighty-seventh Pennsylvania that held large numbers of Gettysburg men.•

°Company K of the First Pennsylvania Reserves was the only Gettysburg company attached to the Army of the Potomac at the time of the battle. Thus it was the only Gettysburg company that participated in the three days' battle.• Fifty-two Gettysburg and Adams County men fought on the same fields where years earlier they had played as boys.

"I am proud of the conduct of Company K at, as well as after, the battle of Gettysburg," wrote Capt. Henry N. Minnigh of the First Pennsylvania Reserves. "And why should I not be? These brave fellows could easily imagine the dangerous surroundings of loved ones during the terrible conflict in their homes within the bounds of the battlefield. Yet not a man left the ranks or fled from duty. And while most of them got home after the battle, by a peculiar device only one failed to return."

ON THURSDAY, JULY 2, both armies reached their maximum strengths, totaling more than 160,000 soldiers. °The Confederates were on the offensive but unable to break through the Union lines on both flanks. Although the Southerners briefly pierced the center on Cemetery Ridge, the attack was ultimately repulsed.•

Henry Eister Jacobs described the next day's battle: "Friday morning seemed to be a time of rest for both sides, as far as our hearing could tell. But at seven minutes past one o'clock, two big guns sounded. My father

John Burns (below), a veteran of the War of 1812, was sixty-nine years old at the time of the battle. He had moved to Gettysburg in 1825 and was a shoemaker. On the first day he took his old flintlock and powder horn and joined the Federal regiments near McPherson's Ridge. He was wounded twice but continued to fight. During the afternoon he was fighting alongside the 150th Pennsylvania when he was shot through the ankle. Remarkably, he recovered from these injuries and became a national hero. His home (above) was photographed by Alexander Gardner.

Among the lore of the battle of Gettysburg are the tragedies of three young people of the town who died within days of each other. Jennie Wade (near right) was the only civilian killed during the battle. She was allegedly engaged to Jack Skelly (far right), a Gettysburg resident serving in the Union army in the Shenandoah Valley. Jennie was staying at her sister's house on Baltimore Street, helping to tend to a newborn. On the morning of July 3, while she was baking bread, a stray bullet pierced two pine doors and struck her in the back, killing her instantly. Skelly had been critically injured near Winchester, Virginia, prior to Gettysburg. He was found by John Wesley Culp (below), another native of Gettysburg, who had moved south before the war and enlisted in the Confederate army. Culp was a member of the famous Stonewall Brigade. When he left the Shenandoah for Pennsylvania, he carried a message from Jack for either Jennie or Jack's mother, depending upon which legend one hears. The message was never delivered because Culp was killed near his cousin's farm, probably on July 2. One of his comrades recalled his death, "I think he was about 22 years old when he was killed." He was the only man killed in action in his regiment. Three other members of his unit later died from their wounds. Skelly died on July 12.

looked at his watch and said, 'We must all go into the cellar.' We complied and then began the terrible artillery duel of Friday afternoon—unequaled, I believe, the sound and fury from the annals of the war. It lasted for an hour and a half."

Jacobs and his family were hearing the prelude to one of the bloodiest and most decisive encounters of the Civil War: Pickett's Charge—the desperate Confederate assault on the Union line that held Cemetery Ridge. °After the massive artillery bombardment, which caused the hills and the fields and the dwellings of Gettysburg to shake and tremble, twelve thousand Confederates moved across the field before the center of the Union line. The Federals hurled back the assault, and more than half of the attacking force were killed, wounded, or captured. That climactic event essentially concluded the battle in favor of Meade's army. Lee and his proud Army of Northern Virginia retreated from the field.•

Earlier that day the battle ended for twenty-year-old Jennie Wade, believed to be the only Gettysburg civilian killed during the fighting at Gettysburg. °A baby boy had been born to Jennie's sister on June 26, just four days before the battle, so she was not at her home at the start of the fighting. On July 3 Jennie was kneading dough to make biscuits for some Union soldiers stationed near her house when a stray bullet, probably from a Confederate sharpshooter, entered the north side of the building where she was standing. The bullet passed through two doors and struck her in the back, under the left shoulder blade. She died instantly, an unfortunate accident of war.

Jennie's death on July 3 was the end of a more tragic story that involved her childhood friend Wesley Culp and her sweetheart, Johnston "Jack" Skelly. All three had grown up together in Gettysburg and enjoyed a very close friendship, with Skelly apparently treating her as his intended. Skelly's photograph was found in Jennie's apron pocket after her death.•

JAS   °A few days before the battle, Skelly, a Union soldier, was badly wounded in a battle in the Shenandoah
WAF   Valley.• °Ironically, one of the Confederate soldiers who encountered the wounded Skelly was his child-hood friend, Wesley Culp, who had left Pennsylvania and was then serving in the Confederate army.• Culp was able to spend some time with Skelly and undoubt-ably was given a message to take to Jennie should he get back to Gettysburg.

Culp was indeed on his way there, but before he could get to the Skelly farm to tell Mrs. Skelly about her wounded son, and before he could find Jennie, he fell in
WAF   the fighting on his family's farm on Culp's Hill. °He was the only member of the Second Virginia Infantry to be killed in action that day.

Skelly himself died on July 12, 1863. Culp never saw Mrs. Skelly or Jennie. Jennie never learned what had happened to Skelly, and Skelly never learned what happened to Jennie. Culp's body was never found by his family.• Eventually Jennie Wade and Jack Skelly would rest only one hundred paces from each other in Gettys-burg's Evergreen Cemetery.

With the fighting essentially over, Henry Eister Jacobs noted, "About midnight Friday the streets began to fill with men. Again, a human tide flowing, flowing, but now like some great current that had passed through innumerable scenes of wreck, bearing its flotsam with it."

BP   °Rain began to fall intermittently for the next several days as Lee led his army in

This was the house in which Jennie Wade was killed. It was one of four so-called double-unit homes built in the early 1840s in Gettysburg. The northern unit belonged to Jennie's brother-in-law, John L. McClellan, who was attached to Company E of the 165th Pennsylvania Infantry. Jennie's sister, Georgia Anna Wade McClellan, had given birth to a son on June 26, four days before the battle, and she was being cared for by her mother, Mary Ann Wade, and Jennie. The southern unit was occupied by Catharine McClain, a widow whose husband had been killed at Hampton, Virginia, in May 1863 while serving in the same company as McClellan.

*As the two armies withdrew from Get-
tysburg, the Army of Northern Virginia in retreat and the Army of the
Potomac in pursuit, the townspeople of
Gettysburg found themselves facing a
herculean task of burying the dead.
While the Federals buried their own
before departing, the Confederates had
little time for such civilities.*

retreat back across the Pennsylvania border and through
Maryland toward the Potomac River.• Leading the Confederate retreat was a seventeen-mile-long wagon train
carrying five thousand wounded. Elements of the Union
army followed the Confederates to the Potomac and
launched some disjointed attacks, but most of the Southerners made good their escape.

BP   °Meade and the Union army had been battered at Gettysburg. Although he angered President Lincoln by not
pursuing Lee, Meade did not want to risk failing in an
attempt to destroy the Confederate army.• He knew Lee's
army was more vulnerable than it had ever been before,
and he presumed there would be time to crush it later.

WAF   °With the departure of the armies from Gettysburg,
the town and the surrounding countryside became one
vast hospital. Twenty-one thousand wounded soldiers
from both armies had been left behind. Meade removed
his army from the town. Thinking he might need more
doctors if another battle erupted unexpectedly, the Federal commander left behind only one hundred army doctors to care for the thousands of seriously wounded
soldiers in Gettysburg.•

BP   °The townspeople were still in shock from the battle
that had raged around them. The war had come to their
homes, had left this horrific destruction on their door-
steps, and then moved on.• Fanny Bealer described the
scene of the following days: "Around us were evidences
of a great battle: The wounded, the dead and dying, all
heaped together; horses that had fallen beneath their

riders, with limbs shattered and torn, dead, wounded, and bleeding; all lying in the streets so far as we could see either up or down. Such was the awful scene spread out before us as we ventured to the front of the house on the morning of the fourth of July 1863."

IN THE DAYS after the battle, the residents of Gettysburg made it a practice to carry bottles of piñon oil or peppermint with them to mask the nauseating stench of dead men and horses decaying in the summer heat. °Fence rails could not be seen because they were thick with green bottle flies that were massing around the wounded.•

The sight of the untreated wounded was not for weak stomachs. "I asked if anyone would like to have his wound dressed. Someone replied, 'There's a man on the floor who cannot help himself; you'd better see to him.' Stooping over, I asked for his wound and he pointed to his leg. Such a horrible sight I had never seen and hope to never see again. His leg was all covered with worms," wrote Sarah Broadhead.

While the wounded were being tended, the dead were so numerous they could not be buried quickly enough. °The grave diggers had to use fence rails to roll the bodies into the graves because the flesh was coming off the bodies. The diggers vomited until there was nothing left in their systems.•

On July 7, 1863, Sarah Broadhead noted: "I am becoming more used to sights of misery. We do not know until tried what we are capable of."

The Abraham Trostle farm was typical of those of the surrounding countryside. Approximately one and a half miles south of Gettysburg, it had been the scene of horrific fighting between William Barksdale's Mississippi brigade and a Federal battery, the Ninth Massachusetts under Capt. John Bigelow. At risk was the Union left flank. After fierce hand-to-hand combat, the artillerists fell back, allowing four of their six cannon to fall into Confederate hands. At the same time the Union battery lost more than fifty horses whose rotting carcasses littered the farm for days before they were cremated.

With thousands of dead to bury and wounded soldiers in need of care, the Sanitary Commission set up temporary headquarters at the Fahnestock brothers' store on Baltimore Street. In 1863 the store was the town's leading dry-goods store owned by three brothers—James, Henry, and Edward—who had acquired the business in 1855 from their retired father, Samuel. At the time of the battle, Edward Fahnestock was serving as a lieutenant colonel of the 165th Pennsylvania Infantry in Virginia. The Sanitary Commission, whose goals included raising the hygienic standards of the camps and improving the soldiers' diet, was allowed to use the building only until Edward's return, which occurred on July 25. By that time, the commission was ready to reestablish its headquarters at Camp Letterman on the outskirts of town.

The corpses of dead men were not all
GAC that fouled the ground. °The battle had also exacted a toll on the animals used by the armies. Approximately five thousand dead animals littered the countryside, and the majority of these were horses. Since there was not a sufficient work force to bury the soldiers, something else had to be done with the animal corpses. The horses, too big to bury, were piled up and burned on pyres made of fence rails doused with kerosene.

These mounds of horseflesh, as big as a room, burned for as long as two weeks. There were reports of people sickened by the smell and some even dying from the odor, the filth, and everything that had been forced into their systems while they worked with the dead, the dying, and the wounded in Gettysburg.• "I fear we shall be visited with pestilence, for every breath we draw is made ugly by the stench," Sarah Broadhead confessed.

In the chaos surrounding the battle and its aftermath, many of the wounded were neglected or even forgotten
CG entirely. °One building of the Lutheran Seminary had been in Confederate hands since the first day of the battle. As many as four or five hundred wounded men had been brought there. Two days after the battle, Sarah Broadhead visited the site to do whatever she could to help. She found that the rain that fell as the battle ended had flooded the building's basement. There she found scores of wounded men floundering in water.• "Men wounded in three or four places, not able to help themselves the least bit, lay almost swimming in water," she wrote in her diary on July 8, 1863.

TC   °Sarah, another woman, and a few nurses carried nearly one hundred men to the fourth floor of the semi-
CG nary building.• °While moving them caused the men a great deal of pain, because many of them had not been treated for their wounds, the women saved their lives•
°without regarding whether they wore blue or gray.•

Although the Lutheran Seminary and the High Street Schoolhouse continued to function as hospitals, by July

15 the Union army began moving the wounded from the homes and churches of Gettysburg to newly established Camp Letterman, a mile east of town. Here, a new general hospital could be served by railroad.

"A line of stretchers, a mile and a half in length, each bearing a hero who had fought nigh to death, told us where our work lay. And we commenced it at once," wrote Sophronia Buckland, a government nurse, describing Camp Letterman on July 18, 1863.

°Judged by a few surviving photographs, Camp Letterman was the best facility the army could create, with tents in orderly rows and attendants standing by, guards in the distance, and decorations on the tents. The patients' cots were on wooden platform floors with sheets on the cots. Those conveniences, however, were not available until at least a month after the battle.

The original army hospitals, such as the Second Corps hospital, were much more primitive. Photographs of the area show muskets jammed into the ground with a rope tied between the trigger guards and a tent thrown over the rope. There were four thousand men in the Second Corps hospital, which was laid out on a hillside along a creek. The rain that fell after the battle caused the creek to flood and to sweep twenty of these men to their deaths; they had been too weak to move to higher ground.•

Camp Letterman was erected on the George Wolf farm and opened on July 22, 1863. The ground was well suited for a hospital. The evergreen ornamentation, shown in the photograph (left) and the engraving (right) above was added for a gala event that occurred on September 23 and remained in place until the camp was deactivated in November. The general hospital included rows of large tents with cots. Drainage ditches were dug, and cooking supplies and sanitary facilities were also provided. Doctors and nurses were brought in to work in the hospital, but many women from the town volunteered to comfort the wounded, dress their injuries, and distribute food. While the commission provided some comfort to the injured soldiers, the medical care was anything but sanitary. One nurse later discribed an operation at the camp. "This surgeon [earlier characterized as drunk] . . . found [it] necessary to take off a section of the bone, and the operation was done in full view of the other patients. . . . After mangling him there for a time . . . they paused . . . to have their photographs taken, the suffering patient lying in this critical condition. . . . For three hours he was kept under the knife and saw." Remarkably, the patient survived the trauma.

With the establishment of Camp Letterman came better conditions and rigorous military order. Frank Stoke of the Pennsylvania militia, a guard at Camp Letterman, described the facility: "The hospital is composed of large tents, which cover eighty acres of ground. It is laid off in streets or avenues, which give it the appearance of a city."

The women of Gettysburg, officially no longer needed now that the military hospital had been built, were annoyed that the army had consolidated the wounded from the three primitive hospitals used since the battle. The removal of the men to Letterman meant the end of the intimate relationships they had shared with their wounded patients.

°Many women found it hard to break the bond they had developed with "their" soldiers, "their" boys. They had taken care of these men when the army had moved on, and suddenly the army told them they were no longer needed. Many refused to accept that. They went to the new hospital and offered their help.•

Fanny Bealer pointed to the difference between the care offered by the townspeople and the institutional care offered by the army: "The tents were filled with wounded men who craved good, nourishing food. So a number of the ladies had a cooking stove taken to the woods behind the seminary. And they would spend every day for weeks cooking and making nice things for the men who were suffering but were not sick and could eat

The amputation scene below (left) is probably posed, with no real operation going on. Amputation was more common in the hours after a battle than months afterward. This image was part of a series of photographs taken in October and November 1863. The white-bearded gentleman is the Reverend Dr. Gordon Winslow, who appeared in more Camp Letterman photographs than anyone else largely because he had been appointed sanitary inspector of the Sanitary Commission following the battle at Gettysburg. Winslow drowned tragically while caring for his son, who was wounded at Cold Harbor, on June 7, 1864.

The mass of tents that made up Letterman (below right) overlooked the town. Although this photograph was probably taken in late September, the camp is far from empty. Interestingly, these same heights had hosted several Confederate batteries during the battle.

SAC

anything that was offered. These men were from both armies and were grateful for all we did for them."

BP °IN THE WEEKS that followed the battle, after the dead had been buried, Gettysburg began receiving the first family members of soldiers who had been killed on the battlefield. They came to see where their husbands, their brothers, and their sons had fallen. Many tried to find the grave of a loved one so the body could be exhumed and taken home.• Unfortunately, not every body had been identified; Civil War soldiers normally did not carry identification tags. The search for loved ones was often futile, but some family members were lucky.

BP °The Union had held the field, so if there was any way that a comrade of a fallen soldier could, he would take a piece of a biscuit box or a fence rail, scribble the name of the dead soldier on it and affix a note to the humble marker pounded in the ground at the head of a grave. Thus it was easier for the families of the Union dead to recover their men.• The Confederate dead were treated with less dignity, often being buried in shallow mass graves with no markings.

"The town is as full as ever with strangers. And the old story of the inability of a village of twenty-five hundred inhabitants, overrun and eaten out by two large armies, to accommodate from ten- to twelve-thousand visitors is repeated almost hourly. Twenty are with us tonight, filling every bed and covering the floors," wrote Sarah Broadhead on July 13, 1863.

Prior to the establishment of Camp Letterman, several intermediate field hospitals, such as the one pictured above, served the wounded in numerous locations around Gettysburg. The temporary nature of the field hospitals mandated the evacuation of wounded as expeditiously as possible, with the less wounded being moved first. Repair of the railroad between Gettysburg and Hanover facilitated the quick transport of all but the most seriously wounded. Between July 7 and 22 more than eleven thousand wounded Federals and Confederates were removed from the town by rail.

A few days after the battle the corpse of a Union soldier was found in a vacant lot in town. His hand clutched a photograph of three children (below), which was published in several newspapers throughout the North in an effort to identify him. Four months later Philinda Humiston came forward to claim the body of Sgt. Amos Humiston (above) of Company C, 154th New York. Before the battle his regiment had numbered three hundred. When the roll call was taken in the evening of July 1 only three officers and fifteen men responded. Most of the remainder had been captured. The three children are, from left to right, Frank, Fred, and Alice.

Elizabeth Thorn was the wife of the caretaker at Evergreen Cemetery. While six months pregnant, she took up the task of digging graves and burying the Union dead. To many in the town, she became °an unsung hero because her husband had joined the army. He was the person responsible for the burial of anybody who died in town.● °She had tried to hire some young men to help her, but nobody lasted more than a couple days doing that kind of work. Over the next three weeks she and her elderly father buried 105 Union soldiers in Evergreen Cemetery.●

David Wills, a local attorney, spearheaded a plan that would honor the fallen Union soldiers at Gettysburg by creating the Soldiers National Cemetery. °The process of establishing the national cemetery in Gettysburg began in July 1863 as the solders were being buried. The task involved hiring someone to return to the battlefield, open up thousands of graves, determine which ones were Union soldiers, then rebury them in the national cemetery. The town required a formal bidding for the contract. The high bid was $8.00 per body and the low bid was $1.59.● The contract went to the low bidder.

By November 19, 1863, the cemetery had interred the bodies of eleven hundred soldiers, only a third of the number that would eventually rest there. Attorney Wills invited the president to the dedication ceremony and asked him to make a few appropriate remarks, but Lincoln would not be the only speaker.

°Edward Everett was the most renowned orator of the day, and he had been ambassador to England and governor of Massachusetts. The speech he offered at the dedication of the cemetery was an hour and fifty-seven minutes long. Lincoln followed him.●

°Lincoln wanted a speech that would be remembered. He needed only two minutes to offer his observations. He felt he had failed in his task. The president need not have worried.● His Gettysburg

Address became one of the most famous speeches ever delivered: "We are met on a great battlefield of that war. We have come to dedicate a portion of that field, as a final resting place for those who here gave their lives that that nation might live. It is altogether fitting and proper that we should do this. But in a larger sense, we can not dedicate—we can not consecrate—we can not hallow—this ground. The brave men, living and dead, who struggled here, have consecrated it, far above our poor power to add or detract."

JAS °The national cemetery that Lincoln dedicated was laid out in a semicircle that was divided into state sections, with each of the eighteen Northern states having state plots. There was also a section for regular soldiers of the U.S. Army and two other sections for 979 unknown soldiers.•

Sgt. Amos Humiston might have been one of those unknown soldiers except for a photograph of three children found clasped in his dead hand. The photograph was published in newspapers all over the North, setting off a search for his widow and orphaned children. His story inspired poetry and music.

"His limbs were cold. His sightless eyes were fixed upon the three sweet stars that rose in memory's skies to

In 1866 plans were made for a soldiers' orphans home in Gettysburg, financed by the sale of reproductions of the "children of the battlefield" photographs and sheet music that had been composed as part of a contest. The first twenty-two orphans arrived in late October, but the orphanage did not officially open until November 20. The Humiston children were among the first to arrive, and their mother served as one of the supervisors. The original building (above), was enlarged in 1869. Philinda Humiston remarried in that year and left Gettysburg with her three children. The home closed in 1877 lacking sufficient funds and under a cloud of accusations concerning the mistreatment of children.

In the months following the battle, thousands of bodies were disinterred for reburial in the Soldiers' National Cemetery at Gettysburg. This October 1863 photograph by Peter S. Weaver (left) shows the bodies of nineteen Federal cavalrymen being exhumed at Hanover. They had been killed on June 30, when Union and Confederate cavalry clashed at Hanover, and had been buried in the Reformed Church cemetery there. Samuel Weaver, the photographer's father, had been named to oversee the removal of all remains for the national cemetery. He stands to the far right, notebook in hand.

303

A half century after the battle, fifty thousand Federal and Confederate veterans of the battle reunited at Gettysburg. On July 3 veterans from both sides reenacted the famous assault against the middle of the Union line—Pickett's Charge (opposite page). During the reunion southerners wore gray and northerners donned dark blue. The veterans in the center are thought to be former Yankees who accompanied several Rebel veterans. This time, however, one can see smiles on their faces rather than the fear and determination that marked them fifty years earlier. The atmosphere was more solemn when the old veterans gathered at the stone wall near The Angle (near right). Several of the old soldiers died on their way home after the reunion. They had wanted to see the ground just once more where they had grasped at immortality.

light him o'er death's sea," is a part of James G. Clark's "The Children of the Battlefield."

In November 1863, Humiston's widow recognized the photograph and came forward. Sales of the children's picture, the poetry, and the sheet music were so great that the proceeds funded the creation of the Soldiers Orphans Home in Gettysburg. Humiston's children were educated there, and his widow became its first matron.

Old soldiers returned regularly to Gettysburg for

JAS reunions. °At the fiftieth anniversary, fifty thousand veterans descended on the town. At the seventy-fifth anniversary in 1938, two thousand old soldiers stayed in a tent camp erected for them on the battlefield. Sponsored by the federal government, few chances were taken: all the Union soldiers were placed on one side of the road and all the Confederates on the other side. There was little chance of anything happening—the average age of the veterans was ninety-five. Not one old soldier died during that entire week, but some died returning home. They had wanted to live for one more reunion.•

For old soldiers and civilians alike, time had quieted the raging passions stirred by the greatest battle of the

GAC Civil War. °The old soldiers had come away hating war, realizing the brutality of it, but the other side of the story was that nowhere else could they ever have that experience again—a unique experience that created bonds of comradeship.•

These old soldiers were the survivors, but six thousand others took no memories away from the bloody field of Gettysburg. They were the fallen, each with family, friends, and loved ones—each dying a personal death. Those men might have seen more than the fighting around them, something that told them their suffering would soon be over. Alice Powers told of her mother's tending to a mortally wounded soldier: "Mother aided one man mortally wounded by a saber cut across his face. He said, 'Angel hands' then died."

The farmers of Adams County returned to their lands, determined to turn the battleground once more into productive fields of wheat, oats, and corn. Occasionally their plow points struck an unexploded artillery shell, and the battle would claim another life. These deaths reminded the citizens of Gettysburg of what they already knew—that the consequences of that three-day battle would last forever.

GETTYSBURG: THE UNSUNG HEROES

THE BLOODIEST BATTLE IN NORTH America, Gettysburg forged the names of several generals into the bedrock of American history: Robert E. Lee, James Longstreet, George E. Pickett, George Gordon Meade, Winfield Scott Hancock. Yet there were more than 160,000 men who formed the two armies pitted against each other for three days on the Pennsylvania countryside, and within their ranks were many unsung heroes who, in Abraham Lincoln's words, "shall not have died in vain" nor be forgotten.

The toll for this three-day battle was almost fifty thousand dead or wounded Union and Confederate soldiers. As these men fell on the battlefield, most were remembered only as statistics, not as the heroes they were. Abraham Lincoln alluded to their contributions in his concluding words at the national cemetery dedication in Gettysburg, "The world . . . can never forget what they did here."

JIR °The greatest tragedy of the Civil War was that both sides were fighting for the same thing: an America for the future. While there were great figures in that war whom history has remembered, there were countless others who were willing to die for something other than themselves. Their stories must be told because they are not merely an inspiration for America; they also formed the backbone of what this nation has become. They are the faces that have

BP no faces.• °They are not as well known as Lee, Meade, Longstreet, and Hancock, who have become part of the mythology of the battle,• but their contributions and sacrifices are indispensable to the story of Gettysburg.

ECB	Edwin C. Bearss
GAC	Gregory A. Cocco
SH	Scott Hartwig
JIR	James I. Robertson Jr.
BP	Brian Pohanka

Robert E. Lee described James Johnston Pettigrew as a brave soldier and an accomplished officer. Prior to Gettysburg, Pettigrew had participated in the bombardment of Fort Sumter, but the only combat he saw after that was at Seven Pines, where he was wounded and captured. Exchanged two months later, he was given a brigade in Henry Heth's newly created division, which led the Confederate advance on Gettysburg. Pettigrew personally reconnoitered the town and reported the presence of Federal cavalry. His superiors—A. P. Hill and Heth—discounted his word, believing the closest Union force was in Middleburg.

James Johnston Pettigrew (Day 1)

FEW OUTSIDE OF North Carolina have ever heard of Brig. Gen. James Johnston Pettigrew, a man who sincerely believed in the South's constitutional right to leave the Union. "Bad times are ahead in this country. It is humiliating to think that after eighty years of freedom, men are to be found declaiming against the American revolution and principles on which it was successfully fought," he wrote.

°Pettigrew, who went by his middle name of Johnston, turned thirty-five years old the day after the battle of Gettysburg. He was a patrician, born to the landed gentry of wealth and distinction. He entered the University of North Carolina at age fourteen and graduated at age seventeen, after which he was granted a professorship at the U.S. Naval Observatory in Washington, D.C. He was fond of mathematics, astronomy, and literature. He was a man with a sharp mind and a deep soul. He was also a romantic who had traveled throughout Europe, spoke six languages, and had studied law.• His friend and fellow scholar William Henry Trescott said that Pettigrew was the epitome of the North Carolina motto: He was a man who desired to be, not to seem.

°Pettigrew was well liked because he did not flaunt his knowledge or talents. He settled in Charleston, South Carolina, and practiced law with his cousin James Petigru (who preferred the old Scottish spelling of the name). In addition to serving in the South Carolina legislature, he became a colonel of militia and captured the first piece of Federal property after the state seceded: Castle Pinckney, a small fort in Charleston Harbor. When the war started, he returned to North Carolina and accepted the colonelcy of the Twenty-second North Carolina Infantry Regiment. In January 1862 he was appointed brigadier general in spite of his protests.•

Pettigrew had been an aide to South Carolina Gov. Francis Pickens and led the militia to confiscate Castle Pinckney in Charleston Harbor. He faced only verbal resistance from Lt. R. K. Meade, himself a Virginian, and an ordnance sergeant. Following the bombardment of Fort Sumter, Pinckney was little used—other than the garrison's being photographed in August 1861 (left)—until Federal prisoners began arriving following the battle of First Manassas.

Five months later Pettigrew was severely wounded and captured at the battle of Seven Pines, Virginia. He was exchanged and returned to the Confederate army in time to participate in the Gettysburg campaign. Although he could not know it at the time, Pettigrew would play a leading role in the opening of the battle.

On June 30, 1863, Pettigrew's North Carolinians were ordered to scout the town of Gettysburg because the division commander, Maj. Gen. Henry Heth, had heard a rumor that the town had a supply of shoes in storage for the Union army. Pettigrew came close enough to the town to see regular Union soldiers, not the militia that he had been told to expect. Mindful of Lee's orders not to bring on a general engagement, Pettigrew turned his men around and went back the way he had come.

°Pettigrew reported to his corps commander, A. P. Hill, and his divisional commander, Heth, that the cavalry he had seen must have been from the Army of the Potomac, which was supposed to be in Middleburg, Virginia, unaware of the Confederates' movement. Hill and Heth did not believe Pettigrew; he was a lawyer, not a West Point–educated soldier like themselves. They thought since Pettigrew had been down in North Carolina, a minor theater of the Civil War, he was not capable of evaluating what he saw. They insisted that all he had seen were home-guard troops.•

The next morning, July 1, 1863, Heth took his entire division toward Gettysburg, but Pettigrew had been right. The Union forces he had seen were two brigades

309

Before setting out for his second invasion of the North, Lee reorganized his army into three corps. First Corps remained under James Longstreet, Second Corps was given to Richard S. Ewell, and the new corps was entrusted to A. P. Hill (above). Hill had a reputation for being high-strung and impatient, and he had attacked the enemy without orders before. He had graduated from West Point in 1847 in the same class as Henry Heth and John Gibbon. Now Heth's men were advancing against Gibbon's former command—the Iron Brigade—on the outskirts of Gettysburg. Hill's corps would oppose Gibbon's division later in the fighting, but when the fighting began, Hill was ill and not on the battlefield.

The target of Johnston's reconnaissance was known more for its thriving carriage industry than for its warehousing dry goods—which allegedly attracted the Confederates' attention. An obscure county seat, Gettysburg had its share of attorneys, bakers, carpenters, clothiers, grocers, inn keepers, printers, and blacksmiths as well as farmers. In this photograph, looking west from the town square, the building at the corner is George Arnold's clothing store and savings bank. Christ Lutheran Church is marked by the cupola that dominates the center of the image. The street acted as a funnel for Federal troops falling back to Cemetery Ridge.

of cavalry under Union Brig. Gen. John Buford. Heth, over Pettigrew's objections, had brought on the general engagement that Lee had not wanted to precipitate until his entire army was at Gettysburg. That afternoon, Pettigrew's North Carolinians were ordered to the woods near the McPherson farm.

°Also in those woods was one of the best units in the Army of the Potomac, the Twenty-fourth Michigan Regiment, part of the Iron Brigade—five battle-toughened regiments of troops from Wisconsin, Indiana, and Michigan. It was Pettigrew's job to drive the Michiganders from those woods. The men of the Twenty-fourth, among the first Federal troops on the field, knew they had to hold their position until the rest of the First Corps came up. They knew they had to hold the Confederates off at all costs. Inevitably, what followed became the deadliest fight in the battle of Gettysburg.•

"The fighting was terrible. Two lines were pouring volleys into each other at a distance not greater than twenty paces," wrote Confederate Maj. John Thomas Jones of the Twenty-sixth North Carolina. °The battle lines were formed at twenty to forty paces from one another, and the men just blazed away at each other, shooting down first dozens, then hundreds of men.•

Henry King Burgwyn

CALLED "THE BOY colonel" for his youthful twenty-one years, Henry King Burgwyn served as commander of the Twenty-sixth North Carolina. He led his men directly at the Michiganders. Ten men fell bearing the colors of the Twenty-sixth, shot down one after another in rapid order. Burgwyn watched in horror as the torn and bloody flag passed from hand to hand. °Finally Burgwyn reached down and picked up the regimental colors himself. He was in front of his men, urging them forward, silhouetted against the sky, when he too was shot and mortally wounded. His men laid him on the ground, and just before he died, he said, "The Lord's will be done. I have fallen in defense of my country."•

Twenty-one-year-old Col. Henry King Burgwyn commanded the Twenty-sixth North Carolina. He was the youngest colonel in the Confederate army. In the afternoon of July 1 his men joined the attack against the Twenty-fourth Michigan and Nineteenth Indiana of the Iron Brigade near the McPherson farm, but the "damned black-hatted fellows" held their ground. Burgwyn watched his color-guard shot down then grabbed the battle flag and was exhorting his men when a bullet struck and killed him. Thirteen color-bearers went down that day. Only 216 North Carolinians answered roll call that night. They had entered the battle with 800 soldiers.

°The Twenty-sixth North Carolina, which had gone into the battle as the largest regiment in the Army of Northern Virginia, had 584 men shot down of its initial 800. The Eleventh North Carolina lost 250 out of 550 men. The Federals had it just as bad. The Twenty-fourth Michigan had the highest number of men killed or mortally wounded of any regiment in the Union army at Gettysburg. Every regiment in the Iron Brigade lost more than half its men during the fighting of the first morning. Out of 1,800 men engaged, the Iron Brigade lost nearly 1,200. Such high casualties could be attributed to the fact that both sides displayed the most sublime bravery that it was possible for American soldiers to show.•

Pettigrew and his command eventually drove the Iron Brigade from the woods. Somehow he survived the battle without injury. Badly in need of rest, Pettigrew's brigade was held back on July 2, but it would be called upon on July 3. Their losses that first day were tremendous, but they would be nothing compared to what lay ahead. For others, the battle had just begun.

°THE REAL HEROES of the war are rarely mentioned in official reports, since they served almost anonymously far down in

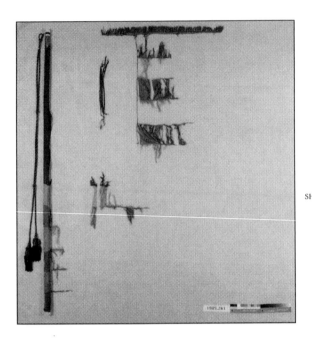

The remnants of the flag of the 143d Pennsylvania (above) survived better than Sgt. Benjamin Crippen, the color-bearer who bore the banner into combat. During the back-and-forth fighting near the McPherson farm, Crippen momentarily found himself alone in the face of Heth's Confederates. Lacking a weapon, he shook his fist at the Southerners. The gesture may have rallied his company briefly, but it cost Crippen his life.

the ranks where gallantry produces gallantry. The men in the ranks rarely received the credit that they deserved.• One example of many gallant gestures at Gettysburg came from a nineteen-year-old Pennsylvania farmer on July 1.

Sgt. Benjamin Crippen

SH °SGT. BEN CRIPPEN carried the colors of the 143d Pennsylvania infantry. On July 1, in the heavy fighting that took place near the McPherson farm, the 143d had reached a point where Confederate attacks were coming at it from two directions. Already having suffered terrible losses, the Pennsylvanians were ordered to retreat. Crippen apparently did not hear the order because he did not fall back.•

BP °As the 143d Pennsylvania was being driven back toward Seminary Ridge, the men saw their flag back near the McPherson farm and attempted to rally around it. Crippen turned to rejoin his regiment, but the Confederates were closing in on him. He turned back to the onrushing Southerners and shook his fist in their faces, some of whom were only paces away. That gesture of defiance cost Crippen his life.• A. P. Hill saw Crippen's gesture and its aftermath and lamented, "It is a shame to kill so brave a man."

Lt. Bayard Wilkeson

As THE FIRST day wore on, the Confederates were holding a solid defensive position when the Union's Eleventh Army Corps, including Battery G of the Fourth U.S. Artillery, came on the field. Nearby, *New York Times* correspondent Samuel Wilkeson had a special interest in the battle. Battery G was commanded by his son, nineteen-year-old Lt. Bayard Wilkeson.

SH °The younger Wilkeson commanded more than one hundred men and was responsible for more than one hundred horses. The vehicles, the equipment, the tactics employed, the decisions that were made, all rested on the shoulders of a nineteen-year-old boy who had the training and the maturity to execute the orders he was given.•

Wilkeson led his battery up to Barlow's Knoll to support the infantry around him. Confederate Gen. Jubal Early brought his infantry and artillery to bear on the Union position with sixteen cannon against Wilkeson's four.

SH °The Yankee battery earned the admiration of the Confederates who were firing upon it. Wilkeson himself was on a white horse, so he was easy to see. He rode about his battery directing the fire of his guns until finally a Confederate shell struck him, knocking him from his horse and mangling him terribly.•

CB °The Union position started to collapse, and the Federals began falling back. Young Wilkeson's leg was hanging only by its tendons. He took out his jackknife, put a tourniquet above his wound, and amputated his own leg. Unfortunately, the loss of blood and the shock were too much for him. He died within minutes. The elder Wilkeson was only a few miles away. His press reports that afternoon were critical of the Union command decisions that had placed his son and his four guns in that advanced position.•

Nineteen-year-old Union Lt. Bayard Wilkeson's battery on the right side of the Federal line was heavily shelled the first day at Gettysburg. Wilkeson's right leg was nearly severed when he was struck by a projectile. He amputated his own leg with a pocketknife, only to die a few hours later. His father, Samuel (below), a correspondent for a New York paper, was in Meade's headquarters when he learned of his son's death.

THE DEATHS OF Burgwyn, Crippen, and Wilkeson illus-
JIR trate something about the waste of war. °Not only were thousands of men lost in battle, but so was the statesmanship they never practiced, the music and art they never produced, the great works of literature they never conceived. The nation lost the sons and daughters these men never fathered as well as what those children might have achieved in their society and their children's children after them.•

SH °The country lost a significant part of a youthful, dynamic generation because the ones who died were the best the country had to offer. The worst soldiers were the ones who hunkered down, who hung back,

313

who were not out front leading and making decisions. It was the brave men in front who paid the highest price with their lives.•

Col. Strong Vincent

ONE BRAVE MAN from the North who fit that description was °Col. Strong Vincent, a lawyer from Erie, Pennsylvania. An 1859 graduate of Harvard, he was an athletic, barrel-chested, powerfully built man who looked the part of a leader. While he was a lawyer by training, his personality was that of a soldier. Like so many others, Vincent had much to lose on the battlefield, including the companionship of a young pregnant wife who had given him her riding crop to carry on the field as a keepsake. They had married on the same day he had gone to war.• Early in the war Vincent took command of the Eighty-third Pennsylvania.

Like most men of his time, Vincent's correspondence with his wife was peppered with statements regarding the righteousness of their cause and the solace their wives should feel knowing that a good husband had performed his duty for his country should he fall in the face of the enemy: "My dear Elizabeth, surely the right will prevail. If I live, we will rejoice over our country's success. If I fall, remember you have given your husband as a sacrifice to the most righteous cause that ever widowed a woman."

°Vincent was a hard-nosed officer whose men did not like him much on the training field, but once they had been in battle with him, they learned that he was the type of officer they needed so they would perform well under fire. He had the ability to command and to command respect.•

In 1862 Vincent was stricken with camp fever, something similar to deadly malaria. °He was ill enough that he should not have gone back to the army, but he was determined to return to his brigade

At the age of thirty-three Brig. Gen. Gouverneur K. Warren was Meade's chief of engineers. On the afternoon of July 2 he was sent to investigate rifle shots in the area of Little Round Top. He found only a signal station but discovered that the left flank of the Union line was unsupported. He quickly sent word to Meade and then began calling up whatever units he could find to fill the gap.

to lead his men. Vincent believed that the Union should be saved and that he had a role to play in preserving it. He also believed that his life was worth sacrificing to do that. So he went back to his brigade when the time came,• and to some extent the Union army was saved at Gettysburg because he did.

BP °Gettysburg was a battle that hinged on the actions, not of senior generals like Lee and Meade, but of subordinate commanders. No part of the battlefield was more illustrative of individual regimental and brigade commanders' rising to meet the crisis than the fight for Little Round Top.•

At the extreme left of the Union line, Little Round Top was a rocky, partly wooded hill rising 650 feet above the countryside. Union Brig. Gen. Gouverneur K. Warren had ridden to the summit on the afternoon of July 2 and seen Longstreet's soldiers advancing toward that part of the line. Little Round Top was totally undefended. Warren knew he had to get some men on those heights or the entire Union line was in danger of being swept away. Normally he would have to go through channels to ask other generals to put men on the slopes, but Warren knew there was no time to follow protocol.

BP
SH °Warren reacted immediately, and he and his staff officers went looking for any units they could find.• °One of Warren's staff officers came across Brig. Gen. James Barnes's division. The first unit in the line was Vincent's brigade. The staff officer addressed Vincent, asking for Barnes. When Vincent was apprised of the situation, he accepted the responsibility of moving his brigade to Little Round Top. He ordered Col. James Rice of the Forty-fourth New York to lead the brigade up the hill while he rode ahead to look at the ground. The North would forever be indebted to Vincent for that move.•

One of Vincent's regiments was the Twentieth Maine commanded by Col. Joshua Lawrence Chamberlain. "Col. Vincent indicated to me the ground my regiment

An 1859 Harvard graduate from Erie, Pennsylvania, Strong Vincent was an attorney before the war. At twenty-six he commanded a brigade during the battle. When word came that troops were needed at the crest of Little Round Top, he acted without orders to deploy his brigade into the void on the Union left. Vincent positioned the Twentieth Maine on the left flank and the Sixteenth Michigan on the right; the Eighty-third Pennsylvania and the Forty-fourth New York solidified the center of the line. Skirmishers were then sent to the front to await the Confederate attack.

Gouverneur K. Warren (above) was born across the river from West Point and graduated from the academy in 1850. He was teaching there when the war broke out. Warren commanded a brigade during the Peninsula campaign and the battles of Second Manassas and Antietam, but at Gettysburg he was chief engineer of the Army of the Potomac and as such did not command troops.

Col. Joshua Lawrence Chamberlain (below) commanded the Twentieth Maine. A professor of rhetoric and languages before the war, he could enlist only after his college granted him a sabbatical for study overseas. Vincent placed him at the end of the line with orders to hold at all costs, which the Twentieth did by means of an unlikely charge when their ammunition ran low.

was to occupy and that a desperate attack was expected in order to turn that position. He concluded by telling me to hold that ground at all hazards," Chamberlain reported afterward.

°The man remembered as the hero of Little Round Top is Chamberlain, but to do so is to forget Vincent, the man who commanded that brigade. It was Vincent who took the initiative to post Chamberlain there at that crucial point.•

°Vincent did not wait for orders from his division commander. Instead he moved to the point of danger to buy time, something that Napoleon said was the most important element a soldier could have. Thanks to Vincent, the Union troops held that piece of ground. It was there also where Vincent was mortally wounded.•

°As the fighting escalated along the front of Vincent's brigade from left to right, he jumped up on a boulder and flourished his wife's riding crop. "Don't give an inch," he shouted to his men. Shortly thereafter a bullet slammed into him and pitched him off the rock. He was carried partly down the slope and lay there bleeding while his brigade teetered in the balance.• The Southerners were hurled back after hours of fighting and after Chamberlain and his regiment had charged the Confederates as a last resort.

Vincent probably never knew of his promotion to brigadier general for his defense of Little Round Top. He died on July 7. °He had wanted to live because of his wife and the imminent birth of his child, but he could not survive his wound. Two months later his wife gave birth to a baby girl. Sadly, the child lived only a year. When she died, she was buried alongside her father.•

Col. Patrick Henry O'Rorke

VINCENT WAS NOT ALONE in rushing troops to the summit of Little Round Top. Another officer to do so was Col. Patrick Henry O'Rorke, of whom one officer later wrote, "Up to that time in my life I had never felt a grief so sharply nor realized the significance of death so well as then. For him to die was to me like losing a brother."

O'Rorke was a native of Cavan, Ireland. His parents had brought him to America as an infant, and he grew up in Rochester, New York. As the top student in high school there, he received an appointment to the U.S. Military Academy. °He entered West Point at age twenty and finished first in the class of June 1861, the same class in which George Armstrong Custer finished last. After graduation O'Rorke went into the Corps of Engineers and served on the Gulf Coast until given command of the 140th New York Regiment.•

°O'Rorke had to overcome a lot of prejudice because the Irish were not held in very high esteem in mid-nineteenth-century America. Nonetheless, he was a man of determination, and those who encountered him were convinced that he was going to make his mark in this country and in the army.

As General Warren came down from Little Round Top looking for troops to defend the heights, he saw O'Rorke and shouted, "Will you bring your regiment? Will you follow me? Will you bring your regiment up on the hill to defend it?" Proper military procedure demanded that O'Rorke consult with his brigade commander who had to go through his division commander who had to go through his corps commander before he could do

As the battle raged on Little Round Top, the Sixteenth Michigan desperately held back the Fourth and Fifth Texas, having beaten off two assaults. The fighting was hand to hand when the Union colors fell. The regiment's three companies on the right and the color-guard started to withdraw to a higher position. Strong Vincent ran forward to stabilize this right flank when he was mortally wounded. The Sixteenth was on the verge of collapse when reinforcements arrived, recently rallied by Warren.

The support that arrived in time to bolster the Sixteenth Michigan was led by Col. Patrick Henry O'Rorke. He was a native of Cavan, Ireland, but grew up in Rochester, New York. O'Rorke graduated at the head of his class at West Point in June 1861—the second class of 1861. In command of the 140th New York at Gettysburg, he responded to General Warren's plea for troops to defend Little Round Top. The 140th New York arrived in time to support the Sixteenth Michigan, but O'Rorke never made it to the summit. The twenty-seven-year-old colonel was killed at the head of his troops.

anything.• Like Vincent, O'Rorke did not stand on ceremony. Instead he raced his regiment up to Little Round Top where Vincent had just been shot.

BP   °In the forefront of the charge up the hill, flourishing his sword, O'Rorke was shot through the neck and instantly killed. His death was a great loss because he was a man who could have possibly finished the war in command of a division. He was a man like Vincent who was destined for promotion had he lived. O'Rorke's wife, Clara, his childhood sweetheart whom he had married in July 1862, was devastated by her husband's death. A devout Catholic, she became a nun and spent the rest of her life in a Catholic order.•

GAC   °MANY HAVE VIEWED the battle at Gettysburg as something exciting, glorious, and wonderful for the Union and as a demonstration of the resolve of the Confederacy. What they ignore are the long lines of graves and unceremonious trenches filled with Southerners and Northerners whose families never knew where they fell or where they were buried.•

Brig. Gen. William Barksdale

MANY WHO DIED at Gettysburg have remained anonymous. Others were well known before the war began. Brig. Gen. William Barksdale was an orphan who

The Round Tops (right) signified the far left of the Federal line. Had the Confederates succeeded in taking Little Round Top, they would have threatened the rear of Meade's forces and would have been able to pry the Northerners from their position. Possession of the Round Tops by Lee would have necessitated the abandonment of the line along Cemetery Ridge. Warren's moves to occupy the heights prevented the line's collapse and cemented the Federals' strong defensive position.

became an outspoken leader for Southern rights. He fought in the Mexican War and served four terms in the U.S. House as a representative from Mississippi.

°Before the war Barksdale was called a "fire-eater," an ardent supporter of states' rights and secession. Of all the fire-eaters and all the men who advocated secession and Southern independence, he was the most prominent soldier to emerge. The others did a lot of talking; Barksdale did a lot of fighting.•

Barksdale joined the Southern army as a colonel. In 1862 he was promoted to brigadier general and given command of four Mississippi regiments. At Fredericksburg, Virginia, in December 1862, Barksdale's sharpshooters tried to keep Northern forces from crossing the river and investing the town. The Union countered with artillery. After two hours, the barrage finally ended when the Northern commanders believed they had driven Barksdale out. °As the Union engineers resumed building bridges across the Rappahannock River, Barksdale's brigade emerged from their cover and opened fire on the engineers again. It was one of the South's great moments, and it took place before the eyes of much of the Army of Northern Virginia. Eventually Barksdale was ordered out of the town and back to the safety of the rest of the army. When he arrived on the battlefield at Gettysburg, Barksdale was a

Forty-one-year-old William Barksdale (above) had been trained as a lawyer and had fought in the Mexican War, but his professional career was that of a newspaper editor and a politician. As a congressman he had been a Democrat and a fire-eater. As a commander he had led troops at Manassas and on the Virginia Peninsula. His brigade—the Thirteenth, Seventeenth, Eighteenth, and Twenty-first Mississippi Regiments—had distinguished itself at Fredericksburg (below), contesting the river crossing.

In the early evening of July 2, William Barksdale rode to the front of his Mississippi brigade, pointed toward the high ground between the two peach orchards, and ordered his four regiments forward towards the Yankee artillery ensconced in the orchards. The Mississippians rose up with a Rebel yell and followed him as he waved his hat, his white hair blowing in the wind. When they neared the Sherfy farmhouse, just west of the Emmitsburg Road, the 114th Pennsylvania—also known as Collis's Zouaves—advanced against them to protect the Federal battery. The fighting at the Sherfy farm is depicted above with Barksdale at the head of the Thirteenth and Seventeenth Mississippi as they clashed with the Zouaves. The Pennsylvanians fell back, forcing the Union artillerists to withdraw to save their guns. With the Federal line broken, Barksdale's unit charged toward Cemetery Ridge. There three New York regiments and numerous Federal batteries responded. In the fighting that followed, the Southern general received several mortal wounds in the chest and fell to ground. He died in Union hands.

well-known soldier, someone who drew the confidence of the army.•

In the attack on July 2 the Confederates charged *en echelon*, in successive waves. Barksdale was anxious to attack. °He was like a caged lion. He kept asking to go in, to join the charge. There were Yankees in his front, and he wanted to engage and defeat them. Finally Barksdale's brigade was ordered to advance around 6:00 P.M. on July 2. The brigade executed what one Southern columnist dubbed the most magnificent charge of the war.•

°Barksdale led his men across the Emmitsburg Road, crashing through the center of the Union Third Corps line, right through the line of red-trousered 114th Pennsylvania Zouaves, and through the Peach Orchard. Three of his regiments swung north and started pushing Brig. Gen. Andrew Humphreys's division up the Emmitsburg Road. The Twenty-first Mississippi kept going straight ahead. In the midst of this onslaught rode a large balding man on a big horse. It was Barksdale waving his hat.•

°Barksdale always went into battle, especially at Gettysburg, with tremendous enthusiasm. One soldier commented on how his face was radiant with joy when under fire. He looked happy and sublime as he led his men through the Peach Orchard.•

SH °Moving against the Mississippians was a New York brigade commanded by Col. George Willard. Willard's brigade confronted Barksdale's. According to one account, Barksdale was swearing and shouting at his men not to give way when he was suddenly struck several times and fell from his horse. His men were forced to retreat, leaving a mortally wounded Barksdale on the field.

"After dark we searched among the dead and wounded until we found him," wrote Pvt. David Parker of the Fourteenth Vermont. "He commenced by telling me that he was dying and that he was leaving a good and loving wife and two sons. If I remember right, eleven and thirteen. He became unconscious talking of his family. He breathed his last about daylight or a little before. After the battle, I marked the spot where he fell from his horse."

Isaac E. Avery (above) was at the head of the North Carolina Brigade—the Sixth, Twenty-first, and Fifty-seventh North Carolina—that joined Brig. Gen. Harry Hays's Louisianans in the Confederate attack on Cemetery Hill at dusk on July 2. The two brigades had to maneuver across rocky ground under fire from Union batteries on the heights, but Avery did not survive this first part of the assault. He was shot from his horse when he was struck in the neck. Before he died, he wrote a last message to his family: "Tell my father I fell with my face to the enemy." Avery's father was a leader of the North Carolina home guard, and he was later killed while pursuing a Federal raiding party.

Col. Isaac Avery

As BARKSDALE SPOKE his dying words, another Confederate soldier was about to give his life for the cause. Isaac Avery was a cheerful, two-hundred-pound businessman from North Carolina. He ran the family farm and helped build the Western North Carolina Railroad. On July 2 Colonel Avery led three North Carolina regiments against the Union right anchored at Cemetery Hill.

JIR °Avery was another soldier who was quite willing to give his all for the cause in which he believed. At Gettysburg he led his men into action as bravely as any professional soldier ever could. Avery was shot at the base of his neck, and he fell to the ground wounded. As he lay there, he asked for pen and paper to write a note to his successor, Samuel Tate: "Major, please tell my father that I died with my face to the enemy."•

A graduate of Harvard, Lt. Col. Charles Mudge headed the Second Massachusetts. On the morning of July 3 his regiment and the Twenty-seventh Indiana were ordered to charge across Spangler's Meadow. Mudge and his officers could not believe the directive, but he turned and said, "Well, men, it's murder, but it's the order." He gave the order, and the Second sprang over a small stone wall and into the open field where they were completely exposed. Mudge was shot down in the middle of the field and died.

GAC

Avery died, but the note made it back to North Carolina and to his father.

°That type of bravery was quite common among soldiers on both sides. They wanted to leave something behind; they wanted their families to know they died doing their duty. That was important to them. They knew their memory would be all their families would have because they also knew their bodies would probably never reach home. Many of them would be buried on the fields where they fell.•

By NIGHTFALL ON July 2 thousands lay dead or wounded. For the survivors the morning would bring not peace but another terrible day's battle. At dawn on the next day, smoke lingered above the bodies strewn about the fields of Gettysburg. Thousands more fell on July 3.

Lt. Col. Charles Mudge

SH °HIS PROFESSORS AT Harvard did not think that Charles Mudge was as serious about his studies as he should have been. He violated all the rules as a student, but he was a good soldier. Mudge became commander of the Second Massachusetts Infantry, one of the early units recruited by the state. The Second saw a great deal of combat before ever reaching Gettysburg.•

Early on the morning of July 3, Lieutenant Colonel Mudge was ordered to lead a senseless charge toward the Confederate lines across an open meadow near Spangler's
SH Spring on the far right, near Culp's Hill. °The order was a classic example that soldiers always have and always will encounter: The person at the top who issues the order does not understand what it means to carry it out because he does not know the real situation at the front.

The reality Mudge and his men faced was an order to charge across a marshy meadow that would force them to move forward carefully and, in the process, make them very easy targets for the Southerners. There was no cover in the meadow, and the Confederates had not retreated from their strong position.

After Mudge received the order, he asked the staff officer, "Are you sure that's the order?" The officer replied that he was. Mudge turned to his men and said, "Well, men, it's murder but it's the order."•

GAC ○Mudge's regiment rushed forward and took the wooded area in only a few minutes, but they lost 136 men while crossing that meadow. During the attack Mudge was shot just below the throat. He bled to death within seconds. Nothing was gained by the gallant charge, but a great deal was lost in the form of good men and officers like the well-respected and well-liked Mudge, who was a clear thinker and a born soldier. He was cut down at a time when he could have done so much for the Union cause.•

James Johnston Pettigrew (Day 3)

THE SLAUGHTER THAT killed Mudge was only one move in the sprawling battle that raged around Gettysburg that last day. What little remained of Johnston Pettigrew's command after the first day's fighting was again called into action on July 3. The three-day conflict was about to take an important turn. The final blow for the Confederacy was the disastrous attack known as Pickett's Charge.

BP ○When some think of the Confederate armies, they think of Virginia—the site of many significant battles and the home of Lee, Stuart, and Jackson—but the Southern state that lost the most men during the war was North Carolina: more than forty thousand. When reference is mistakenly made to Pickett's Charge, a great disservice is done to those North Carolina troops led by Pettigrew who made it past the stone wall at Gettysburg.• "Tell a man in this army that North Carolinians failed to go where Virginians went,

Johnston Pettigrew assumed command of his division after Henry Heth suffered a head wound. When that division began the long march across the Wheat Field toward the center of the Union line, Pettigrew was at the head. He was wounded in the hand but refused to leave the field until the assault ended.

323

From the series of Gettysburg paintings by Edwin Forbes, this image depicts Pickett's Charge from a position along Seminary Ridge looking toward the center of the Union line, which was marked by Ziegler's grove on the left and the large copse of trees on the right. The Federal line itself is delineated by the solid puffs of smoke with the scattered puffs of artillery fire behind it.

and he would think you a fool," said Maj. John Thomas Jones of the Twenty-sixth North Carolina.

JIR °Pettigrew became a hero at Gettysburg. He was a division commander, a brigadier acting as a major general. By rights and protocol, he could have stayed behind the lines as Pickett may have done, but Pettigrew loved his men and his country, and he personally led his men forward. He was in the middle of the field when he was shot through the hand. When the attack was repulsed, Pettigrew stood his ground and was one of the last to leave the field, like a mother hen shooing her young chickens back to safety.•

Pettigrew's brigade numbered 3,000 men on July 1. By July 4, only 835 men remained. The rest were killed, wounded, or missing. Pettigrew survived the charge with his minor wound, but he did not survive the Gettysburg campaign.

BP °On July 14, as Lee's army was recrossing the Potomac, making its escape from Meade's pursuing Federals, a Union cavalry charge came thundering down on Pettigrew's rear guard at Falling Waters, Maryland. Pettigrew fell as he tried to mount his horse. As he struggled back up to his feet, he tried to defend himself, but a Union trooper shot him down.• The Yankee trooper was then pulled from his horse and killed. Pettigrew lingered for a few days before finally dying. His last words were, "It is time to be going."

SH °ONE OF THE things that stand out about the unsung heroes of Gettysburg is that these soldiers always stepped forward when their country called. Whether their allegiance was to the Confederacy or the Union, they offered themselves because they believed in what they were doing. No one could ever offer any more than that.•

BP

°The soldiers who fought at Gettysburg have been memorialized in books, regimental histories, and monuments on the battlefield. It is important, however, to remember those men who fought and fell at Gettysburg not just as monuments or as names in a book or as statistics, but as people. They were people who had lives beyond their military careers. They were not just men in uniform trying to kill other men in uniform. These people were human beings who had wives, children, parents, and hopes and dreams for the future.•

In his address at the dedication of the national cemetery at Gettysburg, President Lincoln knew who they were and what they had accomplished: "From these honored dead we take increased devotion to that cause for which they gave the last full measure of devotion—that we here highly resolve that these dead shall not have died in vain—that this nation, under God, shall have a new birth of freedom—and that government of the people, by the people, for the people, shall not perish from the earth."

By the turn of the twentieth century, monuments, memorials, and statues had been erected to commemorate the great names and celebrated heroes of the Civil War. Many brave souls, however, were not commemorated in stone or marble. Instead, each generation, as it learns the story of Gettysburg and hears the tales of the unsung heroes, must find ways to remember and commemorate the sacrifices made by so many in early July 1863 on the Pennsylvania countryside.

Abraham Lincoln praised the unsung heroes of Gettysburg at the dedication of the National Soldiers' Cemetery, shown above, when he pledged, "From these honored dead we take increased devotion to that cause for which they gave the last full measure of devotion." That has been the challenge for each generation since.

GETTYSBURG: THE PRESIDENT

The BATTLE OF GETTYSBURG HAS come to symbolize the turning point of the Civil War. With more than twenty-three thousand men killed, wounded, or missing out of an army that numbered no more than seventy thousand, the engagement was a stunning blow to Robert E. Lee's Army of Northern Virginia. President Abraham Lincoln, however, did not view Gettysburg as an unqualified victory. To him the battle was a profound disappointment, because he had hoped that it would end the war. Just as he had been frustrated earlier with George B. McClellan following the battle of Antietam, Lincoln was bitterly disappointed when George Gordon Meade allowed Lee to retreat back across the Potomac River into Virginia.

Four months after Lee's retreat, on November 19, 1863, Lincoln transformed his disappointment into triumph at the dedication ceremony of the national cemetery at Gettysburg. His two-minute oration became a defining moment of the war and the greatest speech ever given by an American. His words have become °the closest thing Americans have to scripture in their secular government.° After Lincoln's speech the war was no longer fought just for a political purpose—to keep the Union together. With the Gettysburg Address the war became a moral crusade preserving the ideals of liberty, equality, and democracy on which the country had been founded. °The most compelling element of the address was the feeling that Lincoln had for the men who died at Gettysburg° and the way he portrayed them, not just as political heroes, but as moral heroes. °It helped explain to the

PMZ

GW

JSP

GSB	Gabor S. Boritt
WCD	William C. Davis
REF	Roy E. Frampton
WAF	William A. Frassanito
GWG	Gary W. Gallagher
JMM	James M. McPherson
JSP	John S. Patterson
BP	Brian Pohanka
WGW	William G. Williams
PMZ	Paul M. Zall

327

Gettysburg bore the scars of battle into the fall of 1863. The countryside held thousands of recent graves, and repair work was beginning on fences and homes and buildings around and in town. People were beginning to return to life as usual, but things would never be as they were before July 1. The massive battle that had raged around the formerly obscure county seat had all the gory majesty of one of the world's great confrontations, and efforts were being made to recognize the great loss of life that had transpired on the battlefield these people called home.

American people who they were, what they hoped for, how they hoped to go on, and how they hoped to be born again.•

Four score and seven years ago our fathers brought forth on this continent, a new nation, conceived in Liberty, and dedicated to the proposition that all men are created equal. Now we are engaged in a great civil war, testing whether that nation, or any nation so conceived and so dedicated, can long endure. We are met on a great battlefield of that war. We have come to dedicate a portion of that field, as a final resting place for those who here gave their lives that that nation might live. It is altogether fitting and proper that we should do this. But, in a larger sense, we can not dedicate—we can not consecrate—we can not hallow this ground. The brave men, living and dead, who struggled here, have consecrated it, far above our poor power to add or detract. The world will little note, nor long remember what we say here, but it can never forget what they did here. It is for us the living, rather, to be dedicated here to the unfinished work which they who fought here have thus far so nobly advanced. It is rather for us to be here dedicated to the great task remaining before us—that from these honored dead we take increased devotion to that cause for which they gave the last full measure of devotion— that we here highly resolve that these dead shall not have died in vain—that this nation, under God, shall have a new birth of freedom—and that government of the people, by the people, for the people, shall not perish from the earth.

The Gettysburg Address is only 272 words in length, just ten sentences. Lincoln took two minutes to deliver it. Yet brief as it is, it endures as a cornerstone of national spirit and principle.

°To appreciate the meaning, significance, and importance of the Gettysburg Address, one needs to understand the events of 1863 that led up to it. It was a speech Lincoln chose to use to define the meaning and purpose of the war and what it meant for the future of America and even the world.•

By the spring of 1863 the Union war effort had floundered. In January 1863 Ambrose Burnside had undertaken a disastrous winter campaign meant to accomplish a flanking movement against Lee. An earlier effort to do so had climaxed with a horrendous defeat at Fredericksburg in mid-December 1862. Burnside accomplished nothing with his January campaign, which came to be called the Mud March. Thousands of men were lost to sickness and exhaustion and thousands more deserted. Burnside was relieved of command and replaced with Maj. Gen. Joseph Hooker. In May, Hooker's army was trounced at Chancellorsville.

Within the span of five months, Lee had twice defeated the largest, best-equipped army in the world and the two best generals Lincoln could find. There was no reason to believe the Confederate general would not beat any Yankee general and any army that went up against him.

After two years of war °the Union was no closer to taking Richmond—the announced Federal objective—and no closer to putting Lee and the Army of Northern Virginia out of the war.• During that same time °Lincoln had been frustrated with a series of commanders who would not or could not defeat the

In the aftermath of the battle a number of casualties, particularly Southerners, were left for the townspeople to finish burying. Below, several South Carolinians are laid out near the Rose farm, awaiting burial. Someone had taken the time to write, not carve, names and unit designations on headboards, but the writing appears smeared, possibly due to the rain that began after the battle. Whoever prepared the headboards also apparently tried to place the correct headboard near the appropriate body.

JMM

GSB

WCD

Within a month of the battle, plans were being made for an appropriate burial ground for the Union soldiers who had died at Gettysburg. David Wills (above), an attorney, chaired the committee entrusted with that responsibility. All seventeen Northern states were represented, and a site was selected adjacent to the town cemetery.

The entrance to the town cemetery, Evergreen Cemetery, was marked by a distinctive arched building. Prior to 1853, the only burial grounds in town were in church yards, but the town's growth called for a new cemetery. A site was chosen south of town with an excellent view of the surrounding area. The archway itself was erected in 1855. The image at right is the earliest of the gateway pictures taken following the battle. The earthworks in the foreground and the puddle of water contributed to the belief that this photograph was taken on the morning of July 7. Confederate artillery shelled the strategic hill, pockmarking and shattering headstones. Broken windows and battle scars are still visible in this image. Inside the gatehouse a sign was posted warning that any persons caught discharging firearms on the grounds would be punished.

Confederates in Northern Virginia. In the estimation of the president, nothing would come of the Union war aims until this main Rebel army was conquered.•

°Politically, Lincoln had reached a low point in the spring of 1863 as a consequence of the string of Federal defeats. Because he was the commander in chief, his popularity suffered from the perception that he was leading a failing cause.• Lincoln knew that the South had pointed to his election as the reason for secession, thus he wondered if all of America, as well as his critics, saw him as °the one individual responsible for the American Civil War. At some level of consciousness he believed that was the situation, and this belief fueled his urgency in wanting to end the war. When Lee took his army into Pennsylvania and was defeated, Lincoln saw this as another opportunity to end the war quickly.•

WCD

°By July 4, when it was clear that Meade had won a tactical victory on the field, Lincoln was overjoyed.• "The news from the Army of the Potomac, up to 10 P.M. on the third, is such as to cover the army with the highest honor. To promise a great success to the cause of the Union," the president announced, relieved.

BP
WCD

°The victory at Gettysburg was not the only good news Lincoln received in early July 1863.• °At the same time that Lee was retreating from Gettysburg, U. S. Grant was entering Vicksburg, Mississippi, in the war's western theater. Following a forty-eight-day siege, the taking of Vicks-

SPECIFICATIONS

FOR proposals invited to be handed in at my office in Gettysburg, up to the 22d inst., at 12 o'clock, noon, for the two contracts referred to in the advertisement of this date, (Oct. 15th, 1863.)

FIRST.

For the exhuming and removal to the National Soldiers' Cemetery, of the dead of the Union Army, buried on the Gettysburg Battle-Field and at the several Hospitals in the vicinity :—

The party taking this contract shall receive the Coffins at the Railroad Station, in Gettysburg, and only take them to the field as fast as used each day.

He shall go upon the premises where the dead are buried, under the direction of the person having the superintendence—doing as little damage as possible, and where an enclosure is thrown open, he shall replace it. He shall open up the grave or trench where the dead are buried, and carefully take out the remains, and place them in the coffin, and screw down the lid tight, and nail the head board, where the grave has been marked, carefully on the lid of the coffin. He shall then replace all blankets, &c., that may have been taken out of the grave and not put around the body, back in the grave, and close it up, nearly levelling the same.

He shall transport the remains thus secured to the grounds selected for their burial, on the south side of the Borough of Gettysburg, and deposit them at such a place on the grounds as may be designated by the person having the superintendence of the removals and re-interments.

He shall remove as many bodies to the grounds per day, as shall be ordered by the person in charge, not exceeding One Hundred bodies per day.

He shall exhume all bodies designated by the person in charge, and none others; and when ordered, he shall open up graves and trenches for personal inspection of the remains, for the purpose of ascertaining whether they are bodies of Union Soldiers, and close them over again when ordered to do so.

He shall stipulate the price per body, at which he will contract to perform the work as above set forth. Payment will be made on Saturday evening of every week, for the full amount of the work done.

Bonds will be required in the sum of three thousand dollars for the faithful performance of the contract, with two or more sureties to be approved by me. W***.

After determining the site of the soldiers' cemetery, the immediate task was the exhumation and identification of bodies buried on the battlefield and their reinterment. In October 1863 the Wills committee solicited bids "For the exhuming and removal to the National Soldiers' Cemetery of the dead of the Union Army, buried on the Gettysburg Battle-Field and at the several Hospitals in the vicinity." Thirty-four bids were received, ranging from $1.59 to $8.00 per body. Laborers were hired to do the grisly work of digging up the decomposed remains and placing them in coffins, sometimes with the aid of tongs. Scrupulous care was taken to identify each body. If there were no headboard identifying the buried body, pockets were searched for wallets, letters, and other personal effects. Anything of that nature was preserved for later efforts to contact the family.

burg meant that virtually all access to the central Mississippi River was now denied to the Confederacy. The Southerners could no longer use the river as a route for supplies to reach the East. Thus, strategically, Vicksburg was a more significant victory than Gettysburg.•

°On July 7 Lincoln received official word that Vicksburg had surrendered. A crowd of people gathered at the Executive Mansion, and the Marine Band came to serenade him. The president responded with an impromptu address that sounded very much like the Gettysburg Address he would deliver four months later:• "How long ago was it, eighty-odd years, since on the Fourth of July for the first time in the history of the world a nation by its representatives assembled and declared as a self-evident truth that all men are created equal." °The ideas that he would articulate in November were in their early stages of development in July.•

Amid the revelry and celebration of the news of Vicksburg, Lincoln was experiencing increasing disappointment and frustration with his commander of the Army of the Potomac. Gideon Welles, the secretary of the navy, reported, "The President said this morning that Meade still lingered at Gettysburg, when he should have been near the Potomac to cut off the retreating army of Lee."

°The president believed that after achieving victory at Gettysburg, Meade had several opportunities to win the war by destroying Lee's army. After the fighting had stopped at Gettysburg, several days of rain, which made marching difficult for both sides, had flooded the Potomac, making retreat even more difficult for Lee. That was the time, Lincoln thought, for Meade to attack, and the president urged him to do so. Meade did send his cavalry after Lee, but he cited the heavy casualties the bulk of his army had suffered and claimed that the men were exhausted.•

By July 14 most of Lee's Confederates were back across the river. Just as he had done in September 1862 when he had lost at Antietam and McClellan had refused to attack him a second time on the north side of the Potomac, Lee had slipped away. He had escaped again to recover and to fight another day.

Lincoln and Meade had two different objectives: The president wanted an end to the war, but his general WGW wanted to preserve the Gettysburg victory. °Meade sent a telegram to Lincoln announcing his triumph in Pennsylvania, including the statement, "We have pushed the invader from our soil." Lincoln was dumbfounded• and exclaimed: "This is a dreadful reminiscence of McClellan. The same spirit that moved McClellan to claim a great victory because Pennsylvania and Maryland were safe.

The contract for moving the bodies was awarded to Franklin W. Biesecker at the rate of $1.59 per body. Samuel Weaver supervised the exhumations, and Joseph E. Townsend oversaw the interments. The process of transferring the remains from the battlefield to the cemetery began on October 27 and was completed the following March 18. The image at right is the only known photograph of reburials in the National Soldiers' Cemetery, which the photographer, Samuel F. Corlies, noted as "Reburying Pennsylvania Soldiers in the Cemetery at Gettysburg." The men in the photograph have never been identified. The headboard from the original graves can be seen attached to the coffin, which was a procedure dictated by Weaver.

Will our generals never get that idea out of their heads? The whole country is our soil!"

In frustration, Lincoln wrote to Meade: "My dear general, I do not believe you appreciate the magnitude of the misfortune involved in Lee's escape. He was within your grasp. And to have closed upon him would, in connection with our other successes, have ended the war. As it is, the war will be prolonged indefinitely." Realizing, however, that the letter would probably cause Meade, a new national hero, to resign, he never sent it. °To the end of his life Lincoln believed that Meade's failure to follow Lee was one of the great lost opportunities of the war, which meant more dead, more waste, more war—all for no gain.•

It DID NOT take long before the seven thousand unburied dead at Gettysburg began to have an impact on the town. "When the splendor, the pomp, and the circumstance of battle's magnificently stern array have gone, then the horrible and the ghastly only remain. And remain in their most horrible forms," wrote J. Howard Wert, a Gettysburg civilian.

°July's high temperatures caused the bodies left on the field to deteriorate rapidly. The stench was terrible. The Union army and the people of the town tried to get as many bodies under the ground as possible.• It was a grim curiosity that enabled the grave diggers to distinguish Confederate bodies from Union bodies. The

The establishment of a national cemetery required a dedication, which was tentatively scheduled for late September. The most important element of that consecration was the main oration, and to all involved the obvious choice for a speaker was Edward Everett of Massachusetts (above). He accepted the invitation but asked that the date be set back to allow him enough time to prepare an appropriate presentation and proposed November 19, which the cemetery committee accepted.

Perfunctory invitations to the dedication were sent to political and military officials in late October, including Abraham Lincoln at the White House, shown here as it was when Lincoln occupied it. He supposedly surprised the cemetery committee by accepting. Since the president would be there, the correct response was to ask him to speak. There was concern that his comments might be inappropriate. Thus Wills's November 2 written invitation to Lincoln specified "a few appropriate" comments to "kindle anew in the breasts of the Comrades of these brave dead" an affirmation that the dead "are not forgotten by those highest in authority." Everett, the main speaker, had two months to prepare his speech; the president had two weeks.

Yankees, better fed and fatter, tended to bloat, turn black, and decompose almost immediately in the hot sun. The Rebels, much thinner from heavy marching and a meager subsistence diet, kept their lifelike appearance much longer.

The bodies that were not claimed by loved ones or shipped back home, as most officers were, were usually buried where they fell, an accepted military practice. °Often grave diggers had no alternative but to scoop out a little hole in the ground, roll the body in that hole, put some kind of rude marker over the grave, and hope that the marker would stay there so the body could be identified later by family members if they wanted to recover it.•

°The rain that fell after the battle simply washed the dirt from the bodies. In a matter of a week, the shallow graves were obvious as arms, legs, and bodies protruded from the ground.•

David Wills, an attorney in Gettysburg, was appointed by Pennsylvania's governor, Andrew Curtin, to oversee the care of the state's casualties on the Gettysburg battlefield. A quick assessment of the progress of the work led

On the two Sundays before leaving for Gettysburg, November 8 and 15, Lincoln sat for portraits in Alexander Gardner's gallery (above) in Washington. At the same time, the photographer was also preparing prints for his forthcoming publication, Photographic Incidents of War, *a compilation of photographs taken at Gettysburg in the days following the battle. While in the studio on these occasions, the president may have reviewed the images, which might have deepened his understanding of the devastation of the battle. One of those images was probably the photograph Gardner titled "A Sharpshooter's Last Sleep," reproduced below.*

him to appeal for more help in handling the situation. He wrote the governor: "My attention has been directed to several places where the hogs were actually rooting out the bodies and devouring them. Humanity calls on us to take measures to remedy this." °Wills suggested that a commission be set up to develop a national cemetery in Gettysburg to take care of the dead of all the Union states. Curtin gave him the authority to proceed.•

°Wills's idea introduced a new way of dealing with the military dead. Soldiers would not just be buried where they fell, but buried in hallowed ground, and in many cases in ground where some of them had died. The bodies would be interred in a dedicated place that had been set aside for them, to be honored through all time.•

As the commission reviewed possible sites for the dead from the eighteen Union states, one place seemed uniquely appropriate for this new kind of cemetery. Wills reported: "It is the place where our army had about forty pieces of artillery in action all of Thursday and Friday. It was the key to our whole line of defenses, the apex of the triangular line of battle. It is this spot, above all others, where the honorable burial of the dead have fallen on these fields."

°The plot of ground consisted of approximately seventeen acres adjacent to the Evergreen Cemetery, which was the town civilian graveyard. Wills purchased the property for about twenty-five hundred dollars• and hired William

The sun was setting when Lincoln's train pulled into the Gettysburg depot (above left), and Carlisle Street was filled with people trying to catch of glimpse of the president. David Wills and Edward Everett were among those to greet Lincoln. The only awkward sight was a pile of coffins not far removed from the train platform. The entourage walked a short distance to the town square, or diamond, to the Wills house, which was on the southeast corner.

The Gettysburg that awaited the president was not much different from this 1867 image of South Stratton Street looking toward the German Reformed Church (above right). Muddy streets and plank sidewalks were common. No structures on this road were significantly damaged in the battle; the building in the right foreground is on the property of Henry Rupp's tannery and is being torn down.

Lincoln was taken to a second-story room in the Wills house (above left) to rest before dinner. Meanwhile, the town was festive. People had been pouring into Gettysburg for days. Now they were trying to find food and shelter; every bed, pew, parlor, lobby, and even floor space had been reserved. In the Wills house, dinner had been prepared for twenty-four guests. The group was serenaded from the street, and finally, in response to many calls for some words from the celebrities, Lincoln spoke to the crowd from a window. He withdrew to review his speech and then met with Wills, Governor Curtin, and Secretary of State William Seward before retiring at midnight.

When the president appeared the next morning, the diamond was crowded with people. As he looked south from the town square, he saw the prominent features of the J. L. Schick storefront and the steeple of the Adams County Courthouse (above right). Two lines of soldiers formed an aisle for Lincoln to a small bay horse. The solemnity of the occasion forgave the contrast between the tall man and the short horse.

JSP

Saunders, a landscape architect, to design the cemetery. A leader of the rural cemetery movement, Saunders believed that cemeteries should be places where the living and the dead could commune through nature. °He devised a plan that gave every Union body buried in the cemetery equality by arranging the graves in a semicircle, equidistant from a unifying, central monument. That represented a balance between the democratic desire to treat everyone equally and the desire for a grand, glorious monument that would validate the cemetery.•

REF

°Originally the dead were to have been buried randomly in a semicircle. As the work progressed, however, it became clear that the states placed a high priority on retaining their individual identity by keeping all of the dead from each state together. This was an ironic development. The war was officially being fought by the North to preserve the Union, but the Union forced the cemetery designer to incorporate the Southern tenet of states' rights, with each state having its own plot.•

WAF

While Saunders surveyed and prepared the ground for its lofty purpose, a gruesome task remained. °Someone had to go out on the battlefield, open up thousands of graves, determine which ones were Union soldiers, and then rebury those soldiers in the national cemetery. Before that work was to begin, however, the commission planned to consecrate the ground with a dedication ceremony on October 23, 1863.

The work of reburial had just begun at the time of the dedication. These graves of recently buried are in the Massachusetts section. Unlike the other Northern states, Massachusetts signed an independent contractor, Solomon Powers, to rebury the state's fallen soldiers in the national cemetery. His work required the reinterment of 158 bodies. That task may have been completed at the time this photograph by Samuel F. Corlies was taken.

Invitations to speak were first offered to the leading wordsmiths of the day—Henry Wadsworth Longfellow, John Greenleaf Whittier, and William Cullen Bryant. All three declined. Lacking a poet, Wills looked for a speaker. The accustomed manner for a dedication such as the committee had in mind was an oration, which in the nineteenth century was a type of performance art. °The invitation was extended to Edward Everett of Massachusetts, the best-known orator of the day. Everett had been a congressman, U.S. senator, and governor of Massachusetts. He was a professor at and later president of Harvard

The subject of this photograph by Timothy O'Sullivan, perhaps the most memorable view of Gettysburg, may have been one of the last Confederate bodies on the battlefield. While extraordinary care was taken in the exhumation of the Union dead on the battlefield, the Confederate dead were buried in trenches in lots of a hundred or more. The stone wall had been thrown up sometime during the night of July 2. Little Round Top is visible in the distance.

The distance between the square and the cemetery was only half a mile, and the procession was only about fifteen minutes long. The two photographs above are the best known of the procession from the town diamond to the national cemetery and are likely the work of the Tyson brothers, Charles and Isaac, whose gallery was in Gettysburg. The view on the left is probably a test exposure; the photographer's goal was most likely to capture Lincoln en route to the cemetery. The image on the right depicts the crowd moving toward the cemetery site.

REF University.° °The October date, however, did not allow sufficient time for him to prepare his speech. To accommodate Everett, the committee rescheduled the dedication ceremony for November 19.°

Up to this point the cemetery had been a project borne solely by the states. Lincoln was invited in conjunction with a casual invitation offered to his cabinet and other celebrities to attend a ceremony sponsored by the participating states. No one had suggested that the president should be the main speaker. The federal government was not involved until President Lincoln was invited to speak at the ceremony. Wills's letter of invitation was received by the president on November 2: "It is the desire that after the oration, you, as Chief Executive of the Nation, formally set apart these grounds to their sacred use by a few appropriate remarks."

Everett had agreed to speak several weeks earlier; Lincoln was issued a last-minute invitation to attend. Although he could have refused the invitation on the basis WGW of its short notice, °Lincoln chose to attend, believing that the dedication ceremony of the national cemetery was important. It would give him an opportunity to explain the meaning of the war to the country.° The anticipated attendance of several governors and their representatives also allowed an opportunity for some political fence mending.

BY THE FIRST of November the heady optimism following the Gettysburg and Vicksburg victories had dissi-

This recently discovered image possibly shows Abraham Lincoln in the processional toward the cemetery. A figure in a stovepipe hat is accompanied by one of the parade marshals who stands out in the crowd because of the sash he was wearing. All seventy-two marshals were on horseback and wore sashes.

pated. Early November 1863 was a time of great uncertainty. °The Union war effort was at best tenuous. In September a major battle had been lost at Chickamauga, in northwestern Georgia. In October Lee had also brought the war back to the very outskirts of Washington. The fact that the Confederates could execute such a move sent a clear message to the Lincoln administration that the North was still a long way from victory.• The administration fared no better on the political front, where it had been under attack all year.

°On January 1, 1863, Lincoln had issued the Emancipation Proclamation, attempting to strike against the economic basis of the Confederate war effort—slavery—and to place the Union war effort on a higher moral plane. A great many Northerners, however, saw this as a betrayal of the original purpose for which they had gone to war, which was to preserve the Union. They now thought they were fighting, not to preserve the old Union, but to abolish slavery, which many of them considered an unconstitutional endeavor.• Some generals, such as Maj. Gen. John A. Logan of Illinois, threatened to withdraw their troops from the front. They had been fighting to reunite the Union, not to free slaves. While many generals mut-

339

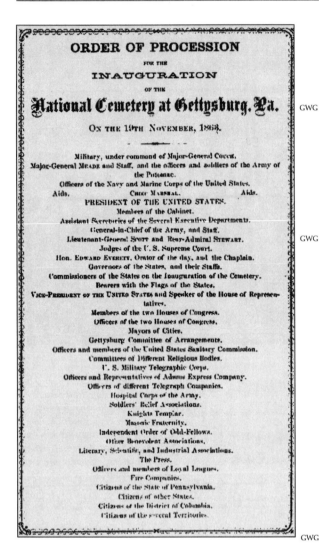

ORDER OF PROCESSION

FOR THE

INAUGURATION

OF THE

National Cemetery at Gettysburg, Pa.

ON THE 19TH NOVEMBER, 1863.

Military, under command of Major-General Couch.
Major-General Meade and Staff, and the officers and soldiers of the Army of the Potomac.
Officers of the Navy and Marine Corps of the United States.
Aids.   Chief Marshal.   Aids.
PRESIDENT OF THE UNITED STATES.
Members of the Cabinet.
Assistant Secretaries of the Several Executive Departments.
General-in-Chief of the Army, and Staff.
Lieutenant-General Scott and Rear-Admiral Stewart.
Judges of the U. S. Supreme Court.
Hon. Edward Everett, Orator of the day, and the Chaplain.
Governors of the States, and their Staffs.
Commissioners of the States on the Inauguration of the Cemetery.
Bearers with the Flags of the States.
Vice-President of the United States and Speaker of the House of Representatives.
Members of the two Houses of Congress.
Officers of the two Houses of Congress.
Mayors of Cities.
Gettysburg Committee of Arrangements.
Officers and members of the United States Sanitary Commission.
Committees of Different Religious Bodies.
U. S. Military Telegraphic Corps.
Officers and Representatives of Adams Express Company.
Officers of different Telegraph Companies.
Hospital Corps of the Army.
Soldiers' Relief Associations.
Knights Templar.
Masonic Fraternity.
Independent Order of Odd-Fellows.
Other Benevolent Associations.
Literary, Scientific, and Industrial Associations.
The Press.
Officers and members of Loyal Leagues.
Fire Companies.
Citizens of the State of Pennsylvania.
Citizens of other States.
Citizens of the District of Columbia.
Citizens of the several Territories.

The procession was led by the Marine Corps band and color guard. The rest of the elements followed in sequence. George Gordon Meade and members of the Army of the Potomac, although invited, were absent. The general had graciously declined the invitation and explained, "This army has duties to perform which will not permit of being represented on the occasion." JMM

tered agreement, the fact that they were professional soldiers rather than politicians-in-uniform, like Logan, led them to keep their opinions private.

GWG °In midsummer 1863 the war became even more complicated for Lincoln because opposition to the draft spread across much of the North.• In July more than 130 blacks, including orphaned children, were murdered in New York City by a white mob enraged that Lincoln GWG expected them to free the slaves. °People who opposed the war on the grounds that they should not be compelled to fight for the Union were joined by those who said they should not be compelled to fight for emancipation. As the fall of 1863 approached, Lincoln needed to capture the essence of what the war was about for his fellow Northerners. He seized upon the invitation to consecrate the dead at Gettysburg as his opportunity to define the war aims of the North.•

Speaking at Gettysburg was so important to Lincoln that he accepted the invitation even though his son Tad was seriously ill. This caused much turmoil GWG in the Lincoln family. °The Lincolns had lost a child the year before, and Mary Lincoln pressured her husband to turn down the invitation. He felt he did not have a choice; he had to place being a father to the country• ahead of his fatherly duties at home.

On November 9, it was announced that Lincoln would attend the ceremony. He had ten days to prepare his comments. °When drafting an important speech of any kind during the war, Lincoln's habit was to compose a few sentences or a paragraph or two during whatever free moments he could find in his hectic schedule. He thought slowly and wrote slowly because he thought deeply. Some of the ideas expressed in the Gettysburg Address had appeared in things he had said earlier in the war, and so it was just a matter of framing the words and the sentences in the best possible way.•

In writing a speech for such a solemn and patriotic occasion, Lincoln naturally drew inspiration from such familiar sources as the Bible and the Declaration of Independence. He might also have found inspiration in something he saw.

JSP °During the few days before the dedication ceremony, Lincoln twice visited the studio of photographer Alexander Gardner to have his picture taken. Gardner had taken photographs of the dead at Antietam and most recently at Gettysburg. Lincoln was in the process of saturating himself in the subject of Gettysburg, and he must have reviewed Gardner's photographs of the battlefield. Perhaps he was moved by them. One of the most famous of these was of a young Confederate sharpshooter lying dead at Devil's Den.•

On November 18, the day before the ceremony, Lincoln departed by train at noon for the eighty-mile journey to Gettysburg. By that time he had completed only the first page of what would be a two-page address.

MM °The chief myth about the Gettysburg Address—that Lincoln wrote it on the back of an envelope on the train as he was going from Washington to Gettysburg—is not true. The story shows how Lincoln was mythologized, making him into something superhuman. Thus the idea of his jotting down these immortal words on the train seemed to fit with the idea of someone who is more than human.•

BP °When Lincoln arrived in Gettysburg, it was not in triumph. The fate of the Union was still to be decided. A Confederate victory seemed as likely as a Federal triumph. Lincoln was lost in thought about the men who had given their lives on that battlefield. Several questions came to mind. Had they died in vain? What ideals

Programme of Arrangements and Order of Exercises

FOR THE INAUGURATION

OF THE

NATIONAL CEMETERY AT GETTYSBURG,

ON THE 19TH OF NOVEMBER, 1863.

The military will form in Gettysburg at 9 o'clock a. m., on Carlisle street, north of the square, its right resting on the square, opposite McClellan's Hotel, under the direction of Major General Couch.

The State Marshals and Chief Marshal's aids will assemble in the public square at the same hour.

All civic bodies except the citizens of States will assemble, according to the foregoing printed programme, on York street at the same hour.

The delegation of Pennsylvania citizens will form on Chambersburg street, its right resting on the square, and the other citizen delegations, in their order, will form on the same street in rear of the Pennsylvania delegation.

The Marshals of the States are charged with the duty of forming their several delegations so that they will assume their appropriate positions when the main procession moves.

The head of the column will move at precisely 10 o'clock a. m.

The route will be up Baltimore street to the Emmittsburg road; thence to the junction of the Taneytown road; thence, by the latter road, to the Cemetery, where the military will form in line, as the General in command may order, for the purpose of saluting the President of the United States.

The military will then close up, and occupy the space on the left of the stand.

The civic procession will advance and occupy the area in front of the stand, the military leaving sufficient space between them and the line of graves for the civic procession to pass.

The ladies will occupy the right of the stand, and it is desirable that they be upon the ground as early as ten o'clock a. m.

The exercises will take place as soon as the military and civic bodies are in position, as follows:

Music.

Prayer.

Music.

ORATION.

Music.

DEDICATORY REMARKS BY THE PRESIDENT OF THE UNITED STATES.

Dirge.

Benediction.

After the benediction the procession will be dismissed, and the State Marshals and special aids to the Chief Marshal will form on Baltimore street, and return to the Court-house in Gettysburg, where a meeting of the marshals will be held.

An appropriate salute will be fired in Gettysburg on the day of the celebration, under the direction of Maj. Gen. Couch.

WARD H. LAMON,

Marshal-in-Chief.

Gibson & Persson, Printers, 511 Ninth st., Washington.

The procession was punctuated every minute by a cannon shot. The drums beat a slow pace. The bands played dirges. The progress was funereal. Just behind Lincoln a group of forty wounded veterans of the battle followed—some on crutches, many with arms in slings—a solemn reminder of the purpose of the dedication.

There was a delay of twenty minutes from the time the procession reached the cemetery until the main speaker took his place on the platform and the ceremonies could begin. In the view above (left), looking to the northeast, the Evergreen Cemetery gateway highlights the left horizon. The speaker's stand is slightly right of center, to the left of the tent, where the crowd seems to swell. Everett had requested the tent as a place to gather his thoughts beforehand and also because he suffered kidney problems. The second image above (right) is probably the most familar of the photographs taken November 19, 1863. It looks southeast toward the speaker's stand and is somewhat closer than the first photo. The raised platform dominates the exposure. Four parade marshals occupy the center, and the flagpole is to the far right.

JMM

WGW

WAF

BP

motivated men to fight like that? How does one voice these ideals? How could he inspire and motivate his generals, his soldiers, and the people to a renewed effort to achieve victory?•

The president arrived at dusk and °stayed with the Wills family, the local lawyer who had initiated the idea for the cemetery and chaired the committee that had overseen the work. That night Lincoln sat in his room and put the finishing touches on his speech.• Only hours later he would deliver his "few appropriate remarks."

NOVEMBER 19, 1863, Dedication Day, began with a grand procession headed by the president from the town square to the cemetery. °Gettysburg had a population of approximately twenty-four hundred; reports that day estimated that from eight thousand to twenty thousand people were in town for the ceremony.•

As the procession entered the cemetery, Lincoln and the other participants saw the work that was still in progress. °By that time approximately eleven hundred Union soldiers had been interred in the national cemetery, which was only one-third of the reburials that would complete the task.• °The grounds were not much more than a little dirt hill marked with the humble graves of these men. Death was still very present here. It was recent; it was in the air.•

It was only in 1952 that a specialist at the National Archives, Josephine Cobb, noticed that the image in the upper right of the facing page showed Lincoln (circled here for effect) and other dignitaries seated on the speaker's platform. The fact that most of the men are bareheaded in the photograph may indicate that the photograph was taken as Everett was being led to his seat by the chief marshal, Ward Hill Lamon. According to accounts of the ceremonies, hats were removed only when Lincoln arrived and was shown to his place on the dais and when Everett was shown his.

On the speakers' platform, overlooking that stark little hill soon to be dedicated as sacred ground, President Lincoln took his place alongside the other dignitaries. After a prayer and a musical selection, Everett rose and gave a two-hour oration. °He did a beautiful job, having understood that his task was to transform the story of the battle into a hugely inspiring moment•: "As my eye ranges over the fields whose sods were so lately moistened by the blood of gallant and noble men, I feel as never before that it is sweet and becoming to die for one's country."

°Everett's theme, a very simple one, was that all the country's political differences were transient. The thing that is permanent is the sense of being one nation.• "These bonds of union are of perennial force and energy, while the causes of alienation are imaginary, factitious and transient. The heart of the people, North and South, is for the Union. . . . The weary masses of the people are yearning to see the dear old flag again floating upon their capitols, and they sigh for the return of the peace, prosperity, and happiness, which they enjoyed under a government whose power was felt only in its blessings."

°When Everett finished, Lincoln jumped up, shook his hand with great enthusiasm, and said, "I'm more than grateful." He understood that Everett knew what the nation needed.•

Readers of Harper's Weekly were given a grand perspective of the ceremonies, the artist taking a view that no photographer could. The main oration began at noon and lasted a few minutes less than two hours. Everett spoke from memory and without gestures, but he modulated his voice for emphasis and occasionally jerked his head with a flourish. He described the battle at length, and his audience, probably the largest assemblage he had ever addressed, seemed focused on each word. Only toward the end did some of them wander off to explore the battlefield.

After the singing of another hymn, the president was introduced. It was two o'clock. Whereas Everett had addressed the crowd in an evenly modulated voice appropriate for a two-hour oration, the president's voice was high to the point of being shrill, and his Kentucky accent grated on some listeners. Nevertheless, Lincoln's tenor voice carried well over the crowd, and his delivery was emphatic. He referred to his written pages only once, and aside from moving the pages, he made no other gestures with his hands. He was interrupted five times by applause.

From the standpoint of the townspeople of Gettysburg, the president surpassed all their hopes that the air around them would in some way be disinfected. The tragedy of the fighting and the debris of the battle were transformed by Lincoln's words into the product of an experiment testing if a government could live up to its lofty underpinnings, which stipulated equality for all. Despite references to "that" battle and the men who died "here," there were no specific allusions to the battle: no names, no sites, no units, no sides. As he lifted the battle to the realm of the abstract, free of the grisliness still apparent on the countryside, Lincoln also lifted up the war. Similarly ignoring sectionalism, states, and slavery, he focused on the ideals that were at stake.

Another view of the crowd shows that the troops that circled the spectators had stacked their rifles sometime during Everett's speech. The line of sight is again looking northeast toward the Evergreen Cemetery gateway with the speaker's stand just off center to the right.

°As a great stump speaker, Lincoln could read a crowd, and he knew that the people attending the dedication ceremony had listened. He gave his address, and the people responded. It went over well, and he knew it at the time.•

°Everett himself wrote a note to Lincoln the next day saying: "I wish I had been able to come as close to the central meaning of the occasion in two hours as you did in two minutes." The great orator admired the Gettysburg Address so much that he asked the president for a handwritten copy. It was one of five requested of Lincoln. °The fact that the president had five copies indicates that there was a demand for the speech almost immediately; there was a recognition that something special had taken place at Gettysburg.•

°The reaction in the press to Lincoln's speech was divided. The Democratic newspapers of the day either underplayed the whole ceremony, did not say much about it, or criticized it.• "Silly, flat, and dishwatery utterances," intoned the *Chicago Times*. "We pass over the silly remarks of the President," was the assessment of the Harrisburg paper. "The ceremony was rendered ludicrous by that poor President Lincoln," sniffed the editors of the London *Times*.

°On the other hand, the Republican newspapers that favored Lincoln printed the speech, and many referred to

In contrast to Everett's mellifluous tones, Lincoln's high penetrating voice carried across the crowd. Some winced at his Kentucky accent. After two weeks of preparation, his remarks required little more than two minutes. Those in attendance could not recall if he read his manuscript or spoke from memory, if he made any gestures, or if he was interrupted by applause or even applauded as he sat down. The president himself, as he took his seat, seemed to think that he had failed.

it in praising tones.• "The few words from the President were from the heart to the heart," wrote *Harper's Weekly.* "A perfect gem, deep and feeling. Compact in thought," celebrated the *Springfield Republican.* "The right thing in the right place," was the response of the *Cincinnati Gazette.* Perhaps the reaction of the *Chicago Tribune* put it best of all: "The remarks of President Lincoln will live among the annals of man."

BEFORE NOVEMBER 19, 1863, the Civil War was being fought over whether the Union should be preserved. With the Gettysburg Address, Lincoln put even more at
BP stake. °His words gave the nation a view of what he himself was undergoing at that time. Increasingly, he came to recognize the moral high ground as the very backbone of the Union war effort, and he put it into
PMZ words that day.• °Lincoln had tried political force, and that had not worked. He still had political enemies. Thus he crafted his desires into words and used the Gettysburg Address to apply moral force.•
GSB   °"Four score and seven years" recalls biblical phrasing, evoking a beautiful language that connotes moral author-ity.• To support his claim to the moral high ground, Lincoln also employed a literary device with spiritual
PMZ connotations. °He built the entire statement around the

metaphor of the family, referring to fathers and conception.• By eloquently weaving this metaphor into his speech, Lincoln did with words what William Saunders did with his design for the soldiers' cemetery. °He talked about a law of nature which stipulates that there can be no life without death and the necessity of death to give rebirth to life to come.•

°Lincoln redefined the meaning of the war with the phrase, "a new birth of freedom." He defined the war as one not merely to preserve the old Union—the Union of 1861—but to create a new Union that would fulfill the promise of the fathers, that would give the nation a new birth of freedom. The United States would move into the future no longer burdened by the hypocrisy of the institution of slavery surviving in a society that proclaimed all men were created equal.•

To Lincoln, the Declaration of Independence was the political equivalent of the Bible. °Starting in the 1850s, he had begun to speak of Thomas Jefferson more frequently, and he knew that the Declaration of Independence was Jefferson's central idea.• On February 22, 1861, Lincoln had said: "I have never had a feeling politically that did not spring from the sentiments embodied in the Declaration of Independence. It gave promise that in due time the weights would be lifted from the shoulders of all men. And that all men shall have an equal chance."

°The connotation of equality to Lincoln was the right to rise in life, to get ahead in the world. This is one of the central meanings of his life and part of the Gettysburg Address.•

With the battle of Gettysburg having taken place close to the Fourth of July, the

An early draft of the Gettysburg Address.

After Lincoln and the other dignitaries departed, Gettysburg became a monument to one of the most significant Northern victories of the war. The work of reburial was completed, and the cemetery matured. Elsewhere the fields of Gettysburg were planted and crops harvested as before. Occasionally visitors came to see the battlefield, but until the establishment of the national park the most explicit memorial to the batle was that of the cemetery. Above (left) the view looks toward the center of the semicircle of graves. The image to the right (above) looks beyond the graves and to the southwest, toward the scene of Pickett's Charge.

BP connection to Independence Day was not lost on Lincoln. °He wanted to define the moral high ground by connecting the efforts of the Federal soldiers and their sacrifice with the founders of the Republic, with the whole ideal that had motivated the founding of America. He wanted to point out that there are times when one's own life is of small account when the stakes are high.•

PMZ By the end of the Gettysburg Address, the application of moral force was undeniable. °By adding "under God," Lincoln gave his speech that little push that raised it to GSB the supernatural level.• °He evidently added this phrase while he was speaking at the cemetery because the original copy does not include it. Lincoln added it at the moment of importance, the moment of truth. He was speaking to fifteen thousand people at the Gettysburg cemetery, but he was also speaking to the entire North. He was speaking to posterity, to all humankind.•

PMZ °Lincoln addressed everyone because he knew that the Northerners were not fighting this war for themselves alone. They were testing whether this form of government—of the people, by the people, for the people—could endure. If so, it would provide a model of freedom for the world.•

JMM °These words have a living meaning because they defined what the war was all about, why it was being fought, and what Lincoln hoped its outcome would be.

They illuminated the larger meaning of the purpose of the United States and its founding ideals:• "That we here highly resolve that these dead shall not have died in vain—that this nation, under God, shall have a new birth of freedom—and that government of the people, by the people, for the people, shall not perish from the earth."

In the Gettysburg Address, Lincoln said, "The world will little note, nor long remember what we say here." He was wrong. His "few appropriate remarks" inspire today just as they did when he spoke them on that cold November afternoon. They inspire because the work that he referred to is still unfinished. The great task still remains, challenging each generation. As long as the American experiment and democratic government continue, this truth will continue marching on.

The Soldiers' National Monument was erected in the cemetery in 1869 at the center of the semicircle of graves, completing the grounds as it had been designed by William Saunders. The photograph above shows the cemetery as it matured in the 1880s—a memorial to the fallen of the battlefield and a reminder "that these dead shall not have died in vain—that this nation, under God, shall have a new birth of freedom—and that government of the people, by the people, for the people, shall not perish from the earth."

VICKSBURG

BC ° *Two* HUNDRED MILES NORTH OF NEW
Orleans on the Mississippi River, Vicksburg, Mississippi,
was in 1861 a city of about five thousand people,
making it the largest city in the state and on all of the
lower river above New Orleans.• Situated on bluffs overlooking the river, Vicksburg was a strategic city and,
according to Abraham Lincoln, the key to controlling
the river and much of the western regions of the Con-
TYC federacy. °To Jefferson Davis it was the nail that held
the two halves of the South together.• To the people of
Vicksburg it was a town rich in history that became the
object of war.

GC °If it had not been for the Mississippi River there
would have been no Vicksburg. The river was the life-
blood of the city commercially because it was a high-
way for America, more important in many respects than
the railroad that came through town. The river had built
the city.•

Vicksburg was founded at a horseshoe bend on the
Mississippi River in 1812 on top of bluffs as high as three
hundred feet. It existed for two reasons: cotton and
steamboats. Cotton was grown on the surrounding plantations and shipped to domestic and foreign ports by the
steamboats that docked at Vicksburg's wharves. By 1860
cotton was king and the steamboat was the royal carriage.
Both did a good business in Vicksburg.

The city thrived on this success. There were agents,
grocers, dentists, clothiers, booksellers, photographers,
cotton brokers, and slave dealers. Just about anything
could be purchased there: French china, liquor, guns,

ECB	Edwin C. Bearss
TYC	Thomas Y. Cartwright
GC	Gordon A. Cotton
WCD	William C. Davis
BP	Brian Pohanka
TJW	Terrence J. Winschel

The plan to capture Vicksburg had begun early in the war since both sides believed whoever controlled the city commanded the river and much of the western territory. As it did in most Southern towns, the war took an awful toll on the people as well as the buildings. This view from the cupola of the courthouse captures the mixture of homes, churches, and shops that made the city comfortable for residents and visitors alike. It was a place of culture, education, and luxury, according to one resident. The city had three newspapers, an orchestra, a repertory company, and a lecture hall that welcomed speakers from around the world.

carriages, even pianos. Up on the hill were fancy hotels, beautiful homes, and churches for the cream of southern society. Down below, along the river, were shanties, brothels, and saloons, all serving the venial needs of the river people.

Lucy McCray, a Vicksburg resident, recalled in her diary: "[Vicksburg] was a place of culture, education, and luxury. Almost every man with a family owned slaves who GC were proud to serve them." °In 1842 a steamboat passenger described the city as he viewed it while he was coming up the river as the sun was setting. He said that it looked like every house on the terrace was ablaze with fire and yet there were no flames. He thought it was the prettiest place he had ever seen.• During the war Confederate Sgt. William Pitts Chambers of the Forty-sixth Mississippi was similarly impressed: "The most beautiful yards and gardens I had ever seen were there, and I also saw finer buildings than I'd ever seen before. The courthouse on the bold eminence is said to be the finest in the state."

The county courthouse dominated the skyline. It was built in the center of town, and a young Jefferson Davis GC had once practiced law in the building. °The clock on top of the courthouse had been built by the Howard Brothers of Boston in the 1850s and installed by a local Austrian-born jeweler, Max Kuner, who had a sense of history and placed a little plaque on the clock indicating that he had installed it during October 1859. The courthouse clock ticked away all during the siege of 1863, keeping both Confederates and Federals on time.•

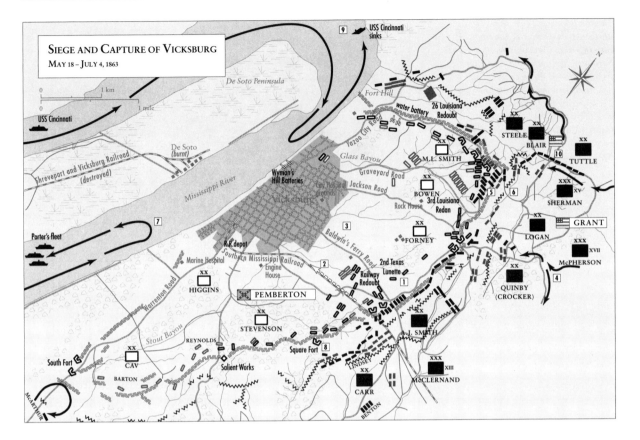

SIEGE AND CAPTURE OF VICKSBURG
MAY 18 – JULY 4, 1863

When the question of secession had been put before the people of Mississippi, those in Vicksburg voted for the status quo. °Vicksburg was pro-Union in its sentiments. In fact, Vicksburg's Warren County was one of only two counties in the state that voted against secession. Vicksburg's residents knew that their livelihood depended on the free navigation of the Mississippi River, and they feared that secession would close the river. They voted their economic interest. Once secession came, however, the citizens of Vicksburg embraced the Confederate cause with both arms.• "As the bugle sounded, and the drums called men to serve their country, the brightest and manliest of [Vicksburg's] sons responded with eagerness," wrote diarist Lucy McCray. "Mothers, wives, and sweethearts little realized what war meant as they kissed loved ones good-bye, thinking that sixty days would bring them back."

The river that gave birth to Vicksburg also made it °a city of unparalleled significance during the course of the

1. **Autumn–Winter, 1862–63:** Confederates construct nine miles of earthworks guarding land approaches to Vicksburg.

2. **May 17, 1863:** Pemberton and two Confederate divisions withdraw into Vicksburg perimeter.

3. **May 18:** Confederates occupy and continue to strengthen Vicksburg defenses.

4. **May 17–18:** Grant's army approaches Vicksburg: Sherman via Benton and Graveyard Roads, McPherson via Jackson Road, McClernand via Baldwin's Ferry Road.

5. **May 19, 1:30 P.M.–dark:** Grant attacks Confederate defenses but is repulsed.

6. **May 20–22, dawn:** Grant positions artillery and occupies ground closer to Confederate perimeter.

7. **May 22, 6:10 A.M.:** Federal artillery and Porter's ironclads bombard Vicksburg.

8. **May 25:** As Confederate defenses prove too strong to storm, Grant calls for siege operations and reinforcements.

9. **May 27, A.M.:** USS Cincinnati is sunk while attempting to gauge strength of Confederate upper water batteries.

10. **May 25–July 3:** Federals strenghten the siege sealing the Confederate garrison within the perimeter.

This rooftop view takes in most of the northeastern portion of the town. The thriving commercial interests of Vicksburg were buttressed by the waterfront. Without the activity on the wharves, there would have been few affluent citizens to demand fine jewelry shops and the latest European fashions. At the same time, rowdy saloons and gambling halls did a brisk business along the river.

Civil War. Confederate cannon mounted on the commanding bluffs overlooking the river protected the city from invasion and also denied that important avenue of commerce to Northern shipping.• The city was naturally protected on the north and east by hills and on the west by the river. °In a sense Vicksburg was the Gibraltar of the Mississippi, a geographically strategic site that had its own identity. Its people were fiercely proud and determined to take on all comers.•

Both Davis and Lincoln knew the strategic significance of the city. Davis knew it had to be held to keep the South together; Lincoln knew it had to be taken to rip the South apart. The Northern president asserted, "The war can never be brought to a close until [Vicksburg] is in our pocket."

The plan to take Vicksburg began two and a half years before it fell. While its citizens did not know it, their city was targeted as a war prize by the North on the day the state of Mississippi seceded from the Union. To the Federals Vicksburg was more than a city: At stake was control of the Mississippi River. The city was also symbolically important. The North knew that the fall of Vicksburg would be a stunning blow to Southern morale.

Shortly before the capture of New Orleans in April 1862, Lincoln called his admirals and generals to Washington to discuss his grand strategy to put down the rebellion. Pointing to a map of the divided nation, he said: "See what a lot of land these fellows hold of which Vicksburg is the key. I am acquainted with that region and know what I am talking about. Valuable as New Orleans will be to us, Vicksburg will be even more so. We may take all of the northern ports of the Confederacy and they can still defy us from Vicksburg. It means hogs and hominy without limit. Fresh troops from all the states of the far South and a cotton country where they can raise the staple without interference. Let us get Vicksburg and all that country is ours."

During the first year of the war, the people of Vicksburg only heard of the fighting in newspaper reports and letters from the front. In May 1862, however, the river brought the war to the city on the hill.

In 1883 Mark Twain observed: "The war history of Vicksburg has more about it to interest the general reader than that of any of the other river towns. It's full of variety, full of incident. Full of the picturesque. Vicksburg held out longer than any other important river town and saw warfare in all its phases. Both land and water. Siege, the mine, the assault, the revolt, the bombardment, the sickness, captivity, famine." Confederate Sergeant Chambers recalled, "When I look back now to that long, bloody and horrible battle, it seems more like a fearful dream than an actual experience." That was similar to a Northern viewpoint expressed by Union Col. Marcus Spiegel, who noted: "I've seen men dying of disease and mangled by the weapons of death. I've seen and experienced hunger, hardships, deprivations."

While the soldiers offered insight into how the battle was fought, the civilians drew upon all they knew to survive. In her diary, Dora Miller wrote: "I never understood before the full force of those questions. What shall we eat? What shall we drink? And where will we be clothed?" Mary Lafurrow added: "Was it a dream? Could I believe that over this smiling scene in the bright April morning the blight of civil warfare could lay like a pall."

Vicksburg never seemed to lack for anything. The landing was rarely vacant, and the river traffic was brisk. The town was also a strategic transfer point for the waterway and the railway. The Vicksburg, Shreveport, and Texas Railroad ended at the village of De Soto, and the goods were ferried from that riverfront depot to Vicksburg's and loaded on the Southern Mississippi Railroad for the remainder of the trip east. Another route brought western goods to the junction of the Red and Mississippi Rivers and then sailed them north to Vicksburg for the rest of the eastward journey.

Union Adm. David Farragut had twice led his ships to Vicksburg. His first venture, in May 1862, turned back when the city refused to capitulate and Farragut lacked the fire- and manpower to take the town. In June 1862 he returned with vessels more suited for river warfare and ran the batteries overlooking the river to link up with a Federal flotilla under Charles Davis. The passing was the first bombardment of the town. The Confederates, in response, set about an attack on the Union fleet. Lt. Isaac Newton Brown oversaw the building of the ram Arkansas. On July 14, 1862, Brown guided the vessel down the Yazoo River toward Vicksburg (right). He caught the Union fleet at anchor and steamed through it, too slow to ram anything but firing his ten guns as rapidly as they could be reloaded. The fight lasted an hour and ended only after the Southern vessel came under the protection of the Vicksburg batteries. The Arkansas disabled one vessel, but every wooden ship in the Federal armada had sustained a hit. The Confederates suffered 12 killed and 18 wounded; the Union counted 17 dead and 42 wounded, but another casualty was Farragut's pride.

TYC °AFTER MAJ. GEN. Benjamin Butler occupied New Orleans, Adm. David Farragut was able to come up the Mississippi. He took Baton Rouge, then set his sights on Vicksburg. Col. J. L. Aultrey, military governor of Vicksburg, defiantly announced: "Mississippians do not know and refuse to learn how to surrender. If Admiral Farragut and General Butler would like to teach them, let them come and try."•

Farragut did indeed "come and try." Sergeant Chambers recalled: "On Sunday, May 18, [1862,] orders were received for all the armed troops to repair to Vicksburg at once. Next morning I walked out on a ridge in front of our encampment, there rolled the mighty Mississippi River. And there, some two miles from where I stood, riding gracefully on the bosom of the turbid stream, were four or five vessels of the Northern fleet. Their dark hulls seem resting on the water, their sides bristled with cannon and over each one, proudly waved the Stars and Stripes. Once the flag of the free, now to us, the banner of subjugation."

After easy victories at New Orleans, Baton Rouge, and Natchez, Union Admiral Farragut and Como. David Dixon Porter supposed they could bombard Vicksburg into submission. For two summer months in 1862 their gunboats launched tons of hot iron at the city. The defenders took the shelling nonchalantly and somehow found hope and comfort in their defiance.

"One bright afternoon, men, women, and children could be seen seeking the hilltops with spy glasses," Lucy

McCray recalled. "From the heights could be seen a black object slowly approaching along the river. Suddenly a shell came rattling over as if to say 'Here I am!' Vicksburg, however, put on her war clothes and cannon were rushed to the river front. Forts sprang into sight in a short time. Whistling Dick, the old Confederate gun, sang defiance."

ᵒThat summer Vicksburg's fate was decided first by the weather, second by malaria and mosquitoes, and third by the appearance of the CSS *Arkansas*, an ironclad that was being constructed on the Yazoo River. The Southern ironclad finally had to escape the Yazoo to avoid being cut off by a Yankee fleet moving down from the north. The vessel was commanded by Comdr. Isaac Brown, one of the most intrepid naval commanders of the war. He steamed his poor, incomplete ironclad through a Yankee fleet of thirty vessels. Brown later described it as having sailed into the heart of a volcano.•

"Down she came one fine morning and passed unscathed through the whole line of our vessels dealing death and destruction as she passed," reported Porter in his postwar memoirs. "The ships poured broadsides of solid shot into her but they rolled from her side like water from a duck's back. That time, the Confederates had the laugh on us."

ᵒThe people of Vicksburg took the *Arkansas*, its crew, and its commander to their hearts. When it finally arrived at the wharf, the city went wild. They believed if this one ship could shame the Yankee fleet, then there was hope

On April 16, 1863, Adm. David Dixon Porter led a flotilla of twelve Northern vessels past the Confederate guns positioned on the heights above Vicksburg (above left). That night many of the townspeople were at a gala ball, including most of the senior Confederate officers. Porter hoped that the event would occupy the Southerners and allow his convoy safe passage. Alert pickets, however, spotted the dark shapes on the river and sounded the alarm. An eyewitness to the ensuing battle wrote: "It was the grandest spectacle of my life. . . . Our batteries were in full play, blazing away at the line of gunboats making their way past them and giving shot for shot. . . . The whole landscape was as light as day. . . . Porter gamely led, and hove-to off the town to send a few shots along its streets, which stampeded the entire population, especially the ball, when the gallant young officers dashed away to their posts, leaving the ladies to their own devices." All but one transport and two barges survived the two-and-a-half-hour ordeal. William T. Sherman was at New Carthage, the Federal assembly point, and greeted each ship as it arrived. In the image above (right) he is pictured in the small boat approaching Porter's flagship, the Benton.

The USS Cricket was part of Porter's fleet that assisted in the siege of Vicksburg. This tinclad had six 12-pound boat howitzers and was manned by forty-eight officers and men. The gunboats and mortar schooners shelled the city from the waterfront while Grant's artillery pummeled it from his land position. Shots from these vessels were thrown high in the air with fuses sputtering, emphasizing the arc of the projectile. The scene was especially dramatic in the evening hours, when the bombardment offered a kind of macabre entertainment for attacker and defender as well.

ECB

that they were going to be able to hold out indefinitely against the Federals.•

While the *Arkansas* provided hope for the people in Vicksburg, it did not stop the naval bombardment. The Yankee shells, however, caused little damage to the city as the naval gunners could not get sufficient elevation to shell the town properly. Likewise, the Rebel cannon could not chase the Federal gunboats from the river. The two sides were at a standoff. "Ships cannot crawl up hills three hundred feet high. And it is that part of Vicksburg which must be taken by the army," wrote a perceptive and frustrated Porter.

By August the river began to recede, and the Union flotilla had to abandon its effort. Soon after, the rich Confederate harvest moved through Vicksburg. In Washington, Lincoln's frustrations became supreme.

°Lincoln was highly concerned about the war effort, so much so that he called for five hundred thousand volunteers. He began looking for new generals to win victories that would help buttress the will of the North. At this point, like the dawn, a man appeared who was determined to take Vicksburg. Maj. Gen. Ulysses S. Grant was gathering his forces for a southern advance along the Mississippi Central Railroad.•

Grant and Porter succeeded in shutting down Vicksburg and stemming the flow of western goods to the East, but the Confederate commander, John C. Pemberton, believed that Grant was pulling back to Memphis as late as five days before Porter's vessels had run past his batteries. Pemberton had even released some of his fifty thousand defenders for service elsewhere. While Porter's move corrected his misconception, he still had no idea of what Grant had in mind.

TYC   °In October 1862 Grant was placed in charge of the effort to capture Vicksburg. By this time, however, he was fighting two wars: one with the Confederacy and the other with the political generals and politicians who wanted his job.•

BP   °Grant was constantly challenged by ambitious rivals like Maj. Gen. John McClernand,• a Democratic congressman from Illinois who was appointed a general by Lincoln. The man lacked any military experience other than serving as a private in the Black Hawk War in the 1830s, but Lincoln needed his political influence. °What prompted Grant to take action against Vicksburg before he was ready was the news that McClernand was going to be taking charge of thousands of troops in Illinois. McClernand wanted to create an independent army that would march into Grant's territory.•

In his memoirs in 1885, Grant recalled: "I was very much disturbed by newspaper rumors that General McClernand was to have a separate and independent command within mine to operate against Vicksburg by way of the Mississippi River. Two commanders on the same field are always one too many. And in this case, I do not think the general selected had either the experience or the qualifications to fight here for so important a position."

ECB   °Grant had to move fast to steal the march on McClernand. Fortunately for Grant, McClernand was distracted

David Dixon Porter commanded the Federal fleet at Vicksburg in 1863. Although he had a reputation for recalcitrance, he teamed wonderfully with Ulysses S. Grant in a rare, workable army-navy coordination.

The USS Cairo (left) was one of seven ironclads called "Pook Turtles" after their designer, Samuel M. Pook. The flat-bottomed stern-wheeler was heavily armed with three 8-inch guns, six 32-pounders, four 42-pounders, and a 12-pound howitzer. It did not participate in any significant action on the Mississippi between its launching in January 1862 and September 1862, when it was briefly taken out of service for an overhaul. The Cairo returned in December to join a diversionary expedition on the Yazoo River while William T. Sherman launched an attack against Vicksburg. On December 12, it struck two mines and sank within twelve minutes with, miraculously, no loss of life. The Cairo was the first warship ever to be lost to mines. In 1956 the vessel's remains were discovered, and it was raised over several years beginning in 1960. Restoration was completed in 1984, when the Cairo went on display at the Vicksburg National Military Park.

Rebel gunners fired their riverfront guns (above left) with great accuracy even during the evening. Special reflectors flashed the light from huge bonfires onto the Yankee gunships. A number of railroad locomotive headlights were also utilized. Southern artillerymen could aim about as well as if it were day. These guns used shot, percussion shell, shrapnel, and grape shot. The batteries were also laid out to minimize the effectiveness of Union naval gunfire (above right), which led Grant to focus on the problem of taking the city from the land rather than the river.

from organizing his army by a wedding—his own. A widower, McClernand set the date of his marriage to his late wife's sister for December 24, 1862.•

With his rival otherwise occupied, Grant put his old friend, Maj. Gen. William Tecumseh Sherman, in charge of the Illinois troops who would have constituted McClernand's force. Then the two launched a two-pronged assault on Vicksburg. The west prong under Sherman attacked Chickasaw Bluffs north of the town. The main thrust, led by Grant, marched through the middle of the state hoping to draw the Rebel army out of their works. Instead, a column of Confederate cavalry

The difficulty of the Union position was not lost on the Confederates. Southern engineers worked for seven months to fortify a nine-mile line with nine forts to protect them from a land attack. On the riverfront they had mounted guns. All avenues were covered. The city was naturally protected to the north and east by hills.

under Maj. Gen. Earl Van Dorn raided Grant's rear at Holly Springs, Mississippi, destroying his supply base and lines of communication. Grant was forced to abort his part of the assault, leaving Sherman alone to fight the Rebels in the swamp.

EC °Late December was a horrible time of year in Mississippi. The weather was miserably cold and wet and hardly conducive to fighting. Sherman learned that war was hell because that was what he found at Chickasaw Bluffs. He lost more than 200 dead and 1,000 wounded as opposed to the Confederate losses of 63 dead and 134 wounded. Sherman did not make any apologies for his defeat. He thought it might have been different had Grant arrived, but he was in an impossible situation. His troops had to wade through deep water and then scale the bluffs that were occupied by the Rebels who were shooting down at them. The battle became a slaughter.•

After withdrawing from the bluffs, Sherman wrote the shortest action report of the entire war: "I reached Vicksburg at the time appointed, landed, assaulted and failed." He was already beginning to develop the style of warfare that would make him famous and feared throughout the South. In October 1862 he had said: "We cannot change the hearts of those people in the South but we can make war so terrible that they will realize the fact that however brave and gallant and devoted to their country, still they are mortal and should exhaust all peaceful remedies before they fly to war."

At the battle of Chickasaw Bluffs, the defenders of Vicksburg made war terrible for Sherman and Grant. Despite the devastating repulse, Grant resolved to move forward, never back. Just as Mississippians did not know the meaning of surrender, Grant refused to learn the meaning of retreat.

Explaining his strategy twenty years later, Grant said: "The problem then became how to secure a landing on high ground east of the Mississippi without an apparent retreat. I then commenced a

Ulysses S. Grant (above) was tenacious and unrelenting in the task of taking Vicksburg. Although the army prized precedent, Grant was always willing to try anything to accomplish his mission. At Vicksburg he tried four strategies: a canal to reroute the Mississippi, a connecting tributary to facilitate joining forces with another army, an expedition through the bayous, and a flanking march that would approach the town from the east.

The Warren County Courthouse (below) was built in 1860 in the Greek Revival style on Vicksburg's highest point. From its prominent setting it could be viewed by both the Union and the Confederate armies, and both sides went by the clock on the cupola.

series of experiments to consume time and to divert the attention of the enemy, my troops and of the public generally. I myself never felt great confidence that any of the experiments resorted to would prove successful. Nevertheless, I was always prepared to take advantage of them in case they did."

These experiments included expeditions through the labyrinthine bayous north of Vicksburg and a futile effort to change the course of the Mississippi River by digging a canal across the De Soto Point peninsula opposite Vicksburg. The object was to force the river into the new canal and away from the town so the Union gunboats could pass up and down the canal at will and out of range of the Confederate guns. The canal-digging scheme was suggested by the president himself. Grant recalled: "Mr. Lincoln had navigated the Mississippi River in younger days and understood well its tendency to change its channel in places from time to time. He set much store accordingly by this canal."

Grant did Lincoln's bidding if only to pacify a president who was quick to fire generals, but the Mississippi was not about to change course for anyone, not even Lincoln. The spring rains never came to raise the river into the canal, and in fact, the river dropped faster than the soldiers could dig below the water level. The canal was a failure. Swamp sickness decimated the ranks of Grant's army. Hundreds of Union soldiers and contrabanded slaves died digging a canal that never filled with water. Still, Grant would not give up, and Lincoln stood by him. "I can't spare this man. He fights," the president said to Grant's critics.

°Grant was not the smartest man in the military or in the White House, but like George Washington during the Revolution, he would be remembered for his persistence. He kept on and on and on. He encountered setbacks, but he never allowed them to stop him. If he had a goal, he achieved it.•

In sharp contrast to Grant's command, the defense of Vicksburg had been entrusted to Lt. Gen. John C. Pemberton. A Pennsylvanian by birth, he had sided with the South. Because he was a friend of Jefferson Davis, he rose quickly in rank, but his rank was not indicative of his abilities as a commander.

John C. Pemberton, the Confederate commander at Vicksburg, was a native Pennsylvanian of Quaker ancestry and an 1837 graduate of West Point. He had seen action in the Seminole Wars and the Mexican War, but in 1861 he sided with his wife's native state of Virginia. He was given command of the Department of Mississippi in 1862 and immediately addressed the problem of fortifying Vicksburg's defenses. Pemberton was not a brilliant commander, but few in his position could have performed better.

One of the homes of the city's more wealthy residents boasted turrets and other Medieval touches. The yard became a camp site and the house was later destroyed by the Federals after the surrender of the town.

°Pemberton's inability to read the strategic situation was a weakness that plagued the defense of Vicksburg throughout the course of Grant's operations. In the early spring of 1863, Pemberton was bombarded with reports from all over: the Federals were here, the Federals were there, and indeed the Federals seemed to be absolutely everywhere. The Southern commander's inability to decipher that intelligence and correctly read the warning signs proved disastrous for the Confederacy.•

°He lacked both organizational skills and the ability to inspire confidence in his men, at least one of which is necessary for a general to be successful. He liked to command from a distance instead of at the front. Grant was just the opposite; he liked being at the front.•

While Grant experimented with finding a good way into Vicksburg, Pemberton fortified the city. The Union navy did all it could to make that as difficult for him as possible. Even the townspeople seemed to grasp the situation more readily than Pemberton. On March 20, 1863, Dora Miller noted in her diary: "The shelling of Vicksburg was on all the time and we had grown indifferent. It does not interrupt or interfere with the other allocations. But I suspect they're only getting the range of different points and when they have them all complete, showers of shot will rain on us all at once."

William T. Sherman, perhaps Grant's most famous subordinate and definitely his friend, had grave concerns about moving the army in the wide flanking maneuver Grant proposed to get at Vicksburg from the east. They would be outnumbered and had no practical route for retreat if defeated. Yet when the two men stood on the bluffs north of the city, Sherman told Grant that until that minute he had doubted his strategy, "This, however, is the end of one of the greatest campaigns in history," even if Vicksburg should not fall.

Many units acquired mascots. Hundreds of dogs went into battle with their masters, and some soldiers had pet raccoons or badgers. One of the best-known mascots of the war was Old Abe, a bald eagle. The previous owner could not care for it, and so he sold it to one of the companies belonging to the Eighth Wisconsin. At the battle of Corinth a bullet severed the rope that held the bird to his perch. It flew along the lines, losing several tail feathers until David McLain, the eagle-bearer, risked his life to recapture the bird and carry it to safety.

The shelling was part of what Grant termed "the reduction" of Vicksburg, but the constant shelling would do no good if the army could not open the eastern or back door to the city. In the spring of 1863, Grant found the key.

WCD   °One of the hallmarks of Grant's generalship was that he always had another idea. He decided that he had to get his army south of the city, march inland to the east, and then come back against Vicksburg from its eastern side. He decided to march his army overland, down the Louisiana side of the river, while sending his fleet south past the batteries along Vicksburg to get below the city.•

To accomplish this plan, Grant needed the navy to ferry his army across the river, but Porter's fleet was anchored above the town. Thus, on a moonless night, April 16, 1863, eight Union ships ran the fiery gauntlet at Vicksburg. Vicksburg's Mary Loch Burrow described the scene: "The river was illuminated by large fires on the bank and we could discern plainly, the huge black masses floating down with the current, now and then belching forth fire from their sides, followed by the loud report."

ECB   °The Confederates sounded alarms and lit the river with burning barrels of turpentine, but the fleet fought its way downriver, losing only one vessel, the *Henry Clay*.•

Several units of U.S. Colored Troops were camped around Vicksburg following the siege. This photograph (right), probably the work of Vicksburg's French and Company, shows the Twentieth U.S.C.T. garrisoned just before Fort Hill. The troops are drawn up on the parade ground in the background. Caves are notable in the foreground, in front of the wagons and stable, and may have been used for storage, which might explain the many barrels clustered around them.

Almost two weeks later, April 28, 1863, Dora Miller recalled: "Another night, eight boats run by leaving a shower of shot. Two burning houses made the river as clear as day." Two nights later, half of Grant's army, forty-three thousand men, were ferried across the Mississippi River. Then, having gained a foothold below the city, Grant executed the most daring move of his career. Instead of waiting for reinforcements from the south, he marched east toward Jackson, the capital of Mississippi. He was moving into the heart of enemy territory without any chance of immediate support and without any clear knowledge of the strength of the enemy.

°Pemberton was confused the whole time. He thought Grant had pulled back to Memphis. When he heard reports of Grant's moving down the west bank, he did not believe them. Finally he realized he was in trouble: a Union army was east of the Mississippi.

Beginning on May 1, Grant initiated a brief campaign during which his army won five battles in eighteen days.• °He was victorious at Port Gibson on May 1, and at Raymond on May 12. Two days later, on May 14, his army captured Jackson. Grant then wheeled his troops west toward Vicksburg, defeating Confederate forces at Champion Hill on May 16 and at Big Black

During the siege many townspeople moved into crude caves dug in the hillsides. The young lady above prays while an intense barrage rages outside; other citizens watched from the mouth of their caves. One of the latter was Mary Loughborough, who reminisced, "I sat at the mouth of the cave, with the servants drawn around me, watching the brilliant display of fireworks the mortar boats were making—the passage of the shell as it traveled through the heavens looking like a swiftly moving star." As the artist depicted it above, those who moved to the caves tried to make them as comfortable as possible with whatever they could bring from their homes.

During the forty-seven-day siege Grant's troops dug into the hillsides (left) and erected arbors for protection from the severe Mississippi summer sun. By mid-June more than one hundred Federal cannon were pounding Vicksburg from the land, and Porter's fleet supplemented the bombardment from the river.

On the morning of May 22, 1863, Federal troops assaulted the Confederate earthworks around Vicksburg. It was thought that the initial attacks had broken through part of the line. The message, however, was erroneous. When Brig. Gen. Joseph A. Mower's Eagle Brigade—so-called for the mascot of Company C of the Eighth Wisconsin Infantry, Old Abe—joined the action, it attacked one of the strongest points in the Rebel line. The Eighth ran into a sunken road, known later as Graveyard Road, and filled the gaps in the line where its predecessors had fallen, but then Confederate canister shot took its toll. The assault was a failure, and all Mower's men could do was wait for night to cover their withdrawal.

River Bridge on May 17. On the basis of these successes and with Vicksburg ahead of it, Grant's army was confident of a quick victory.•

Yet despite his lightning march, Vicksburg still defied Grant. On May 19 and 22 he ordered massive frontal assaults on the Rebel works protecting the city from the east. The attempts were costly failures. He dug a mine shaft under the Confederate lines and blew it up, a tactic he would try again the following summer at Petersburg, Virginia, but the Confederates quickly plugged the hole at Vicksburg, just as they would do at Petersburg.

In his memoirs Grant wrote: "I now determined upon a regular siege to 'out camp' the enemy as it were and to incur no more losses. The experience of [May 22] convinced officers and the men that this was best. And we went to work on the defenses and approaches with a will. With the navy holding the river, investment of Vicksburg was complete. As long as we could hold our position, the enemy was limited in supplies of food, men and munitions of war to what they had on hand. These could not last always."

NOWHERE IN THE Confederacy did civilians suffer more terrible effects of war than during the two-month siege of Vicksburg. Under constant bombardment from Grant's heavy guns, the starving people of Vicksburg were forced out of their homes and into the surrounding hills where they lived in caves.

As early as May 1, Dora Miller noted, "The city just settled at last, and we should spend the time of siege in Vicksburg." °Even before the siege started, in her diary she predicted that it would happen. Dora Miller was a young pregnant bride who had no Vicksburg friends because she was pro-Union. She kept to herself and kept her thoughts private from her neighbors.• "My only consolation is to remember the old axiom, a city besieged is a city taken," she wrote.

Between June 23–25 Federal troops excavated a tunnel under the Confederate works and packed it with 2,200 pounds of gunpowder. The Southerners had heard the digging and surmised what was happening and had began digging a tunnel of their own to intercept the Northerners. They were still digging when the gunpowder exploded. Only six Rebels were killed by the blast because the Confederates had pulled back and waited. Federal troops poured through the crater left by the explosion and toward the Rebel line until forced back to the crater by cannon fire. The Confederates counterattacked, and for hours the combat was hand to hand (left). The Union troops held on to the position for three days and then fell back to their original line. The Northerners lost two hundred men, the Southerners less than one hundred. On July 1 another tunnel charge was exploded that did considerably more damage than the first. Twelve Confederates were killed and more than one hundred wounded, but the Yankee commanders were more cautious and decided not to assault the Rebel works again.

Mark Twain vividly described the scene as he heard it: "Population: twenty-seven thousand soldiers and three thousand noncombatants. The city utterly cut off from the world. Walled solidly in. The frontage by gunboats, the rear by soldiers and batteries. All in a moment come ground shaking thunder crashes of artillery. A moment later, women and children scurrying from home and bed toward the cave dungeons, encouraged by the humorous grim soldier who would shout, 'Rats, to your hole.'"

Emma Balfour, another diarist, wrote: "Tuesday, May 19th. When the general asked me if we were provided with a rat hole, I told him it seems to me that we were all caught in a rat hole." °Balfour had been born in Charles City County, Virginia, and moved to Vicksburg as a young woman. She loved flowers and wrote about them a great deal, but she also wrote about the siege:• "Thursday, May 21st. Last night after the firing ceased as the Yankees passed in speaking distance of our works, our men called out, 'Lend us some coffee for supper won't you? We will pay you when Johnston comes.' They replied, 'Never mind the coffee but Grant will take dinner in Vicksburg tomorrow.'"

Grant's plans were in place, and he confidently noted: "May 23rd. There is no doubt of the fall of this place ultimately, but how long it will take is a matter of doubt. One week is as long as I think the enemy can possibly hold out." He was wrong. For all his might, Grant

The siege of Vicksburg had many assaults, but the bloodiest occurred on May 22, 1863. In front of Fort Beauregard the Twenty-second Iowa had to scale a hill in a shower of bullets and canister. In the painting above the color-sergeant bravely plants the flag as his comrades attempt to breach the Rebel line. At another point in the line the color-bearer of the Ninety-ninth Illinois carried the Stars and Stripes into the line and was captured. Ultimately, the Federal assault on May 22 was a disaster. Grant lost 3,199 men; the Southerners fewer than 500. It was the bloodiest battle of the campaign.

underestimated the Rebel will. Similarly, there was no way he could foresee the hardships his own troops would suffer.

GC °Mississippi summers are unforgettable, ninety-eight degrees Fahrenheit and 98 percent humidity at the same time. It is uncomfortable even without a tiny bug called the red bug, or chigger. Chiggers burrow under a person's skin and cause serious discomfort.•

For forty-seven days the two armies suffered these miserable conditions. Every day Grant shelled the city, and just about every night Billy Yank and Johnny Reb fraternized, trading tobacco, insults, and pleasantries. Between the lines, two brothers from Missouri who fought on opposite sides frequently met. The fraternization also satisfied a more practical need.

"On the afternoon of Monday, May 25th, a truce of two or three hours was arranged in order to bury the dead who lay between the lines," wrote Confederate Sergeant Chambers. "These bodies had become so offensive that our troops could hardly remain in the trenches along those points where the slaughter had been the greatest. Hence, our men gladly assisted in the burial of their fallen foes." Even in an atmosphere of despair, knowing the Union army was just over the hills, the people of Vicksburg found life livable.

"In the midst of all this carnage and commotion, it is touching to see how every work of God save man gives praise to him. The birds are singing as merrily as if all were well. The flowers are in perfection. All save the spirit of man seems divine," wrote Emma Balfour.

Grant did not want the people of the city to find such beauties in their surroundings. "May 31. General, give all your artillery on the enemy for half an hour, commencing at 3:00 tomorrow morning," ordered Grant. On June 2 he altered that order, specifying: "Commence firing at 6:30 o'clock this morning. Fire ten minutes. Stop twenty. Fire again for twenty minutes more." Grant's aim was to break the people and the soldiers inside Vicksburg, to make them anticipate death at any moment of the day. The citizens, however, were not as terrified as he had hoped.

"Mother had a tent pitched outside so that when the mortars did not have the range, we could sit back and watch the shells as they came over. They were beautiful at night," wrote Lucy McCray.

Throughout the siege, Vicksburg hoped and waited for Confederate Gen. Joseph E. Johnston to come to the rescue from Jackson, which he had reoccupied after Grant's May 14 attack on the town. Johnston had been able to build a force of at least thirty thousand men. Every man, woman, and child in Vicksburg was anxious to welcome Johnston's army to town.

"June 18th. Today the _Citizen_ is printed on wallpaper. It says that a few days more and Johnston will be here," wrote Dora Miller. As the siege continued, the people responded to their hardships with a creative resourcefulness. °Before the war there had been quite a few newspapers in Vicksburg. At the time of the siege only one was still in operation, the _Daily Citizen_, edited by J. M. Swords, who tried to bolster the morale of the readers as best he could. Like everybody else, he looked for Johnston's army to come to the rescue.• "June 25th. The

The Vicksburg defenders could not counter the hundreds of Federal cannon posed against them. They did utilize this huge rifled 18-pounder. It had been made at the Tredegar Iron Works at Richmond and was mounted in the city's water battery. A defect in the cannon tube gave its shots an odd sound, and so the gun was nicknamed Whistling Dick. It fired on Farragut's and Porter's fleets. On May 28, 1863, the gun sank the Union vessel Cincinnati. It was finally disabled by Northern fire from across the river. In the photograph above the photographer claimed to have captured Whistling Dick, but legend says the gun was lost in the river.

With his army exhausted and little hope of relief or escape, Pemberton on July 3 offerred a cease-fire to Grant during which a surrender could be negotiated. The painting below depicts the generals between the lines discussing terms, but this meeting did not immediately result in capitulation. The Confederate commander sharply refused to surrender unconditionally. Ultimately, the Federals were generous; Rebel soldiers were paroled rather than taken prisoner. Thus on July 4 Vicksburg surrendered, including 31,600 soldiers, 172 guns, and 60,000 muskets. Since the Confederate rifles were of better quality than the U.S. issues, Grant ordered his officers to replace their weapons with the captured muskets. Some of the captured armament is pictured above.

absorbing question now is where is Johnston and what time will he be here?" asked Swords in an editorial.

Johnston never came. He could never find an unguarded way across the Big Black River, and he was convinced that throwing his men at Grant was futile. He knew he could get no more reinforcements from Richmond because Jefferson Davis was focused on the Virginia front. The reduction of Vicksburg would continue.

"June 25th. A horrible day. Most horrible yet to me because I lost my nerve," wrote Dora Miller. "I am brave and not someone to think of danger till it's over and yet that's not what tears me as for some others. But now, I realize that something worse than death might come. I might be crippled and not killed. That thought broke down my courage."

On July 1 Dora Miller lost her nerve and begged the Union army to allow her to leave Vicksburg as a war refugee. She was a Union sympathizer and eight months pregnant, but Grant refused. "No human being shall pass out of Vicksburg but the lady may feel sure, danger will soon be over. Vicksburg will surrender on the Fourth of July," Grant said.

BY THURSDAY, JULY 2, the situation in Vicksburg was grim. Seventy-one thousand Union soldiers had a death grip on twenty thousand Rebels, a force that had been greatly reduced by men missing,

After forty-seven days of siege Grant's troops marched triumphantly into Vicksburg. The Fourth Minnesota was among the first units to enter the town (left). There was some looting in various parts of the town, mostly by Federal stragglers, army followers, and a few recently freed slaves overreacting to sudden freedom. Other Northerners showed great kindness and took food from their haversacks to share with the hungry Southerners—soldiers and civilians. Porter's fleet also brought in supplies. The victors demonstrated a keen sensitivity toward the vanquished. One of Pemberton's officers recalled that the only cheer he heard on July 4 was "for the gallant defenders of Vicksburg."

wounded, or sick. There was plenty of ammunition but no food. Grave digging seemed to be the only occupation in town. Nevertheless, the *Daily Citizen* still went to press with another defiant wallpaper editorial: "The great Ulysses, the Yankee generalissimo surnamed Grant has expressed his intention of dining in Vicksburg on Saturday night and celebrating the Fourth of

Hospital ships conveyed wounded Union soldiers to and from Vicksburg (below). With the aid of the Sanitary and Christian Commissions, care for the wounded improved. Complete access to the Mississippi River facilitated their timely movement and saved countless lives.

The advance Federal units that entered Vicksburg were preceded by a color guard and a band playing Northern songs. When they arrived at the court-house they were drawn up facing the building. The ceremony of possession of the city was completed by displaying the flags of the Forty-fifth Illinois and of the headquarters of the Seventeenth Corps. Cheers resounded from the Union troops. Grant also rode up to pay his respects to the Stars and Stripes.

A Union camp of African-American troops (below) was stationed at Vicks-burg in 1864. During the siege some Federal black troops were posted across the river at Milliken's Bend, which was manned by one white regiment and three black regiments. On June 7, 1863, fifteen hundred Texans com-manded by Brig. Gen. Henry E. McCulloch approached Milliken's Bend. The Rebels, sensing an easy vic-tory, charged with a shout of "No quarter." A desperate hand-to-hand battle ensued, driving the Union troops back toward the Mississippi. Porter dispatched two gunboats to the scene, and they poured a heavy fire into the rear ranks of the Rebels, com-pelling them to retreat. Of 652 North-ern casualties, 566 were from the African-American regiments.

July by a grand dinner. Ulysses must get into the city before he dines in it. The way to cook a rabbit is first to catch the rabbit."

Saturday night the U.S. Army used the same printing press to publish an extra: "July 4th, 1863. Two days bring about great changes. The banner of the Union floats over Vicksburg. General Grant has caught the rabbit. He has dined in Vicksburg and he did bring his dinner with him."

The city of Vicksburg surrendered on the Fourth of July because Pemberton believed Grant would do any-thing for a symbolic surrender on July 4. The Confeder-ate general from Philadelphia told his subordinates: "I know my people [meaning Northerners]. They are a vain glorious lot. That they will give anything if this city and its garrison surrenders on July Fourth."

Dora Miller noted in her diary: "Sat-urday, July 3rd. I woke at dawn. When I entered the kitchen a soldier was there. I asked him, 'Is it true about the surren-der?' He said: 'Yes. And the men of Vicksburg will never forgive Pemberton, the old grannie. A child would have known better than to shut men up in this cursed trap to starve to death like useless vermin.' When I asked him if he was not being hard on Pemberton, he

Four-Mile Bridge was photographed in 1865 and served as an exchange point for paroled prisoners. The encampment on the far side was the guards' quarters. The site played a role in the Sultana tragedy after the war. On April 24, 1865, twenty-one hundred former Confederate prisoners boarded the Sultana at Vicksburg for passage to Cairo, Illinois. The ship, however, was designed to carry fewer than four hundred passengers. One of its boilers exploded on April 27, and the vessel became a floating inferno. Seventeen hundred died.

replied, 'Some people may excuse him madam, but we'll curse him to our dying day.'"

°CD °Pemberton was probably the most unfortunate man in the Vicksburg story. He did not receive sufficient cooperation from Richmond, and he had no cooperation from Johnston, who was supposed to be coming to his rescue. In the end, Pemberton likely felt he had been abandoned by everybody.• With no hope of assis-

GC tance, °Pemberton had the nerve to accept that further resistance was senseless. Many Southerners hated him for the surrender, but he negotiated a surrender that was not unconditional. He did what he thought was best for the people of Vicksburg and his troops.•

Brierfield, the former plantation of Confederate President Jefferson Davis, was twenty miles south of Vicksburg. He left the estate in the care of his overseers, and they managed to harvest enough of a crop in 1862 to feed several black families that made the house their home. Farragut's sailors were among the first Federals to plunder the property. On July 4, 1864, Yankee soldiers hosted a picnic for former slaves on the grounds and decorated the home with red-white-and-blue bunting.

Grant was indeed anxious to gain the surrender and agreed to parole the Confederates rather than send them to prison camps. Even Pemberton was allowed to go free. In a rare example of a man's recognizing his own limitations, Pemberton resigned his lieutenant general's commission and asked for a colonel's rank in the artillery, which was granted. His last action came in April 1865 when he tried to defend the town of Salisbury, North Carolina, from a Union cavalry raid. He had only a few hundred militiamen against a much larger force of Federals. He lost.

Pemberton (above) was paroled and returned to Confederate service. He resigned his commission in March 1864. He became an inspector of the artillery, and in April 1864 he was placed in charge of Richmond's Defense Battalion of Artillery, training gunners and expanding the batteries along the James River. In January 1865 Pemberton was made inspector general of Southern artillery. As such he visited Charleston, where he had begun his service to the Confederacy in 1861, and then joined Joseph Johnston to reorganize the artillery wing of the Army of Tennessee. After the war he returned to his home near Warrenton, Virginia, and eventually moved back to Philadelphia.

The end of the siege of Vicksburg was almost an anti-climax. In her diary, Dora Miller recorded: "About 11:00 [on July 4], a man in blue came sauntering along. Soon, a group appeared on the courthouse hill and the flag began slowly to rise to the top of the staff. The breeze caught it and it sprang out like a live thing. Now I feel once more at home in my own country."

ECB °Grant felt a great deal of satisfaction at capturing the city. He was a man who had been marked as a failure in life by rumors of drunkenness. At Vicksburg he moved onto a higher plateau with a military campaign that was GC a masterpiece.• °The siege of Vicksburg made Grant's reputation and identified him as the man Lincoln had been looking for to take command in the East. From here Grant would move on to Chattanooga, and from there he would be summoned to Washington by Lincoln to take over command on the Virginia front.•

The Northern president wasted no time in congratulating Grant: "July 13th, 1863. My dear General, I write this now as a grateful acknowledgment for the almost inestimable service you have done the country. I wish to say a word further, when you turned northward east of the Big Black River, I feared it was a mistake. I now wish to make the personal acknowledgment that you were GC right and I was wrong." °Lincoln had realized the importance of Vicksburg when he put his finger on the map in 1861 and talked to his generals about it. He knew they needed Vicksburg to control the river and the railroad. He knew they needed the city to divide the Confederacy in half. It took two years for the rest of the country to realize that Lincoln was right. Vicksburg was the key.•

TYC °With the fall of Vicksburg, all communications to the Trans-Mississippi (the Confederate war department west of the river) ended. Supplies that used to come from Texas through Vicksburg to the rest of the Confederacy ceased. The rest of the Confederacy ended up starving just as Vicksburg did. The war itself lasted two more years, but the capture of Vicksburg marked the beginning of the end. In the opinion of many historians, it was not Gettysburg, the high tide of Confederate movement into the North, that sealed the fate of the

Confederacy. The end was marked by Vicksburg's capture, which was the last link in the Union's regaining control of the Mississippi River.•

The people of Vicksburg did not forget or reconstruct easily back into the Union. Eighty-five years passed between official parades to celebrate Independence Day. Before then the river did something else to embarrass the town. In April 1876, the nation's centennial and Grant's last year as president, the river changed course, leaving the city without its means of commerce. Years later the U.S. Army Corps of Engineers would reroute the river to reconnect Vicksburg with the Mississippi. In 1862 the river had ignored the Federal engineers. Years later, it let them move it.

BP   °Vicksburg witnessed incredible, fearless deeds of sacrifice and a battle of wills between determined people. The shadow of that battle and its memory are still very present in the city. They can be felt.• Certainly, the residents never forgot what they had survived. In celebration, Dora Miller wrote: "It is evening. All is still. Silence and light are once reunited. I can sit at the table in the parlor and write. Two candles are lit. I would like a dozen."

Unlike Gettysburg, where Lee's army was defeated but not vanquished, Grant's victory at Vicksburg was more than just a symbol. It forever closed the Mississippi River to Confederate trade. Lincoln summed up the Union victory with the simple statement: "The father of waters again goes unvexed to the sea."

After the fall of Vicksburg, Grant received an extraordinary congratulatory letter from Abraham Lincoln. In it the president confessed that he had believed Grant had been mistaken in his strategy to take the river stronghold. He concluded, "I now wish to make a personal acknowledgment that you were right and I was wrong."

NOW IN CAMP AT READVILLE!

54th REGIMENT!

MASS. VOLUNTEERS, composed of men of

AFRICAN DESCENT

Col. ROBERT G. SHAW.

 Colored Men, Rally 'Round the Flag of Freedom!

BOUNTY $100!

AT THE EXPIRATION OF THE TERM OF SERVICE.

Pay, $13 a Month!
Good Food & Clothing!
State Aid to Families!

RECRUITING OFFICE.

COR. CAMBRIDGE & NORTH RUSSELL STS., BOSTON.

Lieut. J. W. M. APPLETON, Recruiting Officer.

RWELL & CO., Steam Job Printers, No. 37 Congress Street, Boston.

THE FIFTY-FOURTH MASSACHUSETTS

The FIFTY-FOURTH MASSACHUSETTS Infantry Regiment was the first Northern unit to be manned by black volunteers. This group of men proved in the face of prejudice that African Americans were as smart as, could shoot as well as, could march as well as, and could survive terrible combat conditions as well as any white men. In short, the men of the Fifty-fourth Massachusetts proved they were the equal of any men on the battlefield. Their heroism under fire demonstrated that bravery had no color.

WG °The Fifty-fourth changed the face of the war between the states and the face of social expectations of the nation in one day.• This eventual accomplishment was made all the more remarkable because it came at a time when America, both North and South, was a racist country, when most whites did not pretend to accept people of African descent on any social level. The Fifty-fourth— and all of the two hundred thousand black men who served in the Union army during the last two years of the war—had a special mission: proving to the white race that not only would black men fight, but they would fight as courageously and boldly as their white companions in arms.

When efforts to enlist African Americans into the Union army were started, some critics said that blacks would not be able to march because their feet were shaped differently from a white man's. Others claimed blacks could not be controlled and would act like savages on the battlefield. The brave men of the First and Second South Carolina Volunteer Infantry and the Fifty-

GC	George Coblyn
CC	Carl Cruz
WCD	William C. Davis
WWG	William W. Gwaltney
JH	James Horton
BP	Brian Pohanka
GU	Gregory Urwin

The fight to abolish slavery had begun in the early nineteenth century, but fifty years later there was little to show for the effort. The vast majority of Northerners, like most Southerners, believed that subjugation of African Americans was good economic and social policy. One of the climactic moments in the drawn-out battle for the abolition of slavery was the insurrection led by John Brown in 1859 at Harpers Ferry. This engraving (right) depicts a white mob breaking up memorial services for Brown at the interracial Tremont Temple in Boston on the one-year anniversary of his execution. The event followed Abraham Lincoln's election and coincided with the beginning of the secession crisis, heightening tensions throughout the country and jeopardizing abolitionists and African Americans.

fourth Massachusetts Volunteer Infantry proved all these critics wrong. The First and Second South Carolina regiments, raised several months before the Fifty-fourth from the sea islands around Beaufort, South Carolina, demonstrated that freed Southern slaves had the same abilities to learn as any Yankee volunteers. The Fifty-fourth, the first Union black volunteer regiment raised in the North, demonstrated to racist Northerners that African Americans in the North had just as much stake in the war as anyone else.

African Americans fought in numerous battles from Texas to Virginia. They engaged in the bloody siege of Petersburg, at Olustee, Florida's largest battle, and the last battles fought in Texas and South Carolina. They fought well in virtually every engagement in which they played a role, but at the beginning of the war their potential contributions to the Union effort were ignored. While the South Carolina Volunteers trained in virtual seclusion far from the attention of most Northerners, troops like the Fifty-fourth Massachusetts were under constant scrutiny. This attention did not bring them praise for their willingness to fight in the war. Instead, they comprised the most despised, laughed at, and cursed unit in the army. Yet within just six months of mustering, they all became heroes.

°Most white Americans, both in the North and in the South, accepted the idea of racial inferiority. In the South those ideas were used to support slavery, while in the North those ideas supported racial segregation and discrimination.•

There were four and a half million African Americans in the United States at the time of the Civil War. About five hundred thousand lived as free citizens, with half of those in the North and half in the South. The rest were slaves. In the eyes of the law slaves were articles of property, but they were expensive property. The average cost of a prime field hand could be eighteen hundred dollars or more. Slaves normally had no control over their destiny and were sometimes auctioned when their owner died or suffered financial setbacks. Some of the more skilled slaves, however, such as brick masons, carpenters, and barrel makers, hoped one day to buy their freedom. They could save their portion of the money made by their masters' hiring out their services to business or plantation owners. Slaves were allowed to keep some of the money as an incentive to do good work. For most field

JWG slaves, however, buying their freedom was unlikely.

°Slaves worked from the time that they could see in the morning until they could not see at night. In many respects, slaves were treated similarly to animals. There was no escape from slavery, save the grave.•

Even for those who escaped slavery or were born free and lived in the North, racism was still rampant. Civil rights were few, even in the North where abolition societies

JWG loudly demanded that slavery be abolished in the South.

°The idea of being a free black was best described as being a slave without a master. There were many restrictions on travel, lodging, housing, and property. Blacks could not offer testimony in court. In some areas there were so many restrictions, freemen were often treated much like slaves.•

Slavery was maintained in the South as a benign, patriarchal system—an image perpetuated to some extent by the Union army, which continued to use freed slaves, or contrabands, to harvest crops on captured plantations. The workers lived in the same conditions as before, although the army was generous with supplies and food.

When the first shot was fired at Fort Sumter, there was no question the South was fighting to protect and preserve slavery. The North, however, did not take up arms wcd to end slavery. Abolition was not the issue. °Northern men did not enlist and risk their lives to free Southern slaves; they enlisted to save the Union and to avenge the insult to the flag.• Many in the North had no opinion on slavery. Since they did not work with African Americans, live around them, or have any contact at all with them, they had no interest in or concern about them.

Abraham Lincoln, the man who would be called the Great Emancipator, was not an abolitionist. He was willing to tolerate slavery where it already existed, just to wcd keep the country together. °He publicly stated several times that if he could preserve the nation with slavery he would do it, and if he could preserve the nation without slavery, he would do it. His paramount goal was always the preservation of the Union.•

In so doing, Lincoln ignored one of his most powerful weapons of war, namely, thousands of black men who could fill the ranks and appease many Northerners, including some generals who threatened to take their soldiers home if they had to fight to free slaves. Such threats did not quiet the abolitionists who demanded that Lincoln take advantage of "the Sable Arm" of the black man. After Fort Sumter, abolitionists began mounting pulpits

Wherever the Federal army marched it encountered refugee slaves, such as the group shown here crossing the Rappahannock River. Many slave owners fled when they heard of approaching bluecoats, and slaves knew that freedom came with the "Lincoln men." Several commanders welcomed the newly freed slaves as a source of information on enemy troop deployments and as guides through unmapped territory.

and filling halls, preaching that the best way to win the white man's war was to let the black man fight.

WG °Frederick Douglass, one of the leading orators of the era and an escaped slave whose freedom was eventually purchased by friends, said that three things would come of this war for the black man: first, the cartridge box; second, the jury box; third, the ballot box. Clearly, citizenship was an important part of what these men were fighting for when they did join the Union army.• The white Northern leaders knew this too, which kept them opposed to enlisting African Americans. Douglass, however, was not deterred. In 1862 he suggested: "Once let the black man get upon his person the brass letter of U.S., let him get an eagle on his button, and a musket on his shoulder, and bullets in his pocket, and there is no power on Earth which can deny that he has earned the right to citizenship in the United States."

Douglass was the North's most eloquent and militant champion for black freedom. Early in the war he campaigned relentlessly for African-American enlistment in the army. He lobbied the government and even crusaded in Europe to mold opinion. He traveled so much that his wife mailed him fresh clothes so he could keep up the grueling pace.

WG Douglass recognized °the importance of utilizing thousands, even millions, of black soldiers against the

Wilson Chinn (above), a former slave from Louisiana, displays a collar used for punishment. Northern sensibilities were shocked by the testimony of escaped slaves and the physical evidence of the brutality of slave-owning. The propaganda value of such pictures as the one above was not wasted on abolitionists, and similar photographs were widely circulated in 1863.

For the first half of the war, contrabands were kept in camps in the fields (left). In the North free blacks tried to enlist, but the army declined to recruit them, partly out of fear of what African Americans might do in combat. Lengthy casualty lists and the prospect of a long war, however, influenced Federal lawmakers to reconsider. Lincoln's Emancipation Proclamation facilitated the enlistment of blacks in the North and in those areas of the South occupied by the Union army, but they were formed into segregated units under white officers. Two of the first black regiments were raised from the sea islands around Beaufort, South Carolina.

Horace Greeley, founder and editor of the New York Tribune, *was one of the few white advocates calling for the enlistment of African-American soldiers. In August 1862 Greeley took advantage of his paper's high profile to pressure Lincoln into emancipating the slaves. The president responded in an open letter to the editor, saying that his first goal was to save the Union, not to destroy slavery: "If I could save the Union without freeing any slave, I would do it; if I could save it by freeing all the slaves, I would do it; and if I could save it by freeing some and leaving others alone, I would also do that." After the Southern army was thrown back at Antietam, on September 22, 1862, Lincoln issued a preliminary emancipation proclamation.*

Many Northern commanders were faced with a quandry regarding runaway slaves. Initially, the army had no policy on runaways and left the matter to each commander's discretion. Gen. Benjamin F. Butler, however, categorized slaves as contrabands of war when he learned that they had been involved in the construction of Confederate fortifications. His practice was made law by the Confiscation Act of August 1861. Thereafter Federal commanders set up camps for contrabands and sometimes maintained the camps by hiring out the freed blacks as manual laborers, as depicted here (right). Those employed by the army dug trenches, buried the dead, and worked as personal servants to wealthy officers.

Confederacy. He was once asked if slaves would fight. Douglass responded, "No, the slave will not fight. But if you ask me will the black man fight, the answer is yes."

Most of white America, however, did not consider African Americans as men, much less soldiers. They WCD °believed that blacks were mentally inferior, that they could not learn the drill, bugle calls, or the drum rolls, and that they would not follow orders during battle. In battle, they might turn and run. The other side of white fears was rooted in the belief that blacks were descended from wild, savage barbarians and might not observe the rules of civilized war.•

Oddly enough, the Confederate army was disproving those beliefs about black soldiers. Some free blacks and many slaves accompanied the Southern army, primarily as musicians, teamsters, cooks, and servants. On rare occasions white officers, ignoring laws that prohibited the practice, armed the blacks and put them in the ranks beside the white men, a practice that would have shocked Northerners who were planning segregated regiments. Blacks served with Confederate forces all during the war and left their mark. Several hundred free black militiamen in Louisiana offered to organize into Confederate regiments, but their services were rejected. These so-called Native Guards ultimately joined the Union cause.

As the war moved forward, the Union became bloodied and wearied. In 1862 the North lost thirteen thousand men at Shiloh, twelve thousand at Antietam, and

twelve thousand at Fredericksburg. In the face of these terrible losses, the North was running out of men who were willing to join the army. JH °It was important that African Americans make the point that white America could not win this war alone.•

Finally, Lincoln called on the Sable Arm. On September 22, 1862, the president issued the Emancipation Proclamation, which pronounced that on January 1, 1863, all slaves in the states then in rebellion would be free. That paved the way for black enlistment. African-American soldiers could rally around the flag and help save the country and their race.

THE IMAGE OF black soldiers marching across the land was the white South's worst nightmare. The very idea of a black man with a gun had a devastating psychological effect on the GU Rebels. °Part of the psychological price white Southerners paid for slavery was the fear of slave rebellions. They feared what might happen if a people they had kept in chains and under control were suddenly free and had access to guns.•

The Northerners began to think that sort of fear might play to their advantage. Gov. John A. Andrew of Massachusetts, an ardent abolitionist, announced that he would raise the first African-American regiment from the North, the Fifty-fourth Massachusetts Volunteer Infantry. Andrew argued: "Every race has fought for liberty and its own progress. The colored race will create its own future, by its own brains, hearts, and hands."

Andrew wanted the best men for his regiment. This was to be the model, the vanguard, the noble experiment, and it could not fail. GU °The governor wanted the cream of black Northern manpower, men who had been born free, men who had never known the lash, who had

Racial prejudice was not limited to one section of the country. In the 1862 cartoon above, Alfred Waud drew Capt. Josiah Porter of the First Massachusetts Light Artillery questioning another soldier's servant. The captain asks, "Who the deuce are you, partially developed human?" The black servant replied, "I totes for de Bugler." African Americans who joined the army and navy had to overcome or ignore such stereotypes. In addition to those who believed that blacks were inferior there were those Northern whites who doubted that black soldiers had the will to fight and those who held blacks responsible for the entire conflict.

Robert Gould Shaw was home schooled and educated abroad in his precollege years before attending Harvard in 1856. He was somewhat aimless in his life's pursuits until the war broke out. Shaw first served with the Seventh New York National Guard and then applied and received a commission as a second lieutenant in the Second Massachusetts. His family's influence played no small role in his being offered the colonelcy of the Fifty-fourth Massachusetts.

never had to call anyone "Master." He thought that such men would show more initiative, that they would not be intimidated by their Confederate enemies.•

When enlistment began, the ranks filled quickly. It was hard to resist the call to arms from a man like Frederick Douglass, who lent his voice to the campaign. Who could resist such oratory? "The day dawns. The morning star is bright upon the horizon. The iron gate of our prison stands half-opened. One gallant rush from the North will fling it wide open, while four million of our brothers and sisters shall march out into liberty."

Black men knew this was their chance to make the Civil War one of the most successful slave revolts in the history of the world. °To sit on the sidelines and watch this happen around them and not participate would be unthinkable to any man who could join. The men faced a lot of pressure in their own communities from fathers, sisters, sweethearts, and wives, to go forward and fight.•

The black population in Massachusetts, however, was not sufficient to raise the regiment of one thousand men, so Andrew sent recruiters to Connecticut, New York, Missouri, Pennsylvania, and even Canada. Often gathering places were kept secret and recruits were put on trains under the cover of darkness. Finally, the Fifty-fourth was filled with men who would have their chance to strike at slavery. These were not men who would typically be found in any regiment of whites.

°The typical soldier of the Fifty-fourth was a man who could read and write and had a profession. They were artisans, clerks, barbers, small businessmen, and farmers. They were people who worked for a living. They were not runaway slaves. As freemen they risked a great deal in going to war in the Deep South for their ideals.•

Among the recruits were at least one physician, one druggist, and several printers and engineers. Their literacy rate was higher than the average Confederate. They were also young. Eli George Biddle was barely seventeen when he signed up for the Fifty-fourth. Young as this man was then, he was already a crusader. Biddle's mother had bought the family's freedom from her master in Pennsylvania and then moved her children to Boston. There Biddle was enrolled in the Quaker school.

WCD

BP

GC °His schooling generated within him a powerful, personal consciousness that he had to see his family do better and have a better future. As young as he was, this became a commitment, a crusade.

As part of their daily routine, the children at the Quaker school sang "My Country, 'Tis of Thee" every morning. After thinking about the words of that particular song, Biddle came to the conclusion he should not sing it. His people had not experienced America as a "sweet land of liberty." When he refused to sing, he was warned that he would be expelled from the school. Biddle made his stand, and he took the expulsion.•

Alone and without money, young Biddle walked for miles looking for a recruiter. Finally, he became the youngest man in Company A of the Fifty-fourth. This was Biddle's only way to strike a blow for liberty.

Frederick Douglass also wanted to serve in the regiment, but he was refused by the white organizers. Instead he offered two of his sons to serve for him. Lewis became sergeant major of the regiment.

Finally formed, the Fifty-fourth was ready to begin training. Douglass demanded, "Give them a chance. Stop calling them 'niggers' and call them 'soldiers.'"

GOVERNOR ANDREW HAD his regiment of one thousand young able-bodied African Americans. He needed officers. Of course, they would all be white. °Most white
JH Americans in the 1860s did not believe blacks had the ability to command, so the idea they could be officers was dismissed out of hand. Northerners also had a hard time thinking of blacks as gentlemen. They wondered too how white enlisted men would react in the presence of black officers, and they agonized over the idea of having white enlisted men showing respect to black officers.•

Many African Americans deeply resented the fact that they had to serve under whites in a black regiment, feeling they would still be treated as second-class citizens. Trusted abolitionists like Wendell Phillips, however, urged them to prove themselves, for soon their day would come. In 1863 Phillips reasoned: "If you cannot have a whole loaf, will you not take a slice? For if you are not willing to fight your way up to office, you are not

One of the most profound influences on Robert Gould Shaw was his mother, Sarah Blake Sturgis Shaw (above). She was a strong-willed woman, a deeply devoted abolitionist, and she taught her children that blacks were equal to whites. Robert, however, did not share that belief. Her pleas nonetheless influenced him to accept command of the Fifty-fourth.

Massachusetts Gov. John Andrew (below) was among the first to send troops to Washington at the beginning of the war. In 1863 he announced his plans for the first African-American regiment from the North, which he hoped would be a model for others. He viewed the regiment as "an opportunity for a whole race of men."

worthy of it. Put yourselves under the Stars and Stripes and fight yourselves to the marquee of a general and you shall come out with a sword." That was one of Phillips's milder speeches; he condemned the U.S. Constitution for even allowing slavery, something most abolitionists were too timid to do.

The officers for Andrew's experiment were carefully handpicked. They had to have proven themselves in battle and generally came from powerful and respected families with antislavery convictions. Twenty-six-year-old Robert Gould Shaw fit those requirements. He was a Boston blue blood who had been wounded at Antietam while serving as a captain in the Second Massachusetts, one of the first regiments raised by the state. He came from a wealthy family of conscience. Andrew wanted him as his colonel. °Because Shaw's parents had been prominent in the antislavery crusade, the governor assumed that the son shared the same values.• Ironically, he did not. As a child of privilege, he had spent much of his life away from his family, in the best schools in Europe, before returning to Harvard. Although his mother, Sarah, was a very strong-willed person and a deeply devoted abolitionist who enforced her particular

Massachusetts raised three African-American regiments, which reflected a wide range of class, occupational experience, and education. They were laborers, seamen, farmers, artisans, journalists, students, and teachers and came from Canada, Hawaii, and many states in the North and South. They knew the world was watching, and they were determined to succeed. Their ranks included (below, left to right) Pvt. Abraham F. Brown, drummer boy Henry A. Monroe, and Sgt. Henry Stewart. Brown was a casualty at Fort (Battery) Wagner, eighteen-year-old Monroe survived the war, and Stewart, who had traveled from Michigan to Massachusetts to join the Fifty-fourth, died of disease in September 1863.

philosophy on the entire family,
Shaw did not believe everything she
taught. He did not believe that
BP blacks were his equal. °There was a
certain aimlessness to Shaw before
the war. He was a pampered young
man who had not done well in
school and was not quite sure what
to do with his life.•

Shaw turned down the first offer
to command the Fifty-fourth,
explaining that he had not joined
the army two years before to free
slaves and that he had no commitment to racial equality. To Shaw,
GU this was an offer full of risk. °He
was being asked to do something
unprecedented, to take an enormous risk with his reputation. Until he finally accepted that mission, he did not
know any blacks, at least not as people. Shaw was a man
of his times. His letters were littered with such words as
"nigger" and "darkey," although as he got to know the
men of the Fifty-fourth, he came to respect them. That
kind of language faded from his writings with time.•

In part because of his mother's appeals, Shaw finally
accepted the colonel's commission for the Fifty-fourth Regiment. Training quickly began as recruits arrived by the
hundreds at Camp Meigs in Wheatville, Massachusetts.
The stakes were high, and the work would be difficult.

WCD The heart of the training was °the army drill, a complex set of commands for marching and handling
weapons. The men had to know how to march obliquely
in one direction, turn around while marching, and then
go in the other direction. According to some drill manu-
als, there were nine separate commands just for loading
and firing a weapon. That is why the order of the day for
the soldiers of the Fifty-fourth—which was the same for
all volunteer regiments—was breakfast, drill, some more
drill, a break, lunch, and drill, drill, drill, followed by
more drill.•

The men of the Fifty-fourth were consumed, driven
with the desire to succeed. The weight of their race was

*Even after the Fifty-fourth had com-
pleted its training, there was some
debate as to whether it would ever see
combat. The two soldiers above display
the martial skills they have learned,
but several top Union commanders dis-
agreed over the performance of black
soldiers in combat. William T. Sherman did not believe the African Americans could fight as well as whites. U.
S. Grant, however, stated, "This, with
the emancipation of the Negro, is the
heaviest blow yet given the Confederacy. . . . By arming the Negro we
have added a powerful ally. They will
make good soldiers and taking them
from the enemy weakens him in the
same proportion they strengthen us."*

Like white regiments, the African-American units had their own bands. This photograph was taken while the band was stationed near Washington, D.C. In May 1863 the War Department established the Bureau of Colored Troops. Within three months thirty black regiments were on active duty, and this number doubled by the end of the year. The regiments mustered into Federal service became part of the U.S. Colored Troops (USCT). Rather than return to civilian life, as other volunteers did, several stayed in the service after the war to become professional soldiers.

heavy upon their shoulders. They would even study on their own to succeed in this school of soldiers.

GU   °One of Shaw's captains, Cabot Russell, observed that his men would go out and watch the white troops do guard mounts and pick up the drill manual on their own, outside of the regular drill sessions, just so they could have a little more polish, a little more snap, be a little further ahead in their lessons.•

JH   °The eyes of the nation were on the Fifty-fourth. This was a great laboratory, a great experiment in using African Americans as soldiers. The whites were watching for any hint of unwillingness, inability, or inferiority. On the other hand, African Americans recognized that they could show no weakness, no inability to cooperate. They had to be as perfect as human beings could be.•

Every day, and especially on Sundays, crowds gathered at the camp to watch the novel sight of black men in blue uniforms performing the complex tactical evolutions of the drill. Soon Camp Meigs became more like a
WCD circus ground than a barracks. °Part of the attraction was curiosity; part of it was condescending as some spectators smirked behind their handkerchiefs at the sight of blacks trying to be soldiers.•

Shaw, however, grew to be impressed and proud. His men were proving themselves. The men of the Fifty-fourth were quickly becoming the model for every African-American soldier who would follow.

On March 25, 1863, Shaw wrote: "The intelligence of the men is a great surprise to me. They learn all the details of guard duty and camp service infinitely more readily than the Irish I've had under my command. There is not the least doubt that we shall leave the state with as good a regiment as any that has marched."

In fewer than one hundred days after first commencing their training, the Fifty-fourth received its orders. They were to leave the barracks of Massachusetts for the tents around Beaufort, South Carolina. They were finally off to war, but not before there was a farewell parade in Boston. On May 28, 1863, under a cloudless sky, the Fifty-fourth Massachusetts marched before a crowd of thousands. It was an electric moment.

GU °They energetically sang "John Brown's Body," which was the anthem of the antislavery movement. The friends of antislavery and blacks were delighted to see the men dressed in regulation dress U.S. Army uniforms, carrying state-of-the-art rifled muskets. They marched with great snap, showing that they had learned the lessons of the drill field. In so doing, they made a tremendous impression.• Within four months, they would march into glory and prove themselves heroes.

THE FIFTY-FOURTH FIRST went into camp near Beaufort, South Carolina, where the First and Second South Carolina Volunteers had been raised. After going on a raid to Darien, Georgia, where the cultured soldiers from Massachusetts were appalled at the undisciplined looting of the freed slaves of the Second South Carolina, the time to go into real battle came.

The Federals' first step to taking Charleston was to secure Morris Island, and Fort (Battery) Wagner was the last impediment. After a heavy shelling from Folly Island and the Union fleet on July 11, three Yankee regiments attacked the garrison. The first regiment breached the moat and climbed the parapet where it was pinned down. The other two regiments did not follow, and the attack failed. The Federals responded by pounding the fort for a week and then initating a second attack on July 18 (above), which was spearheaded by the Fifty-fourth Massachusetts.

Led by Shaw, the Fifty-fourth rushed up and over the parapet of Fort Wagner. Despite the heavy bombardment that had preceded the attack, the Confederate defenses were only slightly damaged and the eighteen-hundred-man garrison met the attack with full strength. Hand-to-hand combat ensued. Shaw was shot in the heart and killed instantly. One soldier stated, "The genius of Dante could but faintly portray the horrors of that hell." Overwhelmed, the survivors retreated. Other regiments tried to storm the fort, but they too were thrown back. Fort Wagner was never taken by force; the Confederates later abandoned it.

The Fifty-fourth was ordered to James Island, within ten miles of Charleston. They learned they would eventually be part of the force that would attack Battery Wagner, a formidable log-and-sand fort built near the northern tip of Confederate-held Morris Island. Wagner was the key to Charleston's defenses. If it fell, the Union could use Morris Island to bombard Confederate-held Fort Sumter and the city of Charleston itself.

In 1863 Charleston was a focal point of Union strategy. It was important tactically because it could be used as a base of operations to drive a wedge through the South by striking at railroad lines and river transportation systems. It was also important symbolically because the war had started in Charleston Harbor.

The Fifty-fourth marched for two days and two nights through insect-ridden marsh and sand with too little food and not a moment of sleep to get to Battery Wagner. When they arrived, they were ready to fight. This was the chance for which these sons of slaves had waited. They would take it, no matter what the price. For two tedious and sweltering months, the Fifty-fourth had suffered hardships on the coastal islands of South Carolina

Confederate Brig. Gen. William B. Taliaferro had erected a huge bombproof shelter within Fort Wagner to house 750 men. His soldiers found refuge there when the Federal artillery pounded the garrison. The fort's defenders emerged unscathed to meet the July 18 attack. The next day the Rebels buried 600 Union soldiers, including Robert Gould Shaw, in a common pit. In all, the Northerners counted 1,515 casualties; the Southerners suffered 181 killed and wounded. The photograph to the left was taken after the fort was evacuated on September 6, 1863.

waiting for its chance to go into battle, but South Carolina was nothing like what the men had expected.

"If a person were to ask me what I saw South, I should tell him stinkweed and sand, rattlesnakes and alligators," wrote Corp. James Henry Gooding of the Fifty-fourth. "Tell the honest truth, our boys out on picket look sharper for snakes than they do for Rebels."

The Fifty-fourth, however, had a higher purpose, and the swamps, snakes, and suffocating heat and humidity did not stop them. They were finally in the South and ready to strike a blow. Their first taste of battle came on James Island.

In the early morning of July 16, Shaw's black soldiers heard their first battle cry. Three companies of the Fifty-fourth were on picket duty when a large force of Confederates surprised them, screaming the Rebel yell as they charged. The Fifty-fourth °held their ground long enough to permit the withdrawal of some white pickets to their left who had their backs against a swamp. The Fifty-fourth's stand allowed the main body of Union troops on James Island to fall into line of battle. They gave a good account of themselves• by stopping the enemy and saving another Union regiment, the Tenth Connecticut.

That day the Fifty-fourth proved they could fight, kill, and die like whites. By all accounts they fought bravely. The Fifty-fourth had won their first battle but they had another battle back home to fight. When the black recruits were mustered in, they were promised the same pay as white soldiers—thirteen dollars a month. When the regi-

391

Sgt. William H. Carney, Company C, is pictured here still recovering from injuries suffered at Wagner on July 18. After the Fifty-fourth's color-bearer went down, the twenty-three-year-old Carney seized the flag and achieved the Federals' deepest breach into the garrison. Suffering two wounds, he retreated with his comrades. A member of one of the other regiments saw the injured man and offered to carry the unit's flag. Carney responded, "No one but a member of the Fifty-fourth should carry the colors." For his actions during the battle Carney received the first Medal of Honor awarded to an African American.

ment reached the South, the War Department declared African-American soldiers would only receive ten dollars a month, three dollars of which would be deducted for their uniforms. The Fifty-fourth dearly resented it. °This was a slap in the face. These African Americans were putting their lives on the line just like white soldiers, and the Federal army bureaucrats were officially undervaluing their lives by an official Federal pay policy.•

In protest, the Fifty-fourth—officers as well as enlisted men—refused to accept even a dollar. They waited eighteen long months before the government relented and offered them equal pay. That proved to be too late for some. Just hours after the skirmish on James Island, the Fifty-fourth was ordered to Morris Island. It was a long, dark, and perilous journey at night. When they arrived, they had been on their feet for forty-eight hours without food, sleep, or rest.

°They had to negotiate narrow causeways, little footpaths, and bridges. They were on their feet constantly. The first night it rained, and their uniforms were soaked, which slowed their progress. They were on the move the next night, embarking upon a steamer. The only way to get aboard the steamboat was by rowboat, so most of the men spent hours waiting on the beach, waiting for the rowboat. Again it rained.•

When the men finally arrived on Morris Island, they were wet, worn, and bone weary. It was almost six o'clock at night. Since noon, forty-one Union guns and mortars and nearly a dozen warships had hurled nine thousand shells into Wagner. The Fifty-fourth was near exhaustion, but the attack was about to begin. They did not want to miss it.

°Two Union brigades formed on the beach as darkness fell. All day long the Union ironclads had been shelling Wagner, and the officers told their men the fort had been pulverized by the big guns.• They were wrong.

The artillery barrage, organized by the same general who had successfully destroyed Fort Pulaski outside Savannah, had done little to weaken Wagner. Built of quartz sand and palmetto palms and equipped with a bombproof shelter deep underground, the fort's garrison was almost unscathed. The Union shells merely burrowed

Early in 1864 Gen. Quincy Gillmore was given permission to lead an expedition to Florida. Brig. Gen. Truman Seymour's 7,000-man division landed near Jacksonville. On February 20 Seymour took 5,500 men—the Eighth U.S. Colored Troops, the First North Carolina Volunteers, and the Fifty-fourth—and attacked 4,600 Confederates near Olustee in a campaign to capture the state capital at Tallahassee. Attacking piecemeal, the Federal assaults were beaten back; the Rebels then counterattacked. The valor of the Eighth U.S.C.T. and the Fifty-fourth prevented a complete rout. One witness claimed, "Had it not been for the glorious Fifty-fourth Massachusetts, the whole brigade would have been captured or annihilated." Nevertheless, Union casualties were twice those of the Confederates.

into the sand, exploding harmlessly. The entire barrage had been absorbed by the fort. The Union officers told their men there were only about three hundred Rebels left inside; the truth was there were twelve hundred.

°The Confederates were defiant. They had not been decimated by the bombing. When the attack came, these soldiers had the high ground at the top of the fort's walls, and they had plenty of cannon and ammunition. They also had cleverer commanders. The slope of the fort's walls was such that the fuses on cannonballs could be lit and the cannonballs rolled down to explode into any troops unfortunate enough to be selected to attack the fort.•

Just reaching those walls would be a challenge. Attacking soldiers first had to advance up a barren beach that narrowed near the fort. They then had cross a fifty-foot-wide moat that was filled with five feet of water. Then the soldiers had to scale a thirty-foot rampart of sloping sand. It would be a daunting endeavor for the fittest of men.

The Fifty-fourth was the most weary regiment in Charleston. Yet by all accounts, Shaw's men were willing to storm Wagner. Gen. George C. Strong, who led the brigade in the first wave, asked the Fifty-fourth if it wanted to lead the way, knowing that the moment would be historic. °He told them: "I'm a Massachusetts man like you. I know you're tired. I know that you're worn out. But is there any man here who thinks himself

In February 1865 an advance guard from the 54th Massachusetts was the first Federal unit to enter Charleston, the "seat of secession." Col. Edward N. Hallowell, who had replaced Shaw, was placed in charge of the defenses of Charleston, which included St. Andrew's Parish and the James Island lines. His troops consisted of the 54th, the 107th Ohio, and the 21st U.S.C.T. The soldiers above are recovering from their wounds or illnesses at Aikens Landing on James Island. On June 5, 1865, the 54th was ordered to Charleston where it was quartered in The Citadel. Each morning crowds of former Charleston slaves came to watch the regiment drill in The Citadel square.

Opposite page: A broadside advertises an 1891 lecture series by Henry A. Monroe, a regimental drummer (see the caption on page 386), about his wartime experiences and the history of the Fifty-fourth. He earned a divinity degree after the war and became the pastor of an all-black church in New York City, St. Mark's Methodist Episcopal Church. Monroe's lectures were given during a time of increasing racial strife in the North and a wave of lynchings in the South.

unable to sleep in that fort tonight?" All six hundred of Shaw's troops leapt to their feet and yelled, "No! No!" Then Strong pointed to the color-bearer and said, "If that brave color-bearer goes down, who will pick up the flag?" Again the men raised their hands, jumping up and down with excitement, yelling, "I will! I will!"•

The time was 7:45 P.M. on July 18, 1863. Darkness was coming on swiftly when the Fifty-fourth moved to lead the assault. With the Atlantic Ocean on their right and marshes on their left, the beach began to narrow toward the fort until there was only a tiny passage left. It was there that the Confederates opened fire.

°A storm of shot and shell ripped into the regiment, tearing their ranks. The Fifty-fourth had never faced such concentrated fire before. Lewis Douglass saw shells clearing spaces twenty feet wide, just ripping his comrades apart. The ranks began to break. It was at that moment that Shaw proved his heroism.•

The young colonel brandished his sword and yelled, "Forward, my brave boys," and then began running. °The men cheered, gave a wild shout, and then ran after him. They were bent over double, as though they were running into a hailstorm, but this storm was made of lead and iron.•

Finally they rushed headlong into the huge ditchlike moat. Shaw was still leading, still sprinting into the jaws of death. With Wagner's wall lit up by a cannon flash, Shaw clambered up the thirty-foot sandy slope shouting, "Rush on! Rush on, boys!" Behind him lay a tragic scene of death, and in front of him lay his own.

°Shaw was the first one to get to the top. He stood erect, raised his sword over his head, and yelled "Onward, boys!" At that moment, a North Carolina soldier fired a bullet into Shaw's heart.•

EVEN AS SHAW fell, the Stars and Stripes kept flying. The regiment's national colors, its flag, its symbol of freedom, was kept safe from the enemy by the valor of another man, Sgt. William Carney.

Carney became the symbol of heroism for the Fifty-fourth by being the first African-American soldier to earn the nation's highest award, the Medal of Honor. By the time Colonel Shaw was killed, the men were fighting a vicious hand-to-hand combat with their bayonets. It was pitch dark. Just before the moat, Carney saw the color-bearer go down. He grabbed the flag, held it close, and began to make his way up the parapet.

°He heard men moaning, but Carney could not see them for the darkness. As he climbed, he saw other men whom he assumed were part of his regiment, but in the light of a cannon flash, he saw that they were Rebels.• °Carney took three hits, one serious wound in the shoulder and one in each leg, but he never dropped the flag. He made it to the parapet and only then was he forced to retreat on his knees.• He used one hand to staunch the wound in his shoulder, and he held the flag staff in the other hand.

°Carney planted the flag at the top of the parapet, signifying that these dying and moaning men had not attacked in vain.• Returning, Carney did not stop until he got to the Union field hospital. Torn and bleeding, his wounds were so severe that he never fully recovered, but he did survive. °Just before he fainted, he said to his amazed comrades, "I but did my duty, boys. The dear old flag never touched the ground."•

The few men of the Fifty-fourth who safely scaled the fort's walls battled on the parapets of Fort Wagner for a while before being forced to retreat. The tide had come in, making the moat waist deep. Many of the wounded drowned.

The Union commanders would not give up. The white soldiers of the Sixth Connecticut were ordered into the eye of the storm next. Regiment after regiment and then another brigade were sent up the

A memorial to the Fifty-fourth Massachusetts, sculpted by Augustus Saint-Gaudens, was unveiled on May 31, 1897, on the Boston Common (above). More than two hundred veterans of Massachusetts's three black regiments attended the unveiling. Booker T. Washington was one of the principal speakers that day.

Another memorial to the Fifty-fourth was A Brave Black Regiment: History of the Fifty-fourth Regiment of Massachusetts Volunteer Infantry, *a regimental history written by Capt. Luis F. Emilio (below), Company E and one of the original officers of the regiment.*

sloped walls of Wagner, but their fate was the same as the Fifty-fourth, and the attack was a terrible and costly failure. The carnage was horrifying.

BP °Bodies lay strewn all over the crest of the parapet and piled up in the bastion. They lay sprawled down the slope. It was a scene of terrible slaughter.• More than fifteen hundred Union soldiers were killed or wounded compared to fewer than two hundred Confederates.

The next morning when the Rebels buried the dead of both sides, they singled out the Fifty-fourth and their white officers for special dishonor. They were buried in a GU mass grave with no marker. Shaw °was stripped to his underwear, put on display inside the fort, then dragged outside, and tossed to the bottom of a pit with the bodies of twenty-five of his soldiers thrown on top. When some Union officers asked about the whereabouts of Shaw's body, a Confederate officer replied, "We buried him with his niggers."

The Fifty-fourth paid a high price to put a stamp on the course of American history. Of the 21 officers and 600 enlisted men Shaw led against Fort Wagner, 281 were killed, captured, or wounded. Yet in that one gallant rush the Fifty-fourth transcended the word *hero*, for they had risked their own lives for a better life for others.

BP °That knowing, willing sacrifice of these men for the betterment of an enslaved and despised race was in the truest sense a martyrdom. What the Fifty-fourth did at

Wagner was one of the most noble, self-effacing acts of bravery that ever transpired on a battlefield in the Civil War.•

Because of the Fifty-fourth, other African Americans were allowed to fight. Near the end of the war there were more black soldiers in the field than the Confederacy had in its entire army. Although the Fifty-fourth lost almost half of its men at Battery Wagner, it was not destroyed as a regiment. In February 1864 it alone of all the Union regiments at the battle of Olustee, Florida, stood fast in the face of a Confederate counterassault. Because the Fifty-fourth held, the rest of the Union army was able to retreat. After the battle, near Jacksonville, when the steam engine of a train carrying wounded broke down, the men of the Fifty-fourth pulled the railroad cars with their bare hands.

JH °President Lincoln argued that the contribution of black soldiers in the Civil War was crucial to the winning of that war. He believed the war could not have been won without the involvement and sacrifice of black troops.•

There were some black troops before the Fifty-fourth and certainly there were many others after, but it is this regiment that will always be remembered. These were the men whose flags of freedom were always flying high, and these were the men whose dreams of hope and glory will never die. Because of the Fifty-fourth, nearly two hundred thousand black soldiers fought in the Civil War, with many laying their lives on the altar of freedom. Because of these men, the Civil War was not a war between North and South for the sake of preserving or repudiating the Union, but a battle for racial equality. It was the Fifty-fourth who gave others the chance to win the war of emancipation and to fulfill a promise for a better day for the brotherhood of man.

The battle flags of the Fifty-fourth Massachusetts (above) are preserved in the state capitol. The Fifty-fourth and the other Federal black regiments demonstrated that African Americans could fight and survive the hardships of war as well as any combat unit. Even so, it was not until the Korean War of the mid-twentieth century that U.S. forces were integrated.

397

CHICKAMAUGA AND CHATTANOOGA

⚬⚬⚬

The BATTLE OF CHATTANOOGA ON November 23–25, 1863, marked the beginning of the end for the Confederacy in the western theater of the war. Coming just one month after the South's success at Chickamauga, Georgia, on September 19–20, just a few miles south of Chattanooga, the Union victories around the city at Lookout Mountain, Orchard Knob, and Missionary Ridge proved that Union Maj. Gen. Ulysses S. Grant was a superior field commander to Confederate Gen. Braxton Bragg. Grant's smashing of Bragg's supposedly impregnable defenses was evidence that the South was running out of resources with which to continue the fighting. When Chattanooga finally fell, Georgia and South Carolina could see that they would be next on the Federals' list.

By the late autumn of 1863 the war was starting to go badly for the Confederacy. The single bright spot was a dramatic Southern victory at Chickamauga on September 20, in which the largest Union army in the region was smashed and driven from the field. Elsewhere in the West, the Confederates had lost Vicksburg on the Fourth of July and Port Hudson, Louisiana, on July 9. In the East the South had lost Gettysburg on July 3 and had lost control of the islands around Charleston, South Carolina, by late July. Perhaps the greatest disaster for the South, although it did not appear so immediately, was the appointment of Grant to command all Federal forces in the West.

Having control over all the western theater meant that Grant could direct entire armies toward common objectives, such as the pivotal Tennessee town of Chattanooga,

WCD	William C. Davis
JMM	James M. McPherson
JO	James Ogden
BP	Brian Pohanka
WS	Wiley Sword

Although the poor fields of hardscrabble farms provided some open areas, thick stands of timber and gnarled underbrush dominated the landscape in the vicinity of Chickamauga Creek. Such rough terrain disrupted the formations of attacking Rebel and Yankee infantry but provided good defensive cover. Above, Confederates take shelter behind trees as they pepper unseen bluecoats with rifle fire. The soldiers pictured in the sketch wear ragged clothing, but many Southern troops at Chickamauga were relatively well clad. Lt. Gen. James Longstreet's men wore uniforms of a blue-gray material that repeatedly confused Federal soldiers into thinking they were fellow Northerners.

known as "the gateway to the Deep South." As the two sides prepared for the Chattanooga campaign, they knew that the stakes were nothing less than the survival of the Confederacy. Even the president of the United States, who had little military training, recognized the importance of Chattanooga. "If we can hold Chattanooga in East Tennessee, I think the rebellion must dwindle and die as an animal sometimes lay with a thorn in its vitals," Lincoln observed.

BP °Transportation was vital to both armies, and cities with transportation hubs, particularly those that had both railroads and river transport, were of double importance. Chattanooga was such a place. If the North captured it, the city would become a springboard for the campaigns to come.• °Losing Chattanooga would inevitably mean losing the war.•

WCD

Targeting Chattanooga were the Union's best generals, Grant and William Tecumseh Sherman. The Confederacy's hopes, however, rested with one of its most controversial and least popular commanders—Bragg. It would have been almost impossible to find a man in the ranks who liked the heavily bearded, dark-faced, dour North Carolina native. "No one man that ever lived, I don't believe, ever had as much hatred expressed against him as Bragg," wrote Confederate Pvt. William Fackler in 1863.

WCD °Bragg was an easy man to hate. Well schooled with a degree from West Point in 1837, well experienced at warfare after fighting the Seminoles and Mexicans but seemingly unsure of his own skills, he was a man suspicious of his subordinates. He was constantly at war with himself and frequently with those around him. Bragg was

JMM somewhat paranoid and emotionally unstable.• °A stern disciplinarian, he had men punished for slight infractions and routinely ordered men shot for desertion, sometimes on flimsy evidence.• He did little to try to win his soldiers' admiration and respect, viewing them as little more than slaves who had best do what he told them to do. He developed this view of discipline after

resigning his U.S. Army commission in 1856 to manage his Louisiana plantation, which had more than one thousand slaves. "The very plantation is a small military establishment, or it ought to be. Give us all discipline, Masters, and we shall never hear of insurrection," Bragg wrote in 1859.

°Always pondering why anyone would question his command abilities, Bragg saw enemies behind every door. Militarily, he always seemed to make the wrong decision on the battlefield.• °Under enormous stress during a battle, Bragg would frequently act—or not act—without thinking through the consequences of his actions. One of his contemporary generals said that Bragg, in times of unforeseen circumstances, would rely on the advice of a mere drummer boy,• meaning he would act on just what he knew at the moment, not on information that had been developed before or on the consensus opinions of his other generals.

°The officers in his high command, his corps commanders and many of his division commanders, had come to distrust him and personally to dislike him. If the soldiers in the ranks did not loathe Bragg by the time the siege of Chattanooga was about to commence, they at least did not feel comfortable going into battle under his leadership.• Bragg himself knew that he was not the most popular man in the army, but he underestimated how

Many Southerners viewed Bragg's 1863 triumph at Chickamauga as a strong response to the repulse of Gen. Robert E. Lee's movement into Pennsylvania and the loss of the Mississippi River. "We are gloriously victorious!" Virginian Judith McGuire exulted in her diary upon learning of the outcome of the savage engagement in northwest Georgia. While Chickamauga was unquestionably a major victory for the South, Union Maj. Gen. George H. "Pap" Thomas denied the Confederates the opportunity to destroy the Army of the Cumberland by his stubborn stand on Snodgrass Hill, the action depicted above by artist James Walker. The Union battle line blazes away to the right, while reinforcements rush to join the fray, ignoring groups of skulking and wounded comrades.

401

His left arm still in a sling due to a wound received at Gettysburg, John Bell Hood—acting as commander of Longstreet's Corps while "Old Pete" led the left wing of Bragg's army—recoils in pain as a Yankee minié ball smashes into his right leg during the Rebel breakthrough at Chickamauga on September 20. Hood implored his men to "Go ahead, and keep ahead of everything" as he lay on the ground. His leg was removed that evening.

William S. Rosecrans (below) was beloved by his men, who called him "Old Rosey," but he blundered into the battle of Chickamauga in one of the few instances when Confederates outnumbered Federals. His inability to act after falling back on Chattanooga led to his reassignment.

JMM

WCD

much everyone hated him. "I am somewhat obnoxious to a few," Bragg wrote in one of the understatements of the war.

The reason Bragg had risen to the top ranks of the Confederacy could be traced back to his fine record during the Mexican War of 1846–48. There the young Bragg won the admiration of a fellow officer, Jefferson Davis, and the two remained friends during the twenty-five intervening years. When the Civil War started, Davis, as Confederate president, was Bragg's biggest supporter, standing by Bragg through every controversy and waiting far too long to question his ability.

°Davis liked Bragg and had confidence in him, a confidence that a decreasing number of others in the Confederacy shared as time went on.• Bragg returned the favor by °never challenging Davis, as other Confederate generals frequently did. Bragg always supported the president, always telling Davis what he thought Davis wanted to hear. That kind of loyalty was important to the Confederate president.• Davis's decisions were not always the right course for the Confederacy, but Davis, who fancied himself a military man because of his West Point diploma and Mexican War experience, looked for men who agreed with him. Bragg always did. "The President's attachment for General Bragg could be likened to nothing else but the blind and gloating love of a mother for a deformed and misshapen offspring," wrote Confederate Sen. James Orr, who had no love for either man.

Davis's loyalty was severely tested by events leading up to Chattanooga. In October 1862 Bragg had invaded Kentucky and suffered a major defeat at Perryville. Dr. D. W. Yandell, a Confederate surgeon, said after the battle that Bragg was "either stark raving mad or incompetent." That campaign was followed in December 1862 by another defeat at Stones River, Tennessee. Bragg spent most of 1863 reorganizing and quarreling with his subordinates before trying to maneuver the Federals out of Chattanooga in August. Nothing he did pleased anyone. "If Bragg is kept in command of the western army, the whole country of the Mississippi Valley will be lost,"

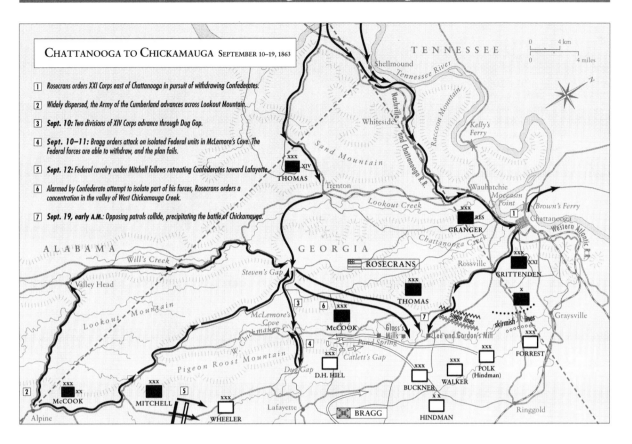

CHATTANOOGA TO CHICKAMAUGA SEPTEMBER 10–19, 1863

☐1 *Rosecrans orders XXI Corps east of Chattanooga in pursuit of withdrawing Confederates.*

☐2 *Widely dispersed, the Army of the Cumberland advances across Lookout Mountain.*

☐3 *Sept. 10: Two divisions of XIV Corps advance through Dug Gap.*

☐4 *Sept. 10–11: Bragg orders attack on isolated Federal units in McLemore's Cove. The Federal forces are able to withdraw, and the plan fails.*

☐5 *Sept. 12: Federal cavalry under Mitchell follows retreating Confederates toward Lafayette.*

☐6 *Alarmed by Confederate attempt to isolate part of his forces, Rosecrans orders a concentration in the valley of West Chickamauga Creek.*

☐7 *Sept. 19, early A.M.: Opposing patrols collide, precipitating the battle of Chickamauga.*

wrote Tennessee Congressman Henry Foote. Bragg could not even find a sympathetic ear from his wife, Elise, who said: "We feel the greatest anxiety. It will be very hard for you to have to fall back when so much was expected from your army."

Pursuing Bragg toward Chattanooga in the autumn of 1863 was the Union Army of the Cumberland under Maj. Gen. William Stark Rosecrans, who was Bragg's opposite number in many ways. Perhaps the greatest difference between the two was Rosecrans's popularity with his soldiers.

BP °Beloved by his troops, who called him "Old Rosey," Rosecrans was conducting a rather brilliant campaign that succeeded in outmaneuvering Bragg at almost every turn, skillfully making use of mountain passes and lines of approach to strike the Confederates at a number of different points, keeping them off balance.• Bragg's frustration with Rosecrans's success was such that on several occasions the Confederate commander

This Harper's Weekly engraving shows Union infantry deployed along the base of Snodgrass Hill, but the stiff composition of the rendering conveys little of the chaos that in reality pervaded the scene. Pvt. John Coxe of the Second South Carolina remembered his regiment weathering a "terrific fire of grape, canister and spherical case" from the Union cannons, while the Palmetto State troops used their "faithful Enfields" with good effect, causing many Federals "to bite the dust for the last time." Coxe further recalled that, after darkness put an end to the fighting, he "ravenously" ate "goodies" from looted Union haversacks regardless of the "dead and dying [that] lay all about."

Braxton Bragg (below) was at the head of the Confederate Army of Tennessee. His abilities rarely matched his tasks, and had he not been a close supporter of Jefferson Davis, he might have been relegated to less important postings. Bragg had confronted Rosecrans at the battle of Stones River in December 1862 but had been roundly defeated. As a result, probably no one was more surprised than Bragg at the Southern victory at Chickamauga, but he quarreled with James Longstreet, and their joint force was short lived.

claimed that his subordinates could have struck back at the Federals but did not, perhaps hoping that not attacking the Yankees would reflect badly on Bragg and cause him to be replaced.

Rosecrans used a roving attack style to win the first showdown at Chattanooga. Bragg had arrived before him, but Rosecrans quickly surrounded the town, catching the Confederates by surprise. Not only was Bragg surprised, he was not even in town. °The Southern general and his wife were east of Chattanooga at Cherokee Springs, a local prewar resort, taking the sulfurous waters to cure some of their ailments. When news of Rosecrans's deployment reached him, Bragg rushed back on August 21 as the Federals unexpectedly opened fire on Chattanooga.

Finally, Bragg did the unexpected: °He gave up Chattanooga without any resistance. He fell back to the south with the excuse, "This was only a city. Getting away from the city, we're no longer stationary. Now, we can maneuver in the open ground." To his credit, that is exactly what he set out to do.•

Bragg was not going to give up Chattanooga quite as easily as it seemed at first. A few miles south of the city, he found a place near Chickamauga Creek where he turned to fight the Yankees. The stream lived up to its Cherokee name, which was said to mean "River of Death."

WHEN BRAGG DECIDED to turn and fight at Chickamauga on September 19, 1863, he had good reason for renewed optimism. Gen. Robert E. Lee had sent one of his favorite generals, Lt. Gen. James Longstreet, and twelve thousand troops as reinforcements. Those men traveled hundreds of miles via bad railroads and, as luck would have it, arrived just in time to join in the battle. Bragg, so long overmatched, now had Rosecrans outnumbered. °It was one of the few major battles of the Civil War where a Confederate force outnumbered its Union counterpart.• Bragg finally felt that he had the upper hand.

The fighting in the dense woods at Chickamauga was fierce and bloody with sixty-six thousand Confederates facing fifty-eight thousand Federals "like two wild beasts coming together," observed one soldier. On the second day, Bragg's army was joined by another new ally— good luck.

°Fortuitously for Bragg, a mistaken order pulled an entire Federal division out of the line and opened a half-mile-wide gap. Compounding Bragg's good fortune, Longstreet's assault was aimed almost exactly at that gap. His men poured through it, cut the Yankee army in half, and gave Bragg certainly the most overwhelming victory any Confederate army ever achieved.•

Accompanying Rosecrans's army was Charles Dana, assistant secretary of war. Afterward he recalled: "The first

During the evening of September 20 and throughout the following day, exhausted, powder-blackened Federal soldiers staggered through the Rossville Gap and into the safety of Chattanooga (above). More than 1,600 bluecoated dead littered the Chickamauga battlefield, while another 9,756 Federals had suffered wounds. Clearly shaken by the debacle, Maj. Gen. William Rosecrans telegraphed President Lincoln that his army's "fate was in the hands of God; in whom I hope." Although "Old Rosey" soon recovered his composure, Lincoln had lost faith in him. On October 19 Lincoln relieved Rosecrans of duty and placed General Thomas at the helm of the Army of the Cumberland.

Occupying a flat area in a rugged mountainous region, Chattanooga quickly grew into an important transportation center after the advent of the railroad. Throughout the first years of the war, trains of the Western and Atlantic, Nashville and Chattanooga, Chattanooga and Cleveland, and Trenton Railroads regularly puffed into the city laden with goods vital to the Confederacy. This photo looks down Market Street toward the Tennessee River. Note that the thoroughfare is infested with stone outcroppings indicative of the rugged topography of the region. The large brick building on the left served as the city's railroad passenger station.

George Henry Thomas (below) was an officer in the regular army before the war. In 1861 his Virginia family expected him to resign his commission and was surprised when he chose not to do so. Nevertheless, his southern roots hindered him in the Federal army. At the battle of Chickamauga, Thomas's men held the line, allowing the army to retreat. For his resiliency in that moment, he was dubbed "the Rock of Chickamauga." Even with that testimony, however, U. S. Grant believed Thomas was slow to implement orders and was somewhat frustrated in his dealings with him.

WCD

thing I saw was General Rosecrans crossing himself. 'Hello,' I said to myself. 'If the general is crossing himself, we are in a desperate situation.'"

BP Rosecrans's army, so accustomed to victory, fell into a panicked retreat, careening back to Chattanooga. °Rosecrans himself and his chief of staff, James Garfield, a future president of the United States, were swept along in the rout.• In his report in the *Cincinnati Gazette,* a correspondent observed, "Men, animals, vehicles became a massive struggling, cursing, shouting, frightened mob."

The Union Army of the Cumberland might not have made it back to Chattanooga at all, except for a brave rear-guard action by troops under Maj. Gen. George H. Thomas at Snodgrass Hill. Thomas and a force cobbled together from determined men held the Rebels at bay so the main part of the army could make its escape. By nightfall, even Thomas was forced to retreat.

°When word reached the Southern people of the victory at Chickamauga, it breathed new life and vigor into them. The second half of the second full year of the war had been the worst months of the war for the Confederacy: Gettysburg, Vicksburg, Port Hudson, and the loss of the Mississippi River itself. Chickamauga was the only bright spot in that otherwise grim picture.•

"The effects of this great victory will be electrical. The whole South'll be filled again with patriotic fervor. Surely

the government of the United States must now see the impossibility of subjugating the Southern people," wrote John B. Jones, a Richmond war clerk.

The men cheered Bragg immediately after Chickamauga. °They all expected, general and private alike, that the Confederate army would march back to Chattanooga to liberate it from the Union army that they had just defeated.• Bragg, however, cut the celebration short when he decided not to pursue the beaten Yankees into town. The Rebels' own casualties, more than eighteen thousand killed, wounded, and captured, had been too heavy, he said. "Any immediate pursuit would have been fruitless with our weak and exhausted forces and the enemy already in position within his lines in Chattanooga," asserted Bragg in his report to Richmond.

The bloodiest two-day battle of the entire war, Chickamauga had been a costly victory for the Confederates. Each side had lost nearly one-third of its army. Of 120,000 soldiers who had taken the field, 35,000 were either killed, wounded, or missing. "The ghastly mangled dead and horribly wounded strewed the earth for over half a mile up and down the river banks," wrote Confederate Col. Thomas Berry.

°The fighting during the war was so rough, so grueling, so exhausting in these engagements that frequently the victor was just as beat-up, tired, and exhausted as the vanquished.• °The battlefield at

Chickamauga was a slaughterhouse. Any follow-up and attack on the Union defenses at Chattanooga would probably not have succeeded.•

Even though they knew how badly their men needed rest, Bragg's generals—especially Longstreet—were furious and disgusted. Here was an opportunity to crush the enemy, and their commander refused to take it. °It was not often in the western theater that the Confederates had occasion to see the backs of their enemies in utter rout and flight. The Confederacy, if it were to win, if it were to achieve a negotiated settlement of some kind that allowed for the existence of the Southern states as an independent nation, had to take advantage of every victory.•

Bragg did not do much to take advantage of his success. Frustrated, Longstreet announced: "I am convinced that nothing but the Hand of God can save us as long as we have our present commander." So strong was the anti-Bragg feeling that twelve of his officers sent a petition to President Davis demanding his removal. The petition, dated October 4, 1863, asserted: "It is certain that the fruits of victory of the Chickamauga have now escaped our grasp. This army, stricken with complete paralysis may deem itself fortunate if it escapes its present position without disaster."

Confederate civilians, including once again his wife, were also quick to criticize Bragg's failure to follow up his

William T. Sherman led the primary force in the attack on the north end of Missionary Ridge. With six divisions totaling twenty-six thousand men, he faced no more than ten thousand Confederates under Patrick Cleburne and Carter Stevenson. The terrain, however, worked to the Southerners' advantage and compensated for their smaller numbers. The Northerners had to descend a hill, cross an open valley, and advance up a steeper hill to gain their objective. Cleburne had placed his artillery well and allowed it to do most of the work against the advancing Federals. When the bluecoats were well within range, the Southern infantry poured volley after volley into the oncoming line, as is illustrated here. Some men even left the safety of their earthworks to attack the bluecoats with clubbed muskets and bayonets. The combat lasted for two hours, with charge met by countercharge and Cleburne at the head each time. When ammunition ran low, the Confederates massed and charged, hurling back a late Northern assault. Finally, Sherman called a halt to the attack and sent word to Grant, but his two-word reply was simply "Attack again." Two hundred men were sent up the slope, and again they were hurled back. Sherman called off any further attacks and ordered his men to entrench; his failure to turn the Confederate right flank made Hooker's attack on the left more urgent.

Douglas Volk's 1906 painting accurately captures the moment during the Union's November 25 attack on Missionary Ridge when the Second Minnesota Infantry, in the words of the regiment's Lt. Col. Judson Bishop, became "completely merged in a crowd of gallant and enthusiastic men who swarmed over the breastwork and charged the defenders with such promptness and vigor that the enemy broke and fled." Many soldiers defined the chaotic nature of the fighting on the ridge as a "soldier's battle," an engagement fought by men operating on individual initiative rather than by the guidance of high-ranking, overseeing officers.

victory. The insightful Elise complained: "I fear our victory is indecisive. We have the glory of some prisoners and cannon. Rosecrans still holds Chattanooga."

Outraged by his generals' insubordination, Bragg began replacing some of them, such as Lt. Gen. Daniel Harvey Hill, a fellow North Carolinian and Stonewall Jackson's brother-in-law. Prior to his assignment to Bragg's army, Hill's querulous disposition had also drawn the ire of General Lee. Bragg was not reticent in criticisms of Hill: "His open and constant croaking would demoralize any command in the world. He does not hesitate at all times to declare our cause lost." Hill was sent back to North Carolina where he sat out the rest of the war, emerging only in the last days to fight at Wise's Crossroads and Bentonville.

While Bragg and his officers went on arguing with each other, the Yankees regrouped and fortified themselves inside Chattanooga. Bragg had given his enemy a reprieve for which he and the South would pay heavily.

AFTER THE CARNAGE at Chickamauga, the Chattanooga campaign turned into a waiting game. The Union forces held the town, but the Rebel armies moved into the surrounding mountains and ridges. From the high ground, the Rebels controlled the enemy's lines of

Lookout Mountain looms over the city of Chattanooga in the photograph above (left). Within days of the Confederate triumph at Chickamauga, Bragg's men had invested the high ground surrounding the river town, hastily digging entrenchments on Missionary Ridge and Lookout Mountain as well as posting an advanced picket line at Orchard Knob, a hillock in the otherwise flat flood plain that lay east of the city limits. In the Harper's Weekly *engraving above (right), bluecoated riflemen use the cover of their log breastworks to boil coffee or keep watch over a field recently denuded of timber. To the right center are three artillery pieces protected by a earthwork known as a "lunette" after its resemblance to a crescent moon. During an enemy charge, these cannons could sweep the cleared field with devastating canister fire and withdraw through the opening in the wall directly behind the position if necessary. Such forbidding gun emplacements were one of the reasons Bragg chose not to launch frontal attacks on the Union position.*

supply. Their strategy was simple—they would starve the Yankees into submission.

°With the usual supply routes cut off, Rosecrans's army became dependent upon a circuitous route over the mountains. The route was so narrow that in places two wagons going in opposite directions could not pass each other. The Union could not get enough supplies into Chattanooga to keep the army fed.• °The route was so primitive, it was estimated that as many as ten thousand horses and mules died in the effort to bring basic supplies into Chattanooga.•

From their vantage points on Lookout Mountain southwest of the city and Missionary Ridge east of the city, the Confederates looked down on the town whose normal population was thirty-five hundred civilians. Now, it had more than thirty-five thousand Union soldiers as uninvited hungry guests.

°The letters and diaries of the soldiers in Chattanooga frequently cited the men's tightening their belts by punching holes in the leather—a clear sign that they were slowly starving. Union soldiers began to distrust their comrades. They kept an eye on what supplies they had and concealed their food. In short, Federal morale suffered during the siege.• August Rymers of the Fifteenth Missouri noted: "Sergeant Eagers went down to the slaughter pen one day where he got hold of two hooves of an old cow. We cooked those hooves five times and drank the hot broth, and thought it was a pretty good meal."

°The living conditions of Bragg's besieging army on the heights were not much better than the Federals'. They were entering a cold, miserable winter, and the Confederates were not well supplied.• Their condition reflected the deteriorating condition of the Confederacy. Robert Watson of the Seventh Florida Infantry noted: "Nothing to eat, but we are well supplied with lice. Many of the regiment are sick from drinking bad water and poorly cooked food."

The outspoken Elise Bragg queried her husband, "Are you going to let your poor army make their beds of stone and lay exposed to the bleak mountain air without a sufficiency of tents, blankets, or clothes?"

Soldiers on both sides felt they shared a common bond of misery, which led them to fraternize with each other. °As was the case any time there was a lull in battle or a campaign, Johnny Reb and Billy Yank managed to set aside the war informally. All along the line where there was an opportunity to do so, the men would exchange things such as newspapers and sometimes even letters from home to family or friends on the other side.• Confederate R. A. Jonnerman recalled, "We even met to swap newspapers, canteens, and tobacco for coffee, and I seen some swap hats and shoes, and talk for half an hour at a time."

As the siege wore on, the toll extended beyond the stomachs of the enlisted men to the mental health of the Union commander, which was becoming questionable to his superiors. Even the president observed, "Rosecrans has been acting confused and stunned, like a duck hit on the head."

°In retrospect Rosecrans was paying the price for the defeat at Chickamauga. He lost all confidence, which led many to believe that he was suffering a mental breakdown.• Lincoln was accustomed to replacing generals in the East; thus he was not long in acting. Rosecrans was

During the harrowing night fighting between Hooker's and Longstreet's soldiers that took place west of Lookout Mountain on October 28–29, most of the action occurred near the hamlet of Wauhatchie. At 2 A.M., however, a sharp fight erupted northeast of this location as Confederate brigades led by Brig. Gens. Evander Law and Jerome Robertson attacked elements of two Federal brigades marching to reinforce their beleaguered comrades. While the Rebels successfully delayed the Yankee column, it cost them dearly, for the firefight ended in a Southern rout. The sketch above depicts Massachusetts and Ohio infantrymen racing through the darkness after their beaten and fleeing enemy.

1. **Sept. 21, 1863:** *Unable to hold Lookout Mountain and Missionary Ridge, Rosecrans withdraws his forces to Chattanooga.*

2. **Sept. 21:** *Bragg's Confederates occupy Lookout Mountain and Missionary Ridge.*

3. **Sept. 25 – Oct. 24:** *To reinforce Rosecrans, Federal XI and XII Corps of Army of the Potomac are transferred 1,233 miles by rail from Culpeper to Chattanooga.*

4. **Oct. 23:** *General Grant is given overall command in the west and arrives in Chattanooga.*

5. **Oct. 26–27, night:** *Gen. Smith and 3,500 men sail down the Tennessee River and march across Raccoon Mountain to Brown's Ferry, chase off Confederate pickets, erect pontoon bridge and cross Moccasin Point.*

6. **Oct. 28–29:** *At Wauhatchie, Longstreet's troops attack Federal XI Corps, but fail to capture the newly opened Federal supply route from Bridgeport, nicknamed the "Cracker-line."*

7. **Nov. 23–24:** *Grant sends Sherman and Hooker to envelop the flanks of Confederate position.*

8. **Nov. 24:** *Stevenson's Confederate division is driven off Lookout Mountain by Hooker's forces, which proceed to Rossville to threaten Bragg's left and rear.*

9. **Nov. 25:** *Sherman's troops attack Confederate right at Tunnel Hill but are repulsed.*

10. **Nov. 25:** *Four divisions of Thomas's corps advance up Missionary Ridge and rout Confederate center, while Hooker attacks the left.*

11. *Bragg's army is defeated and retreats into Georgia.*

BP

pulled out of Chattanooga, and Grant was given charge of the campaign.

WCD

°Grant's presence alone boosted the morale of the army. He had captured Vicksburg, the great fortress city on the Mississippi, just four months earlier. He had captured Fort Donelson earlier in the war, a victory that brought him the nickname "Unconditional Surrender" Grant, a play on his initials.• °He was not an impressive or inspiring man physically, but when Grant arrived anywhere, things began to happen. Order began to spring out of chaos. Security began to emerge out of danger.•

The new Federal commander also had the respect of the Rebel soldiers. Shortly after arriving in Chattanooga, Grant rode out along the river and suddenly found himself facing a Confederate picket line. They easily could have shot him before he had the chance to turn and ride away, but they did not.

Recalling the incident in his memoirs in 1885, Grant confessed: "The sentinel on the post called out: 'Turn

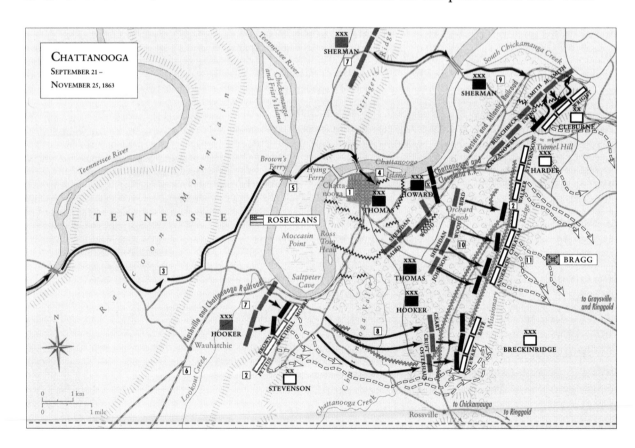

out the guard for the commanding general,' and, I believe, added: 'General Grant.' Their line, in a moment, front faced the North, facing me and gave a salute, which I returned."

While Grant's arrival had animated both armies to some degree, in the mountains around Chattanooga, the Rebels were showing a good deal less respect to their own commander. Bragg and his generals were still arguing bitterly.

°The situation grew critical, causing President Davis to abandon a sickbed in Richmond and make the long, uncomfortable railroad journey to north Georgia to arbitrate the dispute among his generals.•

°It was evident, however, that Davis had already made up his mind to support Bragg against all criticisms. Bragg was still loyal to Davis, and in the winter of 1863 Davis felt obligated to repay that loyalty with loyalty. Realistically, Davis had no alternative. None of the other generals seemed suitable to command the army; they were just as much a part of the poisoned atmosphere as Bragg.• °Davis would have preferred for Lee to take over the western army, but time and time again Lee refused to go.•

With the support of Davis, Bragg retaliated by shifting or demoting his critics, including cavalry com-

The fanciful painting above inaccurately depicts George Henry Thomas—gesturing with his right hand—conferring with Maj. Gen. Joseph Hooker during the battle of Missionary Ridge. At the time of the engagement, Thomas was at Grant's headquarters on Orchard Knob, while Hooker spent the day on the right flank, shepherding his two corps from Lookout Mountain into the fight at the southern end of Missionary Ridge. The rough terrain slowed "Fighting Joe" and prevented him from engaging the enemy until late in the afternoon. When the two generals did communicate during the attack, it was by courier-borne messages.

Before the Federals could scale the steep western face of Lookout Mountain on November 24, they had to cross Lookout Creek. Prior to the attack, work parties erected bridges across this watercourse. A detail commanded by Lt. Col. Eugene Powell of the Sixty-sixth Ohio built such a bridge on the remnants of a ruined gristmill dam. To limit the noise, Powell ordered the Buckeyes to avoid the use of "hammers, nails, or saw," and to tie the walking surface of "rails [and] boards" to the dam's foundation with "pieces of rope." Powell's strategy paid off, and he boasted his troops had made a "good solid foot bridge" without alerting the enemy pickets.

H E BROWN

In the upper left, General Grant, wearing a light-blue overcoat and flanked on his left by Fourth Corps's commander, Maj. Gen. Gordon Granger, and on the right by General Thomas, watches the Union assault of Missionary Ridge from a vantage point on Orchard Knob. Initially, Grant was distressed by the attack, for he had only wanted Thomas's soldiers to take the Rebel works at the base of the ridge to draw attention away from Maj. Gen. William T. Sherman's attempts to turn Bragg's right flank. Thus when the blueclad veterans continued up the slope, he testily asked Granger and Thomas who had ordered the rash charge. "They started without orders," countered Granger, continuing, "[w]hen those fellows get started all hell can't stop them."

mander Brig. Gen. Nathan Bedford Forrest. The mercurial Forrest did not take it well. Outraged by many of Bragg's command decisions, Forrest accosted his commander in front of witnesses and charged: "You are a coward, and if you were any part of a man, I would slap your jaws! If you ever again try to interfere with me or cross my path, it will be at the peril of your life!" Bragg knew that Forrest meant every word and hastened to transfer him from Chattanooga.

Longstreet, another critic of Bragg, was also transferred, taking fifteen thousand men to besiege Knoxville, Tennessee. It was Davis's idea to separate the two and still leave Longstreet with his corps. The problem was that the loss of Longstreet's fifteen thousand battle-tested troops severely weakened Bragg's army.

The ill-advised move did not go unnoticed by the Federals. Grant liked what he saw and later offered his sarcastic compliments to the Confederate president: "Mr. Davis had an exalted opinion of his own military genius. On several occasions during the war, he came to the relief of the Union army by means of his 'superior' military genius."

The Southerners began splitting their forces just as Grant was swinging into action. To break the siege on Chattanooga, he ordered surprise attacks on the Confederate lines downriver.

On a misty October morning, fifty pontoon boats laden with Union soldiers pushed off from Chattanooga. C. C. Bryant of the Sixth Indiana reported: "The men were to lie down in the boats and not a word to be spoken above a whisper. Not a man moved except the fella who did the guiding of the boat."

The boats glided silently past the Rebel lines toward Brown's Ferry, where at dawn the Union troops overran a sleeping Confederate outpost. With the capture of the ferry, the Federals had forced open a new supply route, which the grateful Union soldiers nicknamed "the Cracker Line." The worst of the two-month siege was over. Better news was that reinforcements were on the way, and at the head of the reinforcements was Grant's old ally, Sherman.

°Ever since the battle of Shiloh, where the two of them had stood off the Confederates under adverse circumstances, Sherman had been Grant's right-hand man. Grant had placed a great deal of trust in Sherman, knowing he was a man who would get things done.•

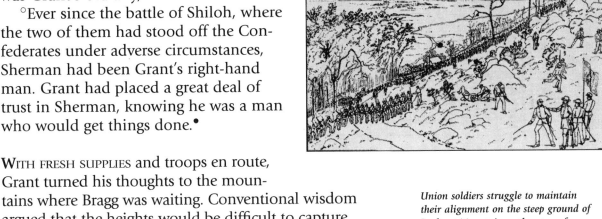

WITH FRESH SUPPLIES and troops en route, Grant turned his thoughts to the mountains where Bragg was waiting. Conventional wisdom argued that the heights would be difficult to capture. When he saw Lookout Mountain, Benjamin Taylor of the *Chicago Journal* wrote: "Glancing at the mighty crest, crowned with a precipice, my heart beats gaily. It could never be taken."

If Grant's army was to challenge the besieging Rebels, it would mean assaulting Lookout Mountain, which had come to have more than strategic significance; it had become a symbol of the siege. °Lookout Mountain was barely eleven hundred feet high, but it was one of the tallest elevations around Chattanooga,• and the steepness of its slopes made it a commanding height. °It seemed grim and somehow threatening because every soldier knew that the mountain had to be taken. The soldiers who were to be given that task looked on it with no little dread.•

On the morning of November 24, 1863, the recently arrived Maj. Gen. Joseph Hooker led ten thousand men up Lookout Mountain. Six months earlier he had led the Army of the Potomac to defeat at Chancellorsville, soundly beaten by Lee in a battle that the Confederates logically had no chance to win. During Hooker's passage to Chattanooga he had beaten off a ferocious attack by several brigades from Longstreet's corps near the village of Wauhatchie in the evening of October 28–29, one of the war's rare night battles.

Union soldiers struggle to maintain their alignment on the steep ground of Lookout Mountain as they press forward their onslaught on the Confederate positions near the Cravens House (visible in the center of the drawing). At the bottom right, bearded Union Brig. Gen. John Geary oversees the attack, sending out an aide with new orders. Just above Geary, Confederate prisoners are escorted to the rear, and in the background an improvised ladder made of planks nailed to a tree trunk leans against the limestone cliffs, known locally as the "palisades," that crowned the mountain. Geary's son, Edward, a Union artillery lieutenant, was killed at his guns during the battle of Wauhatchie.

415

Southern artillerists try to prevent their weapon from being captured, while a fellow gunner fires his cannon in vain at Yankee infantry sheltering behind the lip of Missionary Ridge. Unfortunately for the South, most of the Army of Tennessee's fieldpieces were placed too high on the ridge to fire effectively at the attacking Federals. As Maj. James Connolly of the 123d Illinois bragged in a letter to his wife, Mary: "42 pieces of artillery [were] belching away at us, but they couldn't even scare us, as they couldn't depress their guns to reach us, but had to blaze away far over our heads. We captured all these guns."

The waiting Rebels on Lookout Mountain believed their position was impregnable and jeered when the first Union cannon shots fell short. "We would holler to them, 'Put in more powder!' and other ludicrous remarks. We were enjoying the fun of our fancy security. A number of our men were drunk," wrote Robert D. Jamison of the Forty-fifth Tennessee. The security of the crest, however, soon proved illusory.

WCD °The steepness of the mountain was also an impediment to the Confederate defense. The Southerners were up so high and the slope was so steep, they could not train their cannon to fire on the Federals coming up. Furthermore, Bragg did not have a numerical advantage on Lookout Mountain. The relocation of his forces had thinned his line everywhere, and it was especially thin on Lookout Mountain.•

Another element playing to the advantage of the Federals was that they attacked in a heavy fog, taking the Rebels off guard. This gave the battle for Lookout Mountain the picturesque if somewhat inaccurate title of The Battle Above the Clouds.

JO As the fighting commenced, °the fog or low-hanging clouds seemed to increase, masking most of the fighting from all but the immediate participants. With no view of the action, the Union generals were anxious about their men's progress.• That night the scene became darker still with an eclipse of the moon—seen as a bad

omen for Bragg. Down in the valley anxious Union soldiers went to sleep not knowing how their colleagues had fared on the mountain.

BP °The next morning, when the sun came out and revealed the flag of the Eighth Kentucky flying over the heights, the sight sent a clear message to the troops in Chattanooga that the tide was turning in their favor.• "The troops in the valley grew wild with excitement and rapturously cheered the appearance of the flag," noted Union Gen. Fred Kneffler. "Their hurrahs, like mighty thunder sounded back and forth across the valley." In the end, Bragg had to get his men off the mountain to avoid having them captured and put out of the campaign entirely.

Grant next turned his sights on the last remaining target—Bragg's strongpoint atop Missionary Ridge, a slope east of the city that was not as tall but seemed just as forbidding as Lookout Mountain. "It was conceded that a direct frontal attack on the enemy's works on Missionary Ridge could not be made with a reasonable prospect of success," observed Union Gen. Thomas Wood.

To get close enough to attack Missionary Ridge, Grant's army needed to take an outlying, smaller elevation, Orchard Knob. There was nothing in front of Orchard Knob but open ground. Grant had no choice but to deploy his twenty-four-thousand-man force

Another James Walker panorama portrays the Union bombardment of Lookout Mountain that took place immediately before Geary's infantry began marching toward the mountain's summit. In the center of the picture rides General Hooker, mounted on a white charger. Although many Union soldiers in Chattanooga could hear the fighting on Lookout Mountain, a drizzling rain mixed with the smoke of battle to create a fog that hid most of the action from view. Newspaper reporters, therefore, quickly tagged the engagement with the romantic title of "The Battle Above the Clouds."

After the siege of Chattanooga was lifted, many Northern soldiers hiked to the rocky summit of Lookout Mountain to have their likenesses photographed by Royan Linn, a native of Ohio who had journeyed to Tennessee following the battle of Missionary Ridge. Captivated with the beauty of the region, Linn opened a mountaintop studio where he worked until his death in 1872. His descendents continued to operate the business until 1939. In the photo to the near right, two Union officers, Capt. John C. Wyman (left) and Col. D. C. McCallum pose for Linn's camera. In the photograph next to it (far right) William W. Blackmar, an orderly sergeant in the Fifteenth Pennsylvania Cavalry, strikes a dramatic—and precarious—pose, helped by an unidentified trooper who steadied him against the winds that constantly swirled about the summit. Blackmar later became a lieutenant in the First West Virginia Cavalry, and in 1865, during the battle of Five Forks, he led a daring charge for which he was awarded the Medal of Honor. High-ranking officers were not immune to the lure of acting the tourist and having their image captured by Linn. Below, Maj. Gen. Joseph Hooker sits at a safe distance from the edge of the mountain he conquered. The taking of Lookout Mountain was perhaps the high point of his post-Chancellorsville career.

on the level terrain and send them forward against the Confederates.

It was an awesome scene as the Confederates watched the Federals form their lines of battle on land that could have easily served as a parade ground. Bragg himself pronounced the movement a dress parade in honor of Grant. Suddenly the blueclad soldiers surged toward the Confederate lines, and Orchard Knob was quickly overrun. Most of the Soutehrners managed to get off only one volley before they were lost in the Federal onslaught.

Orchard Knob offered Grant a staging point for the attack on Missionary Ridge. He decided to strike the Confederate left, using Sherman, his most trusted general. The plan, however, failed because opposite Sherman was the best division commander in Bragg's army, a man many thought should have replaced Bragg as its commander—Maj. Gen. Patrick Cleburne. An Irish-born veteran of the British army, Cleburne's reputation was secure in the hearts of his men. They viewed him as one of the bravest leaders they had ever seen.

Fighting under a distinctive blue flag with a white oval in the center, Cleburne personally led a counterattack that hurled Sherman's men back down the hill. The ground was so steep at that part of Missionary Ridge that Cleburne's men could roll boulders down on the hapless Federals. Sherman was finally forced to call off his assault. "The general was in an unhappy frame of mind. It was a stinging disappointment. He gave vent to his feelings in language of astonishing vivacity," wrote German-born Union Maj. Gen. Carl Schurz.

In reserve, Grant still held on to Thomas's Army of the Cumberland—the men who had lost at Chickamauga. Grant had little confidence in them and even less in their general. Thomas was a Virginian who had stayed loyal to the Union. Although he had saved the army at Chickamauga, Grant felt Thomas was plodding and cautious. °Thus Grant viewed the Army of the Cumberland as a secondary force. He did not like that it had suffered defeat at Chickamauga two months earlier, and he had reservations about its military abilities after the two-month siege.•

As Sherman fell back, Grant ordered Thomas to send his men forward to support the pullback. At most, he wanted the Army of the Cumberland to occupy the rifle pits at the foot of Missionary Ridge. The men of the Cumberland, however, had other ideas. °They felt that they needed to redeem themselves for the defeat at Chickamauga. They were anxious to get into this fight to show that they were not a defeated force, as Grant had treated them. They wanted to prove they were still effective and able to bear any burden placed on them.•

°When Thomas's men reached the first line of rifle pits along the base of Missionary Ridge, they knew they would draw the attention of the Confederate artillery on the ridge if they stayed there. They could either go back or push forward, and their pride mitigated against retreat. As they gained the foot of Missionary Ridge, a certain inertia filled the Federal lines. They continued going forward, but they had no orders to proceed.• Company and regimental commanders were puzzled for a few moments as the men started climbing Missionary Ridge on their hands and knees, then the officers started following them up the steep slope.

Officers of various U.S. Colored Troops (U.S.C.T.) regiments, accompanied by two newspapermen, take a break from their duties in Chattanooga to sit for this 1865 photograph. From left to right, they are Col. William B. Gaw, Sixteenth U.S.C.T.; a Mr. Thompson of the New York Tribune; Brig. Gen. Clinton B. Fisk; Capt. T. W. Clark; Lt. J. P. Alden, Fortieth U.S.C.T.; and a Mr. Scribner of the New York Herald. Richard J. Hinton of the Eighty-third U.S.C.T. reclines in front of Fisk.

In addition to ending their investment of Chattanooga, the Confederate disaster at Missionary Ridge cost the Rebels irreplaceable losses in ordnance. More than six thousand rifles and fifty-five thousand rounds of ammunition fell into Northern hands. The photograph above shows three of the dozens of cannons the Federals reported capturing. The fortunes of the Army of the Tennessee looked bleak in the aftermath of its defeat on November 25, and the bulk of the blame for the loss fell on the Southern commander. Bragg "has a winning way of earning everybody's detestation. . . . The army will be relieved to get rid of him. . . . Heavens, how they hate him," penned the famous Southern diarist Mary Boykin Chesnut in early December 1863.

BP °The men of the Cumberland wanted to end this battle once and for all, regardless of what their generals thought. Watching from Orchard Knob, Grant and Generals Thomas and Gordon Granger, whose forces were making this attack, began to realize they had lost control of the battle. What they were seeing—this army clawing its way up the ridge—was not supposed to be happening.•

JMM °Grant queried Thomas if he had ordered his men forward. Thomas said that he had not. Grant asked the same of Granger, and Granger denied it, too. Grant clamped down on his cigar and said that somebody would be in trouble if the unauthorized attack turned into a disaster.• Grant feared that the Confederates would be waiting at the top of the ridge with more than one hundred cannon and would catch his men in a cross fire that they would not survive.

WCD °When Grant saw that the unauthorized attack was succeeding, he quickly set things in motion to follow it up. He was not a man to pass up a serendipitous opportunity.•

The advance up Missionary Ridge was a soldiers'

BP battle. °Every man was for himself in this advance as they crawled from boulder to boulder, firing as they went. That was not how Civil War battles were supposed to be fought. The generals taught the men to fight

420

During the winter of 1863–64, the Federal army turned Chattanooga and the surrounding region into a vast armed camp. The thousands of soldiers and tons of supplies that poured into the area were protected by an elaborate system of forts and gun emplacements designed to thwart any Confederate effort to retake the town. This Parrott gun—a rifled cannon with a extra band of iron applied to the breech for strength—points menacingly down the Tennessee River, awaiting Rebel gunboats that would never come. Chattanooga remained firmly in Union hands for the rest of the conflict.

in orderly geometric formations and to be obedient to and listen for the commands of their officers. At Missionary Ridge no officers were in charge—the enlisted men were on their own. In this battle the officers followed their men.●

Fred Kneffler, a Federal officer scrambling up the slope with his troops, recalled: "There was a savage exultation and a wrathful eagerness to reach the crest. The soldiers pressed upward inexorable as fate."

The Rebels, badly outnumbered and again surprised as they had been at Orchard Knob, began to give way. Their main problem was not a lack of courage but a lack of manpower. °When a man occupies a rifle pit on a hilltop and cannot even see his fellow soldiers on either side, he feels very alone, particularly as he watches fifty thousand of the enemy coming directly at him. The result was that as the Federals climbed up the mountain, Confederate resistance began to break up all along Missionary Ridge. Finally the whole left end of the Rebel line collapsed and ran in flight.●

°Bragg's army disintegrated. He had placed his artillery so it could not be brought to bear on the advancing Federals. The cannon were of no help to the Confederates who had not planned for this kind of spontaneous attack.

WCD

BP

Civilian day-hikers and sketch artists enjoyed the grand view from Lookout Mountain and the rock formation known as Umbrella Rock (seen at the upper right) in more peaceful times. Soldiers also enjoyed the scenery when they could. While stationed in the area, Confederate Pvt. O. T. Hanks of the First Texas and his comrades took the time to have a "trampoose" about Lookout Mountain, even daring to "slide up to the [mountain's] edge" to enjoy the sights below. Hanks also wrote that "at times . . . a heavy fog or mist" would envelope the Texans, and they would "wash" their "faces and hands in the clouds," believing that they "had accomplished a wonderful feat."

The fall of Missionary Ridge was one of the last failures in the accumulated litany of complaints against Bragg. Clearly the morale of his men had eroded to the point where they were not prepared to face the unexpected with a man like Bragg in command.•

Around dusk, only an hour after the impromptu assault began, the flag of the Twenty-fourth Wisconsin was planted on the crest. Three color-bearers had fallen that afternoon, carrying that precious banner into an engagement. The bearer who made it through for the Wisconsin regiment was eighteen-year-old Lt. Arthur MacArthur, who won the Medal of Honor for his gallantry that day. Eight decades later, MacArthur's son, Douglas, would win the same medal as the general commanding all American forces in the Pacific in World War II.

BP °ONCE THE UNION troops gained the crest of Missionary Ridge, there was tremendous jubilation. Some of them cheered, "Remember Chickamauga!"

Among the officers on the ridge was Col. Charles Harker, who had followed his general, Philip H. Sheridan, up the hill. Harker had played a heroic role organizing the Chickamauga defense on Snodgrass Hill. This afternoon he watched Sheridan leap upon a captured Confederate cannon in jubilation. Harker too jumped atop one of the cannon, waving his cap. He did not stay long, having burned his buttocks on the hot iron of the gun.•

Rebel soldiers ran from the ridge in droves. A band was ordered to play "Dixie" to bolster morale, but even that did not work. Nor did Bragg's attempts to rally his WCD men. °Some of the Southerners hurled epithets and jokes at him as they ran past, such as, "I'm moving as fast as I can, General, but in this direction not that." They had no faith in Bragg and did not hesitate to tell him so, even insulting him to his face.•

In his postwar memoirs, Pvt. Sam Watkins of the First Tennessee commented: "Bragg looked so scared, poor fellow. He looked so hacked and whipped, and all along the lines soldiers would raise the yell: 'Bully for Bragg, he's hell on retreat!'"

°After the battle was over, someone asked Grant if he thought that the Confederate position had been impregnable. The general smiled and said, "Well, it was impregnable." Yet his defiant troops had achieved it without orders.•

Bragg's beaten army was chased deep into northern Georgia before it could regroup. By now, even Bragg's own confidence had fled him. He offered his resignation to Jefferson Davis, blaming his troops for running and his generals for undermining his authority. He complained: "The warfare against me has been carried on successfully, and the fruits have been bitter. I fear we both erred in the conclusion for me to retain command here after the clamor raised against me."

°By this time Bragg was so obsessed with assessing blame that he seemed to lose the ability to distinguish the truth from the fictions he created to exculpate him-

As the Union troops swarmed over Missionary Ridge, screaming the vengeful battle cry "Chickamauga! Chickamauga!" they captured legions of Confederate troops, some of whom are pictured above at the Chattanooga railroad depot waiting for transport to a Northern prison. Taken prisoner after being badly wounded, Joseph Riley of the Thirty-third Tennessee left this account of his capture: "I arose [after being shot] and looking back saw the Yankees about 100 yards from me. I tried to run but my legs would not carry me up the slope. They overtook me and I never fired another shot at the Yankees. However, the hardest service ever rendered by a soldier was to be my lot for the next sixteen months—Rock Island [a prison camp in Illinois]."

Infantrymen of the Twenty-first Michigan line up in company formations outside their whitewashed clapboard barracks in Chattanooga. Such elaborate accommodations, built after the siege, starkly contrasted with the squalid living conditions endured by the Yankees before Missionary Ridge. The Twenty-first was assigned to the Army of the Cumberland's engineer brigade during the Chattanooga campaign, providing labor and protection during the construction of their army's vital pontoon bridges.

In addition to new barracks, the Northerners built dozens of warehouses in Chattanooga, some of which are seen in the photograph to the right, turning the city into a vast supply base for Sherman's drive to Atlanta. Such buildings housed everything from weapons to candles for the blue-clad soldiers battling the tenacious troops of the Army of Tennessee over the wooded hills and ridges of northwest Georgia in the spring and summer of 1864.

self from responsibility.• True to form, a forgiving President Davis brought his failed commander to Richmond to be his military adviser. The South was stunned by the loss at Chattanooga, but there was no small rejoicing at Bragg's departure. An editorial writer with the *Daily Richmond Whig* wrote, "This rumor of Bragg's relief was received with as much or more satisfaction by the public yesterday than would the official news of a victory over the Yankees."

JO   °As the commander of the Army of Tennessee, Bragg was responsible for creating the environment that allowed so much dissension to spread throughout the ranks. He
WS   did nothing to counteract it.• Instead, °he was fond of blaming others for his mistakes. Since the war, history has judged him a failure because of his own policies.•

Bragg's assignment to Richmond did not end the controversy over his skills. In the fall of 1864 Davis sent him to Wilmington, North Carolina, to defend that city and Fort Fisher against attack. A Virginia newspaper printed the headline: "Bragg Assigned to Wilmington. Good-bye Wilmington." Later he fought in the battle of Bentonville, North Carolina, where he demanded reinforcements on his side of the line instead of in a part of the battlefield where they could have been better used. The Confederates lost that battle, which they might have won had those troops been rushed into an attack rather than being sent to Bragg.

WCD   °The fall of Chattanooga, especially in such bleak contrast to the great victory at Chickamauga, brought 1863

This massive Parrott rifle (left), capable of firing a two-hundred-pound shell, was positioned in a Union fort constructed atop a high point overlooking the Tennessee River known as Cameron Hill. Lookout Mountain commands the distance. The large garrison cannon and its well-staffed protective earthworks aptly signify the importance the Union placed on maintaining control of Chattanooga. From the fall of 1863 until April 1865, the train whistles heard in Chattanooga's railyards belonged to Northern locomotives pulling loads of men and matériel destined for Yankee armies. Without question, the Confederacy keenly felt the loss of Chattanooga.

to an end as one unremitting tale of woe for the Confederacy. It had lost the "gateway." °Chattanooga became a base and a jumping-off point for Sherman's campaign the following spring to capture Atlanta. °A Yankee army stood poised in north Georgia, on Georgia soil for the first time, ready to move toward Atlanta, with nothing to stand in its way but a demoralized and understaffed Confederate Army of Tennessee. °In that sense Chattanooga was of great strategic importance, for that campaign ultimately brought Union victory in the war.

°The victory at Chattanooga in late November boosted Union morale as it had not been boosted since Gettysburg and Vicksburg that summer. The battle changed not only the course of the war, but also the lives of the two opposing commanders. Grant went on to lead the North to victory and to become the nation's eighteenth president. Bragg spent the postwar years lurching from one failed job to the next, still the target of Southern scorn. Eleven years after the war ended, Bragg suddenly fell dead on a Texas street. Grant was in the White House.

FRANKLIN AND NASHVILLE

The END OF 1864 WAS A DARK TIME for the Confederacy. After burning Atlanta, William Tecumseh Sherman had marched across Georgia and captured Savannah and was preparing to invade South Carolina. Ulysses S. Grant had backed Robert E. Lee into a trench line surrounding Petersburg, Virginia. Food in the South was running out. Sickness was everywhere. Civilians were dying. It seemed that things could not get much more grim. In November 1864 the last Rebel hope had been the Army of Tennessee. Then came the battles of Franklin and Nashville.

JMM °While Sherman moved east from Atlanta on his March to the Sea beginning in mid-November, Confederate Gen. John Bell Hood marched north in the belief that he could recapture Tennessee for the Confederacy. If he succeeded, he wanted to move over the mountains to join his old commander, Lee. Hood believed that he and Lee together could defeat Grant in Virginia. It was an impossible dream.• Before he could join Lee, Hood wanted to return Nashville to the Confederate fold.

WS °Nashville was an important city to the Confederacy. In addition to being the capital of Tennessee, it was a commercial and manufacturing center. Yankee troops had occupied the city since early 1862, shortly after Grant had captured Forts Henry and Donelson. Its occupation by the Union army was an embarrassment RM to the Tennesseans in the Army of Tennessee.• °They knew that the U.S. flag had been flying over the capitol since February 1862. Their mission was to replace it.•

TLB	Timothy Burgess
TYC	Thomas Y. Cartwright
JMM	James M. McPherson
RM	Ross Massey
RLP	Robert L. Parker
WS	Wiley Sword

The proud Confederate Army of Tennessee had its origins in the Provisional Army of Tennessee, a portion of which is pictured here. Isham G. Harris, the Volunteer State's governor, organized the Provisional Army in 1861 during the hectic days following the bombardment of Fort Sumter. From a collection of existing militia units and new recruits, Harris cobbled together a force of twenty-four infantry regiments and ten artillery batteries, supported by quartermaster and ordnance departments and an engineer corps. During the summer of 1861 the troops of the Provisional Army were amalgamated into the newly formed Army of Tennessee.

Hood's Tennessee campaign of 1864 was at once a test of character and a trial of despair. By thrusting north from Georgia into Tennessee, the Confederate Army of Tennessee hoped to rekindle the South's dying flame and recapture Nashville. Some called the Confederate offensive a brave and bold attempt to rescue the South. Others called it a far-fetched work of a foolhardy commander. Whether the campaign was born of courage, desperation, or hopelessness, it climaxed in blood at Franklin and Nashville.

When Pvt. Sam Watkins of Company H, First Tennessee Infantry, published his memoirs in 1882 under the title of *Company Aytch,* he began the story of the battles of Franklin and Nashville with these words: "Kind reader, right here my pen and courage and ability fail me. I shrink from butchery. Would to God I could tear the page from these memoirs and from my own memory. It is the blackest page in the history of the war of the Lost Cause. It was the bloodiest battle of modern times in any war. It was the finishing stroke of the independence of the southern Confederacy. I was there. I saw it. My flesh trembles and creeps and crawls when I think of it today. My heart almost ceases to beat at the horrid recollection. Would to God that I'd never witnessed such a scene."

IYC °For four years the Army of Tennessee had fought gallantly, putting a lot of fear into Grant at Shiloh in April 1862 and Rosecrans at Stones River in December 1862 and Chickamauga in September 1863. At Shiloh it had almost pushed Grant into the Tennessee River. At Chickamauga it had shattered an entire Federal army and sent it reeling back in panicked retreat. The Army of Tennessee was a great army, but it was also a hard-luck army.•

Under Gen. Braxton Bragg it had won victories and then pulled back, creating major disappointments in the ranks. IYC °The men, however, always came back. They prided themselves as the best of their generation from every state of the Confederacy. They possessed the essence of indomitable courage, bolstered by an evident pride that refused to surrender regardless of the odds. These men had been asked to do everything that human beings could be asked to do. Now in November 1864— with the Confederacy obviously starting into a downward spiral that few people believed could be stopped—these men were asked yet again for more than they could possibly do. At the end all they had was glory.•

Capt. Sam Foster of the Twenty-fourth Texas, Cleburne's division, Army of Tennessee, recalled: "November 21. We left camp this morning at sun up and started for Tennessee. General Hood says that we're going into the enemy's country, that we will have some hard marching and some fighting, but that he is not going to risk the chance for a defeat in Tennessee, that he will not fight in Tennessee unless he has an equal number of men and choice of the ground. All this was very nice talk, for we all felt confident that we could always whip an equal number of men with the choice of the ground, and every man felt anxious to go on under these promises from General Hood. Commenced snowing soon after leaving camp."

At age thirty-three, Kentucky-native Hood was the youngest man to command a major army during the war (Lee, by comparison, was fifty-seven). He was an 1853 West Point graduate known more for his bravery than his intellect. He had graduated forty-fourth in a class of fifty-two and had risen only to first lieutenant in the prewar army.

Union Maj. Gen. John Schofield looked more like a college professor than a military officer. Before the war he had, in fact, taught philosophy at the U.S. Military Academy and physics at a university in Saint Louis. Schofield had also been a classmate of John Bell Hood at West Point and had even tutored him. Schofield ranked seventh in the fifty-two-member class of 1853; Hood was ranked forty-fourth. At Spring Hill, Tennessee, a combination of good luck and Confederate mistakes allowed Schofield to evade Hood's juggernaut and make good an escape to Franklin.

The reputation of six-foot-two-inch-tall John Bell Hood soared after he suffered a second wound and the amputation of his right leg at the September 1863 battle of Chickamauga. Throughout the following winter the upper crust of Richmond society feted the recuperating general as the hero of that battle, treating him to standing ovations at numerous parties and balls. Hood's military career and popularity, however, came to an end after his disastrous Franklin-Nashville campaign. Thereafter the Confederacy's social elite either pitied or loathed him as a failed general whose sad face reflected, in the words of Southern chronicler Mary Boykin Chesnut, the "torture of the damned."

JMM °The single most outstanding feature of Hood's character was his aggressiveness as a military commander, starting with his command of the Texas Brigade in the spring of 1862 and extending to the end of the war. He fervently believed in the gospel of attack, attack, attack.•

Hood distinguished himself in June 1862 by personally leading the Texas Brigade in a bayonet charge at the battle of Gaines's Mill, Virginia. The action won a crucial victory for Lee, and Hood became an instant celebrity in Richmond. At Second Manassas and Antietam he led a division with conspicuous gallantry and was appointed a major general. He built on his reputation at the battle of Fredericksburg. His fame garnered invitations to many Richmond parties, where in the spring of 1863 he met and fell in love with Sarah Buchanan Preston, an enchanting, flirtatious beauty nicknamed Buck.

WS °Sally Preston was young, bilingual, educated in Paris, and very much a belle of aristocratic Richmond society.• Diarist Mary Chesnut observed: "Buck, the very sweetest woman I ever knew, had a knack of being fallen in love with at sight and of never being fallen out of love with. But then, there seemed a spell upon her lovers. So many were killed or died of the effects of wounds."

Hood fell immediately under Sally Preston's spell, but he would not have much time to court her properly. During that fateful summer and fall of 1863 he suffered two terrible wounds. The first came at Gettysburg in July. On the second day of the battle, Hood had tried to persuade his commander, Lt. Gen. James Longstreet, to allow his men to flank Little Round Top and attack from the rear. Longstreet refused, explaining that General Lee desired a frontal assault. A reluctant Hood led the attack, and his left arm was shattered by a Yankee shell. °The arm was not amputated but placed in a

TYC

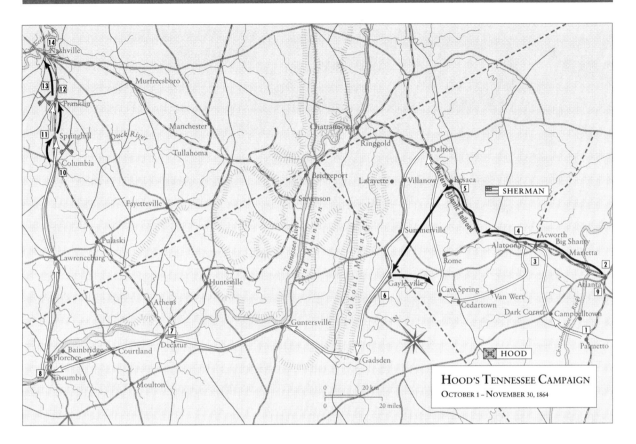

HOOD'S TENNESSEE CAMPAIGN
OCTOBER 1 – NOVEMBER 30, 1864

sling, where it withered. Some less-than-kind critics called it a toothpick.

Three months later at Chickamauga, Hood took a minié ball in the upper right leg, which resulted in its amputation at the hip. At the time, 80 percent of the men who required such radical surgery died. Hood lived.[•] In a war where measles and diarrhea killed tens of thousands of men, Hood had taken two minié balls in less than three months and had survived.

Hood recuperated in Richmond. He also courted Sally Preston, and he did so in the same manner in which he fought his battles—ardently and aggressively. Their affair became her embarrassment. On December 16, 1863, Mary Chesnut recorded: "Buck can't help it. She does not care for the man. It is sympathy with the wounded soldier. Helpless Hood."

In February 1864, instead of being retired, Hood was assigned a corps command in the Army of Tennessee, then headed by Gen. Joseph E. Johnston, who had replaced

[1] *Sept. 29–30: Hood's Confederates cross the Chattahoochee River near Campbelltown.*

[2] *Oct. 2: Leaving XX Corps to hold Atlanta, Sherman pursues Hood.*

[3] *Oct. 3–4: Stewart's Confederate corps captures Big Shanty and destroys railroad between Marietta and Alatoona.*

[4] *Oct. 5: Stewart assaults Federal supply depot at Alatoona, but is driven off suffering 900 casualties.*

[5] *Oct. 13: Hood withdraws to Cave Spring then to Dalton where he captures the Federal garrison.*

[6] *Oct. 14–15: Hood retreats to Gadsden. Sherman follows to Gaylesville, then halts.*

[7] *Oct. 27 – Nov 2: Hood vainly tries to cross the Tennessee River at Decatur. Then resumes his western march.*

[8] *S.D. Lee's corps of Hood's army crosses the Tennessee River at Tuscumbia and occupies Florence.*

[9] *Nov. 15–16: Sherman returns to Atlanta. He now begins the march to the sea.*

[10] *Nov. 21–27: Hood marches to Columbia, which is held by Federal troops under Schofield.*

[11] *Nov. 28: Fearful of being cut off from Nashville, Schofield withdraws toward Spring Hill.*

[12] *Nov. 29: Hood attempts, but fails, to intercept Schofield at Spring Hill; during the night Schofield withdraws to Franklin.*

[13] *Nov. 30: Hood pursues Schofield to Franklin, attacks, and is repulsed.*

[14] *Night: Schofield withdraws to Nashville.*

Soldiers admired Tennessee native Benjamin Franklin Cheatham's willingness to share the dangers of battle with them, even though he had been a general officer from the beginning of the war. At Franklin, Cheatham (above), a major general commanding a corps, watched in horror as his troops frantically built breastworks out of the bodies of dead comrades to protect themselves from the hail of enemy gunfire.

Maj. Gen. Nathan Bedford Forrest (below) led Hood's Cavalry Corps. He was very familiar with the terrain of his native state after three years of terrorizing Union outposts and supply lines in the region and tried repeatedly to give Hood sound strategic advice. The stubborn Hood, however, was unwilling to listen.

Bragg after Bragg had lost Chattanooga in November 1863. All that summer Hood struck at Sherman in the battles around Atlanta and lost every time. Although Hood lost these battles, President Jefferson Davis blamed Johnston, an old political enemy. Finally, Davis replaced the cautious, conservative Johnston with the aggressive Hood.

When Hood took command of the South's second largest and second most important army, he was horribly disfigured, love-forsaken, and perhaps addicted to laudanum, a painkiller derived from opium that was as addicting as heroin. Hood was old beyond his years. At best, he was in command of an army that he had no experience leading. At worst, he was in command of an army that he had the capacity to destroy.

°Hood probably did not know how many U.S. troops he would face in his new command.• Moreover, he had never had to think about strategy. As a brigade and division commander, he had always had a corps commander to point him in a direction and order him to attack. As an army commander, he would be expected to think strategically, something he had never done. While Hood might have recognized his limitations, another factor may also have been at work.

°Before leaving Richmond he had proclaimed himself engaged to Sally Preston, something that she herself denied. Hood wanted to impress her. He perhaps dreamed that headlines in Richmond, such as "Hood Wins Great Victory," would win her love. It would never happen. Although Hood would marry later, it would not be to Buck.•

No one other than President Davis wanted Hood to command the Army of Tennessee. °Lee, who knew Hood well, had advised against giving Hood command of the army.• He had counseled: "Hood is a good fighter, very industrious on the battlefield, careless off. I have a high opinion of his gallantry, earnestness and zeal. I am doubtful as to other qualities necessary." °At another time Lee said of Hood, "All lion and no fox," reinforcing the reputation of a good fighter and a poor planner. Most of Hood's critics believed he should have been retired, that his multiple wounds and problems with painkillers should have disqualified him for command.• Neverthe-

RM less, °the Army of Tennessee had a commanding general who had to be strapped to his horse with a cork leg hanging off the side, who was in constant agony and took laudanum and imbibed alcohol to maintain a semblance of good humor, and who was so helpless that at one point he fell off his horse during the march through Tennessee.•

YC   °The story of Hood's command career would almost be comedic if it were not so tragic. Any number of men were available to take command of the Army of Tennessee: Lt. Gen. William J. Hardee, who had written the textbook on infantry tactics used by both sides; P. G. T. Beauregard, who had been second in command at Shiloh; Nathan Bedford Forrest, the cavalry wizard; or Patrick Cleburne, who was one of the most popular leaders in the entire army.• All were generals who had fought for years with the Army of Tennessee before Hood had arrived from Virginia.

YC   °Hood, however, had a reputation as a fighter, and that was what President Davis wanted.• Hood's men were accustomed to fighting, and after doing battle for Bragg, they were also accustomed to bad generals. Needless to say, they were not happy about Hood. "For the want of a nail, the shoe was lost. For the want of a shoe, the horse was lost. For the want of a horse, the general was lost. For the want of a general, the battle was lost," wrote Watkins of the First Tennessee.

IF ANYONE WAS pleased about Hood's leading the Army of Tennessee, it had to be Grant, who was now in over-

Franklin, Tennessee (above left), was a fairly prosperous cotton-growing village that numbered nine hundred white residents at the beginning of the war. On November 30, 1864, John M. Schofield's harried Federals staggered into town and then "worked like beavers," said a resident, to tear down fences and outbuildings for wood to strengthen their earthworks ringing the southern edge of the hamlet. Northern axes also quickly felled orchards and osage orange hedges in order to create abatis to impede the Confederate charge. "By 10:30 [A.M.] . . . our regiment had the strongest defensive mainline I can recall," claimed Pvt. Adam Weaver of the 104th Ohio.

The Columbia Turnpike, visible in the foreground (above right), split the Carter property in half. The gin house (seen above from the direction of the Confederate charge) stood east of the road, while the house and several outbuildings were west of the thoroughfare. The turnpike served as the axis of the Rebel attack, and some of the bloodiest fighting of the Civil War occurred on the Carter property. A. J. Batchelor of the Thirty-third Alabama remembered stepping on the bodies of dead comrades to reach "the [enemy] works at the corner of the old gin-house." Batchelor probably would have shared their fate had he not been "jerked over the works" and taken prisoner by Union soldiers.

In a terrible irony of war, one of Fountain Carter's sons, twenty-four-year-old Rebel Capt. Theodrick "Tod" Carter (above), was shot down only yards from his family home.

Pvt. Sam Watkins (below) was a veteran of the Army of Tennessee. Despite some embellishment, his postwar memoir, Co. Aytch: A Side Show of the Big Show, is one of the best sources on the western theater from a Confederate perspective and is considered a classic of its genre. During the Rebel debacle at Nashville, he was shot three times and had eight bullets pierce his clothing but somehow avoided capture. Watkins said that Hood "was a good man, a kind man . . . but as a general he was a failure in every respect."

all command of all Union armies. In his postwar memoirs Grant recalled: "Sherman and I rejoiced. Hood was unquestionably a brave, gallant soldier and not destitute of ability. But unfortunately his policy was to fight the enemy wherever he saw him without thinking much of the consequences of defeat."

Grant believed Hood would invade Tennessee rather than follow Sherman across Georgia. To defend Tennessee, Grant called upon the Army of the Cumberland under the command of Maj. Gen. George Henry Thomas. °Thomas was a Virginian who remained loyal to the Union because he had a deep conviction that the United States should be preserved as a single nation. His wife was from New York, and she reinforced his Unionism and his loyalty to the North.•

°Thomas was one of the most successful battlefield generals the Union army had, having won at Mill Springs, Kentucky, when he had an independent command, and having turned in creditable performances at Shiloh, Perryville, and Stones River when under the command of other generals. Thomas had never lost a battle and had won fame at Chickamauga, where he earned the nickname "the Rock of Chickamauga" by holding the Confederates at bay at Snodgrass Hill while two-thirds of the Union army retreated back to Chattanooga.• °Another, less-attractive nickname Thomas had was "Old Slow Trot," a double reference to his weighing more than 250 pounds and his slow and deliberate manner.•

One problem that Thomas could not overcome was that Grant did not like him. Perhaps the distrust went back to West Point where Thomas was three years ahead of Grant, some other service slight, or because of Thomas's supposed caution in the attack. Whatever the reason and despite his proven abilities on the battlefield, Grant did not give Thomas his due.

Serving directly under Thomas was Maj. Gen. John Schofield, an 1853 West Point graduate. He had roomed with Hood at the military academy, and the two men had graduated in the same class. Thomas and Schofield knew Hood well. °Thomas had been an instructor of both Schofield and Hood at West Point, and Schofield had tutored Hood.•

Fortunately for Hood and his soldiers, the Army of Tennessee had many outstanding subordinate officers. The cavalry was led by Maj. Gen. Nathan Bedford Forrest. Three infantry corps were under Maj. Gen. Benjamin Franklin Cheatham, a hard-drinking farmer who had become a credible general. Others included Lt. Gen. A. P. Stewart, a college professor who had attended West Point, and Lt. Gen. Stephen D. Lee, one of the youngest lieutenant generals in the Confederacy at the age of thirty-one and distantly related to the Lees of Virginia. Among the division commanders was the army's shining star, Maj. Gen. Patrick Cleburne.

°Robert E. Lee had called Cleburne "a meteor shining from a clouded sky, the young eagle in the west." He was also called "the Stonewall Jackson of the West."• Cleburne had been born on Saint Patrick's Day 1828 in County Cork, Ireland. After service in the British army as a boy, he immigrated to America at the age of twenty-one, where he first learned to be a druggist and later a lawyer. When the war broke out, he was a lawyer in Helena, Arkansas. °He immediately joined the army as a private, but his leadership qualities soon proved he should be colonel of his regiment. He worked his way up through the ranks of the Army of Tennessee until he reached major general.•

°Cleburne was the epitome of the Army of Tennessee, full of fight yet one of the men. His soldiers could talk to him as easily as they could their own sergeant. They loved him.• He was much like Forrest in that his men

This postwar view (above left) shows Fountain Carter's house after the roofline had been redone. The fighting was an inferno here as the Rebel attack crested at the reserve line of Federal earthworks that traversed Carter's yard. Soldiers fought and died on the porch while the Carter family and several neighbors—twenty-four people in all—huddled in terror in the basement. Carter, who had previously buried foodstuffs beneath the cellar's dirt floor to safeguard them from Federal troops, placed heavy coils of rope in the cellar windows as protection against stray bullets.

The infamous gin house (above right) was defended by Federal brigades under Brig. Gen. James Reilly and Col. John Casement. Confederate Maj. Gen. Patrick Cleburne died here while leading the assault against this position. Of the confused, vicious fighting at the cotton gin, S. B. Miller, a rifleman in Reilly's brigade wrote: "I saw three Confederates standing . . . guns in hand, neither offering to shoot or surrender—dazed as in a dream. . . . I turned my face to the foe trying to clamber over our abatis. When I looked again the three were down—apparently dead; whether shot by their own men or ours, who could tell?"

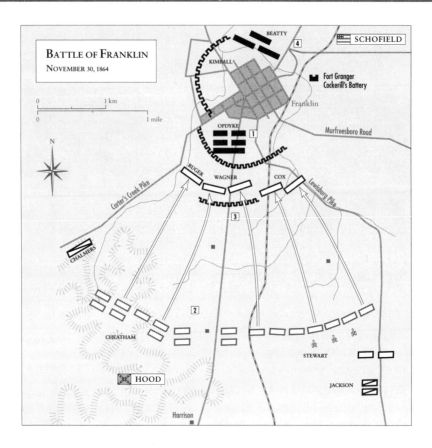

BATTLE OF FRANKLIN
NOVEMBER 30, 1864

1 **Nov. 30, dawn:** The Federals under Schofield arrive and form a defensive line.

2 **Afternoon:** Hood arrives and orders a frontal attack on Federal defenses.

3 After five hours of fighting Hood's forces capture outer works but fail to take main defense lines, eventually his exhausted forces fall back.

4 **Night of Nov. 30/31:** Schofield retreats to Nashville.

knew he would never send them onto any battlefield on which he would not personally go. They trusted him with their lives.

°At Powder Springs, Georgia, on October 4, 1864, Cleburne's division marched up to his headquarters and serenaded him. When asked to speak, Cleburne told the men how important this campaign would be. He told them what would be won if they were victorious and what would be lost if they were defeated. He compared their lot to that of Ireland under British rule. He then looked up into the starry sky, and with all the emotion in his heart, he said, "If this cause that's so near to my heart is doomed to fail, I pray that heaven may let me fall with it, with my face toward the foe, and my arm battling for that which I know to be right."•

°Men like Cleburne led their men into action and shared the dangers along with them. By doing so they felt they could inspire their men to greater courage, to greater effort, to greater success.•

The most visible measure of pride in Cleburne's division was its distinctive flag, °a rectangular blue flag with a white oval moon in the center. Even after the Army of Tennessee adopted the rectangular version of the square Confederate battle flag, or Saint Andrew's cross, which was being used in the East, Cleburne's division demanded to keep its flag and was the only Confederate division, east or west, that was allowed to do so.•

"Friends and foes soon learned to watch the course of the blue flag that marked where Cleburne was in the battle. Where this division defended, no odds broke its lines. Where it attacked, no numbers resisted its onslaught, save only once—there's the grave of Cleburne and his heroic division," recounted General Hardee.

WHEN HOOD INVADED Tennessee, he relied on the one tactic he knew best—a lightning march. By moving rapidly, he hoped to trap part of the Union army that was under Schofield, his former roommate. Hood's opportunity came on Tuesday, November 29, 1864, when he reached the small town of Spring Hill, outside Columbia, Tennessee, south of Nashville.

Col. Emerson Opdycke's brigade of midwestern regiments, although exhausted from serving as the rear guard during the retreat from Spring Hill, hurtled themselves from a reserve position into the teeth of the Confederate breakthrough at the Carter house. Their rash charge halted the Rebels, but only after savage hand-to-hand fighting. J. K. Merrifield, one of Opdycke's "Tigers," saw a grayclad infantryman get clubbed to the ground by one Union soldier while another "put a bayonet on his musket, turned it upside down, and plunged the bayonet into the [prostrate] Confederate." During the fray, Opdycke, as seen here, resorted to bashing away at the enemy with his pistol butt.

Northern troops, well protected by strong earthworks erected in front of the Carter house, deliver a killing fire upon an exposed group of Hood's beleaguered infantrymen in this Marvin Stalnaker rendering. This print properly shows the hipped roof of the Carter house at the time of the battle. In the center of the scene stands one of the Carter's slave cottages. The farm's clapboard office building and brick smokehouse are visible on the left.

Hood's army outflanked Schofield's and cut off the Federal escape route, the road from Columbia to Nashville. Sensing his moment, Hood gave orders to attack, but his instructions were vague and contradictory, possibly because of exhaustion or the medications he was taking for his constant pain. The Confederates skirmished with the Federals, but no clear orders had been issued by Hood to do much more than feel out the Federal position.

ws °Laudanum may have clouded Hood's judgment. He was fatigued, so rather than try to exercise tactical control of the situation, he turned the battlefield operations over to Cheatham and retired to his headquarters to rest for the remainder of the day.• Cheatham, like the other general officers, was not sure what Hood's objectives were, so he did very little to prepare for battle. Specifically, because he was not told to block the road from Columbia to Franklin, Cheatham left the thoroughfare open.

That night Schofield's army marched past Hood's army on the road to Franklin, a town between Spring Hill and Nashville. By morning the Union army was safely ensconced behind earthworks in Franklin. It was

тус one of the more bizarre incidents of the Civil War. °The Confederate campfires were within 150 yards of the road, close enough that the Federals could see the campfires and close enough that the Confederates should have

Another Stalnaker painting portrays the fighting at the gin house, stripped of its siding by Federal troops for use in their breastworks. At the right, next to the flag, Cleburne, only seconds from death, waves his cap. The fighting continued after dark, and Confederate Capt. James Synnamon recollected: "The air was all red and blue flames, with shells and bullets . . . howling everywhere, . . . as we rushed across the cotton fields strewn with fallen men. Wounded and dying men lay . . . in ghastly piles, and when we reached the works at the old cotton gin gatepost, only two or three of my companions were with me. They went into the ditch, but I was tumbled over by a Yankee bullet and was dragged over the field and laid a prisoner by the old gin house."

heard the Federal wagons lumbering past. Some sentries reported what was happening to Hood's headquarters, but neither he nor Cheatham gave any orders to do anything about the apparent movement of the Federals. One scout did check the road, found it clear, and reported so, but he likely stumbled into a gap between the Federal brigades. Some of the Yankees, apparently not fully aware of what was happening, came up to the Confederate campfires to light their pipes and were captured.•

°Spring Hill was a Confederate fiasco. All the elements were in place for a major Southern victory—the Federals were trapped—but the Rebels allowed the Yankee army to just walk away. Even though commanders like Cleburne were poised to make an overwhelming attack that would have captured Spring Hill and cut off the Federal retreat, the attack never occurred, apparently due to a lack of orders from Hood. It never dawned on Hood that Schofield would attempt to march his army past the Confederates. He believed he had trapped Schofield and that one more day would not matter. At the same time, Schofield was very lucky to escape that night.• Afterward, the Federal commander noted: "I must say that I think the mistake was Hood's. Hood went to bed while I was in the saddle all night."

When the Confederate army formed up the next morning to attack the Federals, they discovered there

439

Included among the 6,252 casualties Hood lost on that fateful November day were six dead and fatally wounded generals—a leadership drain the Army of Tennessee could ill afford. From left to right above, they were the aptly named Brig. Gen. States Rights Gist, Tennessee native Brig. Gen. John Adams, Ohio-born Otho French Strahl, twenty-six-year-old Brig. Gen. John C. Carter (who died of his wounds December 10), the "Stonewall Jackson of the West"— Maj. Gen. Patrick Ronayne Cleburne, and the wild-haired Brig. Gen. Hiram B. Granbury. After the battle, the bodies of all but Carter and Gist lay side by side on the porch of Carnton, one of Franklin's most beautiful mansions.

were no Federals to attack. "About two hours after sun up the next morning, we received the order to fall in, fall in quick, make haste. Everything indicated an immediate attack. When we got to the turnpike near Spring Hill, lo and behold, wonder of wonders, the whole Yankee army had passed during the night. The bird had flown," wrote Private Watkins.

°When Hood learned what had happened, he was beside himself with anger for failing to exploit the best opportunity he had to defeat "in detail" part of the Union army.• As Bragg had done so often, Hood absolved himself of all blame for the incident and then blamed the men of his army, viewing the corporate dereliction of duty as a personal insult. This reinforced his idea that his immediate predecessor, Johnston, had ruined the men by having them fight a defensive war around Atlanta. As a result the men had lost their nerve to fight on open ground. In his postwar memoirs Hood asserted: "The discovery that the army, after a forward march of 180 miles was still unwilling to accept battle unless under the protection of breastworks, caused me to experience grave concern. In my inmost heart I questioned whether or not I would ever succeed in eradicating this evil."

°To discipline his subordinates and his army, Hood ordered them to follow up Schofield's retreat to Franklin.•
Before decamping °Hood hosted a breakfast for his generals at Rippa Villa, the Matt Cheairs home, on the morn-

ing of November 30. There he blamed everybody but himself for allowing Schofield to march by unmolested.• More than anyone, Hood blamed Cheatham and Cleburne. He decided they were responsible and their men should be punished.

TYC   Not everyone accepted Hood's verbal thrashing. °After the meeting, as they were leaving, Forrest turned back to Hood and said: "General Hood, if you were a whole man, I'd whip you within an inch of your life!"•

Following the narrow escape at Spring Hill, Schofield ordered his troops to dig in at Franklin. With a nine-hour head start on the Confederates, his army established a seemingly impregnable system of earthworks.

By noon Hood had reached the outskirts of Franklin and personally studied the breastworks thrown up by Schofield. At 2:30 he called a council of war and announced that the Army of Tennessee would make a frontal assault against the fortified Union lines. All of the general officers were stunned. Hood was talking about marching across nearly two miles of open terrain into the face of more than a corps of men who were dug in and waiting for them. Cleburne and Forrest objected.

WS   °Forrest knew from knowledge of the immediate terrain that there was a gap that would allow the army to bypass the Franklin road to Nashville and block Schofield's line of retreat, much as had been done at Spring Hill. He proposed that the army could undo its

441

After the battle an artist sketched the abandoned Union works at Franklin. The killing gradually tapered off as Schofield's surviving troops quietly fell back on Nashville, leaving many of their dead and wounded behind. After spending a cold evening on the battle-field, shivering Confederate troops awoke to horrific scenes of carnage. Casualties were often piled seven deep, and "dead, cold and stiff bodies were laying in every conceivable posture, all with ghastly faces and glassy eyes. At the pike . . . were lying a Confeder-ate and Federal soldier, both with bay-onets sent through their bodies. It was plain to see that they were each other's victims. . . . [The] streets, gutters, sideway[s], doorstones and porticoes [of Franklin] were covered with dead men in blue," shuddered Byron Bowers, a Southern artilleryman.

Spring Hill mistake and once again trap Schofield's army. He urged Hood to take that route.•

°Hood abruptly dismissed Forrest's suggestion, saying: "We will make the fight, and we will make it with honor. You will go in at right shoulder shift, bayo-nets fixed. You will not fire a shot until you overrun the advance line, then shoot and stab the enemy in the back and go into the works with them and drive the enemy into the river at all hazards."• He had only a few cannon and fewer than thirty thousand men who would be exposed with no cover at all. Schofield had thirty-eight thousand men and sixty cannon behind the entrenchments.

Several of the generals tried to dissuade him, but Hood stared them down and repeated that they would make the fight here "rather than at Nashville where they have had three years to prepare." Hood had won his first fame for a frontal charge at Gaines's Mill, Virginia, and may have been remembering that glory.

Filled with this terrible resolve, Hood ordered the battle lines formed, with Cleburne's men positioned in the middle. °Ordered to make the suicidal attack against the center of the Federal entrenchments at Franklin, Cle-burne knew that Hood had written his death warrant.• Brig. Gen. Daniel Govan of Cleburne's division recalled: "General Cleburne seemed to be more despondent than I ever saw him. I was the last one to receive any instructions from him, and as I saluted and bade him good-bye, I remarked, 'Well, General, there will not be many of us that will get back to Arkansas.' And he replied, 'Well, Govan, if we are to die, let us die like men.'"

As the attacking force formed, Schofield himself could scarcely believe what he was seeing—a full-scale Confederate attack beginning as night was coming on. °At 4 P.M. the winter sun was setting in the southwest, the moon was rising in the southeast, and the skyline was red over the plain in front of the Federal entrenchments. The Confederate soldiers even then were calling it "the valley of death" and "the valley of no return."

At that moment twenty thousand Confederates—almost twice the number that had charged the Union center at Gettysburg—divided into eighteen brigades, made up of one hundred regiments, started forward. Most of the field officers were on horseback. Just behind the soldiers came the regimental bands, playing songs to keep up the men's spirits. Thousands of bayonets were fixed and glistening in the dying sunlight. One hundred battle flags were flying. Conspicuous among those rectangular Confederate battle flags was the indomitable blue flag with the white moon that marked Cleburne's division.•

The Federals were awestruck. They described the Confederate movement like a human tidal wave rolling toward them, a big brown-and-gray wall. Adam Weaver of the 104th Ohio remembered: "Four o'clock, the air is hazy, I can honestly hear bands playing, and that eerie defined Rebel yell. May God be with us."

°SOME HISTORIANS HAVE called Franklin the Pickett's Charge of the West, but the Franklin charge was much more difficult. At Gettysburg the Confederates charged one mile. At Franklin they charged two. During Pickett's Charge twelve thousand Confederates executed one charge that lasted

A color sergeant of the Thirty-third Alabama defiantly waves his battle-torn "full moon" flag, the distinctive banner of Cleburne's division, in the painting above. During the battle of Franklin the Thirty-third managed briefly to plant its colors on the Union works near the gin house before being repulsed. Cleburne's once-feared division was shattered by casualties and the death of its beloved leader at Franklin and further gutted by losses at Nashville. After the Tennessee campaign, the Thirty-third ceased to exist; its few, gaunt survivors were integrated with other units.

In the first months of the Civil War, Nashville bustled with Southern martial activity. Factories like the Nashville Plow Works quickly retooled to make weapons for the Rebel war effort, while camps and bivouacs of the forming Army of Tennessee were scattered throughout the city. Units like the Rutledge Artillery, pictured above, posed proudly for photographers in their clean, natty uniforms, confident the conflict would be over in a few short weeks. Such heady days were short lived, for Tennessee's capital fell to Union troops in February 1862.

In a show of military might, Union troops line up for a dress parade in a Nashville street shortly after the Federals occupied the city in 1862 (below right). As the neat, well-maintained buildings on this thoroughfare indicate, Nashville had been a thriving city during the antebellum era, boasting a population of thirty thousand people and fine hotels, universities, and homes. The massive influx of Union troops, however, caused much of the civilian populace to flee and soon changed the character of the town. Yankee soldiers caroused about dingy streets like "Smoky Row," a stretch along the Cumberland River overrun with cheap saloons and prostitutes. By December 1864, Northern entrenchments and forts garrisoned by almost fifty thousand Yankee troops guarded the city.

fifty-five minutes. At Franklin twenty thousand men performed seventeen charges lasting five hours.•

RLP °When the bugle sounded for the assault to start, Cleburne's band struck up "The Bonnie Blue Flag," and Brig. Gen. John Calvin Brown's division, made up mostly of Tennesseans, struck up TYC "Dixie."• °One Irishman in Cockrell's Missouri Brigade recalled that this was the only battle he ever remembered where the "tooters" and the "shooters" went in together.•

WS °The first charge was one of the grandest martial spectacles of the Civil War: twenty thousand men marching across an open valley against prepared entrenchments lined with cannon and thirty-eight thousand Yankee soldiers.• "A sheet of fire was poured into our very faces. The air loaded with death-dealing missiles. Never on this earth did men fight against such terrible odds. It seemed that the very elements of heaven and earth were in one mighty uproar," wrote Private Watkins.

Fountain Branch Carter lived one mile outside of Franklin in a handsome house atop a small hill. On his property was a brick smokehouse and across the road his cotton gin. That afternoon Carter's farm was the center of the Union line. Across the valley, Carter's twenty-four-

year-old son, Confederate Capt. Theodrick "Tod" Carter, mounted his horse, pulled his sword, and said: "This is my home. I can see the house yonder, and I'm going to be there shortly, and I want every man of my regiment to go with me. Follow me, boys. I'm almost home!" Within minutes young Carter fell mortally wounded on the battlefield, shot nine times trying to reach his home. He had not seen the house in four years, not since leaving for the war in May 1861.

As Hood watched from the rear, Cleburne and Brown hurled their divisions at the Federal line. Incredibly, they broke through in two places. At the Carter house, gray-clad soldiers poured through the works, and those in blue mounted a fierce counterattack.

°The Illinois Brigade under Col. Emerson Opdycke, approximately two thousand strong, burst out of their reserve positions. The two lines met like waves crashing together, fighting hand to hand. It was vicious fighting. A Confederate soldier was bayoneted on the front steps of the Carter house, and his Yankee assailant was immediately killed. Another Federal was bayoneted to the ground, but before the Southerner could pull his bayo-

Between December 2 and 3 Hood's weary graycoats settled into earthworks outside of Nashville that were so near to the town that they could plainly view the Tennessee State Capitol (above)—a "fine old building of solid granite, looming up on Capital Hill," remarked one Confederate rifleman. The Rebel force of twenty-three thousand troops was thinly spread over four miles of trench lines, low on ammunition, and living in pits dug in the ground. Hood hoped to incite Thomas into a rash attack, whereby he could destroy in detail the army of "the Rock of Chickamauga." "The enemy will have to seek out our armies and fight them . . . [and] the losses will be on the side of the Federals," contended Hood.

Nashville's prewar prosperity came about partially because the city was a hub and switching yard for several railroad lines that ran northward into Kentucky as well as dispersing to the Lower South. It was this fact that made the city valuable to the Federal army. Hood believed that by recapturing the strategic city, he could hinder the flow of supplies to the Union's western forces, deal a blow to Northern morale, and reenergize Confederate sympathy in Tennessee, thereby gaining new recruits.

WS

TYC

TYC

Standing on the left of the outer line of Union earthworks, Fort Negley (above and at the top of the opposite page) was one of the forts that sheltered Thomas's army and helped defend the southern approaches to Nashville. Being protected by such imposing bastions helped boost the Yankees' assurance of success. One Michigan soldier crowed, "We are strongly fortified and all the Rebel hordes could not take the city by assault." In fact, most of the Union soldiers in Nashville were eager for a chance to attack Hood's force and were worried the bearded Confederate general might retreat without giving battle.

On the cold, foggy morning of December 15, Negley's 32-pound cannon fired the signal shots that began a tremendous bombardment of the Confederate lines prior to the Union attack. One bluecoat asserted that the "firing was so intense and ceaseless that not an individual gun could be distinguished" among the continual roar. After the bombardment, Federal troops surged across the muddy fields toward the Rebel left flank. Although Hood tried to shift reinforcements to this sector of the battle, they arrived too late to push back the Yankees, and the Confederates were forced to retreat to a contracted line farther south.

net from the wound, his head was crushed by a Yankee rifle butt.•

Down by the Carter cotton gin, Cleburne led his men toward a position bolstered by Union artillery °in one of the most ferocious encounters of the entire war. The Federals were firing canister—tremendous shotgun-like blasts of iron balls fired from cannon.• The carnage even shocked the Federals.

°A drummer boy from Cockrell's Missouri Brigade ran up to a Federal cannon and stuffed a split rail into its muzzle in an attempt to disable it. The boy did not know the cannon had not yet been fired. When it went off, the Federals said the little drummer boy with the drum on his back exploded like a tomato.• At approximately the same time, the "bright light" of the Army of Tennessee, Cleburne, was extinguished forever.

"General Cleburne had two horses killed under him in the attack," General Govan testified. "Cleburne then moved forward on foot, waving his cap. I lost sight of him in the smoke and din of battle. He must have met his death a few seconds afterwards." Cleburne went down with a minié ball in his abdomen.

°Against those entrenchments, the spirit of the Army of Tennessee died. Fifty-four regimental commanders were killed or wounded, and six Confederate generals were killed or mortally wounded in the assault: Cleburne, States Rights Gist, John Adams, John C. Carter, O. F. Strahl, and Hiram Granbury. The survivors of the assault described these men as the bravest the world had ever known.•

The six generals were an interesting group, with five of the six being practicing lawyers. Gist, a Harvard graduate, was the cousin of the governor of South Carolina who had signed the Ordinance of Secession. Adams was an 1846 graduate of West Point who rode his horse onto the Federal ramparts before he was riddled. Carter was a law professor. Strahl was a lawyer born in Ohio. Granbury was a Mississippi-born Texas judge.

Hood continued the fight five hours into the night, ignoring reports that his army was being slaughtered. The firsthand account of Private Watkins described the scene: "The death angel was there to gather its last harvest. It was the grand coronation of death."

TYC ° The Federal army retreated at approximately 12:30 that night, leaving their dead and wounded behind. The order was simple: If a soldier could not walk, he was left behind.•

WS ° Hood claimed Franklin as a victory since the Federals had abandoned the field to him, but he knew that he had wasted a great portion of his army—more than six thousand men killed and wounded.• °It was a tactical victory won at a price the Confederacy could not afford.•

RM

WS ° Hood had squandered lives for the sake of his pride.•

In so doing Hood had not endeared himself to his soldiers. One of Cleburne's officers, Capt. Sam Foster, righteously condemned the army commander: "General Hood has betrayed us. This is not the kind of fighting he promised us. This was not a fight with equal numbers and choice of the ground. The wails and cries of widows and orphans made at Franklin, Tennessee, November 30, 1864, will heat up the fires of the bottomless pit to burn the soul of General John Bell Hood for murdering their husbands and fathers. It can't be called anything else but cold-blooded murder."

AFTER THE BATTLE of Franklin, Grant sensed that Hood's army was grievously wounded. Wanting to destroy it, he immediately telegraphed Thomas in Nashville and ordered him to attack Hood and finish

George Thomas lost his family's affection when he remained loyal to the federal government. Although criticized by Grant, the waiting game of "Old Slow Trot" diminished the fighting spirit of the Army of Tennessee, particularly after the onset of frigid winter weather on December 7. The smashing attacks unleashed December 15 earned him yet another nickname: "the Hammer of Nashville."

447

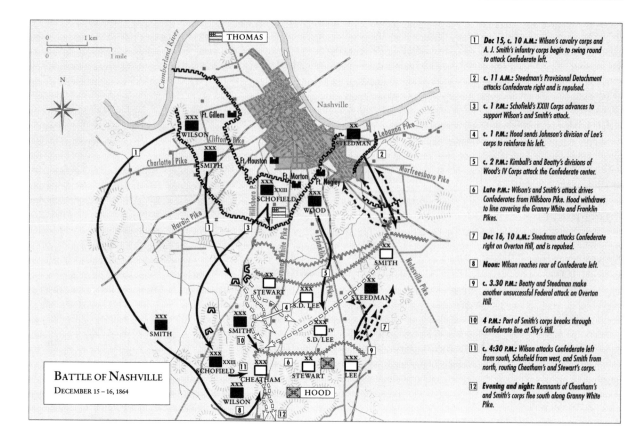

BATTLE OF NASHVILLE
DECEMBER 15 – 16, 1864

1. **Dec 15, c. 10 A.M.:** Wilson's cavalry corps and A. J. Smith's infantry corps begin to swing round to attack Confederate left.

2. **c. 11 A.M.:** Steedman's Provisional Detachment attacks Confederate right and is repulsed.

3. **c. 1 P.M.:** Schofield's XXIII Corps advances to support Wilson's and Smith's attack.

4. **c. 1 P.M.:** Hood sends Johnson's division of Lee's corps to reinforce his left.

5. **c. 2 P.M.:** Kimball's and Beatty's divisions of Wood's IV Corps attack the Confederate center.

6. **Late P.M.:** Wilson's and Smith's attack drives Confederates from Hillsboro Pike. Hood withdraws to line covering the Granny White and Franklin Pikes.

7. **Dec 16, 10 A.M.:** Steedman attacks Confederate right on Overton Hill, and is repulsed.

8. **Noon:** Wilson reaches rear of Confederate left.

9. **c. 3.30 P.M.:** Beatty and Steedman make another unsuccessful Federal attack on Overton Hill.

10. **4 P.M.:** Part of Smith's corps breaks through Confederate line at Shy's Hill.

11. **c. 4:30 P.M.:** Wilson attacks Confederate left from south, Schofield from west, and Smith from north, routing Cheatham's and Stewart's corps.

12. **Evening and night:** Remnants of Cheatham's and Smith's corps flee south along Granny White Pike.

the contest. To Grant's chagrin, Thomas waited. He was in a strong position in the city. He wanted Hood to come to him.

On Thursday, December 1, Hood ordered his battered army to march on Nashville. He would invest the hills around the city, then take it by siege.

RM Assessing the situation from the Petersburg trenches in Virginia, Grant feared Hood might succeed. °Almost paranoid with thoughts that Hood was already crossing the Cumberland River, he badgered Thomas just five days after the battle of Franklin. He suspected Thomas did not have his men in order for an attack against his earthworks. Grant was obsessed with attacking Hood, and he was afraid that Thomas would be too slow.• What Grant did not know was that Hood had wrecked the Confederate army at Franklin.

Again the firsthand perspective of Watkins described a mournful scene: "When the morrow's sun began to

lighten up the eastern skies with its rosy hues, we looked over the battlefield and oh, my God, what did we see, it was the grand holocaust of death. Death held high carnival there that night."

MM
°The city of Franklin became a vast military hospital, with every house, church, and public building turned
TYC into a hospital for the wounded Confederates.• °Some were there for weeks and months. Soldiers were still dying six months after the battle.• Tod Carter, the boy who was going home, died on Friday in the parlor of his parents' home.

On Monday, December 5, 1864, news of the battle reached Susan Tarleton in Mobile, Alabama. That afternoon she was tending her garden when she heard a newspaper boy shout: "Big battle near Franklin, Tennessee. General Cleburne killed." The words made her weep. She and Cleburne had planned to marry before Christmas.

Cleburne's death would be honored throughout the South with verses such as:

> Blow ye breezes, softly o'er him,
> Fan his brow with gentle breath.
> Disturb ye not the peaceful slumber,
> Cleburne sleeps, the sleep of death.
> Rest thee, Cleburne; tears of sadness
> Flow from hearts thou hast nobly won.

Federal troops captured Nashville in conjunction with their movements into the Volunteer State that culminated in the April 1862 battle of Shiloh. The city's loss cost the Confederacy the use of its sprawling rail yards, a portion of which are visible above (left), for the remainder of the conflict. The South's loss was the Union's gain, as Nashville's rail lines brought critical shipments of Northern men and matériel into the interior of the Confederacy's western theater. Such supplies were vital to numerous Federal thrusts into the Southern heartland.

Not all Union soldiers spent their spare time in whorehouses or saloons while stationed in Nashville. Many took advantage of the town's historical sights, such as this Yankee soldier photographed at the tomb of President James K. Polk (above right), who had served as the state's governor during 1839–41 before he became America's eleventh chief executive. The Polk mansion, still occupied by the president's widow, was policed by Federal troops and remained undisturbed during the Union army's three-year occupation.

This photograph of a portion of the Union defense line at Nashville was taken on December 15 or 16 as fighting actually took place in the distance. The fact that these soldiers were loitering about unarmed—note the row of stacked muskets to the left—and the overall casual atmosphere present in this muddy camp while the battle was underway is a strong indication of Thomas's numerical superiority.

Memr'y ne're will cease to cherish,
Deeds of glory, thou hast done.

On the Union side the mood in Virginia was becoming frantic. On Tuesday, December 6, an exasperated Grant again wired Thomas, "Attack Hood at once!" °Thomas replied that he would do so as soon as he was ready. Then an ice storm hit Nashville on December 7, and everything was brought to a halt. When the report went from Nashville to Washington and then to Grant in Virginia that Thomas could not move because of an ice storm, Grant lost his temper. He saw this as merely another excuse for delay by Thomas.•

What Grant could not know was the ice storm hurt the Confederates as much as any attack that Thomas could have mounted. °At least one-fourth, possibly one-third of the Confederate army was shoeless. Many soldiers lacked coats and blankets. The only way they lived was by digging holes in the ground.•

By contrast, Union soldiers living in tents were cold, but they still enjoyed the comforts of the city. °Nashville offered theater companies, circuses, and all types of stores. The city was also well known for its prostitutes. Some of the soldiers had barracks with fireplaces and floors. All in all, Nashville was a good place to be while the Confederates were freezing to

On December 15 debris-cluttered Union trenches, such as this one, were quickly emptied as their inhabitants rushed toward the Rebel lines. From Thomas's headquarters a group of officers nervously watched the charge in "breathless suspense, as the blue line, broken and irregular, but with steady persistence, made its way . . . against a fierce storm of musketry and artillery," wrote Henry Stone, a member of Thomas's staff. Upon the collapse of Hood's left, the tension eased among the Northern high command, and Thomas quickly sent a telegram to Washington announcing the "splendidly successful" attack, the capture of "17 guns and 1,500 prisoners," and promising to "drive the enemy" again on December 16.

death trying to besiege it. Grant, however, did not know this.•

Six miles outside Nashville, Hood established his headquarters at a home called Travellers Rest. His °accommodations were first rate. The home was a wonderful, warm clapboard frame house where Hood enjoyed elaborate dinners while his freezing soldiers in the field survived on scanty rations. The contrast between Hood and his staff and the average soldier in the field was almost cruel.•

By Friday, December 9, 1864, Grant was so angry that Thomas had not attacked that he decided to relieve the Rock of Chickamauga of command. °He issued orders to put Schofield in command, partially due to Schofield's sending telegrams to Washington pointing out that Thomas was too slow. Schofield wanted command of the Union army at Nashville, and he was not above undercutting his commander to get it.•

On a misty Thursday morning, December 15, as Grant prepared to come to Nashville himself, Thomas left his headquarters and told his staff, "Well, boys, we'll go out and settle this little business now. It's about the right time to stop fooling."

Scattered on the foothills of the town, Union wounded and curious locals watched as the Rock of Chickamauga became the Hammer of Nashville. With a thundering

451

Howard Pyle's magnificent 1906 oil painting portrays the intensity and drama of the Union attack on the second day of the battle of Nashville. A Minnesota regiment bears its tattered banners at the double-quick toward Shy's Hill, upon which the left of Hood's second line was anchored. Shy's Hill received its name from the bravery of Confederate Lt. Col. William Shy. The officer refused to surrender as Union troops overran his position, instead picking up a musket and firing at the bluecoated infantry swarming about him. The fierce Rebel only succumbed when he was shot in the head at point-blank range.

flank attack on the Rebel line, Thomas clobbered Hood. By day's end Union troops enveloped the remnant of the Army of Tennessee. The next day the Union army won the battle at Shy's Hill—an elevation named for the brave Confederate colonel who died in its defense.

RM ᵒThe engagement at Shy's Hill was something that all generals dream about. Virtually every Confederate soldier on the battlefield could see Shy's Hill being captured. When it fell, the rest of the Rebel line fell like dominoes. Even the Confederate troops farther to the right, who were not under tremendous pressure, began retreating.•

WS ᵒThey gave way to fear, not a fear of fighting, but the
RM fear of wasting their lives.• ᵒNashville was like no other battle they had ever fought, because the Southerners simply lost interest.• The Confederate Army of Tennessee retreated and never saw its home state again.

The following January 1865, Hood resigned as the commander of the Army of Tennessee. Until the day he died in 1879 during a yellow fever outbreak in New Orleans, Hood believed he left his army in better spirits than when he joined it.

The Army of Tennessee itself marched on to North Carolina to fight under Joseph Johnston again in the battle of Bentonville in March 1865, where it would stage the last great Confederate charge of the war. By then, however, it was an army in name only. At Bentonville it had less than eight thousand men in arms. Two years earlier it had been seventy-thousand-men strong.

MM

°Other events—Sherman's marches through Georgia and South Carolina and Grant's final victories in March and April in Virginia finally brought the Southern military machinery to bay—were crucial in the outcome of the war. The battles of Franklin and Nashville, however, were decisive steps toward the end of the Confederacy, because an entire army was crushed on those fields.•

Sam Watkins concluded his chronicle of his war, saying: "Kind friends, soldiers, comrades, brothers all: the curtain is rung down, the footlights are put out. The audience has all left and gone home. Coming generations and historians will be the critics as to how we have acted our parts. The past is buried in oblivion. The blood-red flag with its crescent and cross that we followed for four long, bloody and disastrous years, has been folded, never again to be unfurled. We have no regrets for what we did, but we mourn the loss of so many brave and gallant men who perished on the field of battle and honor. The tale is told, the world moves on, the sun shines as brightly as before, and the scene melts and gradually disappears forever."

At Nashville, previously stalwart regiments "ran like a herd of stampeded cattle," lamented Confederate gunner E. T. Eggleston, and the horrible, frigid retreat from the Volunteer State further sapped the strength of the Confederacy's western army. Somehow, the less than ten thousand soldiers who remained in the Army of Tennessee managed to carry on through the last days of the conflict, placing their meager battle lines in the path of William T. Sherman's march through the Carolinas. This once mighty Rebel force, however, never recovered from the disastrous Tennessee campaign of 1864.

Bibliography

Bearss, Edwin C. *The Vicksburg Campaign.* 3 Vols. Dayton, Ohio: Morningside, 1985–86.

Berlin, Ira, et al., eds. *Free at Last: A Documentary History of Slavery, Freedom, and the Civil War.* New York: The New Press, 1992.

Billings, John D. *Hardtack and Coffee, or The Unwritten Story of Army Life.* 1887. Reprint, Williamstown, Mass.: Corner House Publishers, 1990.

Burton, E. Milby. *The Siege of Charleston, 1861–1865.* Columbia: University of South Carolina Press, 1970.

Chisholm, Daniel. *The Civil War Notebook of Daniel Chisholm: A Chronicle of Daily Life in the Union Army, 1864–1865.* Edited by W. Springer Menge and J. August Shimrak. New York: Orion Books, 1989.

Coddington, Edwin B. *The Gettysburg Campaign: A Study in Command.* New York: Charles Scribner's Sons, 1968.

Connelly, Thomas Lawrence. *Army of the Heartland: The Army of Tennessee, 1861–1862.* Baton Rouge: Louisiana State University Press, 1967.

———. *Autumn of Glory: The Army of Tennessee, 1862–1865.* Baton Rouge: Louisiana State University Press, 1971.

Connolly, James A. *Three Years in the Army of the Cumberland.* Edited by Paul M. Angle. Bloomington: Indiana University Press, 1959.

Cozzens, Peter. *The Shipwreck of Their Hopes: The Battles for Chattanooga.* Urbana: University of Illinois Press, 1994.

———. *This Terrible Sound: The Battle of Chickamauga.* Urbana: University of Illinois Press, 1992.

Curtis, O. B. *History of the Twenty-Fourth Michigan of the Iron Brigade Known as the Detroit and Wayne County Regiment.* Reprint, Gaithersburg, Md.: Olde Soldier Books, 1988.

Daniel, Larry J. *Soldiering in the Army of Tennessee.* Chapel Hill: University of North Carolina Press, 1991.

Davis, William C. *Battle at Bull Run: A History of the First Major Campaign of the Civil War.* 1977. Reprint, Mechanicsburg, Pa.: Stackpole Books, 1995.

———. *Duel Between the First Ironclads.* 1975. Reprint, Mechanicsburg, Pa.: Stackpole Books, 1994.

Dawes, Rufus R. *Service with the Sixth Wisconsin Volunteers.* Reprint, Dayton, Ohio: Morningside, 1984.

Dufour, Charles L. *The Night the War Was Lost.* Lincoln: University of Nebraska Press, 1994.

Dyer, Frederick H. *A Compendium of the War of the Rebellion.* 1980. Reprint, Dayton, Ohio: Morningside Bookshop, 1978.

Emilio, Luis F. *A Brave Black Regiment: History of the Fifty-Fourth Regiment of Massachusetts Volunteer Infantry 1863–1865.* Reprint. Salem, N.H.: Ayer Company, 1990.

Fowler, William M., Jr. *Under Two Flags: The American Navy in the Civil War.* New York: Norton, 1990.

Frassanito, William A. *Antietam: The Photographic Legacy of America's Bloodiest Day.* 1978. Reprint, Gettysburg, Pa.: Thomas Publications, 1996.

———. *Early Photography at Gettysburg.* Gettysburg, Pa.: Thomas Publications, 1995.

———. *Gettysburg: A Journey in Time.* New York: Charles Scribner's Sons, 1975.

———. *Gettysburg Then and Now: Touring the Battlefield with Old Photos, 1863–1889.* Gettysburg, Pa.: Thomas Publications, 1996.

———. *Gettysburg Then and Now Companion.* Gettysburg, Pa.: Thomas Publications, 1997.

Georg, Kathleen R., and John Bussey. *Nothing But Glory: Pickett's Division at Gettysburg.* Hightstown, N.J.: Longstreet, 1987.

Gibbons, Tony. *Warships and Naval Battles of the Civil War.* New York: Gallery Books, 1989.

Haydon, Charles B. *For Country, Cause and Leader: The Civil War Journal of Charles B. Haydon.* Edited by Stephen W. Sears. New York: Ticknor & Fields, 1993.

Hennessey, John. *The First Battle of Manassas: An End to Innocence July 18–21, 1861.* The Virginia Civil War Battle and Leaders Series. Lynchburg, Va.: Howard, 1989.

Herdegen, Lance J., and William J. K. Beaudot. *In the Bloody Railroad Cut at Gettysburg*. Dayton, Ohio: Morningside, 1990.

Hess, Earl J. *The Union Soldier in Battle Enduring the Ordeal of Combat*. Lawrence: University Press of Kansas, 1997.

Hoehling, A. A. *Vicksburg: 47 Days of Seige*. 1969. Reprint, Mechanicsburg, Pa.: Stackpole Books, 1996.

Holzer, Harold, and Mark E. Neely Jr. *Mine Eyes Have Seen the Glory: The Civil War in Art*. New York: Orion Books, 1993.

Klement, Frank L. *The Gettysburg Soldier's Cemetery and Lincoln's Address*. Shippensburg, Pa.: White Mane Publishing Co., 1993.

Kunhardt, Philip B. *A New Birth of Freedom: Lincoln at Gettysburg*. Boston: Little, Brown, 1983.

Logsdon, David R., ed. *Eyewitnesses at the Battle of Franklin*. Revised edition. Nashville: Kettle Mills Press, 1996.

Lord, Francis A. *They Fought for the Union*. Harrisburg, Pa.: Stackpole Company, 1960.

Lowry, Thomas P. *The Story the Soldiers Wouldn't Tell: Sex in the Civil War*. Mechanicsburg, Pa.: Stackpole Books, 1994.

Marvel, William. *Burnside*. Chapel Hill: University of North Carolina Press, 1991.

Masur, Louis P., ed. *The Real War Will Never Get in the Books: Selections from Writers During the Civil War*. Oxford: Oxford University Press, 1993.

McPherson, James M. *Battle Cry of Freedom: The Civil War Era*. Oxford: Oxford University Press, 1988.

———. *The Negro's Civil War: How American Blacks Felt and Acted During the War for the Union*. New York: Ballantine Books, 1991.

McWhiney, Grady, and Judith Lee Hallock. *Braxton Bragg and Confederate Defeat*. 2 volumes. Tuscaloosa: University of Alabama Press, 1969, 1991.

Murfin, James V. *The Gleam of Bayonets: The Battle of Antietam and the Maryland Campaign of 1862*. New York: Yoseloff, 1965.

Navy Department. *Dictionary of American Naval Fighting Ships*. 1963. Reprint, Washington, D.C.: Navy Department, Office of the Chief of Naval Operations, Naval History Division, 1977.

Nolan, Alan T. *The Iron Brigade: A Military History*. Bloomington: Indiana University Press, 1961.

Pfanz, Harry W. *Gettysburg: Culp's and Cemetery Hill*. Chapel Hill: University of North Carolina Press, 1993.

———. *Gettysburg: The Second Day*. Chapel Hill: University of North Carolina Press, 1987.

Rhodes, Elisha Hunt. *All for the Union: The Civil War Diary and Letters of Elisha Hunt Rhodes*. Edited by Robert Hunt Rhodes. New York: Orion Books, 1985, 1991.

Robertson, James I., Jr. *Soldiers Blue and Gray*. American Military History. Columbia: University of South Carolina Press, 1988.

Rosen, Robert N. *Confederate Charleston*. Columbia: University of South Carolina Press, 1994.

Sears, Stephen W. *Landscape Turned Red: The Battle of Antietam*. New York: Ticknor & Fields, 1983.

———. *To the Gates of Richmond: The Peninsula Campaign*. New York: Tichnor & Fields, 1992.

Small, Cindy L. *The Jennie Wade Story*. Gettysburg, Pa.: Thomas Publications, 1991.

Stewart, George R. *Pickett's Charge*. 1955. Reprint, Dayton, Ohio: Morningside, 1983.

Sword, Wiley. *The Confederacy's Last Hurrah: Spring Hill, Franklin, and Nashville*. Lawrence: University of Kansas Press, 1993. (Formerly entitled *Embrace an Angry Wind*.)

Watkins, Sam R. *Co. 'Aytch': A Side Show of the Big Show*. 1882. Reprint, New York: Collier Books, 1962.

Wheeler, Richard. *Lee's Terrible Swift Sword: From Antietam to Chancellorsville*. New York: HarperCollins, 1992.

———. *The Siege of Vicksburg*. New York: HarperPerennial, 1978, 1991.

Wideman, John C. *Naval Warfare: Courage and Combat on the Water*. New York: MetroBooks, 1997.

Wiley, Bell I. *The Life of Billy Yank: The Common Soldier of the Union*. Indianapolis: Bobbs-Merrill, 1952.

———. *The Life of Johnny Reb: The Common Soldier of the Confederacy*. Indianapolis: Bobbs-Merrill, 1943.

Williams, William G. *Days of Darkness: The Gettysburg Civilians*. Shippensburg, Pa.: Beidel, 1986.

Wills, Garry. *Lincoln at Gettysburg: The Words That Remade America*. New York: Simon & Schuster, 1993.

Wilson, Clyde N. *Carolina Cavalier: The Life and Mind of James Johnston Pettigrew*. Athens: University of Georgia Press, 1990.

Winters, John D. *The Civil War in Louisiana*. Baton Rouge: Louisiana State University Press, 1963.

Wise, Stephen R. *Gate of Hell: Campaign for Charleston Harbor, 1863*. Columbia: University of South Carolina Press, 1994.

Illustration Credits

THE SOURCES for the illustrations in this book are shown below. Credits from left to right are separated by semicolons, from top to bottom by dashes. The following abbreviations have been used throughout:

ACHS	Adams County Historical Society, Gettysburg, Pa.
AHE	American Heritage Engraving, Alexandria, Va.
B&L	Clarence C. Buell and Robert U. Johnson, eds., *Battles and Leaders of the Civil War*, 4 vols. (New York: Century, 1884–88; reprint, Secaucus, N.J.: Castle, 1985).
CHS	Chicago Historical Society
CM	Confederate Museum, New Orleans, La.
HNOC	Historic New Orleans Collection
LC	Library of Congress, Washington, D.C.
Leib	Leib Image Arvices
LV	The Library of Virginia, Richmond
NA	National Archives, Washington, D.C.
OCHM	The Old Court House Museum, Vicksburg, Miss.
SHSW	State Historical Society of Wisconsin
USAMHI	U.S. Army Military History Institute, Carlisle, Pa.
WRHS	Western Reserve Historical Society, Cleveland, Ohio

2: LC (USZ62-14404). 4: LC (B8171-159); CHS (photograph ICHi-27256, Slave quarters at the Scotthouse, Battle of Fredericksburg; Fredericksburg [Virg.]; 1863; photographer—unknown). 5: LC (USZ62-49305). 6: South Caroliniana Library, Columbia, S.C. 7: LC (USZ62-7992). 8: LC (USZ62-12425). 9: *Mary Boykin Chesnut* by Samuel Osgood, oil on canvas adhered to masonite, National Portrait Gallery (L/NPG.9.77), Washington, D.C./Art Resource, New York—LC (USZ62-10704). 10: South Caroliniana Library, Columbia, S.C.; LC (USZ62-156). 11: AHE. 12: South Caroliniana Library, Columbia, S.C. 13: Courtesy of Fort Sumter National Monument. 14: South Caroliniana Library, Columbia, S.C.; USAMHI (RG485-CWP 59.65). 15: LC (USZ62-11149). 16: South Caroliniana Library, Columbia, S.C.—LC (USZ62-33825). 17: LC (USZ62-32160). 18: LC (USZ62-31158)—*B&L*, 1:64. 20: South Caroliniana Library, Columbia, S.C.; AHE. 21: AHE. 22: LC (USZ62-36). 23: LC (USZ62-119586). 24–25: LC (B8184-4797). 25: LC (USZ62-55302). 26: South Caroliniana Library, Columbia, S.C.; courtesy of Fort Sumter National Monument. 27: NA (121-BA-914A). 28: LC (B8184-4799); courtesy of Charles V. Peery. 29: Collection of The New-York Historical Society

(7394); courtesy of Special Collections, U.S. Military Academy. 30: USAMHI MOLLUS Collection (2:L54). 31: Courtesy of the South Carolina Historical Society. 32: LC (USZ62-11148); USAMHI MOLLUS Collection (2:54). 33: LC (B8171-3140A). 34: USAMHI MOLLUS Collection (34:1674). 36: WRHS; CHS (photograph ICHi-08087; Camp of the 1st Conn. Artillery, in sight of the U.S. Capitol). 37: Courtesy of Special Collections, U.S. Military Academy; collection of The New-York Historical Society (58693)—USAMHI (Binder: Civil War Food Eating Commissary); courtesy of Special Collections, U.S. Military Academy. 38: USAMHI MOLLUS (6:278); from James I. Robertson Jr., *Tenting Tonight*, The Civil War (Alexandria, Va.: Time-Life, 1984), 69—LC (USZ62-38); LC (B8171-7222). 39: NA (165-B-2499). 40: NA (111-B-189). 41: Courtesy of Don Troiani—LC (USZ62-37). 42: *Union Assault on Confederate Works* by William Winner, courtesy of West Point Museum Collections, U.S. Military Academy—USAMHI MOLLUS (128:6581). 43: NA (111-B-358)—USAMHI MOLLUS (43:L2123). 44: Courtesy of Don Troiani. 45: LC (USZ62-39368); LC (USZ62-40807). 46: LC (BH82-137)—LC (USZ62-15708). 47: LC (USZ62-8382). 48: LC (USZ62-70890); USAMHI MOLLUS (21:1028). 49: LC (USZ62-91075)—USAMHI Collection (RG985-CWP 130.23). 50: USAMHI Collection (RG4905); *B&L*, 3:99. 51: USAMHI MOLLUS (26:1799). 52: LC (B817-7496); The Library of Virginia (A9-3668). 53: LC (B8178-89). 54: USAMHI MOLLUS (6:L253B); LV (A9-3850). 55: LC courtesy of The Museum of the Confederacy, Richmond, Va. 56: USAMHI MOLLUS (43:L2150A)—courtesy of Don Troiani. 57: Courtesy of Don Troiani. 58: LC (B8184-4132); NA (111-B-252). 59: Archive Photos (#5076); Rochester Museum and Science Center. 60: LC (Harpers Collection). 61: USAMHI MOLLUS (84:422). 62: *4th Alabama* by Don Troiani, photograph courtesy of Historical Art Prints, Southbury, Conn. 64: USAMHI. 65: USAMHI. 68: Leib (232-11). 69: South Caroliniana Library, Columbia, S.C. 70: *Death of Ellsworth* by Alonzo Chappel, oil on canvas, courtesy of the CHS. 71: USAMHI MOLLUS (66:3264F). 72: LC (USZ62-4117); LC (USZ61-505). 73: LV (#A9-3663). 74: *B&L*, 1:231; LV (#A9-5472). 75: LC (B8171-315)—USAMHI MOLLUS (9:L418). 76: LV (#A9-3712). 77:

87). **217:** LC (B8178-39). **218:** *Submarine Torpedo Boat H. L. Hunley, Dec 6 1863* by Conrad Wise Chapman, courtesy The Museum of the Confederacy, Richmond, Va.—South Caroliniana Library, Columbia, S.C. **219:** *Fort Sumter. Interior. Sunrise. Dec 9 1864* by Conrad Wise Chapman, courtesy The Museum of the Confederacy, Richmond, Va. **220:** LC (B8171-3448); LC (B8171-3094). **221:** LC (B8171-3112); LC (B8171-3078). **222:** LC (B8171-3089). **223:** USAMHI MOLLUS (26:1274). **224:** Courtesy of Herb Peck. **226:** USAMHI (RG985-CWD 128.45). **227:** USAMHI MOLLUS (52:L2565). **228:** SHSW WHi(X3)26353; Courtesy of Lance Herdegen. **229:** SHSW WHi(X3)11287. **230:** USAMHI MOLLUS (52:2564A). **231:** USAMHI MOLLUS (52:2564B); USAMHI MOLLUS (52:2564C). **232:** USAMHI MOLLUS (52:2571A). **233:** Courtesy of Milwaukee County Historical Society **234:** USAMHI MOLLUS (52:2563C). **235:** SHSW WHi(X3)26352. **236:** Courtesy of Alan T. Nolan. **237:** SHSW WHi(X3)19923. **238:** SHSW WHi(X3)11030. **239:** SHSW WHi(X3)11028. **240:** SHSW WHi(X3)11291—SHSW WHi(X3)11286. **241:** SHSW WHi(X3)45237. **242:** *Fight for the Colors* by Don Troiani, photograph courtesy of Historical Art Prints, Southbury, Conn. **243:** USAMHI MOLLUS (80:4023). **244:** Courtesy of Lance Herdegen. **245:** SHSW WHi(X3)12862. **246:** Illinois State Historical Library. **247:** Courtesy of Lance Herdegen. **248:** *Give Them Cold Steel* by Don Troiani, photograph courtesy of Historical Art Prints, Southbury, Conn. **250:** LC (USZ62-33815). **251:** LC (USZ62-8880). **253:** *Holding the Line* by Joe Umble, courtesy of Joe Umble—LC (B813-6785A). **254:** *Battle of Gettysburg* by Rufus Zugbaum, from the collection of the Minnesota Historical Society. **255:** *Gen'l W. S. Hancock and Staff* from the Battle of Gettysburg Cyclorama by Paul Philippoteaux, courtesy of Special Collections, U.S. Military Academy; *Wheeler's 13th N.Y. Batteries* from the Battle of Gettysburg Cyclorama by Paul Philippoteaux, courtesy of Special Collections, U.S. Military Academy—LC (B8171-227). **257:** *The First Day of Gettysburg* by James Walker, oil on canvas, courtesy of West Point Museum Collections, U.S. Military Academy. **258:** LC (USZ62-7029); LC (USZ62-18191). **259:** LC (B8171-245). **260:** LC (USZ62-18175). **261:** *Culp's Hill* from the Battle of Gettysburg Cyclorama by Paul Philippoteaux, courtesy of Special Collections, U.S. Military Academy; *Cemetery Hill* from the Battle of Gettysburg Cyclorama by Paul Philippoteaux, courtesy of Special Collections, U.S. Military Academy. **263:** WRHS—*Round Top* from the Battle of Gettysburg Cyclorama by Paul Philippoteaux, courtesy of Special Collections, U.S. Military Academy. **264:** *Men Must See Us Today* by Don Troiani, photograph courtesy of Historical Art Prints, Southbury, Conn. **265:** USAMHI MOLLUS (52:L2567A). **266:** *Lions of the Round Top* by Don Troiani, photograph courtesy of Historical Art Prints, Southbury, Conn. **267:** USAMHI MOLLUS (81:4342). **268:** *Retreat by Recoil* by Don Troiani, photograph courtesy of Historical Art Prints, Southbury, Conn. **269:** *First Minnesota* by Don Troiani, photograph

courtesy of Historical Art Prints, Southbury, Conn. **270:** LC (USZ62-14371)—Leib (56-14). **271:** AHE. **272:** *Band of Brothers* by Don Troiani, photograph courtesy of Historical Art Prints, Southbury, Conn. **273:** USAMHI MOLLUS (23:1123)—USAMHI MOLLUS (23:1108). **274:** USAMHI MOLLUS (23:1102)—USAMHI MOLLUS (75:3534). **275:** LC (USZ62-8379). **276:** LC (USZ62-549). **277:** AHE. **278:** USAMHI MOLLUS (43:2146). **279:** USAMHI MOLLUS (43:2145). **280:** LC (USZ62-14370). **281:** LC (USZ62-8377). **282:** LC (USZ62-38167). **284:** Courtesy ACHS; Courtesy ACHS. **285:** WRHS; Courtesy ACHS. **286:** Courtesy ACHS—LC (B811-2393). **287:** Courtesy ACHS—WRHS. **288:** Courtesy ACHS. **289:** *Battle in the Streets* by Don Troiani, photograph courtesy of Historical Art Prints, Southbury, Conn. **290:** NA (111-B-332). **291:** NA (79-T-2562); NA (79-T-2567). **292:** USAMHI MOLLUS (87:4351). **293:** USAMHI MOLLUS (87:4356)—courtesy of JoAnna McDonald. **294:** USAMHI MOLLUS (129:L6616); USAMHI (RG985-CWP, 25.74)—USAMHI (CS Virginia Box). **295:** Courtesy ACHS. **296:** WRHS. **297:** USAMHI MOLLUS (63:3113). **298:** LC (B8184-5141). **299:** LC (B8184-5351); LC (USZ62-78269). **300:** CHS (photograph ICHi-27257; Amputation scene General Hospital; Gettysburg; Gettysburg [Penn.]; n.d.; photographer unknown); Courtesy ACHS. **301:** LC. **302:** Courtesy of Mike Winey—USAMHI. **303:** Courtesy ACHS—Courtesy Meserve-Kunhardt Collection. **304:** Survivors, Philadelphia Brigade at the Stone Wall and Bloody Angle, Fiftieth Anniversary of the Battle of Gettysburg Commission, RG-25 Records of Special Commissions, Pennsylvania State Archives. **305:** Reenactment of Pickett's Charge, July 3, 1913, Fiftieth Anniversary of the Battle of Gettysburg Commission, RG-25 Records of Special Commissions, Pennsylvania State Archives. **306:** *The Boy Colonel* by Don Troiani, photograph courtesy of Historical Art Prints, Southbury, Conn. **308:** Pettigrew Papers, #592, Selected images of Gen. James Johnston Pettigrew, Southern Historical Collection, The University of North Carolina at Chapel Hill. **309:** LC (B8184-5141). **310:** USAMHI MOLLUS (91:4695)—NA (79-T-2564A). **311:** North Carolina State Archives. **312:** Pennsylvania Capitol Preservation Committee. **313:** Buffalo and Erie County Historical Society—Buffalo and Erie County Historical Society. **314:** LC (USZ62-100659). **315:** Courtesy of JoAnna McDonald. **316:** Brian Pohanka Collection—USAMHI MOLLUS (85:L4298D). **317:** *Don't Give an Inch* by Don Troiani, photograph courtesy of Historical Art Prints, Southbury, Conn. **318:** USAMHI MOLLUS (52:2591)—USAMHI MOLLUS (29:1405). **319:** Leib (56-31)—LV (#A9-9023). **320:** *Barksdale's Charge* by Don Troiani, photograph courtesy of Historical Art Prints, Southbury, Conn. **321:** North Carolina State Archives. **322:** USAMHI MOLLUS (81:4059B). **323:** North Carolina State Archives. **324:** LC (USZ62-14378). **325:** LC (B8184-4426). **326:** LC (USZ61-184). **328:** WRHS. **329:** Connecticut State Archives. **330:** Courtesy Meserve-Kunhardt Collection—LC (B8184-7965). **331:** Special Collections,

Lehigh University Information Services. **332:** Courtesy Jimmer Carden. **333:** Lloyd Ostendorf Collection, Dayton, Ohio—Courtesy Meserve-Kunhardt Collection. **334:** LC (BH837-207)—WRHS. **335:** ACHS; NA (79-T-2027). **336:** ACHS; ACHS. **337:** Courtesy Jimmer Carden—LC (B8184-7942). **338:** CHS (ICHi-27255; Gettysburg-Baltimore Street at junction of Emmittsburg Road and Baltimore Pike; Gettysburg [Penn.]; 1863; photographed by Tipton; LC (B818-10001). **339:** Lloyd Ostendorf Collection, Dayton, Ohio. **340:** Special Collections, Lehigh University Information Services. **341:** Special Collections, Lehigh University Information Services. **342:** LC (B8171-1159B); NA (111-B-4975). **343:** WRHS. **344:** ACHS. **345:** USAMHI MOLLUS (43:L2147C). **346:** ACHS. **347:** LC (USZ62-3117)—LC (USZ62-3118). **348:** ACHS; ACHS. **349:** WRHS. **350:** USAMHI MOLLUS (75:3704). **352:** OCHM. **354:** LC (B8184-10424). **355:** LC (B8171-391). **356:** *B&L*, 3:556. **357:** AHE; *B&L*, 3:497. **358:** LC (B8184-3133)—USAMHI MOLLUS (75:L3704). **359:** LC (B8172-1334)—LC (B8184-3135). **360:** USAMHI MOLLUS (75:L3704F); USAMHI MOLLUS (75:L3704A)—USAMHI MOLLUS (75:L3704C). **361:** USAMHI MOLLUS (52:2551)—OCHM. **362:** OCHM. **363:** OCHM—USAMHI MOLLUS (105:L5448). **364:** OCHM—OCHM. **365:** LC (USZ62-31209)—LC (USZ62-13623). **366:** *Eagle of the 8th* by Don Troiani, photograph courtesy of Historical Art Prints, Southbury, Conn. **367:** LC (USZ62-35907). **368:** LC (USZ62-12757). **369:** LC (B8184-10649). **370:** OCHM—LC (USZ62-13625). **371:** *Fourth Minnesota Regiment Entering Vicksburg* by Francis Millet, from the collection of the Minnesota Historical Society—OCHM. **372:** OCHM—OCHM. **373:** OCHM—OCHM. **374:** Leib. **375:** USAMHI MOLLUS (90:4558). **376:** Massachusetts Historical Society. **378:** Massachusetts Historical Society. **379:** LC courtesy of The Museum of the Confederacy, Richmond, Va. **380:** LC courtesy of The Museum of the Confederacy, Richmond, Va. **381:** USAMHI MOLLUS (108:5590)—LC (B811-154). **382:** USAMHI MOLLUS (127:6549)—LC (USZ62-33456). **383:** Massachusetts Historical Society. **384:** Leib. **385:** Massachusetts Historical Society—Massachusetts Historical Society. **386:** Massachusetts Historical Society; Massachusetts Historical Society; Massachusetts Historical Society. **387:** USAMHI MOLLUS (110:L5677). **388:** LC (B8171-7861). **389:** *B&L*, 4:56. **390:** LC (USZ62-25390). **391:** LC (B816-8025). **392:** USAMHI MOLLUS (95:L4886D). **393:** Massachusetts Historical Society. **394:** LC (B8171-2608). **395:** Massachusetts Historical Society. **396:** Massachusetts Historical Society—Massachusetts Historical Society. **397:** Massachusetts Historical Society. **398:** LC (B8184-10176). **400:** Tennessee State Museum Collection, photograph by June Dorman. **401:** U.S. Army photograph in Tennessee State Museum Collection. **402:** Houghton Library, Harvard University—Leib (639-15). **404:** LC (USZ62-31159)—Leib (52-04). **405:** NA (111-B-

4830). **406:** Tennessee State Archives and Library—USAMHI MOLLUS (54:2685). **407:** LC (USZ62-1266. **408:** LC (USZ62-61448). **409:** *The Second Minnesota Regiment at Mission Ridge* by Douglas Volk, from the collection of the Minnesota Historical Society. **410:** USAMHI MOLLUS (75:L3709); LC (USZ62-59778). **411:** Tennessee State Museum Collection. **413:** Tennessee State Museum Collection, photograph by June Dorman—Tennessee State Museum Collection, photograph by June Dorman. **414:** LV (Prang's War Pictures). **415:** Tennessee State Museum Collection, photograph by June Dorman. **416:** Tennessee State Museum Collection, photograph by June Dorman. **417:** U.S. Army photograph in Tennessee State Museum Collection. **418:** USAMHI MOLLUS (15:3216A); USAMHI MOLLUS (65:3216B)—USAMHI MOLLUS (65:3216C). **419:** USAMHI MOLLUS (65:3217). **420:** LC (B8184-8123). **421:** Tennessee State Archives and Library. **422:** AHE. **423:** Tennessee State Archives and Library; USAMHI MOLLUS (30:1463). **424:** Tennessee State Archives and Library. **425:** Tennessee State Archives and Library. **426:** *Forward the Colors* by Don Troiani, photograph courtesy of Historical Art Prints, Southbury, Conn. **428:** Tennessee State Archives and Library. **429:** Leib (331-02). **430:** LC (B8184-10387). **432:** USAMHI MOLLUS (85:4297A)—Tennessee State Museum Collection, photograph by June Dorman. **433:** USAMHI MOLLUS (136:6984A); USAMHI MOLLUS (136:L6986A). **434:** The Carter House, Franklin, Tenn.—The Valentine Museum, Richmond, Va. **435:** USAMHI MOLLUS (136:6983); USAMHI MOLLUS (136:L6986). **437:** *Opdyke's Tigers* by Don Troiani, photograph courtesy of Historical Art Prints, Southbury, Conn. **438:** Tennessee State Museum Collection, photograph by June Dorman. **439:** Tennessee State Museum Collection, photograph by June Dorman. **440:** LC (B8171-3931); Tennessee State Museum Collection, photograph by June Dorman; Tennessee State Museum Photographic Collection. **441:** Tennessee State Museum, Photographic Collection; Tennessee State Museum Collection, photograph by June Dorman; The Carter House, Franklin, Tenn. **442:** Tennessee State Museum Collection, photograph by June Dorman. **443:** *Pat Cleburne's Men* by Don Troiani, photograph courtesy of Historical Art Prints, Southbury, Conn. **444:** McClung Collection, Knoxville, Tenn.—LC (USZ62-15277). **445:** Tennessee State Museum Collection, photograph by June Dorman—LC courtesy of Tennessee State Museum Collection. **446:** NA (77-F-147-88). **447:** Tennessee State Museum Collection—Tennessee State Museum Collection. **449:** Tennessee State Museum Collection; Tennessee State Archives and Library. **450:** LC (B8171-2639). **451:** LC (B8171-2640). **452:** *Battle of Nashville* by Howard Pyle, from the collection of the Minnesota Historical Society. **453:** *Gray Wall* by Don Troiani, photograph courtesy of Historical Art Prints, Southbury, Conn.

Index